Contents

Project Committee

Co-Directors

Willis Holding, Jr., North Carolina, Chairman, NASPO Research Committee, 1969-73; NASPO President, 1974

David Neuman, Partner, Peat, Marwick, Mitchell & Co.

LEAA Project Monitors

Robert Donlan, 1973

Jack Nadol, 1974

The Council of State Governments

Robert Cornett, NASPO Secretariat

NASPO Study Group

Thomas B. Blanco, Illinois (ret. 1973)

Hugh Carleton, Pennsylvania

Herman Crystal, New Jersey

Frank Pennoni, Michigan

John Short, Wisconsin, Chairman, NASPO Research Committee, 1974

Max Walton, Texas

Peat, Marwick, Mitchell & Co.

Paul M. Carren, Project Manager

Allan R. Betts

Peter M. Bjonerud

James T. Carter

Jan H. Hendler

Advisory Council

Chauncey H. Browning, Jr., Attorney General, West Virginia

Charles A. Byrley, Director, National Governors' Conference

Stanley R. Cowle, County Administrator, Hennepin County, Minnesota

Wilmot E. Fleming, State Senator, Pennsylvania

Harry Gerdy, Regional Counsel, Region 5, General Services Administration

Max E. Greenberg, Attorney-at-law

Albert H. Hall, Executive Vice President, National Institute of Governmental Purchasing

Irving Jaffe, Deputy Assistant Attorney General, Civil Division, U.S. Department of Justice

Ralph C. Nash, Professor, George Washington University Law School

Terry Sanford, President, Duke University

Walter Wechsler, Director, Division of Budget and Accounting, Department of the Treasury, New Jersey

Government is a trust, and the officers of the government are trustees; and both the trust and the trustees are created for the benefit of the people.

Henry Clay

(From a speech given in Ashland, Kentucky, March 1829.)

Foreword

Public purchasing, at all levels of government, is a difficult task. Assuring the best value of goods and services from a multitude of suppliers becomes ever more complex, as technological advances offer increasingly sophisticated equipment and products. The present report is the first comprehensive research effort on this topic, a digest of which was printed in June 1974.

The report traces essential elements of the purchasing process, including the assessment of needs; written specifications; advertising, evaluating and awarding bids; and inspection and testing procedures. It concludes with a review and evaluation of purchasing manuals. Considering the expenditures involved, state and local purchasing officials have a massive responsibility to assure impartiality, integrity, and cost savings in government purchasing.

The Council of State Governments is pleased to publish this report prepared by the National Association of State Purchasing Officials, an affiliate of the Council, and Peat, Marwick, Mitchell & Co., with the financial support of the Law Enforcement Assistance Administration.

Lexington, Kentucky
March 1975

Brevard Crihfield
Executive Director
The Council of State Governments

State and local government purchasing officials may find that many—perhaps most—of the essential elements of public procurement identified in the study appear familiar and elemental, if nevertheless essential. But if this study reinforces the professional's perception of state and local government purchasing, it also enlarges that perception to include a real world of challenge and change. The findings make imperative an expanded and innovative role for the government purchasing official.

For the professional staff and particularly for those on the threshold of a purchasing career, the study is a text, a setting down of the data of common experience. We have the benchmarks against which personal and program development can be weighed.

As the practice of public purchasing has matured, there has been a tendency common with similar support services within government toward an aura of great specialization and professionalism. Management may give full faith and credit to the competency of such a program, but does not necessarily look upon it as an integral part of the top management team. The study brings into focus the role of the purchasing official in government management.

A chief executive was asked to comment on this role.

Preface

Public purchasing is entitled to claim our attention with this study. Sound purchasing operations contribute greatly to the economical and effective operation of our governments and, perhaps of even greater importance at this time in our national history, they are basic to public confidence and trust in government. Furthermore, purchasing is an important, although underutilized, resource for improved program planning and evaluation, and for policy and management generally.

While this study will be used most intensively by those who seek professional development in the field of public purchasing, I recommend the study to management at all levels of government as an exposition of a highly technical and professional support service which serves well and, with our clearer understanding and support, could serve better.

I am honored to present the preface to this major study of public purchasing, not because of any particular personal credentials, but because of the reputation which North Carolina enjoys among her sister States for solid and professional excellence in state purchasing. I therefore accept the honor, not on behalf of myself for my own Administration, but on behalf of my State and the many public servants who have, by years of hard and dedicated service, earned our position of esteem.

Our position is "institutional" and is not synonymous with particular individuals. But one individual, Willis Holding, Jr., clearly stands out. I am pleased, therefore, to be able to pay tribute to Mr. Holding for his enormous contributions to North Carolina and to note the leadership provided by Mr. Holding nationally, including specifically his work in conceiving and guiding the study of which this report is a result.

James E. Holshouser, Jr.
Governor of North Carolina

1. Introduction

This study of purchasing by state and local governments is the first comprehensive research effort on the subject. It is directed to the acquisition and utilization of goods and services and does not treat directly construction and public works contracting. Its purpose is to examine differences in current practices and to recommend those characteristics which promote strong and effective programs. The scope of the research effort extends from state and local laws to written policies and day-to-day practices. This information provides the basis for identifying principles and characteristics found in successful programs.

The principles, concepts, and conclusions presented in this report are not directed to public purchasing officials only. The study encompasses law, regulation, policy, and practice; and so it is directed also to the executive, legislative, administrative, and fiscal elements of government. The enlightened cooperation and support of these echelons of government is needed so that purchasing officials may realize improvements in their programs.

The dollar volume of state and local government purchasing has grown dramatically during the past decade, and it now exceeds that of the federal government. The *Survey of Current Business* reports the following data on purchases of goods and services, exclusive of employee compensation.

	1963	1973
	(In billions of dollars)	
Federal	$38.9	$53.8
State and local	$25.3	$75.7

Despite the considerable amount of money being spent, the study disclosed a dearth of literature on this vast subject, with some of the best of it obscured in law reviews and limited in scope. Therefore, the dimensions, objectives, and methods of this research effort are unique; and this very uniqueness marks the need for the information it presents. While the report was never intended to be a text of public purchasing, it has become a very good syllabus.

The concept of New Federalism—the trend toward giving state and local governments more authority and responsibility in spending funds collected by the federal government—further highlights the importance of and need for this research effort. The federal government's interest in state and local government purchasing is expressed directly through the Law Enforcement Assistance Administration's sponsorship of this study.

The study comes at a time when there is much interest in improving procurement programs. This interest stems from a variety of issues. Today, public purchasing faces greater challenges than ever before in its history. The wave of technology that has characterized the national economy for the past decade or more has brought with it increasingly complex equipment, materials, and systems. Items with a high degree of technology frequently become obsolete in a short period of time by the rapid introduction of new, more refined products. As items become more highly developed, it is progressively more difficult to separate the "frills" from actual requirements and, consequently, to determine the best buy for the money.

The magnitude of public purchasing expenditures brings into focus the principle of accountability. A basic tenet of our society is that public officials having the authority to apply public resources also have a responsibility to give a full accounting of their actions. This accountability relates to the manner in which resources are applied and to the effect of their application, as well as to the specific objects for which public funds are spent. Effective and efficient purchasing programs based on sound principles are needed to give a proper accounting for purchasing activities. Public record and openness are also necessary features which not only act as controls in the system, but also help foster public confidence in government itself.

Governments are faced with the need to provide more and better services to an ever-changing population. Different life styles, attitudes, and levels of sophistication result in different demands to be satisfied. Demands for more and better services by governments cannot be met merely by increasing the already heavy tax burden of the public. Government must stretch its funds and increase its productivity. The challenge of advanced technology and need for increased economy require that public purchasing officials continually update their technical knowledge, information systems, and purchasing techniques.

These conditions impact severely on budgets, the economy, and the marketplace. Until recently, public purchasing functioned in a market where supply and demand were balanced, or where a buyer's market existed. Now, market conditions can change drastically. Basic commodities are in short supply, and purchasing finds itself trying to satisfy increasing demands within the constraints of a tight seller's market. The task of obtaining products when needed, at competitive prices, is a major assignment.

In addition to the challenges of technology, public demands, and the market, purchasing officials must often cope with social, political, and business influences which seek preferred treatment. There is a need for strong statutory or regulatory safeguards to preserve the integrity of the purchasing process and to protect the government against loss caused by the misfeasance or malfeasance of its employees. Good safeguards and controls must exist, but must not be so restrictive as to stifle the professional judgment and personal initiative necessary for purchasing officials to function effectively in the public interest. One of the unique features of centralized public purchasing is the complete openness of its operations, which distinguishes it from private purchasing. But despite this general openness, there have been cases where favoritism has occurred in the awarding of contracts, and favoritism invariably reflects negatively on all public purchasing activities. Public purchasing officials must recognize and resist the pressures of those who attempt to improperly influence purchasing practices.

The need to come to grips with the integrity of public contracting procedures and practices is particularly acute at this time when we see declining public confidence in our institutions of government. A recent survey by the Institute for Social Research shows that the majority of American people believes that many public officials are less than honest in carrying out their official duties.

The National Advisory Commission on Criminal Justice Standards and Goals' (NACCJS&G) *Report on Community Crime Prevention* (January 1973) made three postulates concerning integrity in government.

• The corruption of public officials at all levels of government—federal, state, and local—is perceived as widespread by the American public.

• Such corruption results in a staggering cost to the American taxpayer.

• The existence of corruption breeds further crime by providing for the citizen a model of official lawlessness that undermines any acceptable rule of law.

Simply put, the commission noted that official corruption breeds disrespect for the law.

In its chapter on "Government Procurement of Goods and Services," the commission opens with this observation:

People who are familiar with the operation of government recognize that a principal opportunity for personal profit or political funding is to be found when a governmental unit purchases goods or services.

These many challenges demand professionalism at its best. Yet, the formal education that is the core of most professions does not exist to any degree in purchasing. Experience has been not only the best teacher, but the only one. Although attention to detail is necessary in this, as in any activity, the professional must elevate himself and reorient his approach to concentrate on managing assigned functions and detailed activities, e.g., formulating policies, supervising personnel, and directing programs. Developing a professional staff requires a systematic program encompassing education, experience, and continuous training which permits progression to a professional level.

Over the years, state and local governments have individually adopted a variety of public contracting laws, rules, policies, and practices representing whatever was deemed acceptable and expedient at the time. In some cases, these laws and policies have remained virtually unchanged for years; in other cases, they have been changed piecemeal or in response to a particular problem. As a result, state and local government statutes, regulations, and procedures generally have not developed in terms of any overall understanding, knowledge, or data, and they vary widely among state and local governments.

Yet, at the same time, many improvements have been made by state and local governments in their purchasing operations. Perhaps the most significant of these has been the growth of more centralized purchasing, motivated largely by the recognition of the economies that could be realized. As with the laws, rules, and policies, however, the applications of centralization vary widely. In adopting centralization, primary attention was given to specific types of commodities and to the types of activities which are traditionally associated with the buying function. Many forms of statutory exemptions and exceptions still exist, and various types of commodities and services are still purchased outside the umbrella of central purchasing.

Recognizing variations among purchasing programs in terms of size, resources, and complexity of operations, the study team did not attempt to dictate a single set of procedures. Instead, the study presents purchasing philosophy and principles as the foundations for public purchasing operations at all levels and of all sizes. Although a variety of local conditions may cause differing details of implementation, common acceptance of basic principles is possible and necessary.

These principles are presented throughout the report in the form of suggested statutory/regulatory coverage and are consolidated in the Overview of this report. It was not deemed feasible as part of this study to attempt to distinguish between statutory coverage and regulatory coverage, as they must be subject to local conditions and peculiarities of operation.

Statutory and regulatory requirements need to be implemented, however, and this is best done with written policies of operating practices and procedures. Therefore, this report also presents recommended coverage for a purchasing manual for the central purchasing authority and to using agencies, and a manual for vendors who seek or who do business with state and local governments. A comprehensive but concise statute, supplemented by regulations and written operating procedures adopted and published by the central purchasing authority, provides the soundest structure for effective purchasing programs.

The data gathered in the research of state statutes and regulations are presented in the tables in Appendix A. Detailed information on the results of the nation-wide survey of cities and counties having populations of 10,000 and over is presented in Appendix B. The scope of the study and the methodology used in researching the material are presented in Appendix C. A glossary of suggested terms and definitions constitute Appendix D; and a bibliography composed of a List of General References and a List of Legal Citations that were used in the study constitute Appendix E.

2. Overview

If a distillation can be made of a study which represents months of dedicated effort and intensive cooperation by purchasing officials and other public administrators, it might be said that where there is centralization, openness, impartiality, and professionalism, government is well-served by public purchasing.

This report promotes the principle of a central purchasing authority. Despite the considerable progress made in centralizing purchasing operations, many major types of purchases are still made outside the umbrella of central purchasing, and statutory exemptions and exceptions still exist. Conditions such as these result in a division of responsibilities, diffusion of control, and loss of accountability. **The centralization of purchasing authority is also the centralization of responsibility and accountability, and the central purchasing authority has the perspective of commonweal,** not the special program interests of individual departments. Delegations can and should still be made when using agencies can more appropriately or better perform certain functions or activities. These delegations, however, should be made formally by the central purchasing authority. Since the responsibility for delegated functions remains with the central authority, proper controls can be established and accountability maintained.

The concept of a central purchasing authority fits almost every organizational structure or form of government. It can be applied by the largest of the States and by the smallest of the cities and towns. It relates to governments having boards of control over purchasing, as well as to those having very small purchasing operations. Although the concept of central purchasing may be applied by means of various organizational forms, it is best established at a sufficiently high level of government to permit independent and authoritative functioning with both suppliers and using agencies. Further, to be effective, this authority requires proper recognition and support from officials responsible for total government operations, such as Governors, mayors, councilmen, and commissioners.

Openness requires that all aspects of the purchasing process be available for public scrutiny. Established policies and procedures should be set forth in writing and should be available to the public. Legal notices, public bid openings, and documentation are all part of this requirement. Documentation is a fundamental, but often neglected, aspect of the purchasing process. It is necesary to maintain internal control and to build a complete public record. Proper documentation of actions is especially important when unusual conditions are encountered, or when deviations from established policies are necessary. Where there is public record there is public confidence. This distinguishes state and local acquisition of goods and services from other activities not as openly performed.

Impartiality must be evident in the manner in which suppliers and using agencies are treated. Sound policies and consistent application of policies are necessary to avoid favoritism. Good specifications are needed to ensure competition and to maintain the appropriate quality level for items purchased. Specifications must not preclude qualified suppliers from competing, and they must not incorporate personal preferences which are not germane to an item's intended use. All qualified suppliers who are willing to bid should be solicited, and all bids or proposals must be evaluated on the same basis. In contrast to industrial or private buying, the price of goods purchased is not the overriding indicator of performance in public purchasing. More important is how the price is obtained. Here, fairness and openness are paramount. There is no room for partiality, secretiveness, or deception. Good purchasing and good government are found together.

The attitude and dedication of purchasing personnel are vital factors in the success of a purchasing program. **A dedicated professional individual or staff can produce results far beyond those which might otherwise be expected.** Governments must foster a spirit of professionalism by providing meaningful programs, appropriate authority, and necessary responsibility. Professional development must be encouraged both on the job and by proper training and supervision. Where there is professionalism and conformance to technical and ethical standards, public purchasing can work as it is expected to work in awarding contracts impartially, reducing costs of government operations, and instilling confidence in the integrity of government.

The public purchasing profession is handicapped by a general lack of understanding among people as to how it differs from contracting for public works. Historically, the body of state and local government laws and principles governing purchases of goods and services has been developed around construction and public works contracts. These types of contracts are predicated on the successful bidder's building a structure, for example, or carrying out a similar project of the owner's design, and assume that a number of contractors have equivalent capability so that the owner will receive essentially the same structure regardless of who is the successful bidder. Price is generally the principal determinant.

With most purchases of equipment, materials, supplies, and services, however, the relationship is usually reversed because the purchaser is buying products of the seller's design or capability. Seldom are they custom-made. Except for certain standard items, instead of receiving the same or essentially the same product from all bidders, the buyer receives products with different characteristics depending upon who is the successful bidder. To arrive at best value, purchasing officials must consider individual product capabilities or the quality of the proposed services, as well as bid prices; price becomes only one factor in the total evaluation. This evaluation process must be conducted in accordance with preestablished criteria which deal with differences among commodities.

Effective purchasing programs must have a sound basis in law. The purchasing laws should set forth the basic principles and requirements which must be observed. The research conducted during this study disclosed few statutes that were well-balanced in the principles and details they espoused. Some were so general as to be subject to constant interpretation and dispute. Others were so detailed that they left little or no room for professional judgment and initiative. The study concludes that the laws should address the specific principles of public purchasing, but should not contain detailed operational guidelines for each principle. The laws should provide room for flexibility and judgment so that purchasing officials can serve the best interests of the government under varying conditions.

The flexibility permitted by statute, however, cannot be left entirely to individual discretion. There must be corollary controls, guidelines, and discipline in the system. Therefore, the laws should provide that the central purchasing authority promulgate rules, regulations, and other written policies which set forth detailed criteria and implementing procedures. These written materials should be subject to formal review and approval procedures.

This report also stresses the need for more attention to the management aspects of purchasing. Centralization of authority and proper delegation of routine activities can bring more management orientation to purchasing. Specific attention should be given to managing the major programs of acquisition, quality assurance, disposition, and related functions such as planning, market analysis, value analysis, and to developing new techniques. If purchasing, with its expertise and vantage point, is not charged with and does not take

the lead in these areas, there will be little or no central direction to the programs. Poor management, or no management at all, only leads to inefficiency and waste. Management brings with it structure and controls which, in the long run, produce economy and efficiency of operation.

Much remains to be done in the area of historical analyses of bid-award data to determine the nature and extent of competition which is actually obtained. Such analyses are performed infrequently, and usually on an informal basis. Perhaps the two primary reasons for not conducting more are a preoccupation with the mechanics of the purchasing process and a lack of structured data. Purchasing operations generate considerable files, but usually the information remains in its original state and is virtually unusable to management. A proper program structure which is management oriented is needed, as are good information systems to permit evaluations of historical bid-award information and to provide input to planning, budgeting, and market analysis.

Competition has been and should continue to be the standard in public purchasing, and the formal sealed bid process must remain the primary mechanism for award. The study found no one in disagreement with these basic precepts. Yet, there remain barriers to full and free competition. Some of these barriers are found in law, others in practice. State and local preference laws, for example, still exist in some state and local governments. To the extent that such laws provide a stipulated preference to state and local suppliers, they directly impede open competition. Practices such as establishing price agreements with all suppliers who can furnish given commodities also obstruct the principles of competition. In this case, each qualified supplier simply provides his price, all are accepted and placed on the price list, and using agencies may purchase from any of them. This practice discourages price competition at the outset, and promotes aggressive back-door selling instead.

Although the formal sealed bid process should remain a standard in public purchasing, there is a place for competitive negotiation. This latter process has been misunderstood and sometimes misused. By definition, competitive negotiation is in no way synonymous with single-source procurement. If there is but one supplier for a particular item, consideration should be given to negotiating with that supplier. There are other cases when competitive negotiation may be appropriate, such as when purchasing high-technology items or professional services. Almost all States report problems in applying conventional bidding techniques to these types of procurements because it is difficult to prepare suitable specifications at the outset. Before proceeding with the competitive negotiation process, however, there should be written justification which supports the need to deviate from the normal sealed bid process. Alternate techniques, such as two- or three-step competitive sealed bid procedures, should be considered. If competitive negotiation is found to be necessary, the basic principles of competition, openness, and impartiality must be observed. Statutes should allow for competitive negotiation, but there should be explicit rules and written policies which provide guidance on when and how this technique is to be used.

Public purchasing must not be looked at as a program which is carried out in isolation by each state and local government. Although local conditions may vary, a common body of principles can and should be adopted by all. There is room for much more coordination, cooperation, and exchange of information among state and local governments. Cooperative purchasing and pooling arrangements, which now exist in many areas, are a good example. The States and the larger local governments should take a more positive role in encouraging participation in such programs. Participants, too, must overcome selfish and political interests and willingly accept the commitments necessary to make cooperative endeavors successful. Similarly, much more needs to be done in areas such as specification writing and testing. Intergovernmental systems for gathering and disseminating information on existing specifications and test results and joint use of existing test facilities would greatly benefit all levels of public purchasing. Some States and purchasing associations now publish data on specifications, as does the federal government. But the process lacks direction. There is a need for a formal program which is actively supported by federal, state, and local governments.

Many ideas about public purchasing are based on incorrect assumptions, one of them being that business is generally anxious to bid for government contracts. Actually, this is not the case, for a variety of reasons. First, competition can drive prices so low that only two bids are received and other businesses are not interested in selling at such low prices. Second, during times of product shortages or strong sellers' markets, obtaining one bid may be difficult or impossible, at least on terms acceptable to the government. Third, business customarily seeks accounts which it can retain as long as its prices are competitive and its services satisfactory. Government accounts are dependent on being the lowest responsible bidder, tend to come and go with each invitation and award, and as a result are not attractive to many businesses. Fourth, some government jurisdictions are slow in paying bills. This is a management problem that discourages many firms from competing for that business, and in times of tight money and high interest rates it may limit competition

severely or eliminate it entirely.

The study findings indicate that the characteristics of a strong purchasing program can be identified in terms of a number of essential elements. These are contained throughout the report and are consolidated in the remaining portion of this Overview. Each of these requires basic statutory or regulatory coverage, together with written policies and procedures for their implementation.

Undoubtedly, some state and local governments will observe that they do not have the resources necessary to accomplish these recommendations or that their programs are too small to warrant implementing some of them. The problem of limited resources only highlights the need for good controls, effective and efficient programs, and proper management orientation. All these are stressed in the report recommendations because an objective of this study was to highlight those practices that promote efficiency and effectiveness. In truth, the relative size of a purchasing program has little to do with observing sound and generally accepted purchasing principles. Implementation techniques can be expected to differ because of program size and other factors. Cooperation, coordination, and mutual assistance among governmental units may be necessary in some cases and may aid in fostering a healthy trend which should extend to all purchasing programs. The study findings reinforced the assumption that the principles of good purchasing apply equally to purchasing programs at all levels of government. The objectives are the same, the needs are quite similar, and most of the problems and concerns are shared. The essential elements of a good purchasing program are, therefore, presented to the chief executives, administrators, and fiscal, legal, and purchasing officials of state and local governments for their use in working together to improve their individual programs and the public purchasing profession as a whole.

ACQUISITION: PURCHASING STRUCTURE

This section of the report deals with certain fundamental concepts that act as guiding principles in accomplishing the public purchasing function. First and foremost, it is axiomatic that purchasing programs be built on a centralized authority and with centralized responsibility. Regardless of the size of the governmental unit or the purchasing program, there should be a single central authority that is responsible for ensuring the integrity and effectiveness of the program.

There are a myriad of detailed procedures and activities within purchasing, and their implementation should be delegated when feasible. Similarly, delegations should be made when using agencies can more logically and efficiently make a purchase. These kinds of delegations are consistent with the concept of a management-oriented purchasing authority. When the central purchasing authority does not itself execute all functions, it still must be held responsible, and using agencies must observe statutory, regulatory, and operational policies. Blanket exemptions from central purchasing authority are inconsistent with this precept, and they jeopardize the integrity of the system by diffusing management control. They can be replaced by judicious use of delegated authority.

The central purchasing authority should establish the goals and objectives of the purchasing program. The goals and objectives should reflect the spirit of the statutes and clearly set forth the intended results of the purchasing program. Similarly, a code of ethics should be prepared and published so that all persons, government and suppliers alike, are aware of the professional behavior expected of them.

The organizational position of purchasing in government varies from locale to locale. This report does not set forth any single organizational arrangement, beyond recommending consideration of a policy board and stressing that the central purchasing authority occupy an adequately high place in the governmental hierarchy. It should be given the stature that enables it to coordinate effectively with other departments and with suppliers. Internal organizational aspects are considered within the materials management context of the three major purchasing programs: acquisition, quality assurance, and disposition. The central purchasing authority should be responsible for managing the numerous activities within each of these programs.

The purchasing statute must serve as the basic source of the requirements and principles for the purchasing program. A declaration of policy in the statute can effectively present general principles. While the statute must set forth the fundamental requirements, it should not present detailed criteria and procedures, which are usually better dealt with in regulations and other written policy.

Essential Elements

Suggested Statutory/Regulatory Coverage

The purchasing statute and/or the rules and regulations adopted pursuant to the statute should:

- Establish a central purchasing authority to manage and control all purchasing activities.
- Define central purchasing's authorities and responsibilities, provide for and designate the scope of its delegation authority, and exclude any blanket statutory exemptions.
- Require that using agencies adhere to pertinent

statutory, regulatory, and central operational policies and requirements when purchase authority is delegated to them; also, direct the central purchasing authority to oversee and control all delegated purchasing activities.

- Not be so detailed and definitive as to be unduly restrictive. They should be concise, covering the major elements, and should require that central purchasing promulgate implementing rules and regulations, and written policies.
- Define the organizational placement of the central purchasing authority, ensuring that sufficient authority, independence, and safeguards are provided to foster the goals and objectives of the purchasing program.
- Define words having specific meaning for purposes of the purchasing statute.
- Set forth a declaration of policy for the purchasing program.

Recommended Practices

- Purchasing should be management-oriented and encompass the activities of the acquisition, standards and quality assurance, and disposition programs.
- Central purchasing should delegate activities when they can be more logically, effectively, and efficiently performed by others.
- There should be written policies governing all activities which purchasing delegates to other departments and agencies, including the manner in which such activities will be monitored and controlled by purchasing.
- Purchasing goals and objectives should be established and set forth in writing.
- The organizational placement of purchasing, and its internal functional organization, should be depicted and described in writing.
- There must be a spirit of coordination and cooperation which unites the technical expertise of purchasing and users in effectively carrying out the purchasing program.
- Team buying should be encouraged as an effective technique which improves commodity specialization, assures backup, and allows for group decision-making.

ACQUISITION: PLANNING AND SCHEDULING

There is a growing need for good planning by all governmental elements if their operations are to meet the increasingly rigorous standards of efficiency and economy. Purchasing should participate in both the management and the operational functions of planning and scheduling.

Government leaders and managers should make use of the capabilities and expertise of central purchasing in the early stages of the planning process. Purchasing can provide valuable information on forecasted costs, market conditions, product availability, and changes in technology which could affect government decisions. Purchasing should also participate in budget reviews, facilities planning, and economic analyses. The benefits from early and constant participation in planning and scheduling accrue equally to purchasing and management.

Purchasing's involvement in planning and scheduling on an operational level is concerned primarily with consolidating needs and reducing costs through volume buying. Competent planning and scheduling can also reduce the effects of market fluctuations and supply shortages.

To provide for orderly procurement and to perform effectively in planning and scheduling operations, central purchasing needs a broad base of information. Much information is available in purchasing and using agency files, but it is frequently scattered and unstructured. Consequently, there is a need to develop information systems that will provide data in a format that is useful to purchasing management. Budgets and surveys of both using agencies and suppliers can add to the data base.

Essential Elements

Suggested Statutory/Regulatory Coverage

The purchasing statute and/or the rules and regulations adopted pursuant to the statute should:

- Charge the central purchasing authority with the responsibility for developing and managing a planning and scheduling program.
- Provide purchasing with the authority to review the validity and program appropriateness of purchases.
- Provide that purchasing establish a data information system adequate to carry out its planning and scheduling responsibilities.
- Require using agencies to submit usage and requirements data to central purchasing, as designated by central purchasing.
- Provide that purchasing maintain an ongoing program to consolidate requirements whenever practicable and to utilize term contracting and scheduled purchase techniques, as appropriate.
- Permit the central purchasing authority to enter into multi-year contracts (subject to the availability of funds).

Recommended Practices

- Purchasing should play a role in top-level management planning.
- The central purchasing authority should prepare written policies and instructions covering the planning and scheduling function, including data requirements from within purchasing; data needs from using agencies; timing of the planning and scheduling activities; and areas of authority, responsibility, and liaison.
- Purchasing should use questionnaires, reviews of budgets, and surveys of vendors in its planning and scheduling function.
- Purchasing should exploit and expand the existing financial management information systems in structuring its own information system.
- Cost-savings analyses should be conducted to determine whether or not volume buying is cost-effective.
- Written policies should cover term contracting procedures and practices, including using agency procedures for ordering and providing documentation to purchasing.

ACQUISITION: BIDDERS LIST

Establishing and maintaining a current list of qualified suppliers is an important part of a good public purchasing program. There are differing viewpoints regarding bidders lists. One view is that any supplier should be included on the list, upon request. The other view is that some form of prequalification is necessary to establish, at least, that potential vendors are responsible.

While all state and local governments have some form of bidders list, these two viewpoints have caused widely varying criteria for inclusion on bidders lists. In some cases, suppliers must provide only their name, address, and commodity category. In other cases, detailed questionnaires must be completed. Some type of prequalification is needed because it is impractical and uneconomical to include every applicant on the list, regardless of whether or not he is capable of performing satisfactorily.

The prequalification program must promote fairness and impartiality and should provide for exceptions, such as for new or small businesses. The procedures, evaluation criteria, and forms used must be set forth in writing.

The bidders list must be properly organized and maintained, which includes systematic updating to accurately reflect the current status of competition. The use of a commodity coding system which lists item classification groupings and, as necessary, product functions should be considered.

Responsibility for identifying potential suppliers rests with central purchasing. Methods and techniques to be used should be defined and developed into a regular program. Similarly, there must be policies which address the circumstances under which bidders may be removed from the bidders list, or debarred, as well as reinstated after removal. The objective is to maintain an optimum base of qualified competitors. All policies for inclusion on and deletion from the bidders list should be written and made public record.

Essential Elements

Suggested Statutory/Regulatory Coverage

The purchasing statute and/or the rules and regulations adopted pursuant to the statute should:
- Require that a list of qualified bidders be established and used.
- Set forth the policy for prequalification of bidders.
- Set forth the conditions under which bidders should be deleted from the bidders list, and the attendant procedures to be used, i.e., reinstatement, period of suspension, notice to the bidder, and the right to an administrative review.

Recommended Practices

- The published policy on prequalification should provide for the forms used, type of information to be obtained from suppliers, specific governmental requirements, standards used, and methods of evaluating data received.
- The prequalification program should recognize the need for exceptions and alternate procedures, to preclude inequities.
- If prospective bidders are judged to be not qualified, they should be so advised in writing and be given an opportunity to appeal and obtain an administrative review.
- There should be a written policy covering the organization, structure, and maintenance of the bidders list.
- A long-range objective should be established to achieve uniform commodity codes among state and local governments.
- The program for identifying new suppliers should include such techniques as reviewing trade publications, attending trade shows, conducting market analyses, and exploratory advertising. Each major commodity group should be reviewed at least every two years.
- The written policy covering deletion of bidders from the bidders list should set forth the grounds for such action. It should require that vendor files be centrally maintained and establish a procedure for obtaining using agency input on supplier performance. Guidelines for setting the period of suspension should be set forth. The policy should require the chief purchasing official to review and approve proposed deletions and written notification to the bidder. Reinstatement procedures should be prescribed, the supplier's

right to administrative review should be provided, and documentation requirements should be specified.

ACQUISITION: COMPETITION

The value of open competitive bidding in public purchasing is stressed in this chapter, and is integrated throughout other chapters, as appropriate. Though competitive bidding has long been recognized as one of the best protectors of a healthy and equitable public purchasing system, certain aspects of competition have neither been fully comprehended nor effectively or uniformly implemented throughout the state and local governments.

Most state and local government laws require formal sealed competitive bids for purchases expected to exceed specified dollar amounts. There are historic prerequisites for using the formal sealed bid process. While purchasing officials and vendors alike are generally quite knowledgeable about the formal sealed bidding process, many are not fully aware that **the absence or altered circumstance of one or even more of these elements does not preclude competitive bidding.** Rather, it calls for purchasing officials to exercise initiative, innovation, and judgment to maintain an impartial environment for competition. Consequently, this report stresses the requirement to obtain competition at all levels of purchases. All too often, expediency and convenience override the principle of competition where purchases are below the statutory amounts which require sealed bidding. Where competition cannot be obtained, purchasing officials must have sufficient authority to carry out their responsibilities with judgment. However, there must be more consistency in policies which provide for waivers of competition. Close scrutiny and a well-documented file are also essential.

The major facets of the competitive bidding process, including legal notices, solicitation of bids, and the Invitation for Bids, are discussed in this chapter. Some form of legal notice is required, although most purchasing officials do not believe advertising requirements enhance competition. As a general rule, all bidders on the bidders list for a particular commodity should be solicited. Exceptions to this rule should be recognized and written guidelines should describe the circumstances under which exceptions may be made. The central purchasing authority should be responsible for the final review and approval of Invitations for Bids before they are issued.

At present, most state and local purchasing laws do not provide for competitive negotiation, which is a relatively new concept at these levels of government. Contrary to some beliefs, the use of negotiation is not intended to preclude competition and is not synonymous with single-source procurement. It is averred that competitive negotiation can be advantageously used in certain situations, and that it is in the best interests of the government to so use it.

Essential Elements

Suggested Statutory/Regulatory Coverage

The purchasing statute and/or the rules and regulations adopted pursuant to the statute should:

• Provide that competitive procedures be used for purchases of all commodities and services.

• Require sealed competitive bids for all purchases expected to exceed a predetermined dollar value.

• Require legal notice for all purchases expected to exceed a predetermined dollar amount.

• Require the central purchasing authority to issue Invitations for Bids to a large enough group of potential suppliers to assure adequate competition. Where formal sealed bids are required, the general rule should be that all bidders on the bidders list for the item be solicited. Provision should be made for exception to this general rule if it is not feasible or necessary, under given circumstances. For all such exceptions, there should be a requirement for written documentation which supports the decision not to solicit all bidders on the bidders list.

• Charge the central purchasing authority with responsibility for final review and approval of Invitations for Bids.

• Allow the purchasing official discretionary authority to require a bid security or bid bond adequate to protect the interest of the government and, when security is elected, require equal bid security and bid bond of all bidders.

• Require the purchasing official to establish procedures for maintaining accountability over bid deposits and their refunds.

• Require that the conditions and circumstances under which the requirements for obtaining competition may be waived be set forth in writing.

• Provide for the waiver of competition when certain designated officials determine, in accordance with written rules, that it is required to meet an emergency situation, requiring that such officials consult with the purchasing official whenever practicable before making an emergency purchase, and requiring documentation of the conditions that made the emergency purchase necessary, the method of purchase, and purchase price(s) of the commodities that were purchased.

• Provide for waiver of competition where the commodities or services lack responsible competition, where there are patented or proprietary rights, where standardization/interchangeability is demonstrated as ad-

vantageous to the governmental unit, and where only one source can supply the needed items, requiring that all such instances be justified in writing and approved by the central purchasing authority, in accordance with written rules.

• Permit central purchasing to use competitive negotiation when the conventional formal sealed bid process is determined to be inappropriate, in accordance with guidelines contained in written rules.

• Designate the basic criteria permitted for evaluating bids and proposals and for awarding contracts.

Recommended Practices

• All purchases should be made under conditions which foster competition among a sufficient number of potential vendors.

• The absence of one or more of the historic prerequisites for formal sealed bidding should not be interpreted to mean that competitive bidding cannot be used.

• Written procedures should be established for competitive bidding where the expected value of purchases is less than the dollar amount requiring formal sealed bids.

• Legal notices should generally describe the items or services to be purchased; state where the specifications and bid forms may be obtained, where the bids are to be received, what the deadline is for filing bids, and where the bids will be opened; indicate the type and amount of bid security (if any); and any other information the purchasing official deems necessary.

• Regional bidding may be used if necessary, but rotational bidding is to be avoided.

• The written procedures which set forth policies related to emergency purchases should define "emergency"; specify the authority, delegation, and responsibility policies; outline purchasing procedures; and specify documentation and review requirements.

• There should be written procedures for verifying single-source procurement decisions.

• Purchasing officials must challenge routinely all representations which seem to limit competition on the rationale of "standardization."

• Some form of price or cost analysis must be made for all negotiated procurements.

• In negotiated procurements, negotiations should be conducted individually with each qualified offeror, and minutes of these meetings should be prepared.

ACQUISITION: IMPEDIMENTS TO COMPETITIVE BIDDING

Impediments to competitive bidding may be inherent in the purchasing operation, the result of legislation, or initiated by suppliers.

Purchasing activities must be reviewed to eliminate any features which represent impediments to competitive bidding, such as restrictive specifications, requirements for "most favored customer" clauses, or practices that are partial toward some bidders.

Existing laws should be reviewed, and those which adversely affect free and open competition, such as preference laws, should be amended or repealed. Proposed legislation which can be expected to impact on purchasing should be coordinated with the central purchasing authority to ensure that it does not impede purchasing's ability to uphold the requirements and principles of competition. Impediments stemming from suppliers can only be detected through vigilance, good records, and a program for periodically analyzing the record for unusual bidding or award patterns. Bid-award history files should be maintained to permit such analyses. Policies need to be established to deal effectively with identical bids and dictated contracts, and there needs to be close liaison with the Attorney General in all such matters. Many state and local governments require bidders to submit signed statements that their bids were prepared independently and without collusion. This practice should be continued.

A documented public record is a most effective tool in combatting impediments to competition. Perhaps the strongest deterrent against collusive bidding is active cooperation between purchasing officials and the Attorney General's office, particularly when there are criminal penalties for collusive bidding and the Attorney General seeks to enforce them.

Unusual conditions which affect competition can and do occur, and it is best to provide for these in advance. Typical examples are markets in which one or many items are in short supply and markets in which demand exceeds supply. There are ways to cope with such conditions, but purchasing officials need the authority to adjust and modify their procedures as necessary, lest they violate the law or find themselves unable to proceed.

Essential Elements

Suggested Statutory/Regulatory Coverage

The purchasing statute and/or the rules and regulations adopted pursuant to the statute should:

- Preclude the use of restrictive specifications and "most favored customer" pricing clauses.
- Empower the central purchasing authority, when identical bids are received, to make the award in any reasonable manner that will discourage the submission of identical bids.
- Define the reasons and conditions allowing "schedule contracts" and "multiple awards."

- Require that bidders submit statements of non-collusion with all bids.
- Provide criminal penalties for collusive bidding unless specifically provided elsewhere.
- Empower the central purchasing agency to take whatever action is appropriate to purchase needed items for which acceptable competitive bids cannot be obtained, and require that these actions be justified in writing and documented in files which will be public record.

Recommended Practices

- Proposed legislation that directly or indirectly affects purchasing should be coordinated with the central purchasing authority.
- Procedures should provide for close coordination between purchasing and Attorneys General in dealing with suspected collusion, and purchasing should not proceed without advice of counsel.
- In coordination with the Attorney General, purchasing should develop documentation and records retention requirements.
- There should be a reporting format for reporting suspected collusion to the appropriate governmental element.
- Attorneys General should sponsor periodic training seminars for purchasing officials on how to respond to such matters as antitrust and collusive bidding.
- Consideration should be given to establishing a regional program, under the National Association of Attorneys General, for coordinating and acting on collusive bidding practices.
- Purchasing officials should routinely challenge "customary" price changes which are simultaneously made by all or most suppliers of particular products.
- Written guidelines should be developed to set forth procedures for making awards when identical bids are received.
- Instances of "dictated contracts" should be reported to United States and State Attorneys General.
- A bid-award history file should be maintained.
- There should be written procedures describing the techniques and procedures for analyzing bid-award history data to detect apparent collusive bidding practices.
- There should be written procedures governing the use of option clauses and a requirement that option provisions be set forth in Invitations for Bids.
- Option clauses should specify that they will be exercised at the original contract price.
- There should be written procedures which cover the methods and techniques applicable to the use of escalator clauses.
- Procedures should be established to provide guide-

lines in contracting when suppliers offer only the market price at time of delivery.

• Relief to suppliers under contract should be permitted only when holding them to the contract would be patently inequitable, and then only in accordance with stipulated procedures.

ACQUISITION: RECEIPT, OPENING, AND TABULATION OF BIDS

It is a rule of law that formal bids, correctly identified, remain sealed until the time set for bid opening. The controlling and safeguarding of bids are important to vendors, the general public and, clearly, to purchasing authorities. Procedures relating to these activities should be established and monitored by central purchasing.

Bid openings should be open to vendors and to the general public. This practice fosters confidence in the integrity of the process and discourages collusion and favoritism. While informal bids are not subject to the same requirements, the informal bid process must still be an open one. Records should be maintained which are available to all interested parties, so that the entire spectrum of purchasing is open to public scrutiny.

Whenever feasible, it is best to prepare a tabulation at the bid opening. When this is not feasible, alternative procedures should be established. In any case, the public should have the right to witness bid openings and, as for all public records and documentation, the vendors and public must have access to the prepared tabulations.

Essential Elements

Suggested Statutory/Regulatory Coverage

The purchasing statute and/or the rules and regulations adopted pursuant to the statute should:
• Permit bidders and the general public to attend bid openings.
• Require a tabulation of bids that is recorded and made available to the public.

Recommended Practices

• The central purchasing authority should be responsible for establishing written policies for controlling and safeguarding of sealed bids until the time set for openings.
• There should be written policies governing the methods for tabulating bids, the information included in bid tabulation, and the length of time these records will be retained.
• There should be a policy requiring that a public record be kept of vendors solicited for informal bids and bids received.

ACQUISITION: BID EVALUATION AND AWARD

Purchasing laws and good practice require that factors in addition to price be considered in determining the successful bidder. Consequently, bids must be carefully reviewed and evaluated. By statute, state and local governments require that awards be made to the "lowest responsible," "lowest and best," "lowest responsible meeting specifications," or other similar descriptions. Based on the research performed during this study, the phrase "lowest responsible bidder who submits a responsive bid which is most advantageous to the government" has evolved as the most suitable description of the successful bidder.

Guidelines must be established for determining which bidder is responsible and which bid is responsive and most advantageous. The standards of openness and impartiality are outlined in the statutes, but they must be further detailed in written policies. Although professional judgment must always be used, written guidelines will bring rationale, consistency, and documentation into the process.

Numerous aspects of the bid evaluation and award process deserve attention by central purchasing and are treated in this chapter. Topics such as late bids, alternate bids, mistakes, payment discounts, and one or no bids received are covered. The problems and conflicts with the principles of competition posed by state and local preference laws are also discussed. Statutory and procedural requirements covering the authority of purchasing officials to reject bids in whole or in part deserve attention and due care.

Essential Elements

Suggested Statutory/Regulatory Coverage

The purchasing statute and/or the rules and regulations adopted pursuant to the statute should:
• Provide that awards under the formal sealed bid process be made to the "lowest responsible bidder who submits a responsive bid which is most advantageous to the government."
• Require that the central purchasing authority publish written criteria, policies, and procedures governing the evaluation-award process.
• Establish that any form of state or local preference is neither acceptable nor allowable.
• Allow for discretion on the part of purchasing officials in acting in the best interest of the government when no bids are received or when the response to a solicitation is otherwise inadequate.
• Provide the authority to reject all bids, or to reject any bid in whole or in part, in accordance with written

policies and guidelines, and provide authority to take alternate courses of action, as necessary.

Recommended Practices

Written policies should be developed to provide guidelines for determining successful bidders. These procedures should stress openness and impartiality and require documentation to support decisions made, particularly in cases where awards are made to other than the low bidder, where bids are rejected in whole or in part, or where alternate bids are accepted. The written policies should cover such matters as:

• Guidelines for determining the "lowest responsible bidder who submits a responsive bid which is most advantageous to the government."

• A definition of "responsiveness" and the factors to be considered in making this determination.

• A requirement that the Invitation for Bids set forth the factors that will be used in determining responsiveness.

• The policy with respect to alternate bids and supplemental actions that may be warranted.

• Procedures to be followed when mistakes are discovered in bids.

• Guidelines for determining "substantial conformance" and "minor irregularities" in bids.

• The policy for considering discounts in determining the low bidder.

• The policy regarding late bids.

• Circumstances under which all bids may be rejected, or a particular bid may be rejected in whole or in part.

ACQUISITION: SAFEGUARDS

The principles, procedures, and structure of an effective public purchasing program must not only promote efficiency and economy, but also must provide adequate safeguards against improper and unethical conduct. The best safeguards are the requirements for written procedures, complete records, and public access to these records. Documentation of each step of the process reveals the basis of any deviation and assists in keeping the process open.

The openness of the process should be supplemented by legislative deterrents to specific situations that can destroy the integrity of the purchasing process. People who attempt to influence awards either in offering or accepting rewards should be criminally prosecuted.

Conflict of interest statutes prohibit all concerned personnel from being in positions where self-interest and integrity may come in conflict. Conflict of interest statutes should be inclusive enough to cover all officers and employees of the government, and their spouses,

who could act to influence contract awards. Penalties for violating conflict of interest statutes should parallel those for felonies. Further, any contract which is tainted with conflict of interest should be declared void, even though it might be the most advantageous for the government.

Incidences of kickbacks, bribes, or gratuities should be criminal offenses, and the specific term "giving and receiving" should be included. Legislation should deal with these actions equally harshly.

Circumventing statutory requirements is an offense of a different nature. Obtaining particular brands, making unjustified emergency purchases, and other unlawful methods can nullify good purchasing practices. While not overtly criminal, the harm to the purchasing system can be great. Effective procedures require that the responsibility for such actions be placed squarely on the shoulders of those persons who made or authorized such purchases, and written reprimands should be given to the individuals.

The infiltration of organized crime into public purchasing has not been either widely or fully recognized. An effective working relationship between purchasing officials and Attorneys General and other law enforcement officers is a clear necessity. A major contribution to this relationship is the furnishing of complete documentary evidence by purchasing officials to public prosecutors.

Essential Elements

Suggested Statutory/Regulatory Coverage

The purchasing statute and/or the rules and regulations adopted pursuant to the statute should:

• Provide for public access to and openness of the procurement process by requiring the publication of all purchasing laws, rules, regulations, and procedures; public notice of all solicitations of bids, awards, and major contract changes; documentation of all actions in the procurement process, particularly waivers of competitive bidding; and public access to bid openings and all records except unopened bids, documents on which an award is pending, and vendors' proprietary data.

• Provide for criminal penalties for attempting to influence awards through offers of reward, and for accepting such rewards; and provide that all guilty parties shall be financially liable to the government for any losses that the government incurred as a result of any contract which was so awarded.

• Provide that contracts are void if they result from a conflict of interest; if they were awarded to a person or firm that tried to influence the award by offering something of value to a government employee; or if a contract is awarded by a government official or employee by circumventing statutory requirements.

• Provide that conflict of interest statutes cover all government personnel who are in a position to influence contract awards, including the chief executive, legislators, cabinet-rank officials, department heads, officers, and employees, as well as their spouses.

• Specify the types of actions which constitute conflicts of interest.

• Classify as a felony all violations of the conflict of interest statutes.

• Require immediate dismissal from office for government employees convicted of a conflict of interest violation.

• Provide that, where contracts are declared void because they resulted from a conflict of interest, the public employee involved will be liable to the government for the amount of his profit plus the amount of any loss that the government suffered as a result of the contract.

• Set forth the conditions under which the government may be liable for a contractor's provable costs under a contract which resulted from a conflict of interest.

• Require that the chief purchasing official maintain surveillance to detect "back-door selling" and prescribe suitable penalties for suppliers and government employees who engage in this practice.

• Require a bond to protect the government against all losses caused by malfeasance or misfeasance of government officers or employees who can influence the award of public contracts, if no provision is made for such a bond elsewhere in government legislation.

• Require that a code or standard of conduct be published to govern the performance of government employees, and especially purchasing personnel, in managing, purchasing, or otherwise expending government funds.

• Provide for criminal, civil, and administrative sanctions; penalties; and disciplinary actions for violation of such standards either by government officers or employees, or by contractors or their agents.

• Establish personal liability for government personnel who authorize purchases to be made without following applicable statutes and rules.

Recommended Practices

• The central purchasing authority should prepare and issue written policies and procedures designed to discourage "back-door selling" and to detect and prevent instances of this practice.

• The central purchasing authority should prepare written procedures which set forth the techniques to be used to prevent and detect the circumvention of purchasing laws and regulations. The procedures should provide that official reprimands be issued to government employees who circumvent these laws and regulations.

• The central purchasing authority should establish a program for continuing communication and coordination with the appropriate law enforcement units who are responsible for dealing with organized crime matters.

QUALITY ASSURANCE: SPECIFICATIONS

The preparation of proper technical specifications is one of the most important and most difficult functions in the purchasing process. Specifications describe what is required or desired, and thus are the communication media between buyer and seller. The great variety of items that are purchased complicates specification writing, as does the fact that state and local governments can seldom dictate the exact characteristics of the products they buy and use. This vast and difficult field challenges every purchasing program, and all purchasing officials share the feeling that improved techniques and capabilities are needed.

Specifications should set out the essential characteristics of items being purchased, so that bidders can accurately compute their bids. This requirement relates directly to the suitability of the product for its intended use, and rules out both under- and over-specifying requirements. Specifications also must be nonrestrictive, i.e., they must not unnecessarily limit competition.

Specifications take many forms, including brand names, qualified products lists (also called approved products lists, approved brand lists, or qualified brand lists), comparison of actual samples, designation for a special use, design, performance, and costs of operation analysis. This chapter discusses each of these forms. While specifications based on performance are preferred, and some specifications are better than others, no one type is best for all types of products. There are situations where the use of a certain form of specification is necessary or expedient. Written guidelines should describe each type of specification, its advantages, and its limitations. Appropriate safeguards should also be specified, such as with brand name specifications. These should always include a statement that the brand name is used only to establish a quality level, and that equivalent items will be acceptable. Wherever possible, several brand names should be listed.

Regardless of where specifications originate or are prepared, the central purchasing authority must be responsible for final review and approval. The review process should determine whether or not the specifications are adequate for competition, and whether or not they call for a quality level which is suitable for the item's intended use. To preclude misunderstanding, the authorities, responsibilities, and procedures related to the specification process should be set forth in writing.

Standardization is another significant aspect of the specification process. Most States and many local governments have established programs to develop standard specifications for most or all purchases of a given item. These programs permit more efficient operations and result in lower prices because of volume purchases. The issues pertaining to standard specifications are considered in this chapter of the report including coordination with using agencies, obtaining industry input, and establishing standardization committees.

Much more needs to be done in exchanging specifications and related data among state and local governments. A basic rule in specification writing should be to "look for and use whatever reasonable aids are already available." These aids include specifications already developed by other state or local governments, by the federal government, or by professional organizations. In this area, the most potentially significant program is a cooperative program to write performance standards under the aegis of the Council of State Governments and the National Association of State Purchasing Officials, with funding from the National Bureau of Standards. The impact of this program, if successful, will be tremendous.

Essential Elements

Suggested Statutory/Regulatory Coverage

The purchasing statute and/or the rules and regulations adopted pursuant to the statute should:

• Charge central purchasing with the responsibility for establishing a specification program and a standardization program, with written policies and procedures.

• Provide central purchasing with the authority, under defined conditions and with each action suitably documented, to waive competitive bidding for the purpose of buying articles for experiment, test, or trial.

• Grant the central purchasing authority the power to review, modify, and approve specifications.

Recommended Practices

• To provide a common basis for bidding, specifications should set out the essential characteristics of the items being purchased.

• Specifications should not call for features or a quality level which is not necessary to an item's intended use.

• Planning procedures should call for reviews of equipment items to determine the types of optional items ordered and the frequency of such purchases.

• When optional item needs warrant, the Invitation for Bids should set forth the expected needs and the manner in which the related bid prices will be considered during the bid evaluation process.

• Historical data on optional item purchases should be included when building an information system for purchasing.

• The policies and procedures for handling optional items should be set forth in writing.

• Specifications should include descriptions of the nature and methods of testing to be used, and guidelines for objectively applying test results must be established.

• Written guidelines should be prepared to set forth the different types of specifications and the circumstances under which they are most appropriate.

• Whenever brand name specifications are used, there must be an accompanying explanation that clearly indicates that the specification is not intended to be restrictive and, where possible, several acceptable brand names should be used.

• The use of brand name specifications should be limited insofar as feasible.

• Qualified products lists limit competition to those products on the list, but can be effectively used. When used, actual samples or highly documented files should be kept on each item that qualifies, and qualification procedures should include, where feasible, qualitative ratings or test scores.

• The use of samples is a valuable aspect of the specification process. Samples can also serve as indications of the quality level of delivered goods.

• Design specifications must be carefully constructed in terms of any features that might make an item unacceptable for the purpose for which it is to be used.

• Performance specifications encourage ingenuity, innovation, and cost reduction, and are the preferred type of specification.

• Techniques which foster the determination of best value to the government should be encouraged and further developed.

• Central purchasing should review specifications for restrictiveness and should assure that the appropriate quality level is specified.

• The specification process should be set forth in writing, citing both central purchasing's and using agencies' responsibilities and authorities.

• To avoid organizational conflicts of interest and to assure objective specifications, suppliers should not prepare specifications.

• Because standard specifications allow for more efficient operations and result in lower prices, they should be used wherever suitable.

• When developing standard specifications, using

agency program needs must be considered, and industry input should be obtained.

• The use of specification and standardization committees should be encouraged because, if properly structured, they can be an effective technique for developing standard specifications.

• Standard specifications should be indexed and filed, and procedures should be developed for their review and updating.

• The same format should be used for all standard specifications.

• Maximum use should be made of industry specifications as well as those available from federal, state, and local governments.

• Some means is needed to provide better collection and dissemination of specification data among state and local governments.

QUALITY ASSURANCE: INSPECTION AND TESTING

There must be assurance that the government gets the types and quantities of items called for in the purchase order or contract. Inspection and testing of items delivered by suppliers are important elements of the purchasing system. They cannot be left to an informal procedure that lacks direction and control. They must be formally established and centrally administered by purchasing, even though some of the activities may be properly delegated to using agencies. The inspection-testing program should, therefore, be set forth in writing, preferably in a manual. The procedures should include a mechanism for reporting to purchasing, which should maintain the central files and be responsible for taking the necessary action, including contacts with suppliers. Central purchasing should also identify the outside facilities that are available for testing (e.g., local colleges or universities), as well as any available in-house facilities. Where appropriate, suppliers can be asked to furnish certificates of compliance or certified test results on items delivered.

Essential Elements

Suggested Statutory/Regulatory Coverage

The purchasing statute and/or the rules and regulations adopted pursuant to the statute should:

• Require that central purchasing establish and administer a formal inspection and testing program.

Recommended Practices

• Central purchasing should prepare and publish an inspection manual which sets forth the authorities, re-

sponsibilities, techniques, and standards related to the inspection and testing program. Alternately, this subject could be included in the purchasing procedures manual.

• Government personnel who are responsible for receiving and inspecting items delivered should have ready access to specifications.

• Receiving documents should not show the quantities to be delivered.

• Central purchasing should either make all inspections or, if this function is delegated, monitor the program to assure that established policies are being observed.

• Central purchasing should identify and set forth written guidelines on the types of testing facilities that are available and on alternate techniques such as obtaining certificates of compliance or certified test results from suppliers.

• There is a need to explore the ways in which governments can coordinate the testing of similar items and better communicate test results to each other.

• There should be a formal, written reporting system for complaints against suppliers and for deficiencies noted during inspections.

• Central purchasing should be responsible for acting on deficiency and complaint reports and should be the focal point for contacts with suppliers on such deficiencies.

DISPOSITION

The disposition of surplus items and scrap is closely tied to the acquisition program and to inventory management, and is an important element of the overall materials management concept. Timely identification of surplus and scrap is essential. Although using agencies usually are in the best position to identify unneeded items, they often have little incentive to do so. Consequently, some governments give using agencies credit for the sales proceeds of items released. While central purchasing should have overall policy and procedural control of the identification process, effective coordination between purchasing and using agencies is essential if a disposition program is to work. This coordination should take place within the framework of written procedures setting forth clear guidelines to be followed.

Central purchasing should be responsible for determining the most appropriate disposition method. Transferring items not needed by one agency to another that does need them is the best method of disposal. The "want list" is an effective technique used by some governments.

Obtaining released items under the federal donable and surplus property programs is discussed in this chapter. The effectiveness of the States' efforts in this area could be improved with specialized central attention.

Essential Elements

Suggested Statutory/Regulatory Coverage

The purchasing statute and/or the rules and regulations adopted pursuant to the statute should:
• Charge central purchasing with the responsibility for overall supervision and ultimate control over both the inventory and surplus programs.
• Require that the using agency identify surplus items, declare them as such, and report them to purchasing.
• Provide that the proceeds from disposition be credited to the owning agency.
• Grant central purchasing the authority to dispose of surplus and scrap, or to regulate its disposal, in a manner that it deems to be in the government's best interest.
• Assign central purchasing the task of keeping informed of items available under federal surplus programs (state statute only).
• Grant central purchasing the authority to operate and regulate any state program related to federal surplus programs (state statute only).

Recommended Practices

• Central purchasing should periodically review inventory levels of using agencies to determine whether excess stocks are on hand.
• Written procedures should be prepared and published which set forth central purchasing's authorities and responsibilities in identifying items as surplus, and guidelines for determining the most appropriate disposition method (e.g., transfer, trade-in, sale) for given types of situations.
• Well-defined procedures should be established for transferring surplus property among state or local agencies prior to disposition.
• Want lists should be encouraged as an effective technique in the disposition program.
• If trade-ins are accepted on a particular piece of equipment, the Invitation for Bids should call for bid prices with and without trade-in and indicate that the award may be made on either basis.
• Procedures for and conditions of sale should be documented in writing and published.

COOPERATIVE PURCHASING

There are a variety of arrangements by which two or more government entities buy under the same con-

tract or agreement. The major advantage is to obtain lower prices from volume buying, although this cannot always be achieved. Cooperative purchasing tends to encourage the manufacture of new or modified products which are not otherwise commercially available. The strongest cooperative purchasing programs require that all participants be actual parties to the contract. The weakest programs are permissive arrangements whereby third-party agencies can use a contract whenever and however they choose.

Cooperative purchasing programs have developed unevenly, and some sound principles of competitive bidding have been endangered through loose, optional types of arrangements. Recently, these dangers have been recognized so that commitments have been required of all parties. From a practical viewpoint, the largest participating jurisdiction should be the agreed focal point for contract administration because of its larger and more technically qualified staff.

Not all state and local governments have the same requirements and procedures governing purchasing. As a result, difficulties are frequently encountered in meeting the legal requirements of all participants. All state and local laws should provide authority to purchase cooperatively, but the laws should also provide that cooperative purchasing will be permitted only when the purchasing jurisdiction assuming administrative responsibility conducts its purchasing operations according to the principles of open competition.

Essential Elements

Suggested Statutory/Regulatory Coverage

The purchasing statute and/or the rules and regulations adopted pursuant to the statute should:
• Explicitly provide the authority for intergovernmental cooperative purchasing, under rules and procedures established by the central purchasing authority.
• Provide that governmental units be parties to contracts under cooperative purchasing agreements.
• Provide that cooperative purchasing be permitted only when the purchasing jurisdiction assuming administrative responsibility conducts its purchasing operations according to the principles of open competition.

Recommended Practices

• Participants in cooperative purchasing must agree to abide by all contractual requirements, including prompt payment of invoices.
• Normally, the largest participating unit should administer the cooperative purchasing program.
• When local governments or nonstate agencies are permitted to join in cooperative programs with state

purchasing, their participation should be elective, not mandatory.

• State and large local governments should take a more active leadership role in fostering, designing, and administering cooperative purchasing programs. Programs among local governmental units should be especially encouraged.

• Local entities must consider their responsibilities to serve the public interest and approach cooperative purchasing opportunities with a professional management outlook.

• Local governments should consider extending the concepts of consolidating operational functions to administrative areas such as purchasing, under merged governments or pooling arrangements.

• The long-range benefits of aggregating purchasing power through joint purchases by two or more States should be examined.

PROFESSIONAL DEVELOPMENT

Statute and administrative law, policies, procedures, and organizational structure all mesh to provide the mechanism of public purchasing. It takes people to put this static mechanism into motion. This chapter discusses the roles of people both in and out of the mainstream of state and local government purchasing who, in a variety of ways, participate in the procurement of goods and services.

Although purchasing cannot be called a profession in the strictest sense of the word, with implications of educational discipline, licensing, and professional standards of practice, public purchasers can and should nevertheless perform in a professional manner.

The educational needs and requirements of public purchasers have changed as purchasing has evolved through three identifiable phases. In the 1800s, laws largely concerned themselves with protecting taxpayers against favoritism and fraud, and were patterned after construction and public works contract law. The public purchaser was a technician. The need to get the most out of the tax dollar after World War I and the depression of the 1930s started the movement toward the greater efficiency of more centralized purchasing operations. The need for a more formal purchasing discipline became apparent, and it becomes more urgent as purchasing enters its third phase of development, that of increasing the buying power of the tax dollar through a growing management orientation.

There is not now a formal educational program to prepare the purchaser for this kind of role. Purchasing associations must assume the responsibility for formalizing the body of knowledge that supports good public purchasing practice, and state and local governments must commit themselves to training and professional development. Furthermore, purchasing associations must continue their efforts to promote the necessary structure of uniform principles and standards that will advance uniform application of this body of knowledge. This entire study is itself directed toward that goal.

Some purchasing associations have already established professional certification programs to identify responsible purchasing performance among individuals who have attained a prescribed level of qualification. This study commends that beginning, and urges their consolidation into one national program receiving full faith by all associations in the field. Such a national program, combined with a new commitment to communication with the publics served by public purchasing, is vital to the public confidence so necessary to effective purchasing programs.

Purchasing has evolved from a simple buying function to one of management of public funds requiring knowledge of constantly changing technologies and market conditions, complex information systems, and new purchasing techniques. Without ongoing professional development, public purchasing cannot fulfill the government's needs.

Essential Elements

Suggested Statutory/Regulatory Coverage

The purchasing statute and/or the rules and regulations adopted pursuant to the statute should:

• Provide a statement of intent encouraging affiliation by purchasing officials and their technical staffs with one or more professional purchasing associations.

• Require that government personnel have the authority to prepare and maintain position specifications for the full spectrum of purchasing jobs. These specifications should reflect the current thinking of appropriate associations as to job content and credentials.

• Embody as part of the policy statement in the purchasing law an affirmation of the management role of public purchasing officials. (See also "Acquisition: Purchasing Structure.")

Recommended Practices

• Purchasing associations should incorporate the specifics of career education into position specifications and educational standards for purchasing.

• The need for formal training and educational programs which supplement basic knowledge and experience should be examined.

• The central purchasing authority should provide for specific funding in the departmental budget for training and professional development, including formal course work; an updated departmental technical library; memberships in local, state, and/or national purchasing associations; and travel to observe other purchasing units.

- Associations of public purchasers should lead the way in formalizing a body of requirements and an educational curriculum in the field of public purchasing.

- Ongoing management and administrative work experience should be required of the technical staff. For example, the staff should become members of committees and task forces (i.e., the "purchasing" representatives for such groups), adept at researching and writing policy issue papers, and experienced in preparation of budgets.

- Public purchasers need to establish a viable underlying commonality to ensure that the principles and standards of good public purchasing are applied consistently.

- The need for a single national certification program which is endorsed and supported by all purchasing associations should be addressed.

- The observations, conclusions, recommendations, and other information contained in this report can be used to improve communication with purchasing's public and to evaluate purchasing programs.

3. Acquisition: Purchasing Structure

ESSENTIAL ELEMENTS

Suggested Statutory/Regulatory Coverage

The purchasing statute and/or the rules and regulations adopted pursuant to the statute should:

Establish a central purchasing authority to manage and control all purchasing activities.

Define central purchasing's authorities and responsibilities, provide for and designate the scope of its delegation authority, and exclude any blanket statutory exemptions.

Require that using agencies adhere to pertinent statutory, regulatory, and central operational policies and requirements when purchase authority is delegated to them; also, direct the central purchasing authority to oversee and control all delegated purchasing activities.

Not be so detailed and definitive as to be unduly restrictive. They should be concise, covering the major elements, and should require that central purchasing promulgate implementing rules and regulations, and written policies.

Define the organizational placement of the central purchasing authority, ensuring that sufficient authority, independence, and safeguards are provided to foster the goals and objectives of the purchasing program.

Define words having specific meaning for purposes of the purchasing statute.

Set forth a declaration of policy for the purchasing program.

Recommended Practices

Purchasing should be management-oriented and encompass the activities of the acquisition, standards and quality assurance, and disposition programs.

Central purchasing should delegate activities when they can be more logically, effectively, and efficiently performed by others.

There should be written policies governing all activities which purchasing delegates to other departments and agencies, including the manner in which such activities will be monitored and controlled by purchasing.

Purchasing goals and objectives should be established and set forth in writing.

The organizational placement of purchasing, and its internal functional organization, should be depicted and described in writing.

There must be a spirit of coordination and cooperation which unites the technical expertise of purchasing and users in effectively carrying out the purchasing program.

Team buying should be encouraged as an effective technique which improves commodity specialization, assures backup, and allows for group decision-making.

Public purchasing is that area of government which seeks to provide equipment, materials, supplies, and services at economical prices by seeking competition and evaluating the most advantageous proposals and taking into account the needs and the best interests of the government. A basic distinction between public purchasing and private purchasing is that public monies are being spent, the activity is public business, and records and information related to purchases are open to public inspection. This openness protects against favoritism and fraud because public officials must be prepared to account for and defend their actions against public criticism. The public purchasing organization must have safeguards to cope with social and political influences while, at the same time, providing public purchasing officials with freedom to use professional judgment and personal initiative to function effectively in the public interest.

The structure of the public purchasing authority must be responsive to its unique status: government procurement is an "act in agency," an agency with a special relationship which calls for the purchasing official to act for others, to commit their budgets, and to influence their programs. This distinctive legal position demands that the purchasing function be accorded a peer relationship with other agencies consistent with the accountability it entails.

Purchasing started out primarily as an ordering, then a buying function, but it is clear that it can no longer be that limited in scope. The evolution of complex, high-technology items which are subject to obsolescence in relatively short periods of time requires that public purchasing officials remain up-to-date in their technical knowledge, related information systems, and new purchasing techniques. Also, a successful program must have the flexibility to adjust to market conditions where supply and demand are relatively in balance, or where either exceeds the other. Without this flexibility, the function cannot meet the government's needs to best advantage.

CENTRAL PURCHASING AUTHORITY AND RESPONSIBILITIES

Purchasing-related activities interface with various using agencies and technical disciplines outside the purchasing unit itself, and an effective purchasing program must be built on a clear statement of authority and responsibility. Because public purchasing entails the commitment and expenditure of public funds, it is extremely important that the responsibility for key purchasing activities be clearly fixed. Recognizing that there are various levels of government and various sizes of purchasing programs, **the constant should be a central purchasing authority responsible for assuring that the principles and attendant requirements of the purchasing program are met.** At the state level, and for larger units of local government, the purchasing authority should rest in a central office. In some local governments, purchasing is so small an activity that it may be handled by one individual on a full- or part-time basis. In any case, there should be a single authority in each governmental unit who is responsible for assuring the integrity and effectiveness of the program.

An issue basic to the concept of a central purchasing authority is that purchasing must be management-oriented, rather than simply service-oriented. The purchasing program encompasses much more than just ordering and buying goods and services. Functions such as planning and scheduling, bid solicitation, evaluation, and award are all part of the acquisition function. Public purchasing should also be responsible for contract administration, quality assurance, and surplus property transfer and disposal. The writing of standards and specifications and the conduct of inspections and tests are closely integrated with the acquisition process.

Specifications are needed in preparing Invitations for Bids and in seeking competition, and some type of testing program is necessary as part of the evaluation and award process to determine whether bidders have or have not met specifications.

Statutory Exemptions and Delegations

Some States provide blanket exemptions from central purchasing for designated agencies, commodities, or both. Some agencies have been exempt for historical reasons—traditionally they have been highly autonomous organizations with segregated funding. Other agencies have been permitted to purchase highly technical items on the grounds that they have the program expertise. Neither of these types of exemptions is consistent with the concept of central purchasing. The tradition of long-standing, autonomous, and politically powerful agencies is difficult to overcome, yet it should not override the fundamentals of a sound public purchasing program.

The argument for the purchase of highly technical and specialized equipment by using agencies is not a valid cause for blanket agency exemption. It is not unusual nor inappropriate for a using agency to work extensively on preparing technical specifications and even to assist in the evaluation process. In fact, the nature of some items calls for participation by the using agency. The central purchasing authority will normally not possess all expertise on every commodity purchased, but experience clearly indicates that the final decision ought to rest with central purchasing. Commodity exemptions often involve over-the-counter items such as liquor for resale, and in these instances the central purchasing authority can generally provide for procedures and procedural review.

Purchasing management and the executive and legislative branches must constantly review exemptions and delegations. The valid rationale of yesteryear may well have become today's impediment to effective purchasing and good government. Blanket statutory exemptions jeopardize the integrity of the purchasing program because they diffuse control. If central purchasing is to be effective, it must manage or supervise all purchasing operations. This management and control should include the authority to delegate purchasing activities and thereby effectively eliminate the need for blanket statutory exemptions.

Some governments require that all orders be prepared and issued by central purchasing, while others permit using agencies to prepare and issue orders after a contract has been awarded by central purchasing. In many governments, the purchasing activity constitutes a substantial volume of work, and the purchasing authority would be inundated with paperwork if all acquisitions, however small, came through it. Consequently, these latter purchasing units usually delegate authority to the using agencies for making certain types of purchases, or purchases under a certain dollar amount, and provide for waiving competitive bidding under certain circumstances (e.g., in the case of emergency purchases). In these cases, central purchasing establishes the procedures to be followed, oversees the entire process, and receives copies of the orders placed, which are subject to review.

Local conditions must be considered in determining the types and extent of authority which is delegated by central purchasing. One agency may need an item which is only available locally. Another agency may need certain items immediately and it may be impractical to go through central purchasing. Delegations can and should be made when the activities can more logically, effectively, and efficiently be performed by others, but always under central statutory, regulatory, and operational policies and with the specific guidance of the central purchasing authority.

Although certain authorities may be appropriately delegated to using agencies, **the central purchasing authority must maintain overall legal responsibility for implementing the purchasing program and establishing the policies, procedures, and controls for delegation.** Central purchasing must monitor and review all delegated activities to assure that they are effectively performed by others.

Goals and Objectives

The central purchasing authority is responsible for safeguarding the public interest. While Legislatures can provide the basis for accomplishing this by enacting good purchasing statutes, purchasing officials must apply the laws and principles of good purchasing in a manner that results in decisions which are in the government's best interest. This can best be done by formulating policy and by having the authority to implement that policy through rules and regulations, practices and procedures, and ethical codes of behavior.

Some of the goals and objectives of public purchasing are:

- providing timely, effective, and efficient service to using agencies and to vendors doing business with the government;
- maintaining open communication with the news media;
- controlling and reducing the cost of purchasing supplies, materials, equipment, and services; and
- adopting a materials management and total supply concept of operation.

A wide range of diverse endeavors is necessary if these objectives are to be attained, the broader of which are seldom given continuing and sufficient emphasis. Among these are:

- overhauling and redirecting legislation toward the end of comprehensive purchasing management;
- researching and developing quantitative purchasing performance measures;
- rearranging organizational structure to encourage effective performance and accountability;
- updating and documenting procurement practices and procedures for continuing improvements;
- increasing capability for innovation, with a focus on stated goals and objectives; and
- aggressively pursuing professional excellence and communicating this to operating agency heads, other government officials, and the public.

Comprehensive purchasing management requires that the central purchasing authority be much more than a focal point for consolidating orders. It is also the center for information from using agencies regarding vendor performance, commodity usage, inventory levels, specifications, and the like. Additionally, when central warehousing is necessary, central purchasing is responsible for the decisions concerning stockpiling, inventory control, receiving, and inspection.

If the central purchasing authority is to fulfill its responsibilities, then recognizing and adjusting those constraints which impede it are imperative. For example, the central purchasing authority may be prevented from formulating policy because the statute describing it is so detailed that for all practical purposes it prescribes the purchasing rules, regulations, and procedures. In this case, the statute deprives the central purchasing authority of the discretion and flexibility it needs to best exercise its duties and responsibilities.

ORGANIZATION

Position in Government

Purchasing officials must deal fairly with vendors, coordinate with other government departments, provide timely and quality service, and protect the public interest. To properly accomplish these responsibilities, the central purchasing authority must be able to exercise independent professional judgment. It also must be able to deal with vendors and with all department heads from a position of authority commensurate with its responsibilities. Purchasing's independence and effectiveness can be either positively or negatively affected by its placement within the government hierarchy. Factors such as organizational and management philosophy, tradition, the size of the purchasing program, and resources available to it have a major impact on this issue. There is no one best arrangement; what may work well in one State or local government may not work well in another.

In the 1950s, there was a strong movement to include purchasing in a department of finance or administration as a means of integrating fiscally related functions. This is presently the case in many governments. In the approach receiving the most attention today, however, the purchasing function is a part of an overall general services responsibility. Recent governmental reorganizations in several jurisdictions have taken this direction. In many governmental structures, however, a department of administration actually serves the same purpose as a general services department, so it provides an equally suitable location for the purchasing function.

In one State, purchasing still functions as a separate department, which is not consistent with prevailing reorganization efforts to reduce the number of all departments to 20 or less. In two States, a separate board appointed by the Governor oversees purchasing activities and the activities of various other central services. In two other cases, purchasing is housed in a department of administration with a commission including legislative members serving as the policy body. Though unusual, the latter two arrangements can afford certain strong advantages.

Fundamentally, however, the need is to place the central purchasing authority in the governmental hierarchy so that the number of levels between the chief purchasing official and the chief executive is lessened. The majority of state and local governments studied have one person between the chief purchasing official and the chief executive. In these governments, public purchasing operates as one bureau or division among several within a given department. The chief purchasing official is the individual who is charged with the legal responsibility for purchasing activities. He might not oversee all the day-to-day operations, but he retains responsibility for them.

A major recommendation of the recent Federal Commission on Government Procurement was the establishment of an Office of Federal Procurement Policy. Several States have established boards or commissions which serve a purpose similar to that recommended for the federal level. In States where it has been successful, the purchasing function operates under an independent board or commission which allows the goals and objectives to be pursued relatively free from governmental and outside pressures. (Figure 1 gives an example.) The board or commission serves as the governing body of the purchasing program. It may be composed of government officials and/or private citizens. Members may or may not serve for a specified term, and the terms may or may not overlap. The

FIGURE 1

Example of External Organization
with Governing Board or Commission

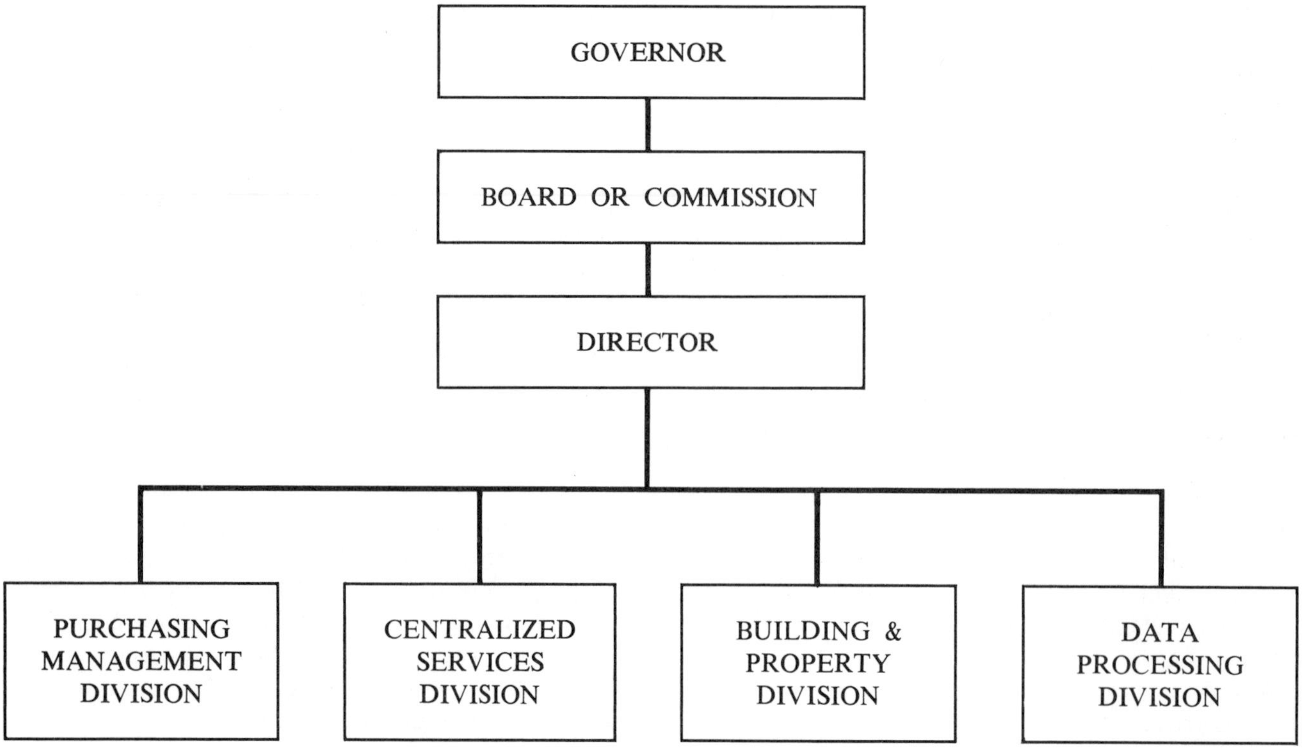

board may appoint a full-time director who serves as the chief purchasing official. The board is concerned with rules and regulations and with the overall direction of the purchasing department. Under this type of organization, purchasing is partially protected from direct external pressures. The board serves as an advocate of purchasing and lends its credibility to the improvement of the purchasing operations. To the extent that government officials serve on the board, a healthy mixture of viewpoints is provided. Overall, such a board can provide a check on purchasing activities, but to be effective it must meet regularly and be actively interested. It functions best as a small body, and care must be taken that its members avoid any conflicts of interest.

For cities and counties where the size and volume of the purchasing activity call for a central office, its goals and objectives are more likely to be met if it is established as a separate unit on equal footing with other major departments. For local governments where the central purchasing authority rests with a single individual, that individual needs sufficient power and responsibility to achieve purchasing's purposes.

It is not possible to set forth a single organizational arrangement that is best for all state or local governments, but a strong recommendation can be made for a policy board. Beyond that, **whatever the organization, the central purchasing authority should occupy a place which provides the stature necessary to coordinate and deal with other departments and agencies effectively and which, at the same time, is designed to prevent decisions which are based on partisan political pressures or considerations, or which would otherwise represent favoritism.**

Internal Organization

In discussing the functional organization for a purchasing program, the underlying concept is one of overall materials management, not merely acquisition. Such a program includes acquisition, quality assurance, and disposal, encompassing consolidation of agency needs for scheduled purchases and term contracts, determination and evaluation of requirements, contract administration, monitoring vendor performance, and reviewing product usage. The levels of sophistication and the quantity and quality of resources (e.g., manpower, funds, facilities, and equipment) available to state and local governments are keys to the issue of internal organization. A recommendation that all state and local governments have a separate and distinct specifications and standards section, for example, is not feasible in a location where one or a few people handle all aspects of the purchasing program.

As shown in Figure 2, the ideal central purchasing authority consists of three major programs. Each of these is further broken down into its major activities. This functional organization generally outlines the kinds of activities that are included under the concept of a central purchasing authority. The need for effective communication and working relationships among all of these activities is paramount if an organization like this is to be dynamic and successful. The organizational placement of purchasing, its internal functional organization, and the key interrelationships with other departments should be depicted and described in writing.

Acquisition Program

The acquisition program encompasses the activities of planning and scheduling; designing Invitations for Bids and soliciting bids; receiving, opening, and evaluating the bids and making awards; expediting; and contract administration. Planning and scheduling is an aspect that needs greater emphasis than it has been given traditionally. This activity should play an important role in budgeting, reducing unit costs through volume buying, consolidating and validating agency needs, and determining how these needs can best be met. Greater attention must also be given to contract administration activities. These activities need to be defined and centrally administered to assure that suppliers meet contractual terms and conditions.

The design of the Invitation for Bids is critical to every procurement. Basic considerations are the terms and conditions which must be prepared to ensure and protect the interest of the government; openness of specifications; requirements for transportation and delivery; and instructions as to how the bidder is to submit his proposal. Solicitation also includes the organization and maintenance of bidders lists, the option of prequalification of suppliers, the need for public notice, and the need, if any, for bid security. Bid solicitation should seek maximum competition for all purchases and fair and equal opportunity for all qualified persons or firms. Bid evaluation and award involve establishing criteria for award and rejection of bids, a determination of the lowest and best or lowest responsible bidder whose proposal is most advantageous to the government, and public awareness of the prices and products obtained.

To the extent that a cooperative purchasing program exists between or among government units, the management responsibility for such a program should lie with the central purchasing authority. The leasing or renting of equipment, and the accompanying lease versus buy decisions, are also a responsibility of the central purchasing authority, as are contracts for repairs and maintenance of equipment, and contractual

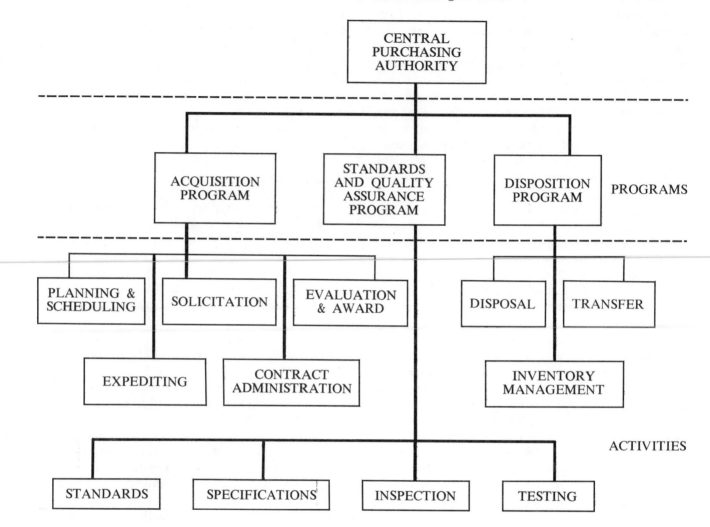

FIGURE 2

Internal Functional Organization

needs such as janitorial and laundry services. Whether or not central purchasing actually handles solicitations and awards of such contracts, or delegates aspects of them to operating agencies, is determined by geographical factors, local conditions, staff size, workload requirements, etc. When they are delegated, it is good practice for central purchasing to design and require the use of a uniform bid solicitation document for each particular type of requirement, including the contract terms and conditions.

Questions sometimes arise about whether purchasing must have all the technical expertise necessary to buy certain items such as insurance or printing. Some purchasing programs have separate sections, including risk managers, that are responsible for purchasing insurance. In other cases, program appropriateness and decisions to self-insure or purchase are made by risk managers outside of purchasing, or by insurance boards. In the case of printing, the laws governing public pur-

chasing apply and there are often special statutes that provide added coverage. As with insurance, some purchasing programs have separate sections that handle the purchase of printing. Items such as these are not too different from many other commodities assigned to purchasing specialists. But it is sometimes more difficult to get the proper technical personnel to do the job. If purchasing cannot get the types of people needed, it must obtain expert advice from individuals outside its own organization. In any case, the actual purchases should be made by central purchasing.

Similar considerations relate to the purchase of professional services, e.g., management consulting, architect and engineering, and medical and legal services. Using agencies must necessarily play an important role in drafting statements of work and in evaluating technical proposals, where such proposals are called for and received. In some state and local governments, the personnel department must determine that the hourly or other rates proposed are within the upper and lower limits of the current hour rates for such services. In some States, the Attorney General must approve the contract before it is signed. Given the need for these types of technical assistance and administrative controls, however, the central purchasing authority should be responsible for the procurement of professional services.

If a state or local government makes a purchase under a "total cost" concept, which takes into consideration initial costs plus maintenance and operating costs, data from using agencies often are needed to make necessary cost comparisons and evaluations. Purchases of high-technology items such as X-ray equipment, telecommunications equipment, and computer hardware and software, usually require the combined expertise of several agencies working together with central purchasing. For example, when procuring computer equipment, experts in automatic data processing would provide certain technical information for preparing and evaluating bids, and the using agency would supply information on the intended use of the equipment. Purchasing, however, would manage the acquisition process. It would be the focal point for preparing the Invitation for Bids, soliciting bids, and evaluating responses. After the award, purchasing would be responsible for the administration and management of all phases of the contract throughout its duration, with reliance on the using agency for information as needed.

There are two additional areas worthy of special note. The first concerns the operation of government motor pools. While the acquisition and disposal of government vehicles should be the responsibility of purchasing, the maintenance and operation of the motor pool should not. This distinction is made because acquisition and disposal are integral functions of a materials management program, while operation and maintenance are not. The same reasoning applies to the operation of a central data processing activity, or of a copying and duplicating center.

The second area relates to the purchase of real estate and buildings, including the leasing of space. The acquisition of real estate is usually governed by a separate set of rather complex laws. It can be argued that real estate is not a biddable item, but this in itself should not be a reason for excluding it from purchasing's responsibility. While real estate is traditionally excluded from central purchasing responsibility, there is no absolute reason to believe that with the assistance of outside expertise, purchasing should not have a responsibility in the purchase and leasing of lands and buildings, with the exclusion of condemnations, rights-of-way, and lands for recreation.

In discussing the acquisition program as it relates to internal organization, the concepts of team buying and rotation are important. Team buying, where more than one person is responsible for purchasing in the same commodity area, is a highly recommended practice. Among other things, it improves commodity specialization by providing several persons who are knowledgeable in the same areas. It assures backup, and it allows for group decision-making with overall responsibility resting with the team leader.

Although some governments rotate buyers as a means for providing backup, this practice is not recommended because many commodities have become so highly specialized that rotation is not feasible. While it is often necessary for more than one person to be aware of current developments in any given commodity area, all purchasing agents need not try to be specialists in all commodities.

Standards and Quality Assurance Program

The standards and quality assurance program embodies the activities of standardization, specification writing, inspection, and testing. Vendor performance and commodity usage are important factors. The activities of developing standards and specifications address the subject of commodity usage, while inspection and testing measure vendor performance. Vendor performance refers not only to whether or not specifications are met, but also to whether deliveries are timely and complete, and whether there are any unauthorized substitutions or other failures in performance. Many government units do not have strong standards and quality assurance programs. In some governments, the writing of specifications is completely outside the central purchasing authority, while in others it is relegated to a status of minor importance within central purchasing. Wherever possible, the four major activities of a complete program should be an integral part of the central purchasing authority.

While the basic duty of the standards and quality assurance effort is to serve as the major technical resource to and to provide technical support for the overall procurement effort, it should be a distinctive organizational entity with its own job descriptions and with well-defined assignments and responsibilities. Too often among both state and local governments this is not the case.

The value of an effective standards and inspection program can be substantial, and in any complex purchasing organization it is an essential component. For States, cities, and counties without the resources for a separate staff, the individual responsible for quality assurance can look to the federal government and to other State and local governments for assistance. Also, a highly effective arrangement can be developed whereby much of the everyday specification work is handled by the specialist purchasing official with a single individual or small technical staff concentrating on standard specifications, inspection, and testing. No matter how limited a government's resources, quality assurance remains a responsibility of the central purchasing authority. In fact, in a broad-based purchasing program, traveling field inspectors can play important roles, especially for large governmental units which serve agencies over a wide geographic area.

Disposition Program

The two primary activities associated with the disposition program are the transfer of surplus property from one agency to another, and its disposal through sealed bids, auction, posted prices, site sales, or by direct negotiation. The latter two methods are usually reserved for scrap or garbage. While some governments trade in used equipment for new equipment, most of them find upon analysis that they receive more return by outright sale.

At the state level, two separate surplus programs exist, State and federal. Consequently, the organizational implications are more complex than at the local levels. Consideration needs to be given to the advantages and disadvantages of combining the state and federal surplus programs. Sharing warehouse and distribution facilities can work to the benefit of both programs by attracting more visits from and providing more exposure for screeners and users from using agencies, and the potential for reducing manpower needs is also a factor. A disadvantage, however, lies in the fact that there is considerable difference between the two programs, both as to the nature and volume of activities. The federal program is more complicated in operation by virtue of the strict federal guidelines, rules, and regulations which must be enforced. These regulations limit eligibility requirements for participation and include detailed utilization and compliance requirements on the part of recipients together with special record-keeping.

However, because the disposal of surplus property is very much a part of the total materials management concept, the advantages of combining the state and federal surplus programs into one entity can outweigh the disadvantages. **The disposal of all surplus property and scrap, whether federal or State, should therefore be the responsibility of the central purchasing authority.**

STATUTORY AIDS

Definitions

Statutory and regulatory material can benefit by a section of definitions, which reduce the likelihood of misinterpretation and misunderstanding. Furthermore, the use of common definitions facilitates communication among governmental units in discussing and exchanging ideas and experiences concerning purchasing operations.

Terms such as "specifications" and "standard specifications" should be precisely defined as should "formal bidding" and "informal bidding." The word "emergency" should have a specific meaning when it refers to the situation that will lead to an emergency purchase, and even the word "purchase" might need definition because questions may arise as to whether it includes leasing, renting, and the acquisition of such things as insurance and printing.

A definitional section can also serve to establish shorthand expressions for clarity and to avoid cumbersome repetitions. For example, in a highly centralized organization where purchasing acquires goods and services for all governmental elements, the term "agency" can well be designated as a substitute for a long list of designations such as department, institution, board, bureau, commission, division, office, which would otherwise be listed repeatedly throughout the statute. The glossary contained in Appendix D contains many useful definitions which can be used in preparing a definitional section.

Declaration of Policy

An effective purchasing system has to be flexible and responsive to changing conditions. Consequently, statutory language should be kept to a reasonable minimum, allowing the purchasing authority to establish administrative rules and regulations concerning the many details of the purchasing process. Extremely exact and restrictive statutes are disadvantageous because by nature they overly confine the purchasing authority's activities, and leave little or no room for creative management and for decision-making under circumstances which cannot be foreseen or predicted.

A section in the purchasing law setting forth the underlying policy of the purchasing statute can serve as a guide to the purchasing official in exercising his discretion in those areas where the statute establishes general principles that he must apply to specific situations. A statutory policy section can also buttress discretionary actions and rules and regulations issued in furtherance of the purchasing statute if they come under legal or judicial scrutiny. Such a declaration of policy or statement of purpose should incorporate the following elements:

• the concept of a central purchasing authority to institute and maintain an effective and economical system for purchasing goods and services;

• the recognition of obligation to the taxpayers, the

using agencies, and the suppliers;

- the enhancement of competition on the basis of fair opportunity and equitable treatment; and

- the obtaining of needed supplies, materials, equipment, and services at favorable prices consistent with quality and reliable vendor performance.

The following "Declaration of Policy" section is paraphrased from an existing statute, and might serve as a general model of its kind.

For the purpose of recognizing and discharging its obligations to the taxpayer, to the using agencies, and to vendors, it is hereby declared to be the policy of the State to provide, through good public administration, a modern and comprehensive purchasing program based upon accepted principles and sound procurement practices, wherein, through full competition on the basis of a fair and equal opportunity to all qualified persons and firms interested in selling to the State, each state agency may obtain the supplies, goods, material, and equipment needed in its operation at competitive costs, consistent with suitable quality and time and probability of performance.

4. Acquisition: Planning and Scheduling

ESSENTIAL ELEMENTS

Suggested Statutory/Regulatory Coverage

The purchasing statute and/or the rules and regulations adopted pursuant to the statute should:

Charge the central purchasing authority with the responsibility for developing and managing a planning and scheduling program.

Provide purchasing with the authority to review the validity and program appropriateness of purchases.

Provide that purchasing establish a data information system adequate to carry out its planning and scheduling responsibilities.

Require using agencies to submit usage and requirements data to central purchasing, as designated by central purchasing.

Provide that purchasing maintain an ongoing program to consolidate requirements whenever practicable and to utilize term contracting and scheduled purchase techniques, as appropriate.

Permit the central purchasing authority to enter into multi-year contracts (subject to the availability of funds).

Recommended Practices

Purchasing should play a role in top-level management planning.

The central purchasing authority should prepare written policies and instructions covering the planning and scheduling function, including data requirements from within purchasing; data needs from using agencies; timing of the planning and scheduling activities; and areas of authority, responsibility, and liaison.

Purchasing should use questionnaires, reviews of budgets, and surveys of vendors in its planning and scheduling function.

Purchasing should exploit and expand the existing financial management information systems in structuring its own information system.

Cost-savings analyses should be conducted to determine whether or not volume buying is cost-effective.

Written policies should cover term contracting procedures and practices, including using agency procedures for ordering and providing documentation to purchasing.

Modern day government is confronted more than ever before with the challenge of meeting the needs of society in continually changing social and economic environments. Replacing old ways with improved techniques and developing and implementing new programs all contribute to an increasing need for skillful planning. Emphasis on planning, from both a management and operations point of view, is even further intensified by the growing concern that government at all levels conduct its operations more efficiently and economically. Planning is an essential ingredient for improving the management of public resources by helping to obtain increased value from the expenditure of taxpayers' dollars.

Planning and scheduling relate primarily to the func-tions of forecasting future needs, formulating programs to fulfill those needs, and scheduling the acquisition and utilization of resources necessary to implement the programs. All organizational elements in each level of government are, in varying degrees, involved interdependently in the planning and scheduling functions. Purchasing should play a key role in the management and operational activities of government planning and scheduling.

Unfortunately, purchasing is often viewed as being exclusively a service agency that can make no significant contribution to the overall objectives of government. Where this view prevails, purchasing has no opportunity to participate in the managerial planning process. It will be shown here that management can benefit by obtaining information and advice from purchasing and that purchasing can fulfill its own responsibilities more effectively as a result of such involvement.

AT THE MANAGEMENT LEVEL

Leaders of governments at all levels should endeavor to draw upon the expertise of purchasing during the planning process. Almost every decision made by States and local governments affects purchasing and materials management, and conversely, the activities of purchasing affect many management decisions. It is desirable, therefore, that purchasing participate in the early stages of management planning. Purchasing can, for example, contribute useful information on forecasting costs of specific programs as they relate to services and commodities. Further, purchasing is familiar with market conditions, materials availability, and technological advancements, and can provide information which is pertinent to determining the feasibility, practicality, cost-effectiveness, make-or-buy decisions, timing, and other planning aspects related to specific programs.

Similarly, purchasing should be called upon to participate in facilities planning. The planning of medical, social, recreational, and administrative centers, as an example, requires forecasting for the acquisition of operating supplies, furniture and fixtures, fuel, equipment, machinery, and countless additional items. Clearly, purchasing's contribution can be valuable in planning and determining the total expected costs of facilities and in arriving at construction schedules which are compatible with the delivery and installation of equipment and machinery.

Purchasing can derive direct benefits from an involvement in the management-level planning process. Its involvement can provide information and insights regarding government directions and trends. Long-range plans can be translated into future requirements, workloads can be scheduled, and attention can be devoted to the acquisition strategies that are most appropriate for current and future market conditions, usage factors, and delivery requirements.

Purchasing also should have a management responsibility, shared with the central budget unit, to review the validity and appropriateness of purchases and to obtain adequate program information and justification from using agencies. This function can be exercised only if provided for by statute.

AT THE OPERATIONS LEVEL

Regardless of the degree to which it participates in the early stages of management planning, purchasing should become deeply involved in planning and scheduling at the operational level. Scheduling at this level is associated with day-to-day purchasing activities and concerns itself primarily with consolidating needs. Generally, planning and scheduling relate to one of the major objectives of purchasing—reducing unit costs through volume buying. Additional economies derived from volume purchasing are savings in overhead costs by reducing the number of transactions, maintaining interchangeable inventories, and eliminating some emergency purchases.

Largely because of increasing economic instability, planning and scheduling have recently taken on another money-saving role. They have become effective tools in reducing the effects of market fluctuations and supply shortages. When, for example, sharp price increases can be identified, it is often advantageous to buy in advance of actual needs, especially when the expected price increases will exceed the additional costs associated with maintaining higher than normal inventory levels. In other instances, where prevailing market conditions portend supply shortages, good purchasing strategy may warrant a deliberate investment in inventories to ensure that government activities and programs continue on an uninterrupted basis. This is particularly true where supply shortages are anticipated for critical items. However, buying in excess of current needs should be conducted only when there is ample evidence that existing market trends clearly reflect spiraling prices and/or shortages.

INFORMATION REQUIRED FOR SUCCESSFUL PLANNING

The central purchasing authority must have information on what has to be bought and how much is needed on an item-aggregate basis from all using agencies before it can plan for orderly procurement. Information concerning the types of commodities and quantities required provides a general indication of the items to be bought in volume. However, this information alone is not sufficient to determine the most economical and practical method of acquisition. Pertinent data on usage patterns, current and future market conditions, inventory levels, and warehouse capacities must be analyzed to determine whether particular items should be bought on a spot basis, under term contract arrangement, or as scheduled purchases.

In summary, a relatively broad base of information is needed so that purchasing can assess which course of action will ensure timely acquisition of commodities at the best prices. However, the study shows that too often the needed information is not readily available and that there has been mediocre success in developing purchasing information systems that collect the right information in the proper format and level of detail to permit meaningful analysis of needs. Historical information considered vital to planning decisions (e.g., the number of purchase orders processed and identified by vendor and by commodity, the dollar volume expended for each commodity, and the amount of the average purchase order) is frequently incomplete and often inaccessible. Surveys show that as a result of not having the appropriate information in a manageable form, the planning process in many state and local purchasing organizations is inadequate; it is often more a matter of intuitive judgment than a structured process.

Not all information needed can be acquired by analyzing the purchasing activities of the past. Planning involves an element of forecasting; consequently, purchasing depends on information external to its operations, such as advance notice from using agencies regarding their expected requirements and government-wide budget information. When this information is received, it is often in a format unsuitable for effective use. Budgets, for example, are frequently so general that purchasing cannot use them as meaningful indicators of future commodity requirements. In other cases, purchasing's accessibility to certain information may be limited. Using agencies often are reluctant to reveal project schedules of future requirements for fear of losing control over their operations. Although most purchasing statutes contemplate that purchasing should obtain such information, the power to do so is largely persuasive, causing purchasing to rely on the voluntary cooperation of using agencies.

Since historical usage data and future requirements are necessary to the planning process, purchasing and other agencies must cooperate in coordinating and exchanging this information. The diversity and volume of commodities handled by purchasing render impossible the effective planning and scheduling of future acquisitions whose demand is based solely on experience and intuitive appraisals of usage patterns. Determining requirements, consolidating needs, and selecting the best acquisition strategy require a continuous and systematic method of accumulating pertinent purchasing information.

The problems of availability and accessibility of data adversely affect purchasing's ability to plan and schedule. The problem calls for **positive statutory language which defines the authority of central purchasing to institute a management information system appropriate to its needs.**

METHODS OF OBTAINING PLANNING INFORMATION

There are four basic methods of obtaining necessary planning information. While many state and local governments already use these methods in one form or another, there is a wide variance in the results obtained.

Using Agency Data

Using agencies identify the items they expect to purchase, the estimated quantities they will need, and the time they will need them, and submit the requirements to the central purchasing authority. Based on the planning data received, central purchasing consolidates the requirements and prepares an initial schedule of purchases to be made. Consolidated needs, required delivery dates, inventory levels, and deliveries yet to be made under existing contracts are factors which are taken into consideration in developing the schedule. While these procedures are usually delineated in statutes/regulations, some more explicitly than others, they are neither consistently nor completely implemented. Some purchasing laws contain, with certain variations, a requirement that on or before a specified date each department submit to purchasing a list of all its estimated needs for designated types of items for the ensuing fiscal year.

In practice, however, the procedures for acquiring information from using agencies often are not well enforced. Purchasing officials must increase their efforts to emphasize and impress upon using agencies the importance of submitting timely and complete information on future requirements. An obvious strategy is to take the initiative by addressing specific questionnaires to agencies and then monitoring responses, as is done in some purchasing programs. Another is to communicate to using agencies the savings that volume buying can generate. This benefit in itself can be an inducement for them to provide purchasing with the necessary data. To obtain the full cooperation of using agencies, however, purchasing needs the support and endorsement of its top management. Obtaining internal support, in turn, depends on how well purchasing keeps its management apprised of the breakdowns in communications with using agencies and of the degree of responsiveness to various purchasing missions. Sometimes the using agencies that are served by purchasing are outside its governmental unit, as in cooperative purchasing arrangements or where nonstate agencies are served by central purchasing. In such cases, statutory direction is needed in many areas, including that of providing planning information to central purchasing. (See chapter on "Cooperative Purchasing.")

Budget Data

Annual budgets, particularly those relating to capital outlays, can be a good source of information concerning forecasted needs. Since most budgets present anticipated expenditures on a program basis by financial accounting category, they often are not readily translatable into specific purchasing requirements. Although budgets are primarily designed for financial purposes, they can, with certain changes in format, provide useful information to purchasing. If, for example, expenditure codes included commodity codes, purchasing could identify specific supply and equipment requirements. Where the budgetary process is computerized, the entire budget could be purged to sort expenditures for supplies and equipment by commodity code and using agency. This technique would provide purchasing with profiles on the types and quantities of commodities required for the coming year. Where systems are not computerized, budgets can still be analyzed to obtain at least broad-based indicators of the general types and volumes of activity which may be expected during the year. In some cases, notably the smaller purchasing programs, much of the same information can be extracted manually from the budget.

Purchasing Management Information System

The first two types of purchasing information focus on agency sources and relate primarily to future needs. Planning for future workloads and identifying items suitable for volume purchasing also require a close examination of the items and quantities bought in the past. This information pertains to what, how much, how often, and from whom commodities were purchased during prior periods. Information of this nature, however, is generally scattered throughout the various bid-award and purchase order files. Information retrieval, therefore, is extremely difficult. Obtaining a profile on a particular commodity, for example, could require a complete purge of all purchasing activity. In some instances, records of past activity are not available, as is usually the case for term contracts where purchasing does not monitor or control the contract activity and, consequently, has no information on the quantities of items actually purchased. There may be no requirement for using agencies to submit copies of field purchase orders to purchasing when buying off established contracts. When this happens, purchasing is forced to go to a less reliable source—vendors—for this information. Vendor reports on contract usage may be the only practical method for some units of government; this option can be greatly enhanced by having contractors furnish copies of invoices.

One approach to improving the availability of commodity usage data is to build on the existing management information system. Typically, the processing of a purchase order involves the recording of an obligation in the accounting records. Where the accounting system is computerized, the encumbrance/obligation routine may be modified to generate cumulative reports on purchase orders processed and to record the details of all purchases by commodity. A report such as this could be updated concurrently with postings to the accounting records.

Not all state and local governments have the data processing capabilities and other resources necessary to develop an automated purchasing information system. There are fundamental modifications that can be made in manual systems to improve the generation of useful purchasing data, such as collecting information on purchasing activity by commodity. This can be achieved by filing all bid-award documents and purchase orders according to major commodity code group, or at least by maintaining a cross-index by commodity. Such techniques can provide the capability to retrieve needed documents and information for a particular commodity without purging the entire file. A commodity profile card can also be established as a record of the important elements of each award. The following illustration depicts one of many acceptable formats that can be used.

COMMODITY PROFILE CARD
COMMODITY X

Vendor	Award date	Bid Award file No.	Qty.	Award amounts	Requesting agency
A	6/25	28919	50	$2,500	Transportation
B	7/4	29101	100	4,500	State police
A	8/2	29256	45	2,000	Finance
C	8/5	30421	30	1,500	State university

Obviously, the use of this technique will depend on such factors as the volume of purchasing activity for particular items. This illustration is an example of an item with a low level of activity. In cases where hundreds of orders are placed against a contract for a particular item, the system may not be feasible.

Survey Data

Another method of data collection relates more to the refinement of information obtained from the other methods described. After collecting using agencies' requirement data, purchasing must determine whether the items can be advantageously bought in volume. An effective means of making this determination is to conduct using agency surveys, usually in the form of a questionnaire asking when the items will be needed throughout the year, where they should be delivered, the level of performance required, and the specifications which will most closely meet the requirements. Information gathered by such a survey can assist purchasing in assessing whether or not the items have a governmentwide application and whether or not a standard specification is suitable.

Although volume buying may be advantageous, suppliers sometimes may not be able to accommodate this form of purchasing. Production capacity and availability of materials and manpower represent some of the barriers. For these reasons, purchasing should also survey suppliers to determine their capabilities for meeting its supply, delivery, and distribution requirements, as well as their ability to respond to standard specifications. Such supplier participation will ensure that the item is biddable on a large volume and standard specification basis by a sufficient number of vendors to provide a reasonable degree of competition.

COST-SAVINGS ANALYSIS

After information pertaining to historical activity and future estimates has been obtained and using agencies and vendors canvassed, purchasing can perform a cost-savings analysis before determining a final course of action. This is necessary because volume buying, when compared to spot purchasing, does not invariably result in a net savings. Certain commodities have fairly stable prices which are not materially affected by changes in purchasing patterns. Additionally, volume buying initially requires more planning and coordination than a single spot purchase and, consequently, added processing costs must be considered. Many items, varying from an electron microscope to a cafeteria serving counter, simply require individual purchases. A comparison should be made between the cost of purchases handled on either a spot or a consolidated basis by central purchasing and the cost of purchases made by using agencies on an informal quotation. It is, therefore, necessary to weigh the anticipated costs and benefits associated with volume buying to determine to what extent savings are available.

TERM CONTRACTING AND SCHEDULED BUYING

Term contracting and scheduled buying are the most widely accepted methods used by state and local governments for consolidating purchases. Term contracting is a purchasing technique that establishes a source or sources of supply for a period of time. Within this definition are a number of conventional arrangements:

- definite quantity for a definite period;
- approximate quantity for a definite period;
- indefinite quantity for a definite period; and
- indefinite quantity for an indefinite period.

The federal government and most state and local governments permit indefinite quantity contracts; a few States and localities, however, permit only definite quantity contracts.

Term contracting can provide certain advantages to both buyer and seller. For the seller, it represents business in volume and presents an opportunity to secure an increase in sales that will be spread over a period of time and thereby to plan ahead. He can view it as a sort of insurance or asset, in that the contract sometimes can facilitate financing arrangements. Term contracting also spares the supplier the administrative time and expense of repeatedly preparing and submitting bids. It can reduce sales expense and permit redirection of sales efforts.

Many of these same advantages can be realized by the purchaser. He can reduce administrative costs by avoiding the highly repetitive activities involved in preparing and issuing Invitations for Bids on the same or similar items, and in receiving, controlling, and evaluating the responses. Widespread use of term contracting permits handling larger volumes of purchases with fewer personnel. The problems and costs of maintaining inventories can be greatly reduced and sometimes almost eliminated through term contracting.

Scheduled buying is a different approach to volume purchasing. It is a spot, or one-time, purchase, but the item(s) is purchased in bulk for all agencies at specified intervals throughout the year. The purchasing intervals are established in accordance with using agency consumption patterns, considering warehousing capacities and seasonal factors. A schedule is then developed whereby particular commodities are purchased.

The type of commodity being purchased affects the decision to use term contracting or scheduled buying. Perishables and other similar items with short shelf lives are usually requisitioned on an as-needed basis. Consolidation in such cases relates more to immediate needs, and the planning cycle is generally limited to the life cycle of the perishable commodity. Consequently, bulk buying for perishable-type items normally occurs several times a year.

Commodity usage is another factor which affects the selection of a purchasing method. Commodities which are typically required throughout the year and used widely among all agencies usually lend themselves to term contracting; items which are required on a seasonal basis or have inconsistent usage are more suited to scheduled buying.

Another factor that influences the selection of the proper purchasing technique is the accuracy with which central purchasing can determine the quantity requirements for a specific commodity. Where the exact quantity required is known, scheduled buying would be preferable. Where quantities cannot be determined accurately in advance and actual usage could vary substantially, term contracting would be more suitable.

The state of the economy and its effect on market conditions must also be considered. A buyers' market generally favors term contracting because suppliers are more willing to accept the buyers' terms and conditions. A sellers' market is usually associated with product shortages and volatile prices, and so it is not conducive to long-term contracts.

When market conditions make term contracting difficult, more imaginative contracting techniques can be used. The wider use of price escalation clauses and shorter contract periods are types of modifications that are used successfully. Legal and administrative problems exist, and state and local governments must resolve these by statute and rule before they can overcome the problems of market uncertainties. A more detailed discussion of these problems, together with recommendations for contracting techniques, is the subject of chapter 7 of this report.

Whether term contracting or scheduled buying is selected, central purchasing must require strict compliance with the established purchasing arrangements. Using agencies must not be allowed to circumvent the contracts except under circumstances unique to the agency and approved by central purchasing. Effective contract administration requires that central purchasing monitor all purchases made by using agencies against established term contracts by requiring them to submit copies of all purchase orders directly to central purchasing. This flow of information will make it possible for purchasing to maintain an up-to-date reading on the contract status. Such information is especially important for definite quantity contracts because cumulative orders can rapidly approach the contract amount, and serve to alert central purchasing to the need for a new contract.

5. Acquisition: Bidders List

Because sources of supply must be identified before bids can be solicited, establishing and maintaining a current list of qualified suppliers is a fundamental part of the public purchasing program. The bidders list provides a systematic means of reaching the greatest number of qualified vendors. Further, such a list, properly managed and impartially used, enhances competition by providing qualified and interested suppliers an equal opportunity to compete for government business.

There are two divergent views concerning bidders lists. One holds that anybody or any firm should be included on the list, upon request. The other view supports the prequalification of bidders. Although purchasing programs can operate under either of these philosophies, prequalification is becoming the more common practice. In the interest of efficiency and economy, bidders lists ought to include only active bidders who are capable of performing. In addition, prequalification relieves some of the need for bid security. The cost associated with bid security is ultimately borne by the purchaser, and savings can be realized where such security can be eliminated.

Because the sealed bid procedure is by far the preferred method of public purchasing, the following text relates to this process. However, the principles apply equally to the procurement of professional services and the procedures for competitive negotiation.

PREQUALIFICATION

To determine who will receive Invitations to Bid, state and local government purchasing offices use a bidders list which is categorized by type of commodity. However, the procedures and criteria used to admit prospective bidders vary among governments. In some state and local governments, for example, the purchasing statute implies that inclusion on the bidders list is automatic for any interested supplier who submits an application giving nothing more than his name, his address, and the commodity in which he is interested. In these instances, little or no attention is given to prequalification. The rationale behind this approach is that prequalification is discriminatory and does not assure equal opportunity for all suppliers to bid on government business, and that rigorous prequalification criteria will inhibit competition by disqualifying new, small, and minority businesses because they usually cannot meet the financial and experience requirements. It is also sometimes argued that prequalification of every prospective supplier is not warranted because:

- He may never submit a bid and therefore would eventually be removed from the bidders list.
- He may never be in contention for an award.
- It is difficult to make a factual determination of responsibility prior to actual contract experience, especially if the supplier has just started his own business.
- Some additional evaluation of responsibility is often needed at the time of award.

In other purchasing jurisdictions, statutes provide that the bidders list include only qualified vendors. But no criteria have been established for determining qualification. Without formally established evaluation criteria, a prequalification program cannot be administered equitably or meaningfully and prequalification is largely a formality.

The Need for Prequalification

If the bidders list is to function as a means of identifying qualified and interested suppliers, some type of prequalification is needed. It is impractical and uneconomical to include on the list every applicant, regardless of performance capability. To do so only unnecessarily increases the size of the bidders list and substantially increases the cost of soliciting bids. The size of a bidders list is not a measure of the extent of competition, and unnecessarily long bidders lists can themselves lead to discriminatory practices such as soliciting bids on a rotational basis. Purchasing must determine supplier responsibility before awarding a contract. When such responsibility can be ascertained in advance, the evaluation-award process can be expedited. Furthermore, it is more suitable to deny a supplier inclusion on the bidders list than to reject him as a nonresponsible low bidder. Finally, prequalification can minimize or even eliminate the need for bonding when soliciting bids since suppliers' capabilities and resources will already have been investigated. This, in turn, can reduce the prices paid for goods and services.

A prequalification program must be structured so that it promotes fair and impartial treatment of suppliers. The application procedures, specific information requirements, and evaluation criteria should be set forth in writing and should be made available to suppliers. The written policies should note explicitly that the program is in no way intended to discourage suppliers from applying for the bidders list. All interested suppliers should be encouraged to apply, with the understanding that all must meet specified minimum requirements.

There may be a need for exceptions or alternate procedures within the prequalification process. For example, it would be unnecessary to apply the prequalification requirements to those suppliers who, by virtue of past performance, are known to be qualified and competent. Similarly, prequalification should not unfairly preclude suppliers from doing business with the government. New or small businesses, for example, could find it nearly impossible to qualify under specific financial and experience requirements. When structuring a prequalification program, therefore, situations such as these must be recognized and resolved. The conditions for exceptions must be defined and set forth in written policy statements. Potential inequities must be identified and a method developed for accommodating them either in the prequalification program or through some other means.

Objectives and Requirements

Purchasing agents or buyers need the guidance of a structured prequalification program to reduce the influence of personal judgment regarding a supplier's responsibility. The program should include a standard applicant information form to ensure that all applicants are treated alike, although the information requested may vary among governmental units. As a minimum, information should be obtained concerning financial standing and responsibility; facilities for production, distribution, and service; and length of time successfully in business.

Central purchasing must review each bidder's application, verifying the information supplied and comparing it to established standards. Supplemental procedures, such as obtaining copies of suppliers' financial statements, visiting their places of business, or contacting other customers are useful and sometimes necessary. The standards must be set in advance, should be specific, and should pertain to each category of information requested. For example, there could be a requirement that a supplier be in business successfully for one year, and that his current ratio (i.e., the ratio of current assets to current liabilities) equal the published norm for that type of business. Once set, the standards, requirements, and evaluative criteria should be made available to all interested suppliers. Whenever a supplier's application is not accepted, he should be advised in writing of the reasons and what he must do to qualify. The supplier should also have the right to an administrative review if he feels that he has not been treated fairly.

Prequalification has a definite place in public purchasing. It is important to both purchaser and supplier and must therefore be governed by written policies and procedures. In addition to the potential savings in administrative, solicitation, and bonding costs, it brings discipline and structure to the process of determining supplier capability and responsibility.

MAINTAINING THE BIDDERS LIST

Prequalification is only one aspect of managing an effective bidders list. Of equal importance are organizing the list and ensuring that it is systematically maintained as accurately as possible. A centrally controlled bidders list is most effective because duplication is avoided and independent control is ensured. It should be cross-indexed at least by commodity code and vendor so that prospective suppliers are easily identified by their respective product lines.

A well-organized bidders list is of little use if it does not represent the most current, available competition. Continual canvassing to identify new sources of supply, therefore, is another part of maintaining a current bidders list, as is the delicate function of eliminating inactive and unsatisfactory suppliers. There must be safeguards to ensure that removals are warranted and are in accordance with published policies and procedures.

Organizing the Bidders List

The bidders list should be organized so that it provides an effective means of soliciting qualified suppliers. The extent to which major commodity groups should be subdivided into item classifications will depend largely on the nature of the item and on the responses received to solicitations. As a general rule, the com-modity code structure should extend to that classification level which consistently produces a good return on bid solicitations. If at least a 50 percent response rate is not obtained, the bidders list is probably improperly categorized.

In structuring the bidders list, major commodity classification groupings must first be established. These groupings should reflect the particular function with which a group of products is commonly associated. Too frequently, this first order of classification is so general that it bears little specific relationship to items in the group (e.g., machinery, which encompasses farm machinery; food processing equipment; concrete machinery; and many others). Different categories of manufacturers are thereby included in too broad a classification, not all of which should receive all solicitations for the classification. Rather than grouping all truck suppliers under one heading, for instance, the list should contain breakdowns such as "four-wheel drive trucks," "pickup trucks," and "tractor trucks."

Proper classifications are useful to the degree that products and suppliers are closely matched. This is done by even further refinement. For example, the classification "floor maintenance machines" could be subdivided into item codes covering brushes and pads, edgers and sanders, power brooms, scrubbing machines, vacuum cleaners, etc. Each classification must be analyzed to determine the proper level of detail for the products it covers. In some cases, there are so many versions of the same product that it is impractical to reduce the major classification group to a lower level.

Product function also should be considered in refining classification groups. When a product is sufficiently unique that variations in style, size, and quality do not materially affect its functional purpose and performance, only one item code needs to be assigned. For example, steel drums come in all sizes and shapes, but they all serve a similar function which is rarely affected by their shapes and sizes. However, items such as generators come in several varieties which may perform quite different functions. In this instance, categorization should reflect as many different types of generators as there are functions.

Suppliers' capabilities will also affect the structuring of the bidders list. A particular classification group may have 30 different associated items, but if the majority of suppliers are known to carry between 80 and 90 percent of the items under the classification, there would be no need to maintain a separate bidders list for each item. However, if the market is fragmented, and suppliers on the average carry only a few of the items under the particular classification, the commodity index should be reduced to its lowest practicable level, and separate bidders lists should be established for all categories. This kind of subdivision provides a bidders list that is manageable and reduces wasteful solicitation.

Indexing System

Some governments have no commodity codes, others have coding systems which bear little relationship to products purchased, and still others have systems which are unnecessarily detailed and complex. Those governments without a coding system should build from the systems used by similar governmental units before developing one completely on their own. All governmental units need to periodically review their indexing systems to determine whether they are still appropriate. **Presently, there is virtually no commonality of commodity code classifications among local governments within a State, among local governments and state governments, or among state governments.** There seems to be little concern over this condition. Uniformity and commonality of commodity codes, however, could provide a basis for better communication and cooperation among governments. This is a long-range objective, but one that should be pursued.

Locating Sources of Supply

Purchasing officials have a responsibility to increase competition by seeking new sources of supply. There must, therefore, be an organized and ongoing program to identify qualified suppliers and get them on the bidders list. Trade magazines such as the *Thomas' Register of American Manufacturers* and the *Chicago Buyer's Guide* are good sources. Attending trade shows, researching license bureau files, and maintaining market information files assist the purchasing office in keeping informed of the market and discovering new suppliers, especially when needed for additional competition.

More extensive measures, such as exploratory or general promotional advertising in national and state trade publications, can also be used. It identifies those products for which additional bidders are being sought and highlights the advantages of doing business with the government. Such advertising also has the benefit of indicating to suppliers and to the general public that the market is indeed open to all qualified suppliers.

Purchasing officials cannot assume that suppliers will take the initiative in seeking business with the government, particularly in a seller's market. The extent of competition obtained, therefore, relies heavily on the government's program to continually search out new suppliers. At least once every two years, purchasing should review each major commodity group to consider the extent of competition being obtained, the

market conditions, and the specific actions which may be needed to expand the supplier base. Presently, very few governmental units have programs of this nature; the analyses and research are informal, and depend largely on the personal initiative of the purchasing agent for his particular commodity area.

Removal From the Bidders List

Just as there is a need to seek new suppliers, there must be a program to identify bidders who should be deleted from the bidders list. Purchasing should consider the bidders' responsiveness as bidders and performance as suppliers. Since removing bidders from the list is a sensitive issue, the procedures and criteria used must be established and published. Typical criteria include a history of no responses or "no bid" responses to Invitations for Bids, default, poor performance, or financial or legal difficulties.

Central purchasing must establish a vendor file to collect information for periodic reviews of bidders' responsiveness, performance, and capabilities. Information concerning response to Invitations for Bids can be gathered within purchasing. Commonly, three or more consecutive failures to bid are considered grounds for removing a bidder from the list. Performance as a supplier can, to some extent, be determined by purchasing agents, but can best be evaluated by using agencies. Matters such as failures to meet delivery dates, failure to meet specifications, and failure to keep promises should be documented in written reports which are sent to purchasing. Purchasing may need to act immediately on these types of incidents, and the reports, as well as a record of all actions and their outcome, should be part of the vendor file. Consistent poor performance is a basis for deleting a bidder from the list. Reports of current financial condition, litigation, if any, and general trends are available from credit sources such as Dun and Bradstreet. Generally, very little has been done in most jurisdictions to develop reports on vendor performance, and even less has been done to establish standards of performance. Lacking such data, purchasing officials naturally are reluctant to proceed on their own in removing bidders from the list.

Just as there is a need for standards of ethics and professional conduct for purchasing officials, there is a need for similar standards for suppliers. The standards should provide for penalties, sanctions, or other disciplinary action (e.g., removal from the bidders list) for violating the standards.

Whatever the grounds for deleting bidders from the list, the seriousness of the action requires that there be safeguards to protect both the integrity of the lists and the rights of the bidders. The following procedures are therefore recommended:

• When removal is for cause (unsatisfactory performance, violation of standards), the chief purchasing official should review and investigate all reasons and evidence supporting the contemplated action and make the final decision.

• When removal from the list appears to be justified, the chief purchasing official should so inform the supplier in writing.

• When removal is based on failure to bid, it should be confined to the list for that particular item(s), and the supplier should be notified in writing.

• There should be complete documentation of the reasons for the action, any contacts with the suppliers, and a record of the review and approval by the chief purchasing official.

Procedures for Debarment and Reinstatement

When a supplier has been removed from the list for no reason other than inactivity, reinstatement to active status should be considered upon receipt of a new application. The act of refiling for inclusion on the bidders list can generally be considered sufficient evidence of the supplier's renewed interest in doing business with the government. This is the policy of most state and local governments.

When a supplier has been removed for cause, reinstatement becomes more complex. Good business practice requires that a supplier be reinstated only on evidence that he has cured the problem(s) that caused his removal; however, there are very few state and local statutes and ordinances that address this subject. Most laws simply indicate a maximum period of suspension, generally one year, beyond which it is presumed that a supplier may be reinstated. In some jurisdictions, the period of suspension for unsatisfactory performance is left to the discretion of the purchasing official. In other cases, the statutes are more explicit, such as requiring permanent debarment in cases of collusion.

The procedures and controls governing the periods of suspension and criteria for reinstatement presently are loosely structured and do not provide needed guidelines. Because there are so many different levels and degrees of inadequate vendor performance, the period of suspension depends on a variety of factors and requires considerable professional judgment. In addition to the peculiarities of each individual case, competitive considerations can also be a factor. Where an item is available from only one, two, or three suppliers, different approaches are necessary in applying disciplinary actions and, at the same time, preserving competition or a source of supply. Therefore, it is inadvisable to arbitrarily establish an exact debarment period. Rather, it is more appropriate to provide general direction and constraints, and permit the chief purchasing official to determine what is most appropriate in each case.

6. Acquisition: Competition

ESSENTIAL ELEMENTS

Suggested Statutory/Regulatory Coverage

The purchasing statute and/or the rules and regulations adopted pursuant to the statute should:

Provide that competitive procedures be used for purchases of all commodities and services.

Require sealed competitive bids for all purchases expected to exceed a predetermined dollar value.

Require legal notice for all purchases expected to exceed a predetermined dollar amount.

Require the central purchasing authority to issue Invitations for Bids to a large enough group of potential suppliers to assure adequate competition. Where formal sealed bids are required, the general rule should be that all bidders on the bidders list for the item be solicited. Provision should be made for exception to this general rule if it is not feasible or necessary, under given circumstances. For all such exceptions, there should be a requirement for written documentation which supports the decision not to solicit all bidders on the bidders list.

Charge the central purchasing authority with responsibility for final review and approval of Invitations for Bids.

Allow the purchasing official discretionary authority to require a bid security or bid bond adequate to protect the interest of the government and, when security is elected, require equal bid security and bid bond of all bidders.

Require the purchasing official to establish procedures for maintaining accountability over bid deposits and their refunds.

Require that the conditions and circumstances under which the requirements for obtaining competition may be waived be set forth in writing.

Provide for the waiver of competition when certain designated officials determine, in accordance with written rules, that it is required to meet an emergency situation, requiring that such officials consult with the purchasing official whenever practicable before making an emergency purchase, and requiring documentation of the conditions that made the emergency purchase necessary, the method of purchase, and purchase price(s) of the commodities that were purchased.

Provide for waiver of competition where the commodities or services lack responsible competition, where there are patented or proprietary rights, where standardization/interchangeability is demonstrated as advantageous to the governmental unit, and where only one source can supply the needed items, requiring that all such instances be justified in writing and approved by the central purchasing authority, in accordance with written rules.

Permit central purchasing to use competitive negotiation when the conventional formal sealed bid process is determined to be inappropriate, in accordance with guidelines contained in written rules.

Designate the basic criteria permitted for evaluating bids and proposals and for awarding contracts.

Recommended Practices

All purchases should be made under conditions which foster competition among a sufficient number of potential vendors.

The absence of one or more of the historic prerequisites for formal sealed bidding should not be interpreted to mean that competitive bidding cannot be used.

Written procedures should be established for competitive bidding where the expected value of purchases is less than the dollar amount requiring formal sealed bids.

Legal notices should generally describe the items or services to be purchased; state where the specifications and bid forms may be obtained, where the bids are to be received, what the deadline is for filing bids, and where the

Continued on next page

bids will be opened; indicate the type and amount of bid security (if any); and any other information the purchasing official deems necessary.

Regional bidding may be used if necessary, but rotational bidding is to be avoided.

The written procedures which set forth policies related to emergency purchases should define "emergency"; specify the authority, delegation, and responsibility policies; outline purchasing procedures; and specify documentation and review requirements.

There should be written procedures for verifying single-source procurement decisions.

Purchasing officials must challenge routinely all representations which seem to limit competition on the rationale of "standardization."

Some form of price or cost analysis must be made for all negotiated procurements.

In negotiated procurements, negotiations should be conducted individually with each qualified offeror, and minutes of these meetings should be prepared.

In government, as well as in private industry, a fundamental purchasing objective is to obtain quality goods and services at minimum cost. Unlike private industry, however, public purchasing has the added responsibility of protecting the interests of the taxpayers and must, therefore, continually function in an environment of public scrutiny. Accordingly, statutes and regulations generally require state and local governments to conduct their purchasing operations on the basis of open competitive bidding. This requirement is intended to secure sound value, to guard against favoritism and profiteering at public expense, and to safeguard the interest of the seller by providing equal opportunities to compete for government business. Open competitive bidding has long been recognized as one of the best protectors of a healthy and equitable public purchasing system. **A unique characteristic of good public purchasing is the underlying principle that more importance is ultimately attached to the ways and means of obtaining prices than to the prices themselves.**

DEFINING COMPETITION

Very basically, the concept of competition presumes the existence of a marketplace in which there is more than one vendor supplying like commodities and/or services. Given this condition, competition can be defined as the process by which two or more vendors attempt to secure the business of a third party by the offer of the most favorable price, quality, and service. Competition exists not only in prices but also in the technical competence of the vendors and in the quality of their products and services. Competition in this sense has multiple levels and requires that the central purchasing authority have the necessary latitude to evaluate each aspect of competition and thereby arrive at the offer that represents the best value. From an economic standpoint, competition in public purchasing is an almost indispensable means for improving the quality of commodities purchased, encouraging innovation among suppliers, increasing the government's latitude of choice and, most importantly, assuring the reasonableness of costs.

SEEKING COMPETITION

Because competition is so critical to public purchasing, **it is essential that all acquisitions be made under conditions which foster competition among a sufficient number of potential vendors. It is precisely upon this principle that the requirements of all purchasing statutes should be anchored.** For the most part, however, laws do not adequately convey the spirit of this principle, since they tend to place more emphasis on the manner of acquiring competition than upon its serving as the standard for all levels of purchases. If the conditions under which competition is to be promoted are not thoroughly covered or are ambiguously stated, misunderstanding and confusion are likely to occur.

Most state and local government purchasing laws provide that all awards for purchases exceeding a stipulated dollar amount be based on formal sealed competitive bids, and this requirement should be continued. Governments periodically review these dollar values, and the trend has been to increase them. The federal government recently increased its dollar value above which formal sealed procedures must be used. As these amounts are increased, a greater total dollar volume of purchases are made under informal bidding procedures. As discussed later in this chapter, competition should be sought for all purchases, even though formal sealed bids are not required.

There are historic prerequisites for using the formal sealed bid process:

• There must be a complete, explicit, and realistic specification or purchase description upon which there can be competitive bidding.

• The specifications must not be subject to changes in requirements or conditions during the period over which the goods or services are to be furnished.

• The specifications must be nonrestrictive, and they must be available to all potential bidders.

• There must be more than one bidder available, willing, and able to compete effectively for the business.

• Sufficient time must be available for preparing a complete statement of the government's needs and terms of purchase, for distributing Invitations for Bids and specifications, for obtaining bids, and for evaluation and award.

• The selection of the successful bidder can be made on the basis of price alone, provided the bidder is otherwise qualified as responsive and responsible.

• Statutes must not preclude competitive bidding for the specific goods or services being purchased.

When all of these elements are present, the resulting process is conventional competitive bidding—a comfortable pattern familiar to government purchasers and prospective bidders alike. **The absence or altered circumstance of one or even more of these elements, however, does not preclude competitive bidding;** they merely call for the purchasing official to exercise initiative, innovation, and judgment to provide an impartial opportunity for competition.

Contemporary government purchasing management has a number of strategies which assure competitive bidding where one or more of the above elements appear to be lacking or constricted:

• Complete, explicit, and realistic performance specifications can be used in lieu of generic or design specifications.

• Two- or three-stage bidding can be used to explore the market and establish commonality for bidding purposes.

• Clear, concise procedures can reveal possible problems at the time of solicitation rather than award.

• Award can be made on documented justification that the bid is the one most advantageous to the government.

While other purchasing techniques are available, the purchasing official should turn to them only as a last resort. Even if the clear intent of most purchasing laws was not to encourage competition through the sealed bid process, the purchasing official should respond to professional pride and to the challenge offered. Furthermore, the public understands and is most at ease with the competitive bidding process.

Competition at All Levels of Purchases

All but one State and most cities and counties have predetermined dollar amounts above which purchases must be made on the basis of sealed competitive bids. Similarly, statutes require in most instances that smaller purchases be made on the basis of some form of informal bidding or quotations. However, this requirement is usually so heavily qualified that it essentially becomes an option. The implication that is frequently drawn from this type of statutory guideline is that competition on purchases not requiring sealed bidding may be sought on the basis of convenience rather than principle. **Barring grounds for a formal waiver of competition, for which laws and rules should make special provision, a decision not to solicit bids or to seek some other form of competition can only be attributed to placing a higher priority on expediency than on good purchasing.**

In other States and local governments, the failure to stress the need for competition at all levels of purchases is even more pronounced where purchasing statutes do not cover purchases below the amount requiring sealed bidding. Here again, the implication is that competition is the standard only where formal sealed competitive bidding is required.

Individually, purchases with small dollar amounts are not material; in the aggregate, they represent a healthy portion of overall purchase expenditures. For this reason, they should follow competitive procedures, and to this end, a few state and local purchasing statutes have wisely adopted provisions to ensure that, even where competitive bidding is not specifically required, every effort is still made to obtain competition.

Absence of Competition

Although competition is the general rule in government purchasing, it is not always possible. Understandably, government operations cannot be interrupted simply because it is not feasible to purchase every commodity or service on a competitive basis. In these situations, the purchasing official must have a sufficient degree of authority to carry out his responsibility of servicing agency needs. Most state and local governments have provided for this authority by setting conditions under which the competition requirement may be waived. In this framework, the purchasing official is vested with the responsibility of determining and documenting whether a proposed purchase meets the prescribed conditions.

There is a need for more uniform practices toward waivers of competition. If the requirement of competition is to develop into a universal principle, with uniform application throughout public purchasing, there must be more consistency in policies which provide for waiving that requirement. A closer look at this problem and some possible solutions to establish more effective policies for waiving competition are presented later in this chapter. In addition, impediments to competitive bidding are discussed in the following chapter.

THE COMPETITIVE BIDDING PROCESS

Although competitive bidding is the preferred method of seeking competition, the receipt of bids alone does not guarantee full competition. An atmosphere of objectivity and impartiality is essential. The management aspect of competitive bidding plays an important role in assuring that the spirit of open competition is maintained throughout the competitive bidding process. The public must be kept apprised of all proposed purchases involving significant expenditures; bids must be solicited in a manner that offers qualified suppliers an opportunity to compete for government business; and bids must contain terms and conditions that will protect the interests of the public and provide an equal basis for competition among prospective bidders.

Legal Notice

Most laws require that all purchases that exceed a specified dollar amount be "advertised" in a newspaper with wide circulation, often in a designated official newspaper in a capital city or county seat. This is usually the same dollar amount as that requiring a formal Invitation for Bids. Most purchasing officials feel that this type of advertising does not enhance competition and that a soundly conceived bidders list is the best means of obtaining competition but, because public purchasing must function with openness, some form of public notice is necessary.

This area is being reassessed by many state and local governments because compliance with most of the current legal notice requirements can be costly. For example, in the 35 States with legal notice requirements, there are statutes specifying that advertisements run for a continuing period of time, contain considerable detail, or appear in more than one newspaper. Requirements such as these are a carryover from earlier days when there was limited communication and less complexity in the purchasing function. In lieu of these requirements, a listing or an abbreviated type of public notice that describes the items being purchased, tells where the Invitations for Bids may be obtained, indicates where and when bids are to be received, and provides any other information the purchasing official feels necessary, is more reasonable. This satisfies the need to keep the public apprised of purchasing activity and invites further inquiry if additional details are desired.

While public works projects are frequently advertised in both the general and specialized media, public purchasing has not generally employed this technique. This study has found that most government entities satisfy the requirements for legal notice, but find no advantage in advertising widely in trade publications.

Soliciting Bids

The purpose of a bidders list is to provide the broadest competition among suppliers who are qualified and willing to furnish items and services needed by state and local governments. **The general rule, therefore, should be that when formal sealed bids are required for a particular item, all bidders on that list should be solicited.** As discussed in the chapter entitled "Acquisition: Bidders List," these lists must be structured and maintained properly. In addition, there must be some provision for exceptions to the general rule, such as emergencies, requirements for local services which would not be of interest to non-local bidders, or requirements for nonstandard items which some bidders on the list are not capable of providing. To preclude any misunderstanding or misinterpretation, the general standard must be that enough qualified suppliers be solicited to assure adequate competition. This requirement should be contained in the statute. Where not all the bidders on the bidders list are solicited, the required documentation must not only justify the action but also show that the maximum practicable competition was sought.

Some government units practice rotational bidding; others use regional bidding. Under the former system, bidders are selected on a rotational basis so that each bidder is solicited in turn over a period of time. The reason given for this practice is that there are too many bidders on the list to solicit them all each time an item is purchased, but the underlying problem is that the bidders list is too broadly categorized or is out-of-date. The solution lies in a well-managed bidders list that assures both equity and economy.

In a regional system, the bidders list is divided into geographic regions. This is done when deliveries must be made to widely scattered points, or where the requirement is of a local nature and it may be impractical to maintain a single bidders list for all locations. When this practice is used, prospective bidders must be advised in advance of the regional structure and be permitted to bid in any or all regions.

Invitation for Bids

The Invitation for Bids (IFB) is the means by which competitive bids are solicited. It is a key document in the purchasing process because it contains the terms, conditions, and specifications to be used by suppliers in preparing their proposals. It also forms the basis for determining bidders' responsiveness and determining the successful bidder. Finally, its terms, conditions, and specifications are incorporated into the contract itself.

The construction of the IFB is critical to competition. As discussed earlier, complete and explicit specifications define the potential for competition, but care must also be exercised so that procedural specifications are as free from restrictiveness as are the technical specifications. The entire tone of the transaction and the future course of any resulting contract are cast in the IFB. Unless sufficient time is devoted to the preparation of the IFB, not only is the competition restricted, but the transaction may be doomed to legal and procedural problems. **Although coordination and assistance among various elements of government may be necessary to accumulate the data for the IFB, final review and approval of it must rest with the central purchasing authority.**

In 35 States, there is a provision for requiring bid security at the discretion of the purchasing official. Some state and local laws, however, still require that some form of security be provided with all bids. Although there is a place for bid security, it is unnecessary to require it as a matter of general policy on all bids. When used for a particular purchase action, the bid security required should be clearly set forth in the IFB and applied equally to all bidders.

WAIVERS OF COMPETITION

Although competition should be required whenever practicable, a degree of latitude should be permitted when competition may not be feasible for specific commodities, services, and circumstances. Single-source items, compatible parts, and commodities and services required on an emergency basis are major categories of purchases which typically cannot be acquired on a competitive basis. The central purchasing authority must be able to use the professional judgment and skill of its staff in determining when a waiver of competition is appropriate and that the waiver is consistent with prescribed policies and procedures.

Although many States and local governments presently refer to "exceptions" to, "exemptions" from, and/or "waivers" of competitive bidding requirements, it is less confusing to use the single term "waiver." The terms "exemption" or "exception" are misleading because they are generally used for a specific commodity which is permanently exempt from a provision normally required of all other commodities. Because conditions and circumstances change frequently, it is unwise and impractical to include blanket exemptions or exceptions

by commodity in statutes. Conversely, the conditions and circumstances for waiving competition are reasonably constant and should be well-defined in rules and regulations.

Emergency Purchases

Emergencies of one kind or another are the most common situations for which requirements for competitive bidding and competition could be waived. The officials who determine that an emergency exists should be limited to those in positions of high responsibility. As a general rule, emergency purchases should only be allowed after consultation with the central purchasing official. This will allow the purchasing official to supply any commodities on hand, obtain those items that he may purchase efficiently, and provide central purchasing's experience to the emergency purchasing that takes place. Thus, central purchasing can coordinate emergency purchases, authorizing those that could be made more practically in the field, but preventing duplicate purchasing in case several agencies request authority to purchase the same commodity or service.

Because acts of God may occur in remote areas some distance from the purchasing department, and at any time of day or night, there should be some latitude which permits delegation of purchasing authority to other department and agency heads. In all such cases, records must be maintained to indicate the types and quantities of items purchased, the vendors from whom purchases were made, and the disposition of the items. Where possible, informal bids should be obtained and recorded. If it is not possible to obtain informal bids, this fact should be recorded, even on an after-the-fact basis if necessary. The complete record of emergency purchases must be routed to central purchasing for a procedural post audit.

Single-Source Purchases

A single-source supplier is the only acceptable vendor who is able to furnish a certain item or service. Although he may need technical assistance and documentation from using agency or central purchasing personnel, the purchasing official is responsible for making all single-source determinations. In doing so, the following factors need to be considered:

• Is there a lack of responsible competition for a commodity or service which is vital to the operation and best interest of the governmental unit?

• Does the vendor possess exclusive and/or predominant capabilities?

• Is the product or service unique and easily established as one-of-a-kind?

• Can program requirements be modified so that competitive products or services may be used?

• Are there patented or proprietary rights that fully demonstrate:

A patented feature providing a superior utility not obtainable from similar products; or

A product available from only one prime source, and not merchandized through wholesalers, jobbers, or retailers where the elements of competition could be encouraged?

Care must be taken to avoid making single-source purchases because there is a bias or preference for a particular product made by a particular company. Central purchasing must look into the intended use of the item and assure that only one supplier is able to provide the item that will satisfy the intended use. The purchasing official should determine that the price is fair and representative and carefully document, in the form of a written memorandum, the reasons for single-source procurements. Negotiating the contract price is called for where the expenditure is substantial, or where there is likelihood of similar additional purchases from the same supplier.

In purchasing equipment or parts, particularly technical equipment, consideration must be given to standardization policies, interchangeability of items, or compatibility with in-place items. Here, product polarization, esthetics, or convenience may motivate the using agency. The purchasing official must challenge routinely all representations that would seem to limit competition on the rationale of "standardization." Each question of standardization/interchangeability requires the purchasing official to seek an interface which will permit competition, preferably by competitive bidding but at least by competitive negotiation. When a single-source award is inevitable, the reasons and action taken must be supported by written documentation. In addition, care must be exercised that all using agencies are treated alike in considering their requests and justifications for waivers.

COMPETITIVE NEGOTIATION

Most purchasing statutes and ordinances provide that purchases exceeding a stipulated dollar amount be made by sealed bidding. These laws seldom allow or provide for purchasing by negotiation. Formal sealed competitive bids, which are opened in public at a specified date and time, reduce subjective judgment in the award process and tend to lessen doubts as to the integrity of the process for expending public funds.

While this process is and should be the standard for public purchasing, there are situations in which competitive negotiation can and should be used. For example, when time is a crucial factor, when the procurement involves high-technology items (e.g., data processing applications, communications systems, complex telemetry equipment), or when the purchase is for professional services, competitive negotiation can be used effectively. Almost all States have experienced problems in attempting to apply conventional bidding techniques in the procurement of these types of items because of the difficulty in constructing suitable descriptive specifications which are necessary for bidders to compete on a common and equal basis. Nonetheless, most state and local government purchasing laws do not provide for the use of competitive negotiation in those cases where the formal sealed competitive bid process is not effective. Competitive negotiation at the state and local government levels, therefore, is a relatively new and innovative concept.

Unlike the conventional bidding process, negotiation generally involves informal discussion and bargaining to reach agreement on price and other terms under a proposed contract. **Contrary to a commonly held belief, the use of negotiation is not intended to preclude competition, nor is it in any way synonymous with single-source procurement.** Critics of the negotiated award process frequently are really criticizing the failure to elicit competition where it could be obtained. When needed items or services are found to be available from only one source, direct negotiation with that source can be useful and advantageous. Whenever this technique is used, the objective should be to purchase to the best advantage of the government, using all the elements of the formal sealed bid process which are appropriate to a given competitive negotiation.

Techniques of Negotiation

Some of the principles that apply to the competitive negotiation process are the same as those that pertain to the formal sealed bid process. For example, a list of qualified offerors should be prepared, public notice of the product or service needed should be made, and qualified offerors should be solicited. Some of the procedures, however, differ in detail from the sealed bid process. A Request for Proposal (RFP) may be used in lieu of an Invitation for Bids. A Request for Information (RFI) may even precede the RFP. The RFP should include a description of the item or service to be purchased, the specific criteria that will be used in evaluating proposals, and other pertinent information such as delivery dates or time frames within which the work must be completed. Since these purchases usually involve nonstandard items or complex services, additional information is frequently needed, such as experience in the line of work being considered (including references), staff capability along with resumes of key individuals who will work on the contract, and a cost breakdown of the proposed price. Price is not normally the major or the determining criterion for award. Consequently, the factors listed above are used in developing the proposal evaluation criteria. These considerations must be carefully developed and a weighting scheme formulated around the most important features of each procurement action. The evaluation criteria must be included in the RFP along with the stated relative order of their importance. Frequently, such criteria are divided into three main categories: managerial capability, technical capability and approach to meeting performance requirements, and competitiveness and reasonableness of price.

The proposal evaluation criteria should be looked upon as the standards that measure how well an offeror's approach meets desired performance requirements, thus permitting an evaluation of the differences between those characteristics and what offerors propose to do. Moreover, such standards match the evaluation of proposals against objective norms rather than against each other. If a scoring system is devised, it must be impartially applied to each proposal. Any departure from the established plan which is prompted by factors outside the system is proper only insofar as the same treatment is extended impartially to all offerors.

The proposal evaluation process should include cost or price analysis. Price analysis represents an evaluation of proposed prices without regard to the separate cost elements and proposed profit amount. Techniques such as comparing proposed prices with each other, with published price lists, and with independent estimates can be used. This type of analysis may suffice when there is adequate competition and prior experience in the item or service being purchased. Otherwise, cost analysis is essential. Cost analysis consists of a review and verification of the cost data supporting each element of proposed cost.

Negotiations should be conducted individually with each qualified offeror, and should be documented by detailed minutes of each session. The objective is to obtain a contract agreement which is most advantageous to the government in terms of factors such as period of performance, type of contract, quality of the items or services being purchased, and price. Proposals submitted by competing firms are not disclosed to the public or to competitors. However, after a contract is awarded, its terms and conditions should be public record.

The spectrum of types of contracts appropriate to negotiated purchases ranges from firm fixed-price contracts to cost contracts. The selection of the type of contract is dependent largely on the definitiveness and stability of the specifications, and the risks involved in either accomplishing the work for the negotiated price, meeting the contract schedule, or meeting a required technical performance. The preference, of course, is to negotiate a fixed-price contract.

Examples of Purchases Appropriate for Formal Advertising and for Negotiation

1. *Two-way radios for police cars.* Fifty radios are required to a specification which several industrial sources have indicated their equipment currently meets or exceeds. The radios are to be delivered and installed over a six-month period, which is within the industry's capability to produce. A warranty for a period of two years after installation is desired. Radios meeting the specification have been manufactured, sold, and used for several years.

Normal method of purchase. Formal sealed bids, because all the prerequisites for this method of purchasing are met.

2. *The design and development of communications network.* A new concept of networking for real-time display of information tied to a central computer using voice interrogation has been conceived as a result of in-house studies. A general description of the concept is available. Several industrial firms have expressed interest in the project, each taking a somewhat different approach toward implementation.

Normal methods of purchase. Since the conventional prerequisites for using the formal sealed bid process are not met, and there appears to be reasonable competition available, two-stage procurement and/or competitive negotiation appear as options. The type of contract awarded would depend on an analysis of risks and the ability of the government and industry to agree on the project's final cost. In general, a project of this scope and lack of specific requirements does not lend itself to definite specifications on which firm prices under formal sealed bidding could be obtained.

Contracting for Professional Services

As part of this study, a brief questionnaire was sent to all state purchasing offices to explore several issues relative to contracting for professional services (i.e., management consulting and architect-engineering), and 34 States responded. Although the questionnaire did not seek to penetrate the complexities of this often sensitive subject, the replies revealed certain interesting facts. For example, in only two of the States responding was central purchasing responsible for the procurement of all professional services. In States where central purchasing was responsible for obtaining management consulting services, for example, it was not necessarily responsible for procuring architect-engineering services. In the majority of the States responding, using agencies were responsible for acquiring both management consulting and architect-engineering services. However, 10 States had designated a separate agency, such as the Public Works Division or the Bureau of Facilities Management, as being responsible for procuring architect-engineering services.

Twenty-one of the respondents indicated that there were no uniform procedures governing the procurement of professional services. Twelve States indicated that there was a uniform procedure, although separate procedures existed for management consultant and for architect-engineering services. Since procurement of both types of services was usually handled by the using agencies, "uniform procedure" was generally interpreted as meaning a consistent procedure for all state agencies to use, depending upon the type of service; it was not interpreted to mean one standard procedure governing procurement of all professional services.

Many of the written procedures addressed themselves not to the solicitation-award process but to post-award practices, such as the distribution of contracts and payment procedures. In general, the written procedures for architect-engineering services were more clearly delineated than those for management consulting services. This may be due to the historical need for architect-engineering services; most of the States that responded awarded more contracts for architect-engineering services than for management consulting services. Architect-engineering services are traditionally obtained on the basis of professional qualifications rather than by any form of price competition. This attitude, however, is changing. The States of Arizona, Florida, Maryland, and Montana, for example, have recently enacted legislation requiring competitive factors in contracting for professional services, including those of architects and engineers. The Florida act, which took effect on July 1, 1973, paved the way. The Maryland act, however, goes further in its requirement for price competition, which both of these professional groups have sought to avoid. Other salient features of these acts are in the following general areas: public announcement of the project, prequalification and certification of firms, selection of certified qualified firms, negotiation, and prohibition against contingent fees. Generally, they assume that it has already been established by the responsible agency that the required services could not be more efficiently and effectively performed in-house, and that adequate funds exist for the services of outside consultants.

Only four of the 12 States that submitted written policy provisions for the procurement of professional services had written procedures specifically for management consulting services. In one State, the procedures were contained in the purchasing manual; in another, in the state administrative manual; and, in still another, in the manual of financial procedures. In States that have written procedures, the definition of management consulting services is usually in terms of what it is not, rather than what it is.

Only four of the States responding had written procedures related to the preparation of Requests for Proposals. Procedures for acquiring management consulting services, in most cases, vary within a State according to the anticipated amount of the contract. However, the dollar breakdown differs from State to State, sometimes by considerable amounts. Among those States' procedures, only two specifically provided for legal notices in state newspapers.

Clearly, therefore, a variety of practices are used in contracting for professional services, and it appears that these practices evolved in response to a variety of needs and that these needs differ from State to State. The most common characteristic is the fragmentation of authority to contract for these services. In the great majority of cases, the authority of using agencies to contract for professional services is a direct authority; it is not delegated via the purchasing laws or a central purchasing authority. Thus, the important aspects of independent review, management, and control seem to be absent. Interestingly, 21 respondents suggested that central purchasing should not be involved in the awards of contracts for professional services. On the one hand, some States reported that they simply did not have the staff, the time, or the expertise necessary to carry out this responsibility. Some other States felt that since professional services were traditionally exempt from competitive bidding and have traditionally been handled by using agencies or some organization other than central purchasing, the practice should remain the same. On the other hand, 12 States indicated that central purchasing should be involved, at least in some review capacity or in prescribing regulations for the using agency to follow.

Tradition, politics, lack of resources, and technical complexity all play a role in the manner in which contracting for professional services is handled today. Several States have recently taken positive steps toward establishing uniform procedures for procuring architect-engineering services, and they typically stress such aspects as the concept of prequalification, the need for competition, the criteria for award, the necessity of public disclosure, and the prohibition of practices of unethical behavior. Other aspects which are surfacing in proposed legislation are truth-in-negotiation certifications, prohibition against contingent fees, affidavits of noncollusion, and cost-plus-a-percentage-of-cost contracting. One State prohibits architects fees that are based on a percentage of construction costs, and provides for a post audit as a means of enforcing the truth-in-negotiation clause.

Consequently, actions are being taken to strengthen

the laws, policies, and practices in this area. Unfortunately, these actions too often are reactionary and deal only with specific problems. This study concludes that it is better to address and improve the entire process of contracting for all professional services than to approach the matter piecemeal. Purchasing officials, administrators, legislators, and using agencies must work together in structuring a sound system using the elements of competition and negotiation. As in other types of contracts, there should be central responsibility with authority to make proper delegations. This responsibility logically rests with central purchasing.

Purchasing officials see negotiations as a challenging and exciting exercise of the 1970s for state and local governments. Although negotiation should never supplant sealed competitive bidding in public purchasing, it should be available for use where the latter does not bring about satisfactory results.

7. Acquisition: Impediments to Competitive Bidding

ESSENTIAL ELEMENTS

Suggested Statutory/Regulatory Coverage

The purchasing statute and/or the rules and regulations adopted pursuant to the statute should:

Preclude the use of restrictive specifications and "most favored customer" pricing clauses.

Empower the central purchasing authority, when identical bids are received, to make the award in any reasonable manner that will discourage the submission of identical bids.

Define the reasons and conditions allowing "schedule contracts" and "multiple awards."

Require that bidders submit statements of noncollusion with all bids.

Provide criminal penalties for collusive bidding unless specifically provided elsewhere.

Empower the central purchasing authority to take whatever action is appropriate to purchase needed items for which acceptable competitive bids cannot be obtained, and require that these actions be justified in writing and documented in files which will be public record.

Recommended Practices

Proposed legislation that directly or indirectly affects purchasing should be coordinated with the central purchasing authority.

Procedures should provide for close coordination between purchasing and Attorneys General in dealing with suspected collusion, and purchasing should not proceed without advice of counsel.

In coordination with the Attorney General, purchasing should develop documentation and records retention requirements.

There should be a reporting format for reporting suspected collusion to the appropriate governmental element.

Attorneys General should sponsor periodic training seminars for purchasing officials on how to respond to such matters as antitrust and collusive bidding.

Consideration should be given to establishing a regional program, under the National Association of Attorneys General, for coordinating and acting on collusive bidding practices.

Purchasing officials should routinely challenge "customary" price changes which are simultaneously made by all or most suppliers of particular products.

Written guidelines should be developed to set forth procedures for making awards when identical bids are received.

Instances of "dictated contracts" should be reported to United States and State Attorneys General.

A bid-award history file should be maintained.

There should be written procedures describing the techniques and procedures for analyzing bid-award history data to detect apparent collusive bidding practices.

There should be written procedures governing the use of option clauses and a requirement that option provisions be set forth in Invitations for Bids.

Option clauses should specify that they will be exercised at the original contract price.

There should be written procedures which cover the methods and techniques applicable to the use of escalator clauses.

Procedures should be established to provide guidelines in contracting when suppliers offer only the market price at time of delivery.

Relief to suppliers under contract should be permitted only when holding them to the contract would be patently inequitable, and then only in accordance with stipulated procedures.

Sound purchasing principles and policies are rules for normalcy. The atypical conditions or situations that occur impede the progress of open competitive bidding and demand that professional and management personnel in purchasing take the initiative in averting or surmounting these impediments. There are no absolute barriers to competition which cannot be overcome by law, rule, policy, or strategy. The following discussion applies to competitive negotiation as well as to competitive sealed bidding.

A most effective tool for combatting the impediments to competition is the documented public record. As this study reiterates, a substantial difference between public and private purchasing is the requirement of openness in government procurement. But to be effective in removing impediments to competition, the public record must also be complete and detailed. Memoranda of oral communications are frequently a necessary part of the record. In a very real sense, the written public record begins with the Invitation for Bid and its supporting documents. It is here that the first steps must be taken to deter impediments to competition.

PURCHASING POLICY AND PROCEDURES

Obviously, impediments to competitive bidding must be eliminated wherever possible within the purchasing operation. Procedures must be established to guard against restrictive specifications and to otherwise assure participation by the optimum number of qualified bidders. This subject is further discussed in the chapter entitled "Quality Assurance: Specifications." Purchasing policy should not be allowed to affect competitive bidding adversely. All bidders must be treated impartially and equally. For example, the same data must be available to all, and bid security, when required, must be required of all bidders. Competition must be encouraged. It is necessary to "sell" prospective bidders on the idea of doing business with government to overcome stereotype concepts such as complexity and restrictiveness. Courtesy encourages participation and competition.

Policy must be examined for its rationale and appropriateness in the contemporary market. For example, some governments insist that their contracts bear a "most favored customer" clause guaranteeing that the prices they are being charged are as good as the lowest price offered by the vendor to any customer. The effect of this procedure, whether or not intended, is to artificially set the low price that bidders are willing to offer. A bidder may be able to give a better price to some purchasers because of lower transportation costs, overstocks in their area, or many other reasons, but he will not do so because it would mean lowering the price to purchasers who demand most favored customer status. These same restrictions on competition apply when most favored customer pricing is used as a benchmark for negotiation. **The use of the most favored customer clause is self-defeating and should be barred throughout public purchasing.**

LEGISLATION

Purchasing policies and procedures that impede competitive bidding may be dictated by legislation such as local preferences, small or minority business preferences, or fair trade law. Such legislation is passed for reasons other than the effectiveness of purchasing operations, and usually without the knowledge that it will make the purchasing process less efficient. Still, to consider such legislation without considering its effect on the purchasing process, or to pass such legislation without looking at the actual effectiveness and effect on purchasing, is to build the legislation on an incomplete foundation. Usually purchasing officials can react to such legislation; but sometimes legislation is passed in response to issues and special interests that generate strong support at a certain time, and then is forgotten except by those who must administer it. When such legislation does not achieve its objectives or has an unwarranted effect on the purchasing process, it takes the efforts of purchasing officials who are willing to speak out and legislators who are concerned about the efficiency of the government to effect remedial legislation. This process has occurred in many States that passed in-state preferences, but subsequently repealed them on evidence that local preference legislation is uneconomical and results in expenditures greater than the revenues it produces.

The repeal of a law is frequently more difficult than its creation. A purchasing official may be tempted to try to live with inappropriate legislation, even "stretching" it to try to accommodate sound purchasing, but such an effort is seldom satisfactory or successful.

Other legislation, especially that which deals with the business community, results in some less obvious impediments to competitive bidding. Although they are directly involved in the business processes of government, purchasing officials are seldom consulted to provide ideas on proposed legislation except when it specifically affects the purchasing process. Legislators and purchasing officials alike frequently do not consider how legislation that affects the business community will affect the government's role as a consumer, either directly or indirectly. Any legislation which affects business can influence the government's ability to obtain competitive bids from firms to which the measure applies. For example, zoning ordinances or occupational licensing legislation can have the effect of keeping out legitimate competition. Consequently, proposed legislation or policy that has business implications should be coordinated with the central purchasing authority.

Hopefully, situations where two government objectives conflict can be avoided. It may be possible to modify proposed legislation or policy to eliminate any negative impact on the purchasing process, without diminishing the desired force or effect of the legislation involved. Fair-trade statutes demonstrate that legislation can be modified to eliminate harmful effects to the public purchasing process without altering the legislative intent. This type of statute allows manufacturers of trademarked, branded, or similarly identified products to set and enforce the prices of their products at the wholesale or retail levels. One need not argue the merits of these statutes because exempting the State and its political subdivisions does not in any way frustrate the purpose of the statutes. In States that passed fair-trade statutes without exempting public purchases, purchasing officials were forced to deal with legislatively sanctioned identical bids because public policy was applied in too broad a manner and unnecessarily violated public purchasing policy. For many years, purchasing officials in these States found it difficult or impossible to overcome the inertia of the statutes and to obtain exemptions for public purchases after the statutes were enacted. More recently, however, a number of States have exempted government from fair-trade laws, and local units of government should check on the current status of any such laws in their respective States.

Legislative committees and executive agencies that deal with areas affecting business should make it a point to routinely inform the central purchasing authority of proposed legislation or policy that will have an impact on business, so that it may submit for consideration comments on the effect of such policy or legislation on the purchasing process. Until such a procedure becomes routine, purchasing officials must continue to try to take the initiative in locating and reviewing proposed legislative and executive actions to see to what extent they may inhibit competition.

BIDDERS' ANTICOMPETITIVE ACTIVITIES

When directing their energies toward protecting the competitive bidding process from bidders' anticompetitive agreements, purchasing officials are involved in a formidable task. Unlike government decisions which are made or proclaimed publicly, suppliers' decisions to act in contravention of the competitive bidding legislation are made secretly. These decisions evolve in a manner intended to hide the agreement because they violate federal antitrust statutes and, frequently, state antitrust statutes as well. A highly useful handbook to help public purchasing officials deal with anticompetitive purchasing agreements by bidders is *Impediments to Competitive Bidding,* published by the Council of State Governments in 1963.

Anticompetitive activities are likely to be criminally and/or civilly actionable upon discovery. Purchasing officials should never proceed to remove these impediments without the advice of counsel, if available, and without close coordination with city and county (district) attorneys and federal and State Attorneys General.

COORDINATION BETWEEN THE CENTRAL PURCHASING AUTHORITY AND THE ATTORNEYS GENERAL

There must be an effective working relationship between the central purchasing authority and the State Attorney General's office, because their functions reinforce each other in the area of suspected collusive bidding. If the Attorney General becomes involved in an antitrust suit, he will need, as evidence, records of past bidding patterns and practices. The following information, which is necessary in an antitrust suit, is generally found in historical purchasing records:

- names of the bidders who were solicited;
- bidders who responded;
- the price each bidder offered;
- the name of the successful bidder; and
- evidence of notice to the general public.

The Attorney General should have some influence in determining the number of years such records are kept so that he may have sufficient historical information to establish evidence of collusion. In addition, the Attorney General should communicate with purchasing officials to determine how he may do this without disrupting purchasing operations.

Because action by the Attorney General will have a beneficial effect on all purchases, there should be established between the central purchasing authority and the Attorney General's office a means by which purchasing officials can communicate to the Attorney General instances of suspected collusive bidding. Communication from the Attorney General's office to all purchasing agents, through seminars, for example, would be useful in explaining which antitrust laws affect public purchasing, how to deal with suspected antitrust violations, and what cooperative procedures have been established between purchasing and the Attorney General's office. The National Association of Attorneys General publishes an *Antitrust Bulletin* which summarizes state antitrust cases, their current status, and their final outcome. This bulletin is an excellent source of information for public purchasing officials.

The United States Attorney General's office is also

interested in possible collusive bidding. In a program intended to discourage identical bidding in all levels of public purchasing, state and local governments are requested to join federal agencies in submitting a brief form (DJ-1510) to the U.S. Attorney General's office when identical bids are received in the competitive bidding process for line items having a bid value greater than $1,000. The information received from these reports is compiled to aid the Attorney General in identifying conspiracies that violate the federal antitrust statutes. The information is also published annually, in a report entitled "Identical Bidding in Public Procurement," in order to discourage the submission of future identical bids. Similar reporting requirements within state and local governments would be useful. The reports would advise the Attorney General, city attorney, auditor, inspector general, or other appropriate government personnel of suspicious bidding practices, identical bids, and evidence of collusive practices which purchasing may be able to detect.

Combining State Antitrust Efforts

Often, State Attorneys General find that they have a greater chance for success in litigation by combining the evidence of collusive bidding from several States and bringing a single class action against the bidders involved. This process could be made even more effective if the States would consider combining their antitrust efforts on a multistate basis. The country could be divided into regions, each having a small staff with the authority to monitor, request, receive, and use for litigation the bidding histories of bidders in various commodities. Information could be exchanged among regions with national coordination taking place under the National Association of Attorneys General. Such a system could be worthwhile not only in combatting collusive bidding practices, but also in collecting triple damages that might be obtained from the successful prosecution of an antitrust suit.

Detecting the Conspiracy

It is difficult to detect an anticompetitive conspiracy, not only because conspirators attempt to hide their actions, but also because such conspiracies can result in many different types of agreements. There have been agreements to sell items at the same price, to adopt formulas to determine prices, to notify the other conspirators if a member intends to change prices, to predetermine the contents of conspirators' bids, and to refrain from bidding on certain contracts. Some anticompetitive agreements, such as using formulas to set the amounts to be bid, may not produce results that are easily recognized as a collusive agreement; in fact, they

may have the appearance of competition. Other agreements may result in bid prices that fall into a distinctive pattern but, unfortunately for the purchasing official who is attempting to detect collusion, the same result may occur by reason of practices which usually do not violate the letter of the law. In some product areas, for example, suppliers may make the same price changes at proximate times because they follow price changes made by acknowledged leaders in the field. **The argument of "custom" should be routinely challenged if this impediment to competition is to be removed or lessened;** otherwise, the only competition remaining in these product areas is based on salesmanship, service, and differences in the products, which may or may not be significant.

Identical Bids

The anticompetitive agreements that purchasing agents can most effectively combat are those in the form of identical bidding. These agreements can only be successful when operated by all the bidders in a market, or by bidders who are sure that they will be submitting the lowest bids. Identical bids may result from various geographic pricing patterns usually based on equalizing transportation charges to meet competitors' delivered prices. Some of these pricing systems are calculating delivered prices from specific set points, such as major manufacturing areas or the location of the vendor closest to the buyer; charging one price within a geographic zone, which may comprise several States or just a part of a State; and charging one price throughout the United States.

Other identical bidding comes about where several distributors of the same manufacturer's products follow price maintenance agreements, such as exclusive distributorships or agency agreements whereby distributors serve as the manufacturer's agent, receive the manufacturer's goods on consignment, and quote the selling price dictated by the manufacturer. Purchasing officials must be familiar with the market for a given product to accurately analyze bids and determine the forces which are operating.

Some bidders refuse to lower prices below a certain level because they claim that the Robinson-Patman Act, a federal statute prohibiting certain discriminatory pricing, requires them to offer the same prices to all customers. When a purchasing official faces this situation, he should inform the bidder that the U.S. Attorney General in 1936 issued an opinion that the Robinson-Patman Act is not applicable to government contracts. [See *Federal Trade Regulation Reporter* (1961), Chicago: Commerce Clearinghouse, Inc., par. 3275.]

When collusive forces are working in the market, the objective of the conspirators is almost always to divide the market among themselves in a particular manner. Identical low bid conspiracies will remain a viable anticompetitive tactic only as long as the method used for making awards divides the government's business in a manner that is satisfactory to the conspirators. Even bidders who are not part of an anticompetitive conspiracy may detect that the government's business will be divided among them when low identical bids are submitted, and may tacitly develop a system whereby they submit low identical bids. Consequently, all identical bids may be considered the sign of a possible anticompetitive conspiracy or the seeds of such a conspiracy; but whether conspiratorial or not, the effect is essentially the same.

The purchasing statute and rules and regulations should allow purchasing officials sufficient flexibility to make awards in a manner intended to discourage identical bids. The methods currently used by many public purchasing systems (i.e., flipping a coin or drawing lots) should be discontinued because they tend to divide the government's business evenly among identical bidders. A grant of authority to make awards "in the best interest of the State (city, county)" would be adequate for purchasing officials, but **a specific statement saying that awards should be made "in any reasonable manner that will discourage the submission of identical bids" carries more weight.**

Written guidelines should be developed to set forth procedures and techniques to be used under this grant of authority, such that specified courses of action are aimed at discouraging identical bidding. For example, the following methods of dealing with the problem have been used successfully:

• Determine and identify the identical bidder whose bid is most technically correct, or whose past performance has been superior. Make the award to him, and then continue to make awards to him as long as identical low bids are received. This procedure eliminates the government's "complicity" in the anticompetitive scheme because the market is not divided among the identical bidders. The biggest strength of this method is that it gives the other bidders economic incentive to submit competitive bids.

• Circumvent the effect of price maintenance agreements by inviting bids on a "package" that includes price-maintained items and non-price-maintained items. Awards are then made to the bidder who submits the lowest price for the total package. Suppliers can lower their bids on items that are not covered by agreement by an amount that actually reflects their willingness to discount the price-maintained items.

• When identical low bids include delivery charges, make the award to the identical bidder farthest from the delivery point and representing the highest transportation costs. (In multiple delivery point contracts, however, this method could be self-defeating because it could divide the market among the identical bidders.)

• Reject all bids and issue a new Invitation for Bids with letters stating that the previous bids were identical and unacceptable.

• Purchase seasonal items during the off-season. Some purchasing agents have found that identical bids are submitted on some seasonal items at the time of year when the largest number of purchases are made. When these items are purchased in the off-season, competitive bids are obtained. Deciding the value of this tactic involves comparing storage costs with the potential savings realized by making off-season purchases.

Oligopoly

There are factors at work which defeat certain long-standing principles of public purchasing. These factors do not relate to temporary product shortages, market prices, and similar aberrations, although these conditions improve the environment for their entrenchment and growth. Rather, they are factors related to firms with commanding market positions who dictate the product specifications, terms, and conditions of conducting business.

It is axiomatic in public contracting that it is the duty of the government to provide common ground, in the form of physical specifications, terms, conditions, etc., as a basis for inviting price competition. However, this is no longer the case in many instances where one or a few firms have powerful market positions, e.g., in computers (hardware and software), copiers, "word processing" systems, duplicators. The effects of oligopoly are multiplying.

Here, sellers dictate the product specifications and the terms and conditions of doing business, and refuse to alter or modify them or the "company policy" on which they are based. The purchaser then has to choose from diverse, rather than common, ground. The concept that competitive bidding is somehow anachronistic has been fostered, and purchasing practices which are loose, if not illegal, are encouraged, e.g., "schedule contracts" and "multiple awards." Some dictated contracts go so far as to abrogate the basic vendor warranty established under the Uniform Commercial Code, i.e., that the merchandise is suitable for the ordinary purposes for which it is to be used. When faced with these situations, purchasing officials should urge the State Attorney General and the U.S. Attorney General to investigate for possible violation of antitrust prohibitions. Purchasing officials should also urge their professional organizations to go on record as opposing such tactics, and to suggest that members not deal with any firm using such tactics (except for maintenance and supply contracts for existing operations), so that national force will confront national force. Finally, acting individually, purchasing officials must continue to make purchases based on competitive bids, to find new sources, or to change requirements if no responsible bids can be obtained.

COUNTERMEASURES

Apparently, many purchasing officials feel that the Attorney General is responsible for gathering evidence for antitrust actions, and that the purchasing office should supply information only when it is requested. Some purchasing officials inform the Attorney General when they suspect collusive bidding, but few of them present the Attorney General with adequate documentation to support their suspicions unless he requests it for the preparation of a case.

The Attorney General's position in this situation can be compared to that of a police department. There are many possible violations of the law that confront him, and the more evidence there is that a violation occurred, the more likely he is to investigate thoroughly. The purchasing official has the raw data, and although a violation may not be apparent as the data are generated, it is in the interest of the competitive bidding process that the material be developed and provided in a form that can be analyzed so that violations may be detected.

Establishing a Bid-Award History File

In order to set up a record-keeping system capable of detecting collusion, bid-award data should be gathered and recorded in a usable format which considers the realities of the market involved. The number of items encompassed by any one analysis should be determined by the specific market in which evidence of collusive bidding is being sought.

The bid-award record should show, at a minimum the suppliers that were solicited, the amounts bid, the numbers of "no bids" and no responses received, and the successful bidder. In a multiproduct market (e.g., the drug market), the information would have to be modified to show the estimated value of the award that each bidder received, as well as the value of the total award, to reveal patterns in the percent of the market that each bidder received. If there were one dominant item in a multi-item market, as would be the case if the government spent 40 percent of the total drug expenditures on one drug, keeping a separate file on that item would be important. In fact, in a multi-item market, patterns in awards could probably be detected by charting several key items individually. An example of a bid-award history file is shown in Figure 1.

Maintaining the Bid-Award History File

With proper planning, a bid-award history file can be easily maintained. Initially, commodity codes can be refined so that later, when an award is made, the proper bid-award history may be found quickly by a commodity code reference. Work-saving devices can be used to reduce the manual copying, which is the most time-consuming element. For example, bid forms (or additional forms) for bidders to fill out can be designed so that a bid-award history file is produced by properly assembling the forms and photocopying them. Obviously, the bid-award file is highly susceptible to computerization, once a system has been developed and tested.

Analyzing Bid-Award Data

A bid-award file brings together the information on awards for one business area. Purchasing officials can analyze these data for patterns that may point to anticompetitive conspiracies. For example:

• Patterns in rotation of low bid among competitive bidders can be detected. If bidders were involved in a collusive anticompetitive agreement, the record might show that although the bids always looked competitive for individual awards, the awards fell into a suspicious pattern (for example, B-C-A; B-C-A, as shown in Figure 1).

• Patterns in geographical distribution of awards can be detected for commodities for which awards are made by region. A map has been used successfully to detect such patterns by designating a color for each bidder and filling in the county or region affected by a contract with the color of the winning bidder.

• "No bid" responses from solicited bidders may reveal a pattern which could be a signal that suppliers have agreed to take turns bidding on contracts. This practice may occur where the items are available from only a limited number of suppliers.

Other suspicious patterns can be detected only through the purchasing official's knowledge of the market. For example, if normally there were a substantial markup from wholesale to retail prices for an item, but the bidding in normal market conditions repeatedly resulted in low bids that were only slightly below retail prices, further inquiry would be in order. The bid-award history also may reveal the approximate time that a conspiracy began by showing a sudden change in bidding patterns. For example, all suppliers might change their pricing policies from one contract to the next, or identical low bids might begin to appear consistently where previously that had not been the case.

When identical bids are received, the purchasing

FIGURE 1
Sample Bid-Award History File

ITEM X

Vendor	Costing Data	Year					
		1971	1972	1973	1974	1975	1976
A	Unit Price ($)	42	41	ⓐ40	43	43	ⓐ41
	Est. Cost ($)	4,200	8,200	12,000	17,200	21,500	24,600
B	Unit Price ($)	ⓐ41	42	42	ⓐ41	41	43
	Est. Cost ($)	4,100	8,400	12,600	16,400	20,500	25,800
C	Unit Price ($)	43	ⓐ40	43	42	ⓐ40	42
	Est. Cost ($)	4,300	8,000	12,900	16,800	20,000	25,200
D	Unit Price ($)	47	47	46	46	45	N.B.
	Est. Cost ($)	4,700	9,400	13,800	18,400	22,500	....
E	Unit Price ($)	N.R.	48	47	47	46	45
	Est. Cost ($)	....	9,600	14,100	18,800	23,000	27,000
F	Unit Price ($)	N.S.	N.S.	48*	48	47	N.B.
	Est. Cost ($)	....	....	14,400	19,200	23,500	....

N. S. = Not solicited.

N. R. = No response.

N. B. = "No bid" response.

◯ = Successful bidder.

* = Bid from bidder who was not on bid list at the time of solicitation.

office should analyze the situation by examining the following factors in the bid-award history file to determine if there are any indications of collusion.

• *Commodity and market analysis*—Did identical bids occur because of the nature of the item (fair-traded, price-controlled)? Are all bidders offering the same manufacturer's product? (If so, the specification might be restrictive, or there might be a collusive price maintenance agreement between a manufacturer and the distributors.) Is there some peculiarity in the present market, such as temporarily limited sources of supply, that has affected the bidding?

• *Number of bidders*—How many bidders responded to the Invitation for Bid? Are the identical bids the only ones received? If several bids were received and only two were identical, one could assume that they were identical by coincidence unless the identical bidders are the dominant suppliers in the market. Additional analysis and observation of future bidding on this item are indicated. If two or three manufacturers are represented, collusive price maintenance agreements are a possible cause.

• *Number of items involved*—Does the bid relate to a single item or delivery point, or are there numerous items or delivery points involved? If multiple delivery points are involved, are the bids identical for each? Are unit prices identical for each item?

• *Historical bid prices*—Are there discernible trends or patterns? Have there been instances of identical bids either for the items involved or with the bidders involved? If identical prices were bid in the past, were awards made by a method that may have encouraged, rather than discouraged, continuation of the practice?

• *Price analysis*—As appropriate, an independent price analysis should be made as a test of the reasonableness of bids received. Catalogs, market surveys, prices being paid by other users, and other similar indicators should be considered.

The conclusions reached from such analyses will help the purchasing official decide whether he should inform the Attorney General that there is evidence of collusion, as well as other actions he might take.

A bid-award history file, therefore, can present valuable information in a manner that facilitates analysis to determine if there is evidence of apparent collusion. It can also present other important information which is useful in managing the purchasing system. For example, the number of responses to bid invitations and the degree of competition over a period of time are readily apparent, as is the incidence of bids from suppliers who were not on the bidders list. Price trends for various items are shown. The frequency of awards to other than the lowest bidder and the items for which such awards occur will be revealed. Determinations of which companies do a great deal of business with the government are made easier. Slight variances in the format of the bid-award history file can add other important information that can further serve the varied management needs of the purchasing system.

Additional Practices and Procedures

Procedures and practices should be designed to make the purchasing system as effective a force as possible in dealing with anticompetitive collusive practices. Twenty-two States and many local governments, for example, require all bidders to submit signed statements that their bids are made independently and without collusion with other bidders. Some systems require separate notarized statements of noncollusion. This serves as an affirmation by the bidder that he has not participated in a collusive anticompetitive agreement and reminds him of the government's concern that the bids it receives are the result of true competition. **Such certifications need to be enforced with specific statutory provisions, such as conspiracy or collusive bidding statutes, which set forth penalties for collusive practices.**

Simple direct action may be one of the best tools available for dealing with collusive bidding. For example, a purchasing official who suspected a collusive price maintenance agreement solicited a bid from one of the firms involved soon after a new manager was hired who was not aware of the agreement. This produced an aberrant bid that was excellent evidence that such an agreement did, in fact, exist. When collusion is suspected, a concentrated effort to identify and recruit new bidders may achieve realistic prices through renewed competition. Taking the initiative to make some inquiries of suppliers who are not members of an anticompetitive conspiracy, or even participants in a suspected conspiracy, may provide information which can be useful in improving purchasing tactics and initiating action against the conspiracy.

Inquiries can be made to determine why a major firm that normally would have bid on a large contract did not do so. If the reasons given are unsatisfactory, if the practice of not submitting bids persists, or if a pattern of several bidders' refraining from submitting bids on successive contracts is detected, the purchasing official should take further action. He could, for example, compare his records of awards with those of his counterparts in neighboring political entities to see if there were evidence of business being divided geographically in a total area that includes several cities, counties, or States. Whenever a firm is suspected of refusing to bid because of its participation in an anticompetitive conspiracy, the purchasing office should not routinely remove the firm from the bidders list. In fact, it should assure that the suspected firm is always solicited, to create a record of the firm's refusal to bid. This type of information can be useful in any antitrust action that may be taken.

When no bids are received from one or more major bidders, restrictive specifications may be a possible cause. The suppliers should be contacted to determine why they did not bid. If restrictive specifications are the reason, the nature of the restrictiveness should be assessed. Consideration should then be given to whether broadening the specification would lower the quality of the item involved below an acceptable level. If it would not, and if time would allow it, the specification should be rewritten and new bids solicited.

The strongest deterrent against collusive bidding is active cooperation between the purchasing officials and the Attorney General's office. This is especially true when there are criminal penalties for collusive bidding and the Attorney General seeks to enforce them.

MARKET CONDITIONS

As noted earlier, purchasing policies and procedures are rules for normalcy. Given normal conditions, specific laws and rules can be adopted, and detailed implementing policies can be written to provide for effective and well-controlled operations. At the same time, it must be recognized that unusual conditions can and do occur and that it is best to provide for these in advance. Perhaps the best example of an unusual condition is a market in which basic commodities are in short supply, demands exceed supply, and production costs are extremely volatile. In such a market, it is difficult and, at times, even impossible to employ the same purchasing techniques which are geared to a normal, competitive market. There are ways to cope with an abnormal market, but purchasing officials need the authority to apply these techniques lest they violate the law or simply conclude that purchases must be deferred.

To avoid any misunderstanding, it must be made clear that purchases will be made by competitive bids whenever possible. Even unusual market conditions should not routinely be considered a basis for deviating from this fundamental principle of public purchasing.

In those cases where it is impossible to follow precisely the established competitive bidding procedures, the purchasing files must be documented to show the condition that existed and procedures that were followed. Various types of conditions have been encountered and various techniques used by purchasing agents in obtaining needed items. Some of these techniques have been successful, and others have not.

Shorter Term and Definite Quantity

Term contracting is an accepted technique that is commonly used in public purchasing. The contracts usually are for a period of one year and frequently for indefinite quantities. In a tight market, however, suppliers often are reluctant to commit themselves for this length of time and for indefinite quantities. Some governments have succeeded in continuing to use term contracting by offering shorter contractual periods and/or definite quantities. Except for some additional administrative time, shorter-term contracts usually retain the advantages of the one-year contracts. Using definite quantities poses some problems because estimating exact requirements in advance is often difficult, and underpurchasing or overpurchasing is always a possibility. The former condition can be alleviated by spot purchases, as necessary, although prices paid on spot purchases will most likely be higher. If requirements are overestimated, it may be possible to cancel some of the deliveries, particularly in a market where prices are rising. If not, the additional quantities must be stored by the government until they are needed.

Options to Renew

Options to renew a contract are sometimes mentioned as a means of protection in a market of rising prices; however, this generally is not true. Furthermore, depending on the manner in which contracts are renewed, the practice could well be in violation of the competitive bidding statute. In order to comply with competitive bidding requirements, option provisions must be set out in the Invitation for Bids, to ensure that all bidders compete on an equal basis. The IFB should specifically state the number of terms for which the contract can be renewed and whether or not the options may be exercised unilaterally. In order to maintain the integrity of the competitive bidding process, it seems necessary that options be exercised at the original contract price, and this too should be specified in the IFB. The negotiation of new prices for each new period is undesirable, probably not in compliance with the competitive bidding statute, and susceptible to collusion. Suppliers could bid unrealistically low prices for the first term and then do their utmost to compensate for

this by negotiating equally unrealistically high prices for later terms.

In general, options to renew do not seem to provide much comfort in a period of rising prices. Knowing the specific option provisions to which they must bid, suppliers will undoubtedly include anticipated price increases in their bids; this is good business practice. If market conditions are not too volatile, some competitive price advantage may be possible. In a highly volatile market, however, suppliers either will be unwilling to bid on a contract with options or will grossly inflate their bids as a hedge against an uncertain market.

Escalator Clauses

If the market becomes so unstable that it is impossible to obtain firm bids using normal contracting techniques, escalator clauses are a useful device in stimulating suppliers to bid. Escalator clauses permit contract prices to be increased under certain stated conditions. As with options, the detailed conditions and procedures must be set forth in the IFB.

There are various conditions that can be attached to escalator clauses, and the detailed procedures and requirements can vary from contract to contract. Generally, however, they should cover the point in time during which the clauses are operative; the conditions under which the clauses may be exercised; the general types of increases that will be considered; the method of determining that a price increase is in order; and the documentation, review, and approval procedures. Oftentimes, contracts provide an initial one- to six-month period within which the escalator clause cannot be used. In other words, the contract price remains firm for the specified period of time. Many escalator clauses place a limit on the amount by which the contract price may be increased. These are good practices that should be used when structuring the provisions for an escalator clause.

The justification for a price increase is frequently linked to an indicator, preferably one that is not controlled by either the buyer or the seller, like a report on market prices by an independent reporting service or the federal government. In some cases, clauses allow price increases based on the vendor's published prices if it can be shown that the prices apply equally to all customers. In industries where labor represents a major part of contract costs, price increases have sometimes been allowed following negotiation of new labor contracts. Obviously, the independent indicator is the best to use. Other factors tend to be more subjective and require much more analysis before there can be some assurance that a bona fide increase is in order.

Escalator clauses should also provide that suppliers

submit to the purchasing official detailed data showing the basis for and the amount of proposed price increases. The purchasing official or his representative should be authorized to evaluate the data and, if necessary, to examine the supplier's pertinent books and records. The clauses should specifically state that no adjustments will be made to compensate a supplier for inefficiency or for errors in judgment, that only bona fide cost increases will be allowed, and that no increase in profit will be permitted. Written instructions are necessary to outline the procedures to be used in evaluating and approving proposed increases. These procedures should provide that data submitted by suppliers, as well as documentation for review and approval or disapproval of the action, be public record.

As a general rule, if properly handled, escalator clauses can be used in complete conformity with the competitive bidding requirements. However, the clauses must be carefully structured and can be very difficult to administer. They should only be used as a last resort, and then only if the need to use them can be justified with convincing documentation. Considering the formal procedures and documentation which are necessary to the process, the clauses often are not very attractive to suppliers.

Market Price at Time of Delivery

There have been times when production costs have been so uncertain and supply so short that suppliers will not bid at all. In such cases, market conditions have been so unstable that suppliers would agree to sell certain items only at the "market price at time of delivery." In such cases, purchasing officials must either try to work with the market as it is, or defer the purchase. If the items are critically needed, purchasing officials must proceed, using the best techniques and practices possible. Some degree of control can be obtained by at least requiring that an independent market index be used as the basis for setting prices. It may also be possible to stipulate that the award will be made to the supplier who offers the most advantageous combination of price and delivery.

Unusual market conditions do occur and purchasing officials must have the authority to deal with them in the best possible manner. If statutory support is not provided, purchasing officials are placed in the position of either not taking action or operating with a fear that their actions may be in violation of the statute. It is not feasible to write laws or rules that specify procedures for every possible situation. The law should, however, give the purchasing authority the power to take whatever steps are necessary to purchase needed items when competitive bids cannot be obtained. Clearly, there is a need for supporting the written policies and procedures that cover deviations from normal competitive bidding (i.e., review and approval, justification and documentation requirements, and contract approvals). Similarly, written guidelines should be established for using option and price escalation clauses.

Market Conditions Affecting Contract Performance

Market conditions can impact not only on the competitive bidding process but also on performance by suppliers who are on contract. If market prices increase substantially, it is not unusual for suppliers to seek relief from the government, and cases such as these are difficult to resolve equitably. The general rule must be that suppliers will be bound by the terms and conditions of the contract. To do otherwise would make a mockery of the competitive bidding statute and could provide an opportunity for collusion. However, there are, in practice, cases where holding a supplier to the contract would be patently inequitable, e.g., the supplier would go out of business. Some type of relief must be allowed in such cases, and this would represent an exception to the general rule. These situations call for conservatism on the part of the government. The facts and reasons for seeking relief must be thoroughly documented by the supplier and carefully reviewed by the government before a decision is made. Written guidelines should govern the process and stipulate who has the approval authority, and what appeal procedures are available if the request for relief is denied.

8. Acquisition: Receipt, Opening, and Tabulation of Bids

ESSENTIAL ELEMENTS

Suggested Statutory/Regulatory Coverage

The purchasing statute and/or the rules and regulations adopted pursuant to the statute should:

Permit bidders and the general public to attend bid openings.

Require a tabulation of bids that is recorded and made available to the public.

Recommended Practices

The central purchasing authority should be responsible for establishing written policies for controlling and safeguarding sealed bids until the time set for openings.

There should be written policies governing the methods for tabulating bids, the information included in bid tabulation, and the length of time these records will be retained.

There should be a policy requiring that a public record be kept of vendors solicited for informal bids and bids received.

The central purchasing authority must establish formal procedures to safeguard bids until the time set for opening to ensure the integrity of the bidding process and to promote public confidence. Public bid openings are the rule for sealed bids, and records should be kept on all bids received. Current practices for carrying out these functions vary widely, and all are not equally effective. Factors such as the size and organizational structure of the purchasing program and its available resources affect the procedures used in receiving and controlling bids. Therefore, although all governmental units need not follow the same procedures, there are minimum standards that should be observed. Purchasing's responsibility for the receipt, handling, and opening of bids is never perfunctory.

CONTROL OVER BIDS RECEIVED

The sealed bid process is predicated on the assumption that all bidders submit their bids without knowledge of the prices offered by their competitors. Without this condition, suppliers are given the opportunity to prepare bids which are just low enough to beat their competitors, yet higher than the best price they would have offered without the knowledge of their competitors' bids. While purchasing officials cannot prevent conspiratorial exchanges of price information among suppliers prior to bid submission, they can control bids after they have been submitted to assure that prices are not prematurely disclosed. The system has to be established and monitored by the central purchasing authority, even though some of the detailed activities are properly performed outside of purchasing. It should be kept in mind at all times that opening a sealed bid prior to the designated time can have serious legal implications.

Some large purchasing programs delegate the receipt and control of bids to a central records or services section within purchasing, or even to a unit outside the purchasing activity. A few States require that copies of bids be sent to both purchasing and the office of the Auditor General. While such a requirement establishes a formal means of independent checks and balances, it has disadvantages. For example, a bidder could inadvertently fail to send a copy of his bid to the Auditor General, or his bid could arrive late at one or the other of the offices because of postal delays. Such occurrences cause major problems, engender complaints and appeals, and can result in the disqualification of low bids which otherwise would provide savings to the government.

State and local governments can seldom afford the luxury of enough personnel to allow for the complete segregation of bid-handling duties. In most governmental units, therefore, bids are received by the purchasing unit, often by the purchasing agent who is handling the solicitation.

Responsibilities and procedures for the receipt and control of bids should be set forth in writing. The procedures should require that all bids be date and time stamped, particularly since many bids are hand delivered and therefore bear no postmark. A designated slot and secured box should be provided for depositing bids and a certain individual should be responsible for controlling the bids while they await opening. Since formal bids, by rule of law, must remain sealed until the bid opening, proper identification on the outside of the bid envelope has special importance. This should include the solicitation number, the opening date, and the bidder's name or identification number. The use of vendor identification numbers permits purchasing to keep a tally of those bidders who replied and those who did not.

PUBLIC BID OPENINGS AND DISCLOSURE

Both bidders and the public have a right to know the nature and extent of competition obtained in response to solicitations of bids. Consequently, the sealed bid process calls for bid openings which can be attended by the general public as well as by bidders. In this way, the attendees will know who bid and the prices bid, and can satisfy themselves that a complete and accurate account has been made of all bids received. This type of openness reduces the likelihood of collusion and favoritism, and fosters increased confidence in public purchasing.

Even though the public may have a right to attend bid openings, frequently the only persons present are government representatives. Some States, therefore, require that a designated third party witness bid openings, such as a representative of the Auditor General's office, the Treasurer's office, or some other fiscal agency. Where this kind of procedure exists, however, it seems to have come about by reason of some abuse or untoward action in the past.

Although informal bids which are not received in sealed envelopes need not be subject to the same bid opening process, **the informal bid procedure must also be an open one.** Records should be kept of the suppliers solicited, the bids obtained, and the successful bidder. These records should be available to any interested party so that the entire spectrum of purchasing activities is open to public scrutiny.

BID TABULATION

State and local governments use a number of different means for recording the bidders and their bid prices. In some instances, bids are tabulated when opened; in other cases, they are tabulated later, during the bid evaluation; and, in a few state and local governments, there is no formal tabulation or listing of bids, as such. Insofar as feasible, it is best to prepare a tabulation as the bids are opened. Such a practice protects purchasing from accusations that bids were altered or not considered. The tabulation becomes a permanent record of all bids received, showing the bidders' names, prices, delivery offered, terms of payment, and perhaps some unusual or pertinent factor. There should be an established records retention policy and the records should be available to the public.

Preparing a tabulation at the bid opening may not be practical in many cases. For example, some bids cover hundreds of separate items, and the time required for recording all prices on a separate tabulation sheet is prohibitive. Alternate procedures, therefore, are necessary. Some state and local governments, for example, use various duplicating techniques to record bids. Others format the Invitations for Bids so that the commodity and quote sections of the bids are detachable and can be laid out for visual comparisons. In other cases, the bid sheets themselves are strung together in an overlapping fashion to show only the item, name of bidder, and item price. Either the original or a copy becomes a permanent record which can be referenced if questions arise concerning a particular solicitation. Consequently, although it may be impractical for the public to witness such tabulations being made, it still may observe the opening of bids and have access later to the tabulation.

9. Acquisition: Bid Evaluation and Award

ESSENTIAL ELEMENTS

Suggested Statutory/Regulatory Coverage

The purchasing statute and/or the rules and regulations adopted pursuant to the statute should:

Provide that awards under the formal sealed bid process be made to the "lowest responsible bidder who submits a responsive bid which is most advantageous to the government."

Require that the central purchasing authority publish written criteria, policies, and procedures governing the evaluation-award process.

Establish that any form of state or local preference is neither acceptable nor allowable.

Allow for discretion on the part of purchasing officials in acting in the best interest of the government when no bids are received or when the response to a solicitation is otherwise inadequate.

Provide the authority to reject all bids, or to reject any bid in whole or in part, in accordance with written policies and guidelines, and provide authority to take alternate courses of action, as necessary.

Recommended Practices

Written policies should be developed to provide guidelines for determining successful bidders. These procedures should stress openness and impartiality and require documentation to support decisions made, particularly in cases where awards are made to other than the low bidder, where bids are rejected in whole or in part, or where alternate bids are accepted. The written policies should cover such matters as:

Guidelines for determining the "lowest responsible bidder who submits a responsive bid which is most advantageous to the government."

A definition of "responsiveness" and the factors to be considered in making this determination.

A requirement that the Invitation for Bids set forth the factors that will be used in determining responsiveness.

The policy with respect to alternate bids and supplemental actions that may be warranted.

Procedures to be followed when mistakes are discovered in bids.

Guidelines for determining "substantial conformance" and "minor irregularities" in bids.

The policy for considering discounts in determining the low bidder.

The policy regarding late bids.

Circumstances under which all bids may be rejected, or a particular bid may be rejected in whole or in part.

THE EVALUATION PROCESS

Following tabulation, bids must be formally reviewed and evaluated, since purchasing laws and good practice require that factors other than price alone be considered in determining the successful bidder. Public purchasing statutes describe the low bidder with such words as "lowest responsible," "lowest and best," "lowest responsible meeting specifications," or "lowest and most advantageous." The courts interpret these provisions as allowing the awarding authority reasonable

discretion and judgment in determining who is the successful bidder. Once made, the decision normally will not be questioned by the courts unless it appears to be arbitrary, capricious, or fraudulent.

On the one hand, the wording of the term used to describe the successful bidder may seem relatively unimportant as long as there are suitable guidelines for making the determination. On the other hand, it is a key provision of the purchasing statute, one that not only serves to guide award decisions but also serves as a reference in litigation and disputes. **This study found that the phrase "lowest responsible bidder who submits the responsive bid most advantageous to the government" has evolved as the most suitable definition of the successful bidder.** The phrase "most advantageous" is the most useful base on which to develop criteria for the analysis and evaluation of bids.

When awards are made to other than the lowest bidder, the facts and bases for the award should be well documented and remain available for public scrutiny. A well-documented record protects purchasing officials from criticism of decisions which, lacking good documentation, might later appear to have been based on favoritism.

It is impractical to set forth in the law precise and uniform criteria to be used in evaluating bids. For one thing, factors can be simple or complex according to the nature of the item, as in the differences between paper clips and electronic computers. In spite of such differences, the evaluation and award process must follow established criteria and procedures. If this highly sensitive aspect is left to an informal process which relies on individual judgment, the system is open to many pressures and inconsistencies which can improperly influence awards.

Guidelines for evaluation and award should encompass a determination of who submitted the lowest bid, whether the low bid is responsive, and whether the low bidder is responsible. A careful analysis must be made to assure that the low bid conforms substantially not only to the physical specifications, but also to the terms and special conditions of the bid solicitation. If it does not, the same process must be applied to the next low bid, and so on, as necessary.

Openness, impartiality, and reasonableness are the standards in this process. Openness requires that evaluation procedures be documented in writing and be made available to all prospective bidders and to the general public. It also requires that evaluation criteria be thoughtfully developed and stated clearly in Invitations for Bids. Impartiality requires that all bidders be treated alike in the evaluation process, so that favoritism, however unintentional, does not control. Finally, the award determination must stand the test of reasonableness, which calls for an ordered process.

Written guidelines will not eliminate the need for professional judgment. They do, however, express the rationale, consistency, and documentation that support the process. Selecting the "lowest responsible bidder who submits the responsive bid most advantageous to the government" is a multiphase evaluation. It is precisely at this stage of the purchasing cycle that the underlying concepts that foster competition—offering the most equitable means of obtaining quality goods and services at fair and reasonable prices—will be either asserted or aborted.

RESPONSIBILITY OF BIDDERS

The government must have some assurance that the successful bidder will be able to perform satisfactorily under the contract. Financial stability, production capability, and the ability to deliver on time should already have been determined in large measure in the prequalification program. Where a particular solicitation is routine, this undoubtedly would suffice. But there is a need for making a conscious decision that no further inquiries are needed. For example, if a low bidder is well-known, has performed satisfactorily in the past, and has the items in his regular product line, he most likely could be judged responsible for the award. However, the purchaser must be certain that these elements are considered, and not allow a careless decision to be made.

Occasions will arise, however, when inquiry into a bidder's responsibility during the bid evaluation process is necessary. For example, if the government has never before done business with the low bidder and he has not been prequalified, some investigation is in order. There must be assurance that the bidder is a proven dealer in the commodity and that he may be relied on to perform satisfactorily. Very importantly, he must not assume that he can make a bid and, if successful, go shopping for a product to furnish at the bid price. Even with well-known manufacturers, additional inquiries may be in order. An established manufacturer may bid on a new product or line of products that he has not produced or marketed previously, or he may bid on a particular item for which his performance on other contracts has been less than adequate.

Determining responsibility, therefore, involves prequalification, past performance, and numerous other supplier capabilities. Often, too little consideration is given to these aspects and formal guidelines generally do not exist. This deficiency is a weakness found in virtually all purchasing operations.

RESPONSIVENESS

Even when a low bidder is responsible, his bid must also be responsive to the specifications, terms, and conditions in the particular Invitation for Bids. A responsive bid is one which is in substantial conformance with the IFB; essentially void of contravening terms, gratuitous additions, and unilateral mistakes or obvious errors made in calculating or presenting figures; and reasonable in price. On the one hand, the determination of responsiveness is largely dependent on the requirements set forth in the IFB. On the other hand, extreme care must be taken to assure that all relevant factors are properly assessed in determining the bidder's responsiveness and the most advantageous bid.

Alternate Bids

Alternate bids may be submitted for a number of reasons and can pose major problems. Bidders may intentionally submit alternate bids if, for example, they suggest a change in the terms, conditions, or specifications of the IFB. Often, they may simply bid on a product which varies with the specifications but which is the nearest thing they have to offer. Sometimes the items being purchased are subject to rapid technological changes, and it is difficult to keep the specifications current. Other times, bidders may offer a newer, more advanced, or perhaps better product than that called for in the IFB. Such alternate bids usually indicate some peculiarity or deficiency in the market or in the purchasing system. Purchasing personnel must keep abreast of technological developments in product lines and update specifications as conditions warrant. If design specifications cannot be kept current because of technological changes, performance specifications may solve the difficulty.

As an interim measure, alternate bids can be called for in the IFB. It is far better to address the issue in advance than to react to an unanticipated alternate bid. At any rate, purchasing personnel must be alert to the possibility of alternate bids and assure that the decision to accept them or reject them is fair to all parties. As a rule, if such a bid is not responsive to the IFB, it should be rejected. If alternate bids are accepted, and an award is made based on an alternate bid, the file should document the bases for this decision. Here, too, reasonableness and impartiality are the criteria, and favoritism must not be permitted.

One type of alternate bid can be especially frustrating to the purchasing office. Some large corporations with powerful sales positions seek to do business only under their own terms and conditions. Where these are contrary to the government's laws, rules, or policies, the result may be an impasse. The government should insist upon the right to control the conditions under which it commits public funds.

Mistakes and Errors

There are no data currently available on the frequency and magnitude of mistakes and errors made in bids. However, mistakes do occur, and their treatment should be covered by written policy.

The sealed competitive bidding process presumes that all bids are submitted without knowledge of the prices being offered by competitors. Consequently, problems arise when a bidder discovers that he has made a mistake serious enough for him to either seek correction or withdraw entirely. The handling of such situations depends on when the mistake is discovered, when the discovery is communicated, how obvious the mistake is on the face of the bid, and how material the mistake is to the intended offer.

A few States do not accept bids that contain corrected errors or erasures. Although this policy seems harsh and can cause the State to lose advantageous bids, it provides a kind of protection. Most governments, however, take a more realistic approach and accept bids if erasures and corrections are initialed by the person who prepared the bid.

When a bidder finds he has made a mistake after the bid has been submitted but before it is opened, he should be permitted to make formal changes or to withdraw his bid before the bid opening without revealing the amount of the bid. Preferably, he should submit a corrected sealed bid in person or by mail, but time and distance may make this impractical. Most States will accept corrections which are telegraphed prior to the scheduled bid opening time. Formal written procedures should govern correcting or withdrawing bids.

Once the bids are opened, mistakes pose a more serious problem because corrections might well be made using knowledge of competitors' prices. All changes made after bid opening, therefore, threaten the spirit and purpose of competitive bidding. As a broad rule, changes should not be allowed after bids are opened. There are, however, valid reasons for exceptions, which have been recognized both by Attorneys General and by the courts. These include obvious errors—for example, where a decimal point is obviously misplaced. Also, it is a fairly common policy that where there is a mistake in the multiplication or extension of unit prices, the unit price governs.

Situations arise where the low bid is substantially below the prices of other bidders. On the one hand, there is no sure way to know whether the low bidder has made an unintentional mistake or simply a mistake in judgment. On the other hand, it is not reasonable or fair to enforce a bid which is so low that the bidder will incur severe loss if awarded the contract. These situations call for sound judgment and established policies based on a rule that the government will not impose an unconscionable hardship. Generally, the problem can be handled by setting the bid aside or allowing it to be withdrawn. But allowing changes in a bid should always be avoided; they can never be allowed to prejudice the rights of other bidders or the public.

Frequently, a distinction is made between "substantial nonconformance" which means that a bid is nonresponsive, and "technical irregularities" which may be waived. Seldom, however, are there guidelines for making this distinction. Predominant here are impartiality and legal considerations. **Any deviation which gives a bidder an unfair advantage over his competitors must not be waived during the evaluation process.** Other seemingly insignificant "irregularities" could present legal problems later (e.g., bids being undated or improperly executed). Consequently, written guidelines must cover this area to assure fair treatment based on the consistent application of established policies.

Payment Discounts

Most States take cash discounts or discounts for prompt payment into consideration when evaluating bids. This practice is proper so long as the IFB states that discounts will be considered, and the government's payment cycle reasonably assures that the discount will be earned. Because of the slow processing of invoices, however, many state and local governments frequently cannot meet suppliers' prompt payment terms. Nonetheless, they may still take the discounts. This procedure is clearly improper and should be discontinued. Purchasing officials must assure the public that the only discount terms that will be considered are those that the government can expect to meet. This procedure will encourage suppliers to bid realistically and will ensure that when discounts are a determining factor, they will be earned and thus substantiate that the successful bidder was, in fact, the low bidder.

Preference

Many state and local governments have laws or policies that require giving preference to local or in-state products or bidders. While there may be variations in preference provisions, the intent is always the same: to favor in-state or local bidders. Even where it is not provided by law, preference to local bidders is given by many local governments and perhaps a few States as a matter of practice.

The percent preference always gives local bidders a definite advantage, as illustrated below.

Bidder	Bid price	Preference		Price on which award is based
		%	Amount	
A	$10,000	5%	$500	$9,500
B	$9,850	......	....	$9,850
C	$9,675	......	....	$9,675

Bidder A, the local bidder, submitted the highest bid but, because of a 5 percent preference, was given the award at a price of $10,000.

Eleven States still have statutes which provide from 1½ to 10 percent preference to in-state bidders. Some of the reasons presented are that increased tax revenues are generated by doing business within the jurisdiction, that new jobs are created, and that businesses are encouraged to locate within the jurisdiction. Without addressing the relative merits of these assumptions, the dangers and disadvantages of this type of preference greatly outweigh any advantages.

From a legal viewpoint, preference is arguably unconstitutional as a barrier to interstate commerce. Another view shows that preference is in direct conflict with the principles of competition and precludes the purchaser from obtaining the best competitive price. Many bidders who otherwise would be interested are discouraged from competing and potential sources of supply are reduced. Preferred bidders feel more secure and have less incentive to submit their best prices when a free competitive market is absent. The result is higher costs to the taxpayer. For example, a survey made several years ago by a National Association of State Purchasing Officials committee showed that prices usually were increased by the amount of the preference percentages, and eventually by more than this amount.

As a form of retaliation, some States apply a reciprocal preference, whereby out-of-state bidders are penalized by the amount of preference they are given in their home States. One State is prevented by law from doing businss with suppliers whose home States employ in-state preference, and its decision several years ago to enforce this statute caused several States to repeal their preference laws and practices. All of these conditions support the conclusion that **preference provisions and practices should be eliminated from public purchasing.** Governing bodies and Legislatures must recognize that preference is promoted by business and special interest groups, that the net effect is costly, and that efforts to establish or maintain preference need to be resisted.

Where preference is used only without "loss or sacrifice in price or quality," that is, where all other factors are equal, it can be defended as reasonable and acceptable. This is a common and valid practice used by some States to break tie bids.

Before leaving this subject, a few words are needed on the subject of "Buy America," which relates to U.S.-foreign trade, and gives preferences to U.S. products and firms over foreign firms. Under various pressures, several state governments have attempted to adopt Buy America principles either by law or by practice. Such attempts have only resulted in problems, legal debate, and rulings of unconstitutionality when brought before the courts. Since Chief Justice Marshall, foreign trade policy has been declared the province exclusively of the federal government. State statutes and policies, therefore, should avoid any Buy America provisions or practices.

Late Bids

Late bids by their nature raise the issue of unacceptability. Any bid received at the place designated for submission after the time set for opening of bids is a late bid. Most States have a policy of rejecting all late bids, regardless of the circumstances, and this is a good general rule. It is easy to administer and, more importantly, eliminates potential disputes concerning the justice of awarding a contract to a bidder who did not follow bid instructions.

In other States and local governments, late bids may be accepted if it can be ascertained beyond a reasonable doubt that the circumstances which caused the bid to be late were beyond the bidder's control and that the bid was submitted without prior knowledge of the contents of competing bids. The determining factor is the time at which the bidder relinquished control of the bid. For example, if the bid was mailed in sufficient time to have arrived prior to bid opening, but was delayed in the mail, or if it was delivered by a messenger who went to the wrong room, the bidder could not have gained any advantage. The theory behind accepting late bids of this type is that rejecting them would be unfair to the bidder and, more basically, that the public would be denied the savings that might be afforded by considering them.

Although the general rule should be to reject late bids, some discretionary authority is in order. The problem can be handled successfully and advantageously with good management. Specific rules should be prepared, outlining the detailed policy and procedures to be used. The rules should require documentation of the reasons for accepting or rejecting a late bid, and the method for disposing of rejected late bids. These rules should be made available to bidders and to the general public.

ONE OR NO BIDS RECEIVED

Occasionally only one bid, or perhaps no bids, will be received in response to a solicitation. These situations can indicate serious internal problems or market difficulties and must be investigated. There are various reasons why only one bid might be received, but award should not be made routinely to the sole bidder, if available competition is lacking. Bids may be called for again, or where it is decided to proceed with the sole bidder, a price analysis should be performed to assess the reasonableness of the bid, and negotiation should be considered and employed, as appropriate.

When one or no bids are received, the technical specifications should be reviewed to determine whether they are so restrictive that no one will bid, or whether they "spec out" all otherwise qualified suppliers but one. Market conditions should be analyzed, and may disclose that a seller's market (i.e., suppliers do not need or want additional business) exists, or that unrealistic or overly stringent delivery dates were specified. The possibility of collusion should not be overlooked. A review of the bid-award history for the item may be revealing, particularly when there was competition in the past. Direct contact with suppliers who normally bid is usually a good approach in determining why they did not bid.

REJECTION OF BIDS

Purchasing officials must have the power to reject bids in order to safeguard the public interest and to deal effectively with conditions such as unsatisfactory bids and suspected collusion. In some cases, the rejection of bids may be almost routine because it is demanded by obvious circumstances. In other cases, the purchasing official may believe that all bid prices are unreasonably high. Care and judgment are always needed in deciding whether or not an only bid or all bids should be rejected. Under any circumstances, this is a serious and sensitive determination.

Rejection of bids carries two distinct meanings. One concerns whether a bid is submitted on time and in good order; if not, it may be rejected without any further consideration. The other concerns a bid which is given full consideration but which is not the successful bid. Depending upon the circumstances, it may be necessary to reject an individual bid in whole or in part, or to reject all bids. Late bids, substantial nonconformance, high prices, major irregularities, and other similar conditions can call for rejecting the bids. The need for the authority to reject bids in part is sometimes overlooked. Where a solicitation covers a number of different items, a bid may contain some sort of irregularity on only one or a few of the items bid. If there is no established policy for dealing with this type of situation, protests can arise from any of the bidders, regardless of the manner in which the case was handled.

If it is necessary to reject all bids, several courses of action must be considered. The reasons for rejection will influence the next step. If all bids were rejected because of suspected collusion, for example, it is unlikely that resolicitation will be effective. In such cases, the best solution may be to buy in the open market or to negotiate a price if the items are needed without delay. Statutes and rules should provide all necessary authority for such alternate actions. Where bids are rejected because they exceed the funds available, readvertising for a lesser quantity may be a solution. To avoid rejecting bids because of the amount of funds, the terms and conditions in the IFB can provide for reducing the quantities awarded if a lack of funds should require.

Statutes can and should provide the basic authorities just discussed, but the need for detailed rules and policies is obvious. If bids are rejected for conditions not specifically covered in the written rules and policies, documentation is imperative, and some type of post review is in order. Sound implementation policies prevent bids from being rejected by an unqualified authority, for an immaterial motive, arbitrarily, or in error.

10. Acquisition: Safeguards

ESSENTIAL ELEMENTS

Suggested Statutory/Regulatory Coverage

The purchasing statute and/or the rules and regulations adopted pursuant to the statute should:

Provide for public access to and openness of the procurement process by requiring the publication of all purchasing laws, rules, regulations, and procedures; public notice of all solicitations of bids, awards, and major contract changes; documentation of all actions in the procurement process, particularly waivers of competitive bidding; and public access to bid openings and all records except unopened bids, documents on which an award is pending, and vendors' proprietary data.

Provide for criminal penalties for attempting to influence awards through offers of reward, and for accepting such rewards; and provide that all guilty parties shall be financially liable to the government for any losses that the government incurred as a result of any contract which was so awarded.

Provide that contracts are void if they result from a conflict of interest; if they were awarded to a person or firm that tried to influence the award by offering something of value to a government employee; or if a contract is awarded by a government official or employee by circumventing statutory requirements.

Provide that conflict of interest statutes cover all government personnel who are in a position to influence contract awards, including the chief executive, legislators, cabinet-rank officials, department heads, officers, and employees, as well as their spouses.

Specify the types of actions which constitute conflicts of interest.

Classify as a felony all violations of the conflict of interest statutes.

Require immediate dismissal from office for government employees convicted of a conflict of interest violation.

Provide that, where contracts are declared void because they resulted from a conflict of interest, the public employee involved will be liable to the government for the amount of his profit plus the amount of any loss that the government suffered as a result of the contract.

Set forth the conditions under which the government may be liable for a contractor's provable costs under a contract which resulted from a conflict of interest.

Require that the chief purchasing official maintain surveillance to detect "back-door selling" and prescribe suitable penalties for suppliers and government employees who engage in this practice.

Require a bond to protect the government against all losses caused by malfeasance or misfeasance of government officers or employees who can influence the award of public contracts, if no provision is made for such a bond elsewhere in government legislation.

Require that a code or standard of conduct be published to govern the performance of government employees, and especially purchasing personnel, in managing, purchasing, or otherwise expending government funds.

Provide for criminal, civil, and administrative sanctions; penalties; and disciplinary actions for violation of such standards either by government officers or employees, or by contractors or their agents.

Establish personal liability for government personnel who authorize purchases to be made without following applicable statutes and rules.

Recommended Practices

The central purchasing authority should prepare and issue written policies and procedures designed to discourage "back-door selling" and to detect and prevent instances of this practice.

The central purchasing authority should prepare written procedures which set forth the techniques to be used to prevent and detect the circumvention of purchasing laws and regulations. The procedures should provide that official reprimands be issued to government employees who circumvent these laws and regulations.

The central purchasing authority should establish a program for continuing communication and coordination with the appropriate law enforcement units who are responsible for dealing with organized crime matters.

Structures and procedures in the purchasing process are established not only for effectiveness, but also to guard against improper actions by government personnel and suppliers. Centralization, for example, takes purchasing authority from using agencies, which might be inclined to purchase on the basis of personal preference, and transfers it to an office which is assigned the duty of being objective in purchasing items that meet actual requirements and are in the government's best interests. Requirements for competitive bidding, solicitation of qualified suppliers, and award to the lowest responsible bidder are intended to prevent awards based on arbitrariness, favoritism, kickback schemes, or other fraudulent arrangements. Central control over specifications eliminates undue restrictions which could favor certain suppliers. When the size of the purchasing staff permits divisions of specification writers, purchasing personnel, and inspection and testing personnel, the likelihood of even unconscious favoritism can be further reduced.

The discussion in this chapter of the report may seem harsh in prescribing absolutes in restrictions and penalties. The goal, however, is the conservation of public funds and public confidence. The slightest erosion of absolute honesty, integrity, and openness is far more damaging in public purchasing than in most other public pursuits, and the mere shadow of doubt impacts as severely as overt misconduct. **Hence, safeguards must be virtually fail-safe.**

PUBLIC INFORMATION

The best safeguards for the integrity of the purchasing process are written procurement procedures, complete records on each purchase, and public access to these records. Many scandals involving the expenditure of public funds have taken place in an atmosphere of secrecy, with awards being made by a vaguely defined process without any justifying records. Purchasing records must document each step of the process—the process involved in establishing the specification, what the specification was, who was solicited, who responded, what the responses were, who received the award, what the contract terms were, how the contract was performed, and the bases for changing contracts. The record should show the basis for any deviation from the normal process, such as making an emergency purchase or making an award to other than the low bidder. **Except for unopened bids, trade secrets, and bids on which awards have not yet been made, all purchasing records should be available to the public upon request.** In addition, all purchasing laws, rules, regulations, and procedures should be published. This is the general rule of most centralized purchasing systems. Experience with this procedure

reveals that interested business representatives do request purchase records from time to time, and that such requests result in little or no disruption of the purchasing process. Requests for information can be handled by clerical personnel. Not only do public records help keep prospective bidders informed, they can also aid in demonstrating to the public that the purchasing processes are being conducted honestly.

By the nature of public purchasing, it is appropriate that sealed bids be opened in public. Forty-six States and many cities and counties make such bid openings accessible to the public. Those who do not should do so; there is no reason to deny or to limit attendance at bid openings.

CORRUPT INTEREST IN PURCHASES

The overall openness of the purchasing process should be supplemented by legislative deterrents to specific situations that can destroy the integrity of the purchasing process. Parties who can influence the award of a contract should not have any personal interest in that contract. Attempts to influence awards through offers of reward, as well as acceptance of such offers, should be criminal offenses. Many state and local governments have general legislation covering conflicts of interest, bribery, kickbacks, etc. Most States, however, feel it is best to have specific statutes dealing with these situations as they relate directly to the purchasing process. General conflict of interest and bribery statutes can suffer from the paradoxical faults of being so broad that their application to a specific situation is uncertain, but not broad enough to cover every specific transgression against which they were directed. Thirty-six States have conflict of interest sections in their purchasing statutes, and 37 have sections in their purchasing statutes or rules and regulations prohibiting the offer or acceptance of things of value to influence an award.

Conflict of Interests

Conflict of interest statutes prohibit people entrusted with the government's business from being in a position to profit from government contracts. In such a position, they would be constantly torn between self-interest and objectivity. Because of the difficulty of determining whether a contract is indeed tainted with self-interest, the statutes usually invalidate any contract that could have been influenced by the self-interest of those who are the subject of the statute.

Conflict of interest statutes should cover all officers and employees of the government who could act to influence the award of a contract. Although it is argued that strong conflict of interest statutes exclude many capable persons from certain types of participation in government, adequate protection in this area is essential. Questions of whether the statute should be more or less strict should be resolved in favor of strictness.

Conflict of interest statutes now in effect reveal a wide variance in delineating the persons subject to the statutes, as well as the prohibitions placed upon them. Persons who are subject to conflict of interest laws range from only the chief purchasing official, to every officer and employee of a governmental entity. Close relatives of primary subjects of the statute may also be included. Because contract awards may be expected as political rewards by their supporters, the chief executive, all legislators and cabinet rank officials, and department heads and their non-civil-service or non-merit-system assistants should all be covered by conflict of interest prohibitions. Although the subordinate of a person in a position to influence an award may not exert influence, he may be able to exert favoritism. Consequently, the prohibitions should apply to any officer or employee of central purchasing, and to any officer or employee of any agency involved in a contract. As a minimum, the spouses of all of these persons should also be under the same prohibitions.

Some statutes prohibit certain individuals from having specific types of involvement, such as conducting an outside business and signing a contract with their own agency, or signing a similar contract with any government agency. Stringent statutes prohibit persons from appearing before an agency within two years after termination of employment with the agency, or giving assistance for two years after employment with the government in a transaction which, within the previous two years, was under the person's official responsibility. Again, as a minimum, legislators, non-civil-service or non-merit executive personnel, and all purchasing personnel should be prohibited from being agents for bidders and signing contracts with the government.

Statutes often prohibit relationships with businesses that sell to the government, including those of partner, board member, officer, or employee of a corporation. In addition, holding an amount of stock significant to make one biased is prohibited. Once it is decided that a person should be covered by a conflict of interest law, the legislation should attempt to cover all types of involvement that could cause bias in favor of vendors. One statute even prohibits negotiating or discussing prospective employment with a business that sells to the government.

Among the penalties for violating conflict of interest statutes are civil damages of three times the loss to the government, criminal penalties of a minor felony, removal from office, and a permanent bar from holding office or employment with the government. In most

conflict of interest situations, the individual involved realizes that a conflict of interest exists. Because of the serious damage that such a situation does to the integrity of the purchasing system and to the government in general, classification as a felony is appropriate. In those rare cases where the individual involved might not have known of the conflict, he will be protected by the requirement that his guilty intent must be proved in court beyond a reasonable doubt before he can be convicted of a criminal offense. Statutes should provide for immediate dismissal from office upon conviction and a bar on government employment unless the conviction is overruled.

Some courts have ruled that even though a contract resulting from a conflict of interest situation might be the most advantageous for the government, the contract is void. Others have stated that if the contract results from sealed competitive bidding, then the conflict of interest statutes should not apply. The first view is the more appropriate. If a person can submit a bid and then be in a position to influence the award, he may attempt to use his influence to have the low bid bypassed. The same is probably true where a legislator, executive officer, or employee disqualifies himself from acting on a contract in which he has an interest. This should not give validity to the contract, since a person who disqualifies himself from official acts does not necessarily disqualify his influence.

Every contract resulting from a conflict of interest should be declared void, and the public employee involved should be liable to the government for the amount of his profit plus the amount of any loss that the government suffered as a result of the contract. Contracts resulting from conflicts of interest must not be profitable. However, some innocent people, such as uninvolved stockholders in a corporation in which a government employee held a significant amount of stock, might be unduly injured if the vendor were not allowed any recovery under such a contract. Consequently, the government should limit its liability on such contracts to the provable costs of the contractor.

There is yet another form of conflict of interest which may not be of the same magnitude of transgression as those conflicts which can occur in the mainstream of the purchasing community, but which nonetheless should be of concern to those involved in public purchasing. This variation is inelegantly described as "back-door selling," i.e., oversell at the user level. This is not necessarily, or even very often, a question of bribery or gift-giving or of any other technically illegal act, but rather the practice of some vendors in the careful care and cultivation of purchasing personnel which draws public employees into a network of obligation. As a result, purchasing personnel consciously or unconsciously become advocates of a particular product. While centralization of purchasing authority definitely offsets this kind of product polarization, the task of the public purchasing official is made infinitely more complex by such marketing techniques. Present laws or administrative procedures offer little remedy for the purchasing official in taking direct action against this type of influence.

Kickbacks and Bribes

There is not as much diversity in the approaches of statutes which cover attempts to influence an award by offering something of value to government personnel. A wide range of terms is used to describe the types of offers which are prohibited. A composite list includes any promise, obligation, contract for future reward or compensation, emolument, gratuity, contribution, loan, reward, rebate, gift, money, or other thing of value. Some statutes which contain long lists of what is prohibited fail to include the important term "giving and receiving." Laws should deal with these actions equally and harshly. One statute sees fit to create a presumption that when an interested party makes any gift to purchasing personnel, the gift is made and received for the purpose of influencing purchasing decisions. This statute shifts the burden in a trial to those who give and receive the gift, so that they have to prove the lack of criminal intent rather than the government's having to prove that there was criminal intent.

Acts of giving and accepting something of value to influence the award of a contract should be criminal offenses, whether the exchange has the intended effect or not. Contracts with a party or a firm that tried to influence the outcome by offering something of value to any government personnel should be declared void. Unlike the case of conflict of interest where innocent individuals might be involved, in cases where something of value is exchanged to influence a purchasing decision, the receiver is culpable, and the management of the firm whose representative made the tender can reasonably be presumed to have known about or condoned his action. This presumption should be made into a statutory rule. Unless the firm can prove that its agent acted entirely on his own, with the result that no individual in the management of the firm was or could reasonably have been aware of his actions, the government should be released from current and future financial obligations to the firm involved based on the tainted contract. If it can be proved that the agent acted on his own, the government should be liable only for provable costs. All guilty parties should be financially liable to the government for any losses that the government incurred as a result of the contract. In many jurisdictions, government officials and em-ployees who can influence awards are bonded, and the government can recover the value of any monetary damage it may suffer due to their malfeasance or misfeasance.

CODE OF ETHICS

The nature of their duties makes it necessary for purchasing officials to remain independent, free from obligation, and above suspicion. A written code of ethics for both purchasing officials and vendors can greatly assist in achieving these objectives. Such a code can delineate the relationship between central purchasing employees and vendors' representatives, and set forth the standards of conduct expected of government personnel. All persons involved can then be aware of the mode of behavior expected of them.

CIRCUMVENTING STATUTORY REQUIREMENTS

Obviously, any purchasing program is greatly harmed by actions involving bribery, kickbacks, conflict of interest, or similar acts. When such cases of corruption are discovered, strong direct action is usually taken to rid the system of the people involved and to prevent a recurrence of the situation. However, when using agencies merely circumvent the purchasing laws and rules, the situation can appear trivial compared to a case of bribery or conflict of interest. In most purchasing systems, when such unlawful purchases are discovered, the measures taken to prevent their recurrence are not adequate, and the problem repeats itself. The total effect, though less spectacular than instances of corruption, actually may be more harmful to the purchasing system.

Often, circumvention simply takes the form of efforts by using agencies to obtain a particular brand, or to avoid the competitive bidding process by acquiring an item immediately. Methods used involve such ploys as ordering an item from a vendor without requisitioning in the prescribed manner, taking emergency purchase measures in situations that are not in fact emergencies, and splitting requirements into smaller amounts to get below the dollar limit for which competitive bidding is required.

Strong appropriate action is not customary on the part of most governments in dealing with violations of this kind. Nor is the action usually directed to the source of the problem—the persons who authorized the purchases. The appropriateness of action that can be taken, other than by the courts, depends upon whether the illegality of the purchase is detected before or after payment has been made. Split purchases may not be discovered until after they have been delivered and paid for. Some purchasing laws call for after-the-fact approval or review of emergency purchases, and circumvention of the law may therefore not be discovered until after the transaction has been completed. When this is the case, the most effective tactic is a strong reprimand from the Legislature or the chief executive, warning of action to be taken if the practice recurs. Such reprimands seldom happen, however. In some governments, central purchasing and auditors regularly report instances where the purchasing and auditors regularly report instances where the purchasing statute has been circumvented; lack of effective follow-up only permits the practice to continue.

Central purchasing can correct the problem if the transgression is discovered before payment. Such a discovery may occur if approval from central purchasing is required prior to payment. In many systems, central purchasing must approve completed emergency purchases before payment can be made and, in this way, it can be aware of any abuses of emergency purchase provisions. It is not uncommon, however, for purchasing officials to ratify unauthorized and improperly made purchases under emergency provisions because of a lack of clear authority or a disinclination to engage in disputes with other agencies. Even those purchasing officials who attempt to discourage circumvention of the purchasing legislation seem to do so ineffectively. They refuse to approve a payment, appear adamant for what they consider an appropriate time, and finally give approval. The thinking behind this course of action appears to be: (1) ethically, the vendor who delivered goods or performed services should be paid for them; (2) when the vendor has trouble getting his money he will not sell to using agencies unless he is sure that they have the authority to make a purchase; and (3) while the vendor is worried about getting paid, he will harass the using agency who will learn from this experience not to repeat the transgression. This tactic does not, however, reach the direct cause of the problem—the individuals in the using agency who made the purchase.

The few purchasing systems that are successful in dealing with this kind of problem are those that place the responsibility squarely on the shoulders of the using agency personnel who made or authorized the purchase. The legislation in these jurisdictions provides that any such purchase does not obligate the government, and that a person making a contract, or the head of the agency involved, is financially liable to the vendor. By refusing to give his approval, the purchasing official can force the using agency personnel to either pay for the purchase or go to the Legislature and ask for a "moral obligation payment" to the vendor. This type of statutory provision provides effective control.

ORGANIZED CRIME

One threat to the integrity of the purchasing process that has not been widely or fully recognized is the infiltration of organized crime into legitimate firms that do business with the government. This problem should no longer be ignored or assumed nonexistent. Some purchasing programs, in the prequalification process for their bidders lists, attempt to screen businesses which have convicted felons as officers or board members, but few go beyond this sort of review. More effort is necessary if public purchasing is to avoid business relationships with criminals. Whether purchasing can disqualify a firm whose performance record is good because of past illegal actions on the part of employees or stockholders, is debatable. Nevertheless, the problem of governments doing business with criminal elements needs to be addressed. The public interest needs to be defined and public policy enunciated. Until then, the purchasing office can contribute any knowledge or data it may have through liaison with law enforcement agencies.

Because information on organized crime activity is tightly controlled, the purchasing official should open a line of communication with the law enforcement unit that deals with organized crime. The Attorney General's office, the local police, and organized crime units have special access to information on the subject. Apparently, however, these law enforcement units have not often taken any initiative to contact government purchasing offices, because little dialogue presently exists between the two groups. Establishing communications can be helpful to all the government elements involved. The law enforcement unit can give purchasing officials information upon request and can relay pertinent information that it knows will be useful to central purchasing. Central purchasing can inform crime units of suspicious occurrences in the market and supply information that could be helpful in investigations of organized crime.

As an example, central purchasing may be able to supply good documentation of an illegal market division engineered by a business affiliated with organized crime. In the other direction, purchasing can use information from the law enforcement unit to deny government business to firms that have organized crime figures in influential positions. In *Lefkowitz* v. *Turley,* 1973, the U.S. Supreme Court said that a State may cancel current relationships and disqualify from future contracts with public agencies, for an appropriate time in the future, architects who refuse to answer relevant inquiries about the performance of their contracts with the State if the architects have been granted immunity from the use of the answers in a criminal proceeding against them.

To begin the two-way communication, the organized crime unit could brief purchasing agents on the types of information available, how to request the information, and how to recognize organized crime. Information that might serve to disqualify firms with organized crime connections from doing business with the government should be sent routinely to central purchasing. For example, if a gambling raid has been successfully conducted on a firm whose parent firm makes sales to the government, this information should be forwarded to central purchasing even if none of the officers or board members of the parent firm were directly implicated.

The use that purchasing can make of information from a crime unit depends on the applicable purchasing laws and the nature of the information received. Purchasing statutes, as well as the general rules of law, permit awards to be made taking into consideration more than price alone. Existing statutory language that appears to further support in not dealing with firms affiliated with organized crime directs that consideration be given to "the character, integrity (and) reputation" of the bidder. Still, these broadly worded pronouncements do not allow purchasing agents a free reign in selecting successful bidders, and a more definitive statement about doing business with organized crime is needed. In the end, of course, the courts can review the action taken by the purchasing official to ensure that he did not go beyond his legislative grant of authority. Generally, the courts will uphold his action where the purchasing agent acts on the facts before him without fraud, arbitrariness, or abuse of discretion.

The problem in dealing with organized crime figures who have not been convicted of felonies lies in obtaining facts. Because of the great potential for abuse, the courts almost certainly would not allow the disqualification of a bidder solely on the word of a law enforcement agent. Still, conviction of a crime is not necessarily required before a bidder may be disqualified. One court, ruling under a statute that called for award to the "lowest responsible bidder, as will best promote the public interest," held that a bidder who was under indictment for grand larceny in the course of performing a previous government contract could rightfully be denied the award of another contract for which he was the lowest bidder (*Zara Contracting Co. v. Cohen,* 1965). In another case, under a statute providing for award to the "lowest responsible bidder," the court ruled that if the awarding body believed, based on evidence that it in good faith deemed satisfactory, that a bidder had defrauded the government on a previous contract, it could declare the bidder not responsible even though he had not been convicted in court (*Williams v. City of Topeka,* 1911).

11. Quality Assurance: Specifications

ESSENTIAL ELEMENTS

Suggested Statutory/Regulatory Coverage

The purchasing statute and/or the rules and regulations adopted pursuant to the statute should:

Charge central purchasing with the responsibility for establishing a specification program and a standardization program, with written policies and procedures.

Provide central purchasing with the authority, under defined conditions and with each action suitably documented, to waive competitive bidding for the purpose of buying articles for experiment, test, or trial.

Grant the central purchasing authority the power to review, modify, and approve specifications.

Recommended Practices

To provide a common basis for bidding, specifications should set out the essential characteristics of the items being purchased.

Specifications should not call for features or a quality level which is not necessary to an item's intended use.

Planning procedures should call for reviews of equipment items to determine the types of optional items ordered and the frequency of such purchases.

When optional item needs warrant, the Invitation for Bids should set forth the expected needs and the manner in which the related bid prices will be considered during the bid evaluation process.

Historical data on optional item purchases should be included when building an information system for purchasing.

The policies and procedures for handling optional items should be set forth in writing.

Specifications should include descriptions of the nature and methods of testing to be used, and guidelines for objectively applying test results must be established.

Written guidelines should be prepared to set forth the different types of specifications and the circumstances under which they are most appropriate.

Whenever brand name specifications are used, there must be an accompanying explanation that clearly indicates that the specification is not intended to be restrictive and, where possible, several acceptable brand names should be used.

The use of brand name specifications should be limited insofar as feasible.

Qualified products lists limit competition to those products on the list, but can be effectively used. When used, actual samples or highly documented files should be kept on each item that qualifies, and qualification procedures should include, where feasible, qualitative ratings or test scores.

The use of samples is a valuable aspect of the specification process. Samples can also serve as indications of the quality level of delivered goods.

Design specifications must be carefully constructed in terms of any features that might make an item unacceptable for the purpose for which it is to be used.

Performance specifications encourage ingenuity, innovation, and cost reduction, and are the preferred type of specification.

Techniques which foster the determination of best value to the government should be encouraged and further developed.

Continued on next page

Central purchasing should review specifications for restrictiveness and should assure that the appropriate quality level is specified.

The specification process should be set forth in writing, citing both central purchasing's and using agencies' responsibilities and authorities.

To avoid organizational conflicts of interest and to assure objective specifications, suppliers should not prepare specifications.

Because standard specifications allow for more efficient operations and result in lower prices, they should be used wherever suitable.

When developing standard specifications, using agency program needs must be considered, and industry input should be obtained.

The use of specification and standardization committees should be encouraged because, if properly structured, they can be an effective technique for developing standard specifications.

Standard specifications should be indexed and filed, and procedures should be developed for their review and updating.

The same format should be used for all standard specifications.

Maximum use should be made of industry specifications as well as those available from federal, state, and local governments.

Some means is needed to provide better collection and dissemination of specification data among state and local governments.

The term "specifications" as used in this section relates to the technical and descriptive requirements of a product and to its intended use or application. It does not encompass the terms, conditions, or other contractual matters which must be set forth in an Invitation for Bids. Specifications describe what is required or desired and, thus, what the successful bidder is to furnish. They are the communication media between buyer and seller, and the basis on which bids are prepared. The degree to which specifications are open or unrestrictive directly affects the type and extent of competition obtained. In addition, specifications provide a control to assure that the proper quality level is purchased (i.e., that the quality level is suited to the item's intended use and that unnecessary features or "frills" are not included). Specifications are public records; they serve to keep the purchasing process open by allowing the public to see exactly what is being purchased. Most importantly, specifications are used during the evaluation of bids to determine whether or not bids are responsive. Any bid that does not substantially meet the requirements set out in the specifications cannot be considered for the award. Unsuccessful bidders and internal management can use the specifications in a post-award review to assure that a proper award has been made.

CONSTRUCTING A GOOD SPECIFICATION

Specifications are one of the most important elements of the purchasing process. The preparation of good specifications is, according to purchasing officials, probably the most difficult function in the process. Some of the difficulty stems from the fact that state and local governments can seldom dictate the exact characteristics of the products they buy and use. Individually, their requirements are not sufficient to justify special production runs to a special design or specification. Consequently, specifications must be prepared around manufacturers' standard products. This would be an easier task if the specification did not have to satisfy competitive bidding requirements. Considering these requirements, therefore, the preparation of a specification that contains a good description of the product and allows for healthy competition is a formidable task.

The immense variety of items that is purchased by state and local governments further complicates specification writing. Specifications must be written for such diverse items as shipments of beef, microscopes, policemen's uniforms, X-ray machines, filing cabinets, and emergency communications equipment. The range of needed expertise must be commensurate with this range of items. Specifications seldom remain static and there is no assurance that they will be suitable for future purchases. Products are improved, new products are introduced, and the government's needs change. Consequently, the functions of preparing and updating specifications must be ongoing.

The vast and difficult field of specification writing

challenges every public purchasing program, and all purchasing officials share the feeling that improved techniques and capabilities are needed. **All programs need a greater exchange of information and assistance from each other to increase their knowledge, save valuable time, and reduce duplication of effort.** Governments with more highly developed programs can help by taking the lead in intergovernmental cooperation and specification sharing. Those systems with less capability can benefit greatly by using the materials and resources developed by others.

To provide a common basis for bidding, specifications should set out the essential characteristics of the items being purchased so that all bidders know exactly what the government wants to buy and can accurately compute their bids. If some essential requirement is left out of the specification, the award may be made without determining whether the successful bid meets government needs, and it may not become apparent until much later that the product purchased is unsuitable for the intended use. Situations such as these are sometimes never resolved to anyone's satisfaction. On the other hand, the unstated requirement may be taken into account during the evaluation process, after the bidding is closed. But here the impartiality that is so vital in the evaluation phase is compromised and unsuccessful bidders would have grounds for protest. It is readily apparent, therefore, that when an essential requirement is omitted from a specification, the competitive bidding process is relegated to one of competitive guess or chance. For this reason, if such an omission or error is discovered in time, the purchasing official should reject all bids, correct the specification, and solicit new bids.

Assuring that specifications contain essential requirements relates directly to the aspects of proper quality level. In purchasing, "quality" means the suitability of a product for the intended use; it does not carry the common connotations of "good" or "bad." Either overspecifying or underspecifying is wasteful. Items purchased should be able to perform as necessary and to be as durable as needed, but they should not have any unessential frills or status features. For example, a request for a concert grand piano for teaching students would be inappropriate, even if the teacher or using agency had a strong preference for the concert instrument.

Requiring unnecessary features can also result in a specification that is so restrictive that it defeats the objective of fostering competition. For the purpose of this discussion, a restrictive specification is one which unnecessarily limits competition. By definition, any specification sets certain limits and thereby eliminates from competition those items that cannot comply. Restrictive specifications, however, eliminate items that

would be capable of satisfactorily meeting actual needs. Furthermore, by reducing the potential for competition, they increase the potential for collusion.

The issue of optional items and the proper means of providing for them in specifications periodically surfaces. Optional items are features which may be adapted to a piece of basic equipment (e.g., automobiles or communications equipment), may enhance performance or capacity, or may represent only luxury-type accessories. Because the prices of optional items can represent as much as 20 percent of the price of the basic equipment and because this expense may or may not be recoverable at the time of disposition, optional items are important cost considerations. This difficult area requires the attention of purchasing personnel; there needs to be improvement in current practices. Decisions concerning optional items should not be delayed until bids have been received and are being evaluated and should not be left to the imagination or discretion of individual purchasing agents. Careful planning and proper structuring of specifications and IFBs are keys to the successful purchase of optional items.

In some state and local government purchasing operations, the IFBs call for prices on the basic equipment and on either all optional items or those most often ordered, but the costs of options are not considered in the evaluation of bids. In these cases, the prices for options represent, in effect, an agreement that the successful bidder will invoice them at the quoted prices. This practice fails to address the issue of which bid, options included, offered the best price.

A few States have adopted the policy of considering only those bids containing prices for options that are within 10 percent of the prices published in specified catalogs and rejecting all others. This practice provides some comfort because it limits the markups on optional items and sets fixed prices for those options which are purchsaed at a later date. However, it still does not resolve the issue of lowest total price.

Optional items can significantly affect the total price paid for equipment. Consequently, purchasing must identify the types of equipment for which optional items are regularly ordered, the specific options that are involved, and the frequency with which they are purchased. An evaluation of these data will indicate whether or not solicitations should request prices for optional items and, if so, just which items should be listed and how the prices will be used in evaluating bids. Expected usage factors can be developed for individual optional items, or a weighted factor can be used to cover them all. These factors, as described in the IFB, are then used in evaluating the bids. For example:

Bidder	Price bid for basic equipment	Optional Items			Total effective price
		Bid price	Expected usage factor	Expected purchase price	
A	$3,300	$1,450	80%	$1,160	$4,460
B	$3,400	$1,100	80%	$ 880	$4,280

The total effective price is the sum of the bid prices for the basic equipment and the prices of those optional items that will most likely be purchased.

One of the barriers to the proper treatment of optional items is the lack of readily available historical data. Such data should be included when building an information system for purchasing. Another concern that arises is that awards should not be based on assumed or expected purchases of optional items which may not occur. However, usage factors for optional items which are based on valid historical data and updated for current estimates of anticipated needs are as reasonable and valid as any other budget or planning data.

An alternative which avoids any uncertainties associated with expected usage is to request that users determine in advance their specific requirements for optional items. These requirements can then be used to develop standard specifications which embody options most commonly used. Some States and local governments have adopted this approach and have, for example, several different standard specifications for related products, such as for passenger cars. This carries the disadvantage, however, of possibly higher prices because of the lower volumes purchased. A further refinement would be to develop performance specifications which set definite performance characteristics, and which apply to all using agencies.

Because options represent considerable expense, methods should be developed for handling them and for determining the degree to which they should be considered in solicitations; this is a planning function. Moreover, the nature of this issue requires established policies and written procedures to reduce the likelihood of favoritism and resultant protests. While general procedures for treating optional items can and should be uniform, details such as how optional items or usage factors can be equitably considered will vary from item to item. The written procedures should provide guidance in making these determinations and should stipulate that, insofar as practicable, the IFB clearly set forth both the optional items and the usage factors that will be considered when evaluating bids.

Impartiality in selecting the successful bidder can be enhanced by establishing objective tests for determining whether or not bids meet specifications. Public scrutiny and vendor interest will combine to assure that such objective tests are properly applied. When subjective tests must be used to determine the successful bidder, the nature and method of testing should be described in the specification to afford the bidders as much information as possible for preparing their bids and to keep the bidding process open. If subjective tests are used, an objective method of applying the results should be established.

If a specification promotes both equality of opportunity to bid and objectivity of selection of the successful bidder, then the specification is serving its intent. Naturally, there must be an effective means of identifying potential bidders; but after this, a straightforward, fair evaluation founded on a good specification will persuade them to bid.

TYPES OF SPECIFICATIONS

Specifications take many forms, some of which are better than others. The general types of specifications commonly used include brand names, qualified products lists (also called approved products lists, approved brands lists, qualified brands lists, etc.), comparisons of actual samples, designation for a special use, design, performance, and costs of operation analysis. Some of these are not good specifications, but they are used when it is expedient or necessary to do so. Purchasing and other government officials must recognize and understand the concepts, uses, and limitations of the different types of specifications.

Because of the difficulties and frustrations associated with specification writing, there is a tendency to become lax and satisfied with the easiest alternative. But purchasing officials must strive constantly to move toward a better type of specification. An examination of the present state-of-the-art shows that improvements are being made in the specification process. There is, for example, more interest in performance specifications, and techniques to disseminate technical data and related information among governmental units are being explored. These are encouraging signs of serious recognition by the profession of the work that needs to be done thoughout this complex area.

Brand Name Specifications

"Brand name" specifications cite a brand name, a model number, or some other designation that identifies a specific product of a manufacturer as an example of the quality level desired. Items equaling or surpassing this quality level are understood to be acceptable. Although brand name specifications are not considered good specifications, they have a legitimate, though limited, place in public purchasing and are probably used to some extent by all state and local governments.

Where the time and resources necessary to develop another kind of specification are not available or cannot be justified, usually because of the low dollar value represented by the purchase, a brand name specification can be used and the efforts of specification writers placed elsewhere.

When brand name specifications are used, they should indicate beyond any doubt that the brand name is used merely as a specification and not as a statement of a preference for the specific product cited. Far better than using one brand name is using several brand names, all of which are acceptable. The specification should always be accompanied by a phrase such as "or equal," "approved equal," or "similar in design, construction, and performance," to indicate that items equivalent in quality to the specified brand names will be acceptable. This intent can be further explained in the IFB by a statement such as:

Any manufacturers' names, trade names, brand names, or catalog numbers used in the specifications are for the purpose of describing and establishing general quality levels. Such references are not intended to be restrictive. Bids will be considered for any brand which meets or exceeds the quality of the specifications listed for any item.

To aid in communicating the desired quality level to bidders, an effort should be made to use a brand designation that either is known throughout the industry or whose specifications are readily available. Otherwise, the brand name specification will truly be restrictive. If a vendor does not know which of his products is comparable to the designated brand name, he cannot bid intelligently and may not bid at all.

Although it would seem that the use of a specific brand with no further description would inhibit vendors of competing products to bid, this is often not the case. Vendors customarily know their competition and can frequently tell without too much difficulty which of their brands or models will be considered equal. Still, a bidder cannot be completely sure what features of the item will be considered crucial in making the award. This can be alleviated if the IFB names the salient characteristics to be used in comparing brands and determining the award. But the specification should also make it clear that these factors are not the total consideration. Brand name specifications are not subject to thorough pre-analysis, and some other factor(s) may also be important.

Brand name specifications, therefore, can cause problems in three major ways. They may lessen objectivity in the process of evaluation and award; they may reduce equality of opportunity among bidders; and they often discourage competition. Consequently, the use of brand name specifications should be limited as much as possible.

Qualified Products List

A qualified products list is a form of specification in which various brands are examined, approved, and placed on a list. When an IFB is issued, the bidding is limited to vendors whose products are on the list. The purpose of this type of specification is to determine in advance those products which comply with specifications or otherwise are acceptable. The evaluation of bids is greatly simplified, and the price and the performance capability of the bidder become the determinants. One of the main reasons that qualified products lists are established is to avoid the problems that occur when the low bidder offers a product whose conformance to specifications is unknown and difficult to ascertain.

The criteria and the methods for establishing and maintaining a qualified products list vary widely for different types of products. For an item of heavy construction equipment, a written specification might be prepared and similar models from different manufacturers tested in the field to determine which of them meet the performance requirements. For obtaining musical instruments, a committee of musicians acting as advisors to the purchasing authority might test different brands of an instrument according to certain criteria. In the case of truck tires, a number of brands might be tested under controlled conditions and determinations made on their performance. For ready-mixed paints, laboratory tests may be used to accept or reject a brand.

Some items take a long time to test. For such items, the need for immediate supplies, the possibility that the second lowest bid may have to be evaluated, and other similar handicaps weigh heavily on all concerned parties. With a qualified products list, if delivery is not a factor, an award can be made immediately to the lowest bidder. There are no appeals or disputes with a bypassed low bidder whose bid was not responsive. Any questions from suppliers whose products were determined to be unacceptable were handled prior to issuing the IFBs.

Another advantage of this approach is that it reduces the amount of testing in the long run because simultaneous tests can often be run on several brands. Once a product is accepted for the list, it does not need another test until either the specification or the product changes. Actual samples and/or highly documented files should be kept on each item that qualifies. These can be used as a contract standard so that contract quality can be enforced if a supplier delivers substandard goods.

The need for enforceability results not only from the concern of receiving substandard goods, but also from a problem inherent in the process. The lists specify acceptable products by brand name, model number, or whatever designation is necessary to precisely identify a certain product. Sometimes manufacturers modify the quality of a product without changing its model number or other designation. This means that the product may still be shown as acceptable even though it may no longer meet specifications. Although manufacturers or their representatives agree to inform purchasing if they make any such changes, the added assurance of having a documented standard of quality is necessary.

While the use of qualified products lists often enhances uniform testing and simplifies the award process, there are also disadvantages. On any given solicitation, competition is limited to the products on the list. Over a period of time, those products tend to gravitate to marginal levels of quality. This, however, can be overcome by including in the qualification procedures, where feasible, qualitative ratings or test scores and evaluating bids by equating these numerical ratings with the bid prices to arrive at optimum value. For example, if a truck tire must pass a use test of a minimum average of 25,000 miles to be qualified, and the six brands which pass the tests range in averages of 25,000, 26,000, 29,000, 30,000, 32,000, and 36,000 miles, then these figures and the price bid on each can be used to determine the lowest average cost per mile.

This kind of effort to equate performance and price can also aid in overcoming another disadvantage—that of looking behind rather than ahead. In dealing only with products already on the market, qualified products lists do not ordinarily encourage or take advantage of innovation, except where they use performance standards as the principal criterion for qualification.

Samples

The use of samples is a valuable aspect of the specification process which almost universally falls short of its potential. In some instances, the comparison and testing of samples can effectively substitute for a detailed specification.

Examples of this have been found in such items as waxes and floor finishes, paints, disinfectants and germicides, file cabinets, tires, cleaning agents, classroom furniture, and art materials. Under this procedure, bidders are invited to offer their price and a sample of the product against a general descriptive specification. The unidentified samples are then subjected to various kinds of comparisons ranging from visual inspection and evaluation to chemical and physical laboratory tests to in-use applications. Data and relative performance results are documented, and determinations are made on the best value.

Samples can also be of great value in assuring compliance and satisfaction after award but before production. For truck chassis or band uniforms, for example, final award of a contract may be contingent upon the successful bidder's producing a pilot model or prototype that is acceptable to the purchaser. In this way, many problems can be solved before the units are manufactured and delivered. If agreement on the pilot or sample cannot be reached, the contract can be awarded to another bidder.

Wherever samples are obtained and used in evaluation or award, the samples should be retained for checking and comparing deliveries for compliance. Retaining samples to serve as a benchmark on quality for delivered goods is a sound safeguard. Samples destroyed in testing are an obvious exception. Detailed questionnaires completed by the bidders, which elicit exact information about the products they are offering, can supplement samples or, in many cases, can substitute for samples. Valid judgments can be made by comparing data as well as by comparing the products themselves.

Designation of Special Purpose

It is sometimes necessary to purchase an item for a special purpose when no items of that kind are normally produced or marketed. For instance, there may be a need for sewing machines to teach blind people to sew. In such a case, the purchasing official may use the normal specification accompanied by a questionnaire asking what modifications bidders would offer to make to their product to make it most suitable for the particular need. Designating the features of the most appropriate standard manufactured product would be restrictive, and writing a unique specification would probably result in no responses because the demand for the item would not be sufficient to warrant retooling or special production. In such cases, therefore, prospective suppliers compete based on an impartial evaluation of the alternatives offered by all who respond.

Design Specifications

Design specifications set the requirements for the item to be purchased by detailing the characteristics that the item must possess. "Design" in this connotation means that the specification is so detailed that it describes how the product is to be manufactured. This is the most traditional type of specification. It has been used historically in public contracting for buildings, highways, and other public works. Its use is essential where a structure or product is to be made to meet the purchaser's design.

Design specifications are not as applicable, however, for purchasing products designed by the manufacturer or seller. A major danger in using design-type specifications under this circumstance is the tendency to call for certain or exact characteristics of one or two products known to be satisfactory, and thereby be restrictive to them.

Even the use of minimums and maximums under this type of specification presents problems. In an effort to encourage competition, a design specification may be expressed in terms of tolerances or minimum standards chosen from various acceptable products. But, a specification that is written in this manner can cause other problems. For example, a specification may take the minimum acceptable level for one feature from product A, and the minimum acceptable level for two other features from products B and C. Although any of the three products may be able to satisfactorily fill the functions of the specified item, a single product with all three minimum features may not be satisfactory even though it would meet the specification.

A similar circumstance might arise if tolerances, rather than minimums, are specified. If five different makes of equipment have different wheelbases and different weight distributions that make them all stable, a design specification that would allow all five vehicles to be bid might call for a wheelbase and weight distribution falling within a range set by the two extremes among these five. A sixth vehicle with a wheelbase and weight distribution that fell within the tolerances set by the specification might be much less stable than the other five, even though it meets the specification. These examples illustrate that design specifications must be carefully constructed in terms of any feature that might make an item unacceptable for the purpose for which it is to be used. Unless the article is custom made, this is often extremely difficult or impossible to do without being restrictive.

Good design specifications cannot be written for some items because the full detail required often cannot be reconciled with the actions necessary to encourage full competition. This is frequently the case when dealing with patented products. For items that are neither patented nor custom made, a suitable modified design specification can meet the criteria of a good specification. Here, only the essential features are set out so that bidders have a reasonably equal basis on which to compute their bids. All nonessential details are eliminated. Adherence to the specification can be determined objectively. Of all types of specifications, however, those based on performance are preferred.

Performance Specifications

The popularity of performance specifications has developed steadily in recent years. As the name indicates, these specifications set out the performance requirements a product is to meet. Using this concept, the end result is the priority consideration and, in contrast to the design approach, the manufacturer or producer is given great latitude in how he can accomplish it. This encourages ingenuity, innovation, and cost reduction.

Performance requirements describe the capabilities that are necessary to satisfy the intended use for the article. Tests or criteria are developed to measure a product's ability to perform and to last as required. Performance specifications generally provide the best approach to specification writing.

A contradiction of sorts is inherent in recommending performance specifications, considering the recognized traditional attitude of seeking to buy only items of proven quality. This might result occasionally in delays in buying innovative products, but there need not be delays in trying them out, and caution about committing or investing heavily in them probably always will be sound public policy. A helpful bridge between these positions is for central purchasing to have the authority, under defined conditions and with each action suitably documented, to waive competitive bidding for the purpose of buying articles for experiment, test, or trial.

Clearly, no one type of specification is best for all types of products. Thus, in an IFB covering hundreds of items of automotive parts, the use of brand names "or equivalents" is satisfactory. For the purchase of lead pencils, samples and trial may serve best; for magnetic computer tape, a qualified products list; for an X-ray machine, a modified design specification; for gasoline, a performance specification; and for an air compressor, a combination design-performance specification. Specifications can include both design and performance features. A design specification can and frequently does contain performance requirements, and vice versa. Characteristics of both are used as prerequisites and as limiting factors in developing qualified products lists.

Performance and Cost

Public contracting is predicated on the principle that the low price bid is the succesful bid unless it is not in compliance or is defective, or unless it can be shown that it is not the best or most advantageous bid. The burden is upon the purchaser, therefore, to disqualify a low bid or to make an ascertainment of fact that another bid is in the best interest of the government. This requirement is a necessary protection of the public against favoritism, fraud, and wastefulness.

There is an ever-increasing number of methods for obtaining and evaluating competitive offers to determine which bid is the most advantageous. Among them are the use of performance specifications, performance evaluation criteria (by testing or otherwise comparing technical data), life-cycle costing, and a variety of ideas inherent in the concept of value analysis whereby cost can be calculated in terms of function.

The essence of all of these approaches is to endeavor to relate performance and price. In doing so, they are both varied and similar, and at times overlapping. Where equipment carries a high original cost, such as electronic computers and earth-moving machines, the comparative costs of lease versus purchase also become important determinations.

As purchasing officials have begun to emphasize performance considerations, they have developed techniques for making judgments of optimum value. These provide for evaluating bids on a price/performance basis. In effect, minimum specifications, which serve the valuable purpose of allowing maximum competition, set limits, not absolutes, below which quality is not acceptable. Quality above that level can be given economic consideration.

Examples of this approach are becoming numerous, with perhaps two classic ones serving as illustrations. One State has a contract for automotive and truck tires for which the bids are taken on a guaranteed mile basis. The cost per mile of each bidder on each size and type of tire is computed easily. The IFB also requires the bidders to offer a servicing capability and a price for the return of the tire carcass of each size. The best and most advantageous bid can, therefore, be logically and reasonably determined. Such a contract has a major disadvantage—the cost of extensive record-keeping.

Another State purchases window air conditioners on the basis of the cost per million Btu's over the life of the compressor or hermetically sealed unit. Bidders must furnish verified performance data via a questionnaire on Btu output, wattage consumption, and other operating characteristics, as well as a bid price for the machine and certain options and features. From these data, Btu cost can be easily calculated.

The advantages of being able to ascertain value in terms of price/performance relationships is obvious. Historically, it has been the practice to buy coal by Btu or heat output value, although it is priced, invoiced, and paid for by the ton. Therefore, this system represents an improvement in many product categories over the everyday practice of making awards to the lowest price bidder, even though the practice requires some estimating. The difficulty in making greater use of it stems from problems of isolating and defining the performance factors of a particular type of product clearly enough to cost them into an overall computation. Doubtless, these factors will be developed by further trial and experience.

It is important to recognize that this approach introduces a different philosophy in both the writing of specifications and the evaluation of bids. The customary procedure has been to concentrate on similarities among like products as the requirements of a specification and to ignore their differences. But performance standards and price/performance evaluations provide equivalent consideration for product differences, both inferior and superior. The result is a more accurate determination both of total value and of significant differences than is possible under a minimum or conventional specification approach.

Some industrial purchasers and, to a lesser degree, state and local governments use a technique called value analysis in determining which bid is most advantageous. Value analysis is used to determine which item will satisfy the required function at the lowest total cost of ownership. Probably the most common and, when properly used, most effective applications of value analysis is life-cycle costing. This application takes into account the operating, maintenance, and other costs of ownership, as well as the acquisition price. Considerable planning and effort are required to use life-cycle costing, and it can be applied only to items which have a measurable service life and can be tested for design and performance characteristics. Also, there should be assurance that there is an existing or potential competitive environment. Certain information is needed to determine whether items are suited to this technique, to construct the specifications, and to evaluate bids. This includes the specific performance characteristics and requirements; the nature and cost of repairs and the time required for repairs; and the frequency and causes of failures. Performance elements can then be established and weights assigned to each element. The performance elements, testing methods, and cost factors to be considered, and the weights and formulas to be applied must be set forth in the specifications, so that bidders understand and have confidence in the objectivity of the method.

There are many variations in life-cycle costing applications, some of which are promoted by manufacturers. For example, some manufacturers offer a guaranteed ceiling for repair costs over a designated period or number of operating hours. Others offer a guaranteed repurchase price at the end of a specified period or number of operating hours. While they seem attractive, such offers must be carefully weighed against historical information on the extent of use, the useful life, and repair costs experienced for the items. The potential resale value of the items as surplus must be weighed against offers of guaranteed repurchase prices, and the legality of accepting such offers must be considered.

When a guaranteed repurchase price is offered, the

situation is very similar to leasing arrangements, with the notable difference that title to the item is transferred in the former application, and the government must pay the entire amount at the outset. Consequently, the potential benefits of leasing must also be considered, particularly for items such as electronic data processing equipment and other high-value equipment. In short, life-cycle costing, applied properly to the proper items, may provide savings to the government. However, it requires considerable planning and much more technical analysis and effort than traditional procurement.

CENTRALIZATION AND SPECIFICATION DEVELOPMENT

Sound management requires that there be central control over specifications. Responsibility for the correctness, competitiveness, and suitability of specifications is a necessary duty of the central purchasing authority, although a specification may originate with the using agency, an architect or independent engineer, a governmental entity, a professional society or association, or the central purchasing authority itself. Without central control, every using agency would set specifications for its own purchases, which would sometimes be the same items. This would obviously be unorderly, inconsistent, and unmanageable. Cooperation between purchasing and using agencies concerning the efficacy and suitability of specifications is essential. The initiative for assuring this cooperation belongs to central purchasing.

Cooperation is often made difficult by an attitude concerning budgets which generally exists among using agencies. The agency point of view, oversimplified and perhaps overstated, is that it is authorized to spend to the limits of its budget. If funds permit, it feels it should be able to buy the most expensive product. Purchasing's point of view, on the other hand, is to refrain from buying better quality or greater amounts than are actually needed. This difference in attitudes is a persistent undercurrent even in calm waters.

Twenty-three States have published policies calling for a review of the quantity and/or quality specified in using agencies' requisitions. Forty-two States and many local governments have standardization programs. All state central purchasing offices recognize their controllership role in developing specifications, although it is not always exercised directly or consistently. Though the central purchasing authority has this responsibility over specifications, it is still up to the using agencies to determine the items they need. Since central purchasing is a service to the using agencies, it, too, is concerned that they obtain the correct items to satisfy their needs. Central purchasing is also charged with the duty of seeing that specifications encourage competition when practicable. This presents various degrees of misunderstanding between the using agencies and the central purchasing authority, which often must modify suggested specifications to make them less restrictive. Consequently, to preclude misunderstanding, the specification process should be set forth in writing, citing both central purchasing's and using agencies' responsibilities and authorities.

Too often, there is a direct vendor involvement in the specification process at the using agency level, and every effort should be made to prevent this. Although using agencies may initiate the descriptions of items needed, there must be an independent body which assures that the specification that finally accompanies the IFB is not restrictive and does not call for features or for a level of quality not needed for the item's intended use. It is important, therefore, for consistency, accountability, and enforceability that purchasing have final approval of specifications before they are used for bidding purposes. As a part of this responsibility, where standard specifications are involved, central purchasing should have authority to deviate from the standard in cases where using agencies have legitimate reasons to obtain a different level of product. Because of the potential for disagreement and conflict, these authorities should be assigned by statute.

SPECIFICATION WRITING

The detailed procedures used in writing and reviewing specifications vary according to the size of the purchasing operation and available resources. Even in the smallest program, however, the central purchasing authority must see to it that using agency specifications are reviewed for restrictiveness. In central purchasing operations having purchasing agents who specialize in commodity areas, the purchasing agents review the specifications and the using agencies help in writing them. Other purchasing units have a staff of people whose major duties are concerned with specifications and who also may be responsible for purchasing some commodities. Their duties relating to specifications vary among the purchasing systems, from checking for restrictiveness to writing all specifications or developing standard specifications. Larger central purchasing operations normally have specification units that deal exclusively in developing specifications, usually standard specifications and technical specifications that need special attention.

In all but the smallest central purchasing operations, purchasing officials write specifications to some extent. As central purchasing staffs get larger and more specialized, more of the specification writing duties are taken from the using agencies and, as specification staffs get larger and more specialized, more of the specification writing duties are taken from the purchasing agents. Because there are so many areas in which expertise is needed, no central purchasing program has specification writing staffs that can cover all the areas of in-depth technical competence that is necessary in writing specifications. Consequently, even in those central purchasing operations having the most specialized specification writing staffs, there are purchasing agents with special experience and expertise who write many or all specifications in their commodity areas with little or no assistance from the specification writing staff. Even in those systems with the largest number of specification writers, there are using agencies who write many of the specifications for items that they use.

Persons hired to work with a purchasing staff as specification writers should have qualifications that make them special assets in that capacity. If they do not have an engineering, chemistry, or other technical background that will afford a special competence in the fields with which they will be involved, there is no reason why the purchasing agents who specialize in those commodities should not write the specifications.

STANDARD SPECIFICATIONS

Items for similar use frequently are purchased on a recurring basis by a particular using agency or by several using agencies. Where using agencies write specifications for items they purchase, similar items are purchased under many different specifications. Centralization allows such situations to be detected, because all purchase records for each commodity are gathered in one place. To eliminate the time and effort required to write and review a different specification each time purchases of such items are made, 42 States and many local governments have established programs to develop standard specifications that can be used for most or all purchases of a given item. If a standard specification can be established, it allows more efficient operations by substituting one purchase for the needs that were formerly filled by several purchases, and results in lower prices due to the consolidation of smaller purchases into a volume purchase.

The term "standard specification" should be distinguished from two other similar terms. "Standardization," for example, is a process that establishes a norm for an item with respect to size, shape, color, or some other attribute that is essential. Standardization results from selection or limitation from a broader field. If there are trucks that carry many different maximum loads, a government might standardize on a quarter-ton truck for light work, and a two-and-one-half-ton truck for heavy work. A "standard" is a norm, resulting from a standardization process that is accepted by a certain group. The standard may deal with part of an item or the entire item. The size of electric outlets is standard throughout the country. The dimensions of certain light sockets are standard throughout the industry so that a light bulb from manufacturers X, Y, or Z can all fit into the same lamp.

To determine which items are suitable for standard specifications, purchasing must know the number of times items are requisitioned and the purchasing volume of the items. Most public purchasing operations rely on the purchasing agents to make this determination. An accurate view of the volume of purchases can be obtained quite easily by those purchasing programs which have refined commodity codes. Normally, a clerical unit receives all requisitions and logs them in for control purposes. If the pertinent commodity codes and quantities requisitioned were recorded in the log, a simple addition can provide the volume of purchases in a given period. Items ordered on a recurring basis in a volume that represents a high dollar expenditure can then be identified as potential candidates for standard specifications. The standardization program should begin with those items where the greatest saving can be expected because of less work and lower prices resulting from volume purchases.

The development of standard specifications involves changes that must be made with an eye on the consequences. Using agencies may not get precisely what they would have specified had they written the specifications themselves. Consequently, specification writers should check to see that the proposed standard specifications will not inhibit the programs of the using agencies. Although this seems to be done generally in most public purchasing systems that have standardization programs, in those instances where using agencies were not consulted during the standardization process, they later expressed resentment and less desire to cooperate. This does not mean that the using agencies should have a veto power. **Central purchasing still must have the final authority for approval, which includes being able to eliminate unnecessary frills that using agencies may request.**

Industry representatives should also be contacted for input to the standardization process. Through their own self-interest, they will point out what parts of the proposed specifications they think they cannot meet. Experience has shown that industry representatives can also provide useful technical input, such as whether any requirements in the specification or terms may be unrealistic, and point out changes that may result in savings to the government. Many purchasing officials feel that they get the best response from industry representatives by holding a meeting on specification development. When the competitors are all in the room together, partisan rhetoric is reduced.

Using agency and industry representatives who are consulted should be those with the knowledge and experience necessary to give the required input. In some cases, industry engineers rather than sales personnel should be consulted for technical input. Also, the actual users should be contacted to see how certain items have functioned on the job. With input from using agencies and industry, purchasing can make those adjustments that will enhance competition while keeping the quality at an acceptable level. Input should be solicited while the specification is being developed, and then the proposed standard specification should be circulated to using agencies and industry representatives for comments and suggestions before it is finalized.

To formalize the solicitation of input, many central purchasing operations establish specification and standardization committees. Usually these committees are comprised of high-level administrative personnel, and often they appoint subcommittees to deal with specific commodity areas. On the whole, they are unsuccessful, usually because of the way they were established. The most common reason for the failure was that people having little or no technical knowledge of commodity areas were asked to deal with them. Another reason was that some people were asked to sit on too many subcommittees, or too many subcommittees were formed at one time. Logistical problems of getting using agency representatives together in one area of a large State on a particular day also defeated some committee programs.

In some cases, committees did some work initially, but once the standard specifications were developed, they became dormant. In others, the committees are ineffective, routinely approving all actions taken by purchasing. But in several locations one or two committees or subcommittees dealing with specific commodity areas are still functional and, in one case, 20 subcommittees on specific commodity areas are active and functioning successfully. In the latter case, the central purchasing operation has no separate specification writing staff. The personnel on the subcommittees are generally using agency personnel. One subcommittee member, describing his positive reaction to the committee system, explained, "It makes us part of the purchasing division." Some subcommittees have both industry and using agency representatives. Others, such as those dealing with specifications based on chemical formulae, have only representatives from industry. One subcommittee has even attracted an expert who represents neither industry nor a using agency.

In some States, the committees have been effective because they met in conjuction with other annual meetings. For example, all janitorial or custodial supervisory personnel of one State have annual meetings. Other committees have been able to draw attendance by hav-ing programs, such as a speaker on landscaping for a committee dealing with groundskeeping equipment and supplies. When it is practical, the committee system for getting using agency or industry input into the development of standard specifications can be a useful tool.

Once they are finalized, standard specifications should be indexed and filed so that they may be found whenever they are needed. If there is a commodity code that is adequately refined, a very useful tool is a booklet that can be easily updated showing which commodity code numbers have standard specifications, approved brands lists, qualified products lists, or a term contract established for them. If such a booklet were circulated among the requisitioning personnel, it would be a handy reference of items for which specifications have already been developed. In addition, it would prevent using agencies from sending requisitions to central purchasing for items on contract that they could order directly from the contractor.

Standard specifications do not mark an end to the need for specification work in the commodity areas involved. Most purchasing authorities do not have a schedule for updating standard specifications, or a system for showing when they were last reviewed. For new standard specifications, periodic reviews that incorporate the comments of using agencies should be made for the first two or three years. After that, changes in the specifications should be made whenever using agency complaints indicate that the specification is unsatisfactory, or whenever the specification writers become aware of industry changes which indicate that a change in the standard specification should be made. Older standard specifications also should be reviewed according to a schedule to see if there are any necessary changes that did not otherwise come to the attention of the purchasing authority. The system for indicating that the specification was reviewed need be nothing more than a notation on the file copy showing the date and the initials of the reviewer, if no changes are necessary. If changes are made, an amendment or new specification with the date of revision must be issued.

Another simple but valuable technique that many purchasing systems do not use is to have all standard specifications follow the same format. This makes it easier for anyone who deals with several of the government's standard specifications, because information of a similar type appears in the same section of each standard specification. The use of a consistent format for standard specifications would make processing them easier for people within a system; the use of such a format by several systems would facilitate the exchange of information on standard specifications, and perhaps even coordination in the review and updating functions. A suggested format is set out in the *Standard Specifica-*

tions Preparation Manual which was published by the Council of State Governments in 1966.

AIDS IN DEVELOPING SPECIFICATIONS

Specifications have not been developed for many items, and other specifications take much too long to develop. **Too often, there is a feeling of isolation when searching for data to use in developing a specification, and too often specification writers— whether they be technically trained personnel or purchasing specialists—simply do not know where to obtain the information they need.**

The first rule of specification writing should be, "Look for and use whatever reasonable aids are readily available." Even small purchasing units without specification staffs can marshal the government's resources and gather the proper material for establishing good specifications. One practice that can help is to use all of the government's expertise, even though it may not be directly related to the use for which the specification is being developed. For example, communications experts at a university may be able to assist in writing specifications for a communications system for government emergency vehicles, or personnel from a hospital may be helpful in writing specifications for police crime lab equipment. If central purchasing can gain the cooperation of government experts, their guidance in assuring that the specifications are in proper form and are not restrictive should lead to a sound specification.

Another extremely important rule is to obtain standards and specifications from sources, other than manufacturers, that have done significant work in the field. Too often government specification writers spend time doing work that has already been done well by other specification writers. If government specification writers would identify and use the material that has resulted from the efforts of others, they could cut their workload considerably and free themselves for other work. For example, one can obtain a year's subscription to the *Index of Federal Specifications and Standards* at the price of $14.00 from the Superintendent of Documents, U.S. Government Printing Office, Washington, D.C. 20402. Other standards or specifications can be obtained from national standards associations or from some professional organizations. Some of these might be accepted industry standards. In addition, state and local governments readily send out their specifications on various items when they are requested by other governments. The material that could be gathered may not necessarily be suitable for adopting, but it should serve as a basis for specification development. Parts could be adopted, some could be adapted, and others could show what important points should be emphasized in the specification being developed.

NATIONAL EFFORT

For years, public purchasing officials have been declaring that a cooperative effort on a national level to develop specifications or standards would be a highly desirable undertaking that could result in significant advances in the specification area. Some attempts have been made at such cooperative programs, but they never produced any significant results because of inadequate funding and staffing. A cooperative program to write performance standards has begun a limited operation under the aegis of the Council of State Governments and the National Association of State Purchasing Officials, with funding from the National Bureau of Standards. The significance of this program, if it succeeds, will be tremendous. Development work will be performed by some specification and other personnel from various state and local governments, leaving their counterparts in other governments free to work on standards or specifications for other items.

12. Quality Assurance: Inspection and Testing

ESSENTIAL ELEMENTS

Suggested Statutory/Regulatory Coverage

The purchasing statute and/or the rules and regulations adopted pursuant to the statute should:

Require that central purchasing establish and administer a formal inspection and testing program.

Recommended Practices

Central purchasing should prepare and publish an inspection manual which sets forth the authorities, responsibilities, techniques, and standards related to the inspection and testing program. Alternately, this subject could be included in the purchasing procedures manual.

Government personnel who are responsible for receiving and inspecting items delivered should have ready access to specifications.

Receiving documents should not show the quantities to be delivered.

Central purchasing should either make all inspections or, if this function is delegated, monitor the program to assure that established policies are being observed.

Central purchasing should identify and set forth written guidelines on the types of testing facilities that are available and on alternate techniques such as obtaining certificates of compliance or certified test results from suppliers.

There is a need to explore the ways in which governments can coordinate the testing of similar items and better communicate test results to each other.

There should be a formal, written reporting system for complaints against suppliers and for deficiencies noted during inspections.

Central purchasing should be responsible for acting on deficiency and complaint reports and should be the focal point for contacts with suppliers on such deficiencies.

A notable deficiency in many public purchasing systems is the lack of a centrally administered inspection program. This condition exists even in some central purchasing programs that are quite innovative in other aspects (e.g., computerization and development of specifications). Often there is a feeling that a formal program is unnecessary. Three explanations are presented for this view. First, as a general rule, suppliers will not purposefully or routinely make nonconforming deliveries, so the few instances that do occur do not warrant the effort needed to detect them. Second, using agencies will do an adequate job on their own to ensure that deliveries conform to specifications. Third, deliveries must be conforming to specifications or central purchasing would hear many complaints.

State and local governments that have established centrally controlled inspection programs have invariably uncovered large numbers of nonconforming deliveries at the inception of the programs. Situations such as three-gallon containers in lieu of the five-gallon containers that were specified, improper components in equipment, diluted chemical compounds, and equipment being dropped off when the contract called for installation are typical of the occurrences that were detected. The incidence of nonconformance was substantial enough to prove that it cannot be assumed that suppliers usually conform to specifications.

Experience has also shown that while some using agencies take great care in inspecting delivered goods, most simply assume that the items conform to specifications. This occurs most frequently where central administration is lacking. Even when receiving personnel attempt to inspect deliveries, sometimes all they can do effectively is look for damage because they have no guidelines to follow and sometimes they are not even given a copy of the specifications. Without a formal program, therefore, it seems there can be little assurance that inspections are made and that they are thorough. Furthermore, the system that lacks formality and direction is highly susceptible to collusion.

An absence of complaints from using agencies should not be taken as an indication that a formal program is not needed. Many types of nonconforming deliveries can only be discovered by inspection, or they will not be discovered at all. If receiving personnel carelessly sign an invoice for 20 five-gallon containers of an item, when actually 20 three-gallon containers were received, payment will be made for five-gallon units and the ultimate users may never realize that an incorrect quantity was received. When quality has been cut slightly, the savings to a supplier may be great, and the change may never become apparent to the user. For example, a nonconforming item may only cause a problem infrequently, when it is operating under the most difficult conditions (e.g., a trash bag which is slightly thinner than specified). Similarly, a slight change in the performance of the item may not be noticed (e.g., slightly diluted floor wax). The resulting problem may occur much later and may not be attributed to the lower quality of the item. A lack of complaints, therefore, could indicate poor or nonexistent inspections. Some using agencies indicate that they do not file complaints because effective action is not taken on them. Although this generally is not the case, an attitude like this further supports the need for central control, which includes reporting complaints, taking action, and providing feedback to using agencies.

Governments without central inspection programs do not heed a basic rule of the marketplace, "Let the buyer beware." This rule came about not only because of inadvertent mistakes but also because of unscrupulous suppliers who will use system weaknesses to their advantage. Where inadequate inspection programs exist, the opportunity for an unscrupulous supplier is obvious. He will compute his bid on an item of lower quality than that specified so that he can underbid his competitors. If there is no indication that he is not a responsible bidder, he will probably get the award. Governments that instituted central inspection programs found that this apparently occurred with some frequency because the number of nonconforming deliveries that were discovered when the inspection program was begun decreased sharply and remained at a very low level once the program became fully operational.

Experience also shows that in order for a government to beware in the marketplace, the task must be recognized as a specialized responsibility. When the inspection process is centrally managed and controlled,

with uniform rules and procedures, many problems can be overcome. Proper steps will be taken to inspect deliveries, and receiving personnel will have the guidelines and information necessary to make a proper inspection. A formal system will evidence concern for assuring the quality of goods received, and using agencies will be encouraged to submit complaints. Requiring proper receiving records and periodic checks by central inspection personnel, auditors, or other government authorities will reduce the possibility of collusion between suppliers and receiving personnel. The checks and controls of a formal system are a good means of thwarting unscrupulous suppliers who attempt to defraud the government.

PLACEMENT IN CENTRAL PURCHASING

Authority over a central inspection program logically falls within central purchasing, and is at least implicit in most purchasing statutes. The requirements of open competition, properly drawn specifications, and all the safeguards connected with the central purchasing program are meant to ensure that tax dollars are spent prudently. It would be incongruous to assert that the public purchasing system, which must ensure that awards are made to suppliers who are capable of providing the items specified, should not be concerned about whether the items actually delivered conform with specifications. **In order for its authority over quality assurance to be complete, therefore, purchasing must be authorized to establish and oversee an inspection program which ensures that items meeting specifications are delivered.** If there is any ambiguity in the purchasing statute as to whether central purchasing has this authority, a direct grant of authority should be added to the statute.

Reinforcing the need for central control over inspection is the fact that the chief purchasing official is, or should be, the contract administrator. This responsibility gives him a direct interest in and need for ensuring that inspections are performed promptly and well. If there is an unreasonable amount of time between delivery and inspection, the delay may have nullified the government's right to demand that unsatisfactory performance be corrected. Not performing an inspection promptly may also cause problems in making a successful claim against a supplier when problems are finally detected. For example, if an item is already in use when an inspection is made, and the item is found to be damaged, it may be impossible to prove that the damage did not occur during use. Also, items which are placed in inventory may become intermixed with other items, making it impossible to identify which supplier furnished the faulty items. To properly accomplish their contract administration responsibilities, therefore, purchasing officials must ensure that inspections are made in a timely manner and in accordance with established policies and procedures.

INSPECTION MANUAL

An excellent means of making certain that thorough inspections will be conducted is to set forth procedures, techniques, and standards either in a separate inspection manual or as part of the purchasing procedures manual. These instructions should specify authorities, responsibilities, and inspection methods. However, very few state and local governments have inspection manuals, and most States devote only a few sentences to inspection in their purchasing manuals.

Because the most basic requirements of good inspection often are neglected, the manuals should cover even the obvious procedures, such as checking for late deliveries, damaged goods, and discrepancies that can be detected with the five senses. The manuals also should discuss other inspection techniques, the equipment that should be used, the facilities available for tests that cannot be performed at the using agency location, and the procedures to be followed when nonconforming deliveries are detected. Receiving personnel should have ready access to the specifications of items they inspect.

Some receiving documents show the quantities that are to be delivered, and receiving personnel check the delivery against these quantities. A better method is to exclude the quantities from receiving documents and require receiving personnel to inventory the items and record their tallies on the receiving report. An independent party compares the quantity delivered with the quantity ordered prior to payment, thus strengthening internal controls.

STAFFING AND TESTING FACILITIES

Seventeen States and some local governments have, as a part of the central purchasing authority, special teams who inspect goods received. In 18 States, the inspection function has been delegated to using agencies, with central purchasing making spot checks or special inspections in unusual circumstances. The program seems to be most effective when central purchasing has personnel who perform either all the inspecting or at least regular spot checks. In addition, central purchasing can conduct periodic training classes that include simulated practical situations, problems, proven procedures for resolving them, and new and improved inspection techniques as a means of improving the quality of inspections.

Some inspections can only be performed with special equipment or through laboratory tests. Twelve States and some local governments have separate testing facilities that can accommodate most of their product tests.

These purchasing operations usually use the facilities for other supportive work, such as developing specifications, testing items for which approved brands lists are being developed, and evaluating samples. Some testing programs even call for testing an item at the manufacturer's plant during production to assure that he is following the specifications.

Obviously, not every state and local government has the resources to establish a testing facility of its own. Nonetheless, each purchasing program should include a testing program using in-house capabilities and other available means. For example, arrangements can be made for local colleges or universities to do some of the testing. For food items, even those governments that have their own testing facilities use the services of the U.S. Department of Agriculture, whose agents grade foods on the processing site to ensure that they meet specifications. Bidders can be required to submit samples of randomly chosen items off the shelf or off the assembly line and have them tested by national organizations in order to have their bids considered. In other cases, suppliers can be required to submit certificates of compliance or certified test results with each shipment. Although tests run by local or regional private laboratories are usually quite expensive, they can be used when there is a need for a test and no preferable alternative is available.

Since most governments buy many similar items, a coordinated testing program might be feasible. By combining resources in a joint effort, governments that could not afford testing facilities on their own may be able to participate in a joint testing program. **On a broader scope, nationwide programs for collecting and disseminating test data would not only assist smaller governments but also eliminate much of the duplication among governments that do have testing facilities.** If uniform standards were developed, as discussed in the chapter, "Quality Assurance: Specifications," uniform testing procedures could be adopted. With this kind of coordination, it might later be possible to designate on-site inspectors at the manufacturers' facilities to make sure that shipments to client governments meet the standards.

ORGANIZATION

Purchasing programs that have an inspection and testing staff should keep them functionally separate from the purchasing agents and specification staff. This segregation of duties will provide a check in the system and inhibit any favoritism in item selection and evaluation. One group would write specifications, another would make awards, and a third would evaluate delivered goods for conformance to the specifications.

Although there must be formality in the process, the

inspection staff should have some latitude in scheduling spot inspections to cover the spectrum of items received and the using agencies served. Copies of all award documents should be sent to the inspection staff so that they can effectively plan their inspections. The purchasing official should manage the operation and ensure that inspections are conducted in accordance with established policies. The inspection staff should be able to respond to complaints from using agencies by inspecting items upon request. Other areas of coverage will become apparent to the inspection staff on its own and through communication with purchasing agents. Items that affect the safety of citizens and wards of the government, items that have caused problems in the past, new products, or items for which future problems might be anticipated should be given particular attention.

INSPECTION AND COMPLAINT RECORDS

Instances of nonconformance with specifications, noncompliance with contractual terms and conditions, or other types of complaints concerning suppliers' performance should be recorded and referred to central purchasing. Most States and many local governments use complaint forms. A file of complaint forms and information on the action taken can serve as a record to help purchasing agents deal effectively with suppliers. The complaint records can be used as criteria for deleting suppliers from the bidders list and in deciding which of two low tie bidders should get an award.

All records of complaints, actions taken, and the final resolution should be filed centrally so that they are accessible to all who have a need to review them. In some systems, each purchasing agent keeps his own complaint file on all the suppliers who are on his bidders lists. This procedure could reduce the usefulness of information that deals with suppliers who sell several products that may be handled by different purchasing agents. It seems best to arrange and index complaint files so that all complaints about an individual supplier can be quickly collected. Where complaint records are kept with other vendor records rather than centrally filed, the complaint information should be identifiable so that it may be easily retrieved when it is needed. A simple device for doing this is to put complaint records in colored folders that contrast with those used for other records.

An effective reporting procedure provides for periodic reviews and check points for action. Guidelines should be established indicating that when a certain number of complaints about a supplier have been received within a certain time, his record should be reviewed and action taken. The actions could include visiting the supplier to discuss his performance, writing letters that caution him against continued poor performance, and informing him of the criteria for removing him from the bidders list. Obviously, factors such as the number of complaints, the seriousness of the complaints, and the supplier's cooperation in rectifying situations that resulted in complaints would be considered in deciding on the proper action to be taken. The guidelines should relate only to individual commodities, since suppliers may perform well with one commodity and poorly on another.

Complaints signal poor performance which, if serious, should be the basis for withholding payment to the supplier. Inspection and complaint procedures should provide that in such cases copies of the reports be sent to the finance department to stop payment until the problems have been corrected. Some purchasing programs do not permit payment on deliveries of certain categories of items (e.g., equipment or items exceeding a specified dollar amount) until they have been inspected and found to be acceptable.

COMMUNICATION WITH SUPPLIERS

Inspection procedures should cover the manner in which complaints or unsatisfactory deliveries will be resolved with suppliers. In some systems, the inspector contacts the supplier to arrange for him to correct the deficiencies. The inspector makes whatever arrangements he feels are appropriate under the circumstances. In other purchasing systems, inspectors only report the situation to the purchasing agent, who then initiates action with the supplier. Both methods seem to function very well in some cases and moderately well in others, but having inspectors handle supplier contacts carries out to the fullest the internal check that results from the segregation of duties.

The fact remains, however, that nonconformance with specifications, poor performance, or other complaints require that decisions be made on the best means of correcting the situation. These decisions are the direct responsibility of central purchasing. It may be necessary to revise a delivery schedule, cancel a contract, or initiate a new purchase action. A written notice to the supplier or even removal from the bidders list may be in order. All these are properly within the purview of central purchasing.

Purchasing is responsible for admitting firms to the bidders list and therefore must be aware of all complaints in order to know firsthand the extent to which suppliers will cooperate with the government when difficulties arise. This is part of purchasing's contract administration responsibilities. For the benefit of suppliers, there should be one element in the government that is authorized to act in an official capacity on all aspects of a purchase. If suppliers must deal with different agencies on different aspects of a sale to the government, the process can become frustrating and time-consuming, especially when complaints are involved.

Some systems provide that the inspector advises the supplier of deficiencies noted and gives him a specified number of days to perform according to the contract. If he does so, an information report is sent to purchasing; if further action is necessary, the purchasing agent himself contacts the supplier. This approach keeps the purchasing in the mainstream, but allows for the quickest action when the supplier takes immediate corrective measures.

Inspection serves as a guard against an unscrupulous vendor's ability to circumvent the competitive bidding process by delivering inferior goods. The integrity of the purchasing process demands that deliveries be made as specified, except for deliveries with some minor non-conformance, such as a slight undershipment that can be accepted with an appropriate reduction in price without inconveniencing the using agency. If a supplier cannot deliver the item specified, he should not have bid. Once it is determined that items that do not meet the specifications have been delivered, the supplier should be asked to replace them with goods that do meet the specifications. If he is unable to do this, it may be necessary to resolicit or to purchase the items on the open market, depending on the urgency of the need. In urgent cases, it is appropriate to charge the defaulting supplier with the difference between the original contract price and the repurchase price, if it is higher.

13. Disposition

The disposition process deals with two categories of items—surplus and scrap. Surplus items are those that exceed present and reasonably near future needs but are still useful. Surplus is generated when excess quantities are purchased or use has decreased, and inventory levels are too high; when items are replaced by newer ones; when programs are changed or discontinued; or when items no longer serve the purpose for which they were purchased. Scrap represents property that is of no further use to the government because of the effects of use, time, or accident. The disposition function is closely related to the acquisition program and to inventory management, and is an important element of the overall materials management concept.

IDENTIFYING SURPLUS AND SCRAP

Timely identification of surplus and scrap is essential to an effective disposition program. Delayed identification results in higher storage and maintenance costs and possible deterioration of the items. As part of its inventory management responsibility, purchasing should periodically review inventory levels of operating departments and other using agencies to determine whether excess stock is on hand. Some people feel that using agencies can best determine, on the basis of their program needs, which items are excess. Although there is some validity to this observation, using agencies usually have little incentive to declare items as excess, and there is a tendency to hoard items for an undefined but possible future use. To overcome this tendency, some governments have found it very effective to give using agencies credit for the sales proceeds of items released. It is important that purchasing have overall supervision and ultimate control over both the inventory and surplus programs. But this authority should not be viewed as one which places purchasing in conflict with using agencies, nor as one that will lead to indiscriminate or unfounded actions. The system works well in those purchasing programs that now have this authority. In some cases, inspectors who work for purchasing and inspect vendor deliveries also identify surplus items. Written procedures must set forth guidelines for identifying apparent surplus items and for assuring that they are indeed surplus, and close coordination between purchasing and using agencies is essential if a disposition program is to be really successful.

METHODS OF DISPOSITION

After items are found to be surplus or scrap, the best method of disposition must be determined. Depending on the nature of the items and the needs of other agencies, items may be transferred; sold by auction, sealed bid, or posted price; or destroyed. Destruction is rarely necessary. Using agencies are not normally in a position to determine the best method of disposition, nor need they be. Since disposition is a nominal function of using agencies' operations, they may have a tendency to dispose of items by the least troublesome means. Central purchasing, on the other hand, has the vantage point and the capability to carry out the disposition function to the best advantage of the government and should therefore be responsible for it.

Transfer

The best way to dispose of items no longer needed by one agency is to transfer them to an agency that does need them. Using agencies should report all excess items to central purchasing, which should have a systematic procedure for determining whether transfers can be made. In one State, copies of using agencies' requisitions are processed through the surplus property section, which determines whether there is surplus property on hand to fill the need. Other techniques include periodically circulating lists of currently available surplus items and "want lists" maintained by the surplus and scrap section. Want lists enumerate items that using agencies need but cannot afford, or do not want to purchase new and are willing to wait for. To encourage using agencies to avail themselves of this service, the lists should be compiled from any type of

requests, written or telephoned, and using agencies should be assured that an expression of a need is not a commitment to accept an item. The value at which the property is transferred should be set by mutual agreement between the agencies involved, or at a fair value set by central purchasing.

Transfer of surplus items between agencies is both efficient and economical. For example, in one system a using agency had some equipment that was technologically obsolete. Since this agency was involved in research and needed the most modern equipment, it requested the obsolete equipment be traded in. Central purchasing found that the best trade-in offer would provide only a nominal amount. Further investigation disclosed that another department could use the equipment for teaching purposes but could not afford it at its original price. The equipment was transferred, and the relinquishing agency received credit for the amount of the trade-in offer.

Transferring items can be an especially effective technique when imagination is used to find new functions for items. In one case, for example, central purchasing transferred an excess fire engine pumper to another agency which could use it for watering roads on detours to keep dust down. As another illustration, mechanical Plexiglass drums originally used for lottery drawings were transferred, after attempts to sell them had failed, to prison shops, where the Plexiglass was used for security windows, nameplates, shelving, and hobby shop material.

When intragovernmental transfers cannot be made, some governments have lists of priorities for transfer or sale to another government or to other tax-supported activities within the State. Some governments even maintain want lists from these governmental units and activities. Thus, surplus property transfer is another means of intergovernmental cooperation. If items cannot be transferred, they can be traded in or sold, depending on the nature of the item, its condition, and the market.

Trade-In

When using agencies need to purchase an item to replace obsolete equipment, it is sometimes possible to trade in the obsolete equipment. Unfortunately, trade-in is sometimes used as an expedient because it is an easy method of disposal and some value is realized. If trade-ins are accepted on a particular equipment item, the Invitations for Bids should call for bid prices with and without trade-in and indicate that award may be made on either basis. The best trade-in offer can then be compared with the expected sale price for the obsolete item. This procedure requires market analysis as a basis for determining the approximate value that would be realized if the item were sold rather than traded in. Experience shows that outright sale, either by auction or by sealed bids, generally produces a better return than trade-in.

Sale

Auctions. Auctions can be a useful means of selling certain types of surplus property. Auctions are advertised to the general public and, in some cases, notices are circulated to government employees. Auctioneers are usually hired to handle the proceeding. Interested parties can inspect the items either at the auction site or at the user's location. Governments use various other methods of providing information on items to be sold, such as descriptive ratings of the condition of equipment, giving odometer readings of vehicles, listing known defects, and providing pictures of the items. Some States hold auctions at several different locations to bring the opportunities for buying closer to more people.

Sealed Bids. Many purchasing programs sell most of their surplus and some scrap items by sealed bid. Sealed bid sales are similar in many respects to sealed bid purchases. A public notice of the sale is made, bid lists are kept by type of commodity, a date is set for public bid openings, and the government retains the right to reject bids. Interested parties must be given an opportunity to inspect the items being sold, and some form of descriptive literature on the items is usually available. Overall, the sealed bid procedure reaches the largest number of prospective bidders.

Sale of Scrap. Almost any surplus property can be sold as scrap. A potentially profitable technique that is used too infrequently in selling publicly owned scrap material is separating the scrap into its component parts or materials. This may be an involved process, but the sale of components or materials will often bring a much higher return.

Conditions of Sale. The government does not sell surplus and scrap as a public service venture, but to realize the best value it can from items for which it has no further use. Consequently, the government should make it clear to all buyers that it takes no responsibility and makes no guarantees for items sold. To be fair, the government should describe the conditions of the items and list known defects but, beyond that, it should be made clear that the responsibility rests with the buyer. Conditions of sale, such as the following, should be published in advertisements and in notices posted at the site of the sale:

- It is the buyer's responsibility to remove the items within a reasonable time after the purchase.
- No guarantees or warranties are given by the government for the items.
- Known and major defects are listed, but the government makes no claim that all defects are known.
- No sale will be invalid due to defects discovered in the item after the sale.
- The government assumes no responsibility once the items are sold.

Federal Surplus

The federal government, like some state and local governments, releases some excess property through intergovernmental programs. Certain restricted state functions dealing with education, civil defense, and public health are allowed to receive federal surplus under the federal donable food and surplus property programs. Because the class of donees is restricted, many States allow the donees to participate individually in the programs. The effectiveness of the efforts in this area, as in others, could be greatly improved by specialized central attention, which could either develop into a large program or be simply a central point for information. The well-developed programs use inspectors to screen items regularly at various federal locations and to operate tractor-trailer trucks to transport desirable items to a central warehouse, where state donees can inspect and acquire them. In States where this program is administered closely with the state surplus program, the users have to express their needs to only one governmental unit. The storage function of both programs is performed in the same facility, although items from the state and federal programs must be kept physically separated, and the users can examine both groups of items in one trip.

Currently, the entire federal surplus program suffers from two major weaknesses, both organizational. Administration at the federal level is divided variously among the Department of Health, Education and Welfare, the Department of Defense, the General Services Administration, and others. Responsibility for the program in the States is similarly fragmented. What must occur if the program is to avoid present wasteful duplication of effort is to center policy and day-to-day administrative responsibility within a single agency for both the federal government and each State.

14. Cooperative Purchasing

ESSENTIAL ELEMENTS

Suggested Statutory/Regulatory Coverage

The purchasing statute and/or the rules and regulations adopted pursuant to the statute should:

Explicitly provide the authority for intergovernmental cooperative purchasing, under rules and procedures established by the central purchasing authority.

Provide that governmental units be parties to contracts under cooperative purchasing agreements.

Provide that cooperative purchasing be permitted only when the purchasing jurisdiction assuming administrative responsibility conducts its purchasing operations according to the principles of open competition.

Recommended Practices

Participants in cooperative purchasing must agree to abide by all contractual requirements, including prompt payment of invoices.

Normally, the largest participating unit should administer the cooperative purchasing program.

When local governments or nonstate agencies are permitted to join in cooperative programs with state purchasing, their participation should be elective, not mandatory.

State and large local governments should take a more active leadership role in fostering, designing, and administering cooperative purchasing programs. Programs among local governmental units should be especially encouraged.

Local entities must consider their responsibilities to serve the public interest and approach cooperative purchasing opportunities with a professional management outlook.

Local governments should consider extending the concepts of consolidating operational functions to administrative areas such as purchasing, under merged governments or pooling arrangements.

The long-range benefits of aggregating purchasing power through joint purchases by two or more States should be examined.

Cooperative purchasing is a rather loose term that refers to a variety of arrangements by which two or more governmental entities buy under the same contract or agreement. Since cooperative purchasing programs necessarily extend across jurisdictional lines—a county and the cities and towns within it, or two adjoining county governments—statutory authorization is required. Generally, this is a specific act for each specific instance. There are several types of cooperative purchasing and several forms within each type, and they come into being for several reasons.

By far the most frequent reason for such an arrangement is to seek lower prices through combined requirements and larger volume. This result, however, is not always achieved. Certain types of requirements, such as tire recapping, can become less attractive to bidders as volume increases beyond certain points. In periods of product shortages or labor difficulties, large-volume contracts are avoided rather than sought by manufacturers and distributors.

Another reason for aggregating purchases is to try to create a demand large enough to encourage the manufacture of new or modified products which are not otherwise commercially available. This can provide an effective incentive, though again it does not always work.

A third reason often stems from action by a State Legislature to allow local governments and other organizations to purchase under state contracts. For a while, this concept was used by the federal government; it extended contracts and prices to activities holding federal grants of one kind or another, and to state and local governments in general. This kind of thinking and practice circumvents competitive bidding, weakens the validity of contracts, and is fraught with dangers.

FORMS OF COOPERATIVE PURCHASING

The soundest cooperative purchasing programs require that all participants be actual parties to the contract. This means, for example, that an eligible non-state unit that wishes to buy automobiles under the State's contract must advise state purchasing of its election to do so, and must agree to be bound contractually in the same manner as a state agency. Such a requirement protects the principle that a bidder know whose business he is bidding for and, if successful, whose business he has earned. Programs of this kind are operating successfully among a variety of relationships including state and local governments, state governments and certain agencies which otherwise are exempt from the state purchasing authority, county and municipal governments, and county and county governments.

The weakest programs are merely permissive-type arrangements whereby a third-party agency, such as a local government, can use a contract, such as a State's, if, when, and how it chooses. The state contract prices become, in effect, ceiling prices against which nonstate agencies can bargain. Such practices place the successful bidders, who have won state contracts in open competition, in the position of having their contract prices presented as targets for others to negotiate with or play against. Additionally, they give sealed bidding the character of an auction, a concept which the courts have rejected. Obviously, any appreciable amount of this "second bidding" discourages bidders from offering their most favorable prices on state contracts. Moreover, in times of unfavorable market conditions, the uncommitted third-party users can increase demands on contract suppliers to the point of severely impairing the ability of state agencies, who are bound by the contracts, to obtain their needs. Loose purchasing arrangements of this type can have political appeal but they are fundamentally unsound.

More acceptable are programs which, while permissive, afford a protection for open competition. Under these plans, a local government has the option of buying under the state contract or taking its own bids; that is, it is relieved of competitive bidding only if it orders under the state contract.

Another method of cooperative purchasing is based on central warehousing. Customarily, the largest of the governmental units involved will buy in carload and truckload quantities, and smaller governmental units can either order or pick up certain types of items from the warehouse. These items are usually limited to categories such as canned fruits and vegetables, and janitorial, housekeeping, office, and general maintenance supplies. This type of cooperative purchasing, like the contractual commitment type discussed earlier, protects the principles of competitive bidding because the bidder will know the commitment covered by the Invitation for Bids and by the award.

Highly successful cooperative programs have come about among contiguous counties and municipalities, such as in certain areas of Florida, Minnesota, and Ohio. Some of these programs represent cooperative purchasing in its best form. These arrangements are favored by geographical proximity and the comparative ease of distributing goods and services. An order of paper towels, for example, can be divided and unloaded by the participants from a freight car in a short time. Less common are arrangements involving two or more cities only, or counties only.

Programs between States and their local governments have developed unevenly. Often, the principles of competitive bidding have not been adequately guarded, resulting in some very loose, optional types of arrangements. The more recent programs, however, recognize these deficiencies and stipulate that if a political subdivision elects to participate in a particular contract, it does so by estimating its requirements and committing itself to order accordingly. On the other hand, if it elects not to participate it must solicit bids under its competitive bidding law. In at least one State, California, the local government or school board must submit all requests to participate in the State's annual contracts in the form of standard purchase requisitions. The requisitions set forth quantities and indicate that these have been authorized by a resolution of the governing board.

Among other things, requiring authorization by a governing board guards against a major problem, the timely payment of bills, that is encountered when outside agencies are permitted to order from contracts established by two other parties. Unfortunately, governmental agencies are not known for paying invoices promptly. Often this is caused by cumbersome accounting procedures which require several approvals for each check or warrant. While the State has some control over the payment process of its own agencies and institutions, it has little or no control over the payment cycle of local governments, school boards, regional libraries, and other entities that may be authorized to order from the state contracts. Delinquent payments by contract participants almost invariably result in higher prices to the State itself on subsequent bids.

Since cooperative purchasing usually involves indefinite quantity contracts, certain legalities need clarification. There are questions as to whether an indefinite quantity contract is enforceable except as a requirements contract, whereby the purchaser is committed to order his normal requirements during the period of the agreement.

THE NEED FOR MORE COMPREHENSIVE LAWS

Obviously, not all state and local governments have the same requirements and procedures governing purchasing. Differences exist in requirements for public advertising, solicitation techniques, procedures for receiving and opening bids, and standards for determining the successful bidder. Therefore, when two or more purchasing jurisdictions seek to combine their needs for mutual advantage, difficulties are often encountered in meeting the legal requirements of all participants. This is particularly true where laws fail to provide the kind of flexibility that allows departure from established practices. The enactment of new laws or amendments to existing laws is necessary in these cases before cooperative purchasing between governmental entities can be effectively undertaken.

All state and local purchasing laws should explicitly provide the authority to purchase cooperatively with other jurisdictions. While such a provision has been incorporated in some purchasing laws, little is ever mentioned concerning the degree to which a jurisdiction must comply with its own purchasing laws when entering into a cooperative purchasing arrangement. Silence in this area is confusing and often leads to questionable legal interpretations.

At one end of the spectrum, for example, there is a tendency to assume that a purchasing official cannot assign his purchasing authority to another jurisdiction unless that jurisdiction has requirements and safeguards that are equal to or more rigorous than his own. Considering the divergence of policies and practices that currently exist among States, cities, and counties, this viewpoint makes cooperative purchasing an academic concept rather than a real practicality. Even when a state government, which generally has more comprehensive and highly developed purchasing practices, administers a cooperative program, there is always the possibility that incompatibility will arise between the State's purchasing practices and those of the local governments. Administrative differences of this nature unnecessarily complicate cooperative purchasing efforts.

The absence of caveats and guidelines in the authority to engage in cooperative purchasing is sometimes misconstrued as a blanket exemption from having to comply with one's own purchasing requirements and standards. Under this interpretation, purchasing jurisdictions are expected to accept the policies and practices of the state or local government administering the cooperative arrangement as satisfactory substitutes for their own policies. An obvious danger exists when the administering jurisdiction has standards and practices that are substantially less demanding than those of the other participating jurisdictions. Entry into cooperative purchasing arrangements under such circumstances can cause purchasing jurisdictions to circumvent the basic principles of their own purchasing laws.

Provisions for cooperative purchasing must, therefore, be designed to eliminate interpretations which are either so rigorous that they effectively preclude any widespread use of cooperative purchasing, or so tenuous that they allow one jurisdiction to adopt standards of a lesser quality from another jurisdiction. This can be aided substantially by requiring that cooperative purchasing be permitted only when it is known that the purchasing jurisdiction assuming administrative responsibility conducts its purchasing operations according to the principles of open competition. As long as cooperative purchases are made in a competitive manner, requiring that a sufficient number of bidders are solicited to ensure competition and that awards are made to the lowest and best bid, the procedures and practices for acquiring this competition can be left to the rules and regulations of the administering jurisdiction.

SELECTING AN ADMINISTRATIVE FOCAL POINT

In cooperative purchasing arrangements, one purchasing jurisdiction normally is designated to administer the acquisition process. However, deciding which participating jurisdiction is to assume this responsibility is often difficult. It is not uncommon, for example, for smaller participants to be reluctant to relinquish their purchasing authorities. This can generally be attributed to a false fear of losing independence and autonomy, and it represents a formidable barrier. Since cooperative purchasing arrangements are voluntary, and since they typically provide greater savings to the smaller jurisdictions, this attitude has little justification. From a practical point of view, it is usually advisable to assign the responsibility to the largest participating jurisdiction, since it is likely to have a larger staff and higher technical capabilities.

THE NEED FOR ACTION

Cooperative purchasing has many advantages and can serve to foster intergovernmental cooperation. Aside from the economies of volume buying, it can greatly assist in reducing the duplication of work done in such areas as preparing specifications, soliciting bids, and testing products. Properly structured laws are needed to grant the authority to engage in cooperative purchasing programs. But the programs will not succeed without adequate leadership and a spirit of cooperation.

State and large local governments can and should take a more active leadership role in designing and administering these programs. Some States, for example, survey local jurisdictions when determining which items are candidates for term contracting. The surveys show whether or not the local jurisdictions buy these items and in what quantities. Copies of specifications are also requested as input to the State's program of developing standard specifications. In addition, some States conduct periodic workshops for state and local purchasing personnel to exchange ideas and information and to improve efforts at cooperation.

Perhaps of more importance, local governments must do their part. They have many avenues for cooperative efforts, especially among each other, but they must overcome their fear that they will be subordinated to another government and their strong preference for local suppliers. Local entities must, first and foremost, consider their responsibilities to serve the public interest and to approach their purchasing mission with a professional management outlook. They must be willing to make contractual commitments and adhere to the principles of competitive bidding. They must be willing to support consolidated purchasing whether through merged governments, pooling arrangements, or other forms of cooperative purchasing practices.

Some local governments are already consolidating operational functions such as police, fire, and sanitation, under merged governments. Extending this concept to administrative areas such as purchasing could pave the way for significant advances for many smaller and medium-sized governmental units.

The pooling of efforts and resources is a natural forerunner to consolidated operations under merged governments. This concept presents many possibilities for creative innovations. For instance, given the minimum optimum size for a local government to accommodate a full-time purchasing officer, the pooling of purchasing functions among several contiguous governments could be quite effective. As another example, the management information systems of several governments, if computerized, could be consolidated under time-sharing arrangements. Pooling arrangements can also be applied to specialized technical functions such as commodity cataloging, specifications, inspection and testing, training, economic analysis, buying strategies, and disposing of surplus and scrap.

There are some new forms of cooperative arrangements being explored which could prove fruitful. One is the rather obvious idea of two or more States joining together in a common contract for some particular commodity or service. Such an endeavor raises both legal questions, which may not be difficult, and economic questions, which may be complex. The long-range impact of aggregating purchasing power in this manner has not been examined.

An accelerated effort is under way in a somewhat different field of cooperation, involving the federal, state, and local governments. This highly promising program for exchanging information on specifications on many individual products is aimed toward reducing much duplication of effort and concentrating energies to develop performance standards which will serve as incentives for manufacturers to innovate and offer more suitable products with greater value.

A milestone will have been achieved if this study helps to promote a recognition of the positive potential for interdependency in public purchasing. Improvement in and enrichment of the procurement process is linked inextricably to each level of government. Local governments, therefore, have a tremendous opportunity and even a responsibility to work more effectively with other governments. Intergovernmental cooperation must be encouraged, facilitated, and nourished at the state and intermediate levels of government to benefit individual purchasing programs and to obtain maximum benefits from available resources. In the final analysis, no matter how a tax dollar is levied, in the eyes of the taxpayer it is public money and deserves to be spent thoughtfully and responsibly.

15. Professional Development

ESSENTIAL ELEMENTS

Suggested Statutory/Regulatory Coverage

The purchasing statute and/or the rules and regulations adopted pursuant to the statute should:

Provide a statement of intent encouraging affiliation by purchasing officials and their technical staffs with one or more professional purchasing associations.

Require that government personnel have the authority to prepare and maintain position specifications for the full spectrum of purchasing jobs. These specifications should reflect the current thinking of appropriate associations as to job content and credentials.

Embody as part of the policy statement in the purchasing law an affirmation of the management role of public purchasing officials. (See also "Acquisition: Purchasing Structure.")

Recommended Practices

Purchasing associations should incorporate the specifics of career education into position specifications and educational standards for purchasing.

The need for formal training and educational programs which supplement basic knowledge and experience should be examined.

The central purchasing authority should provide for specific funding in the departmental budget for training and professional development, including formal course work; an updated departmental technical library; memberships in local, state, and/or national purchasing associations; and travel to observe other purchasing units.

Associations of public purchasers should lead the way in formalizing a body of requirements and an educational curriculum in the field of public purchasing.

Ongoing management and administrative work experience should be required of the technical staff. For example, the staff should become members of committees and task forces (i. e., the "purchasing" representatives for such groups), adept at researching and writing policy issue papers, and experienced in preparation of budgets.

Public purchasers need to establish a viable underlying commonality to ensure that the principles and standards of good public purchasing are applied consistently.

The need for a single national certification program which is endorsed and supported by all purchasing associations should be addressed.

The observations, conclusions, recommendations, and other information contained in this report can be used to improve communication with purchasing's public and to evaluate purchasing programs.

Statute and administrative law, policies, procedures, and organizational structure all mesh to provide the mechanism of public purchasing. It takes people to put this static mechanism into motion. This chapter discusses the roles of people both in and out of the mainstream of state and local government purchasing who in a variety of ways affect and implement the procurement of goods and services. This discussion will be primarily concerned with the effective level of performance of state and local government purchasing personnel, and with the necessary orientation for those who must support purchasing programs through an executive, legislative, or management role.

Discussions dealing with the effective level of performance and the effort necessary to achieve and maintain that level frequently bog down in semantics. There has been and will be much discussion as to whether purchasing, private or public, is a profession. There is great difficulty in arriving at agreement on the definition of "profession," "professionally," and "professional," as these words might be used vis-a-vis the level of performance in public purchasing.

All too frequently, the word "profession" is used interchangeably with occupation or vocation. For the purposes of this chapter, a deliberate and even arbitrary limitation is placed on the definition of profession. Three criteria are essential to this definition: (1) a discipline of education with an established level of knowledge; (2) a process of formal licensing either within a professional association itself and/or by the government; and (3) the establishment of discipline and regulation to that standard of discipline, again by a professional association and/or the government. These are the criteria of the formal professions, e.g., medicine, law, and engineering.

Given these criteria, purchasing is not a profession. It is safe to say that the practitioners of purchasing, at least in the public sector, would not want to be members of a profession with these limitations.

But if public purchasing is not a profession, this is not to say that public purchasers should not act, and indeed be required to act, professionally, i.e., to exhibit conduct characterized by and conforming to technical and ethical standards. It is also appropriate, notwithstanding the definitive limitations placed on the word "profession," to say that public purchasers performing professionally are, indeed, professionals.

There is little doubt that those charged with public purchasing responsibilities strive to maintain professionalism in their work in order to improve their image and, thus, gain recognition and status. In purchasing as in other fields, there are attitudes of pride, value and worth, standards and ideals, and specifics of conduct and performance in all activities. The ingredients of technical and ethical standards in public purchasing include an essential level of knowledge and a competent application of that knowledge, a personal and public discipline of performance, and the acceptance of the responsibility and accountability inherent in public purchasing. There are people both within and without public purchasing, however, who feel that stature is unattainable without the badge of "profession." For those committed to this idea, this chapter may prove a disappointment.

THE ESSENTIAL LEVEL OF KNOWLEDGE

Educational Basics

Formal curricula to prepare for the practice of purchasing in the private sector is somewhat limited. **The opportunity to pursue an educational discipline leading to a specific educational degree in public purchasing is virtually nonexistent.** Present generations of public purchasing agents have come to their careers almost always inadvertently and often accidentally. Certainly, they have come to their careers prepared in a variety of ways educationally, including many as licentiates in such formal professions as pharmacy and engineering, with grounding in principles of business or public administration, but almost always without any specific formal education in government procurement practice.

The absence of specific discipline leading to a degree in public purchasing does not mean that institutions of higher education do not provide the opportunity to generally satisfy the educational background needed in public procurement. Courses in business administration, accounting, fiscal management, public administration, political science, business law, and computer sciences are all important ingredients of the necessary background. A sampling of these with concentration in one or more is reasonable preparation for a career in public purchasing. Work in the liberal arts is also needed to establish the intellectual curiosity of an adequately rounded education.

Despite the availability of this course work, a formal career education in public purchasing remains a mosaic of happenstance and personal choice. It is recommended, therefore, that the specifics of career education be incorporated into position specifications and into educational standards which are or can be established by purchasing associations.

For the part-time public purchaser or for those who come to the field later in a career, there is an opportunity for furthering one's education by correspondence courses, seminars, and institutes offered by colleges and universities. The orientation of much of this continuing education is towards industrial purchasing, but the government procurement officer can find substantial value in these opportunities.

The educational needs and requirements of public purchasers have changed as purchasing has evolved through three identifiable phases. The first period dates back to the 1800s when laws concentrated heavily on protecting taxpayers against favoritism and fraud. The laws were patterned largely after statutes governing contracts for construction and public works. The public purchaser was almost exclusively a technician involved in practices that demanded little educational preparation.

Shortly after World War I, the second stage, a movement to centralize purchasing, began. The economic depression of the 1930s with the need to get the maximum out of the tax dollar provided impetus in this direction. Centralization called for more highly developed operations, and the need for a formal discipline of purchasing education became apparent.

Purchasing is now entering a third phase in which emphasis is being placed on purchasing management. It must continue to assume a more active role in the executive decision-making process, and government management must acknowledge the significant contributions that can be made by purchasing. There are data and expertise that purchasing should provide to the decision-making process in much greater depth and detail than takes place at the present time. Decisions of whether or not a government can or should acquire a given configuration of items or what kind, amount, or degree of capability, should not be made without considering the experience and expertise in purchasing. Purchasing should also be a major adviser in areas of feasibility studies, considerations of alternatives, and cost-benefit and cost-effectiveness analyses.

Continuing Education and Training

This role as an integral part of management requires not only a basis of formal education but also maintenance and improvement of the level of performance on an ongoing basis. There is no question that the experience born of day-to-day operations contributes mightily to the enlargement of knowledge and expertise of a government purchasing office. Valuable as this experience is, however, it represents at best an unstructured form of continuing education. There is a need, then, for formal training and educational programs which supplement basic knowledge and experience.

This requirement is not now well met in state and local purchasing. State purchasing officials report that 11 States have programs of in-house training for the entire technical staff, and three States provide their own training for new employees. Twenty-five States indicate that they rely upon others for continuing educational programs, and 10 States indicate that they have no formal program at all. The results of a nationwide survey of 1,047 counties and 545 cities show that only 9 percent of the counties and 13 percent of the cities have ongoing programs.

These statistics reveal a serious deficiency in the way purchasing activities perceive the need to raise their level of competence. While the surveys did not go into great detail as to the extent of continuing education provided by others beyond the purchasing activity itself, it appears that much of it is through institutes and seminars offered by universities and colleges on an as-available basis, without a great deal of long-term structure to the program. These programs need to be shaped and formalized by a body of requirements which probably can be best expressed through the various associations of public purchasers. State and local governments, in turn, must provide funding for training and professional development, including memberships in professional associations, establishment of technical libraries, travel to comparable purchasing units, and formal course work.

Paraprofessional Development

Another aspect of professional development arises from the fact that while the recognized professional, a doctor for example, practices his profession, not all those in the field of medicine are doctors or professionals. Similarly, legal secretaries and law clerks are not considered professionals in the same sense as those for whom they work. Purchasing also requires divisions within the discipline. Those with suitable education, training, and experience occupy positions of authority and responsibility. Others (i.e., those in clerical, staff, and routine administrative positions), although working in the field of purchasing, cannot be said to be functioning professionally as the term is here defined.

Nevertheless, the requirement for ongoing training and education among this group is also important. It is important not only to ensure conventional continuity, but also to respond to various social forces such as current "Affirmative Action" and "Balance of Work Force" requirements.

Uniformity of Principles and Standards

Professions are built around bodies of knowledge that have been reduced in one fashion or another to an accepted set of rules or principles and standards. These bodies of knowledge are both formalized and uniform. They are used consistently by all professionals regardless of the time or place in which they may be practicing. Uniformity is especially important if the work is to be recognized as a unique discipline with consistent application under the same or like circumstances.

Public purchasing can be measured against the long-established professions in these parameters because there is an extensive body of knowledge pertaining to the practice. However, there is little uniformity among the federal, state, city, county, and other governmental units in the application of this knowledge. This does not mean that public purchasing must become monolithic and have identical practices and procedures for every purchasing jurisdiction. Different jurisdictions have different problems. Flexibility in practice is necessary in public purchasing. **There remains a need, nevertheless, for public purchasers to join in a concerted effort to establish a viable underlying commonality to ensure that principles and standards are applied consistently. This entire study is directed toward that goal of identifying both the principles which define objectives and purposes, and standards as the means to accomplish them.**

Professional associations of public purchasers are developing the necessary structure of uniform principles and standards. There are local-, state-, and national-level associations which represent the gathering together of public purchasers to achieve these purposes, to expand the knowledge of public purchasing, and to define a personal and public discipline of performance. Purchasing officials and their technical staffs should be encouraged to become active members of one or more professional purchasing associations as a means of broadening their professional insights and of contributing in the efforts to better the profession.

CERTIFICATION

Recognition of the need for identifying responsible purchasing performance among individuals who have attained a prescribed level of qualification is evidenced by the fact that many national purchasing organizations, such as the National Institute of Governmental Purchasing (NIGP), the National Contract Management Association (NCMA), and the National Association of Purchasing Managers (NAPM), offer various certification programs. These programs provide opportunities and requirements for purchasers to demonstrate their capability to fulfill established criteria required in purchasing and related fields. Although these programs all promote the recognition of a candidate's professional competence in the field of purchasing, they have varying requirements for educational experience. Written and oral examinations are generally required with specified mixes of academic credits and experience. Most of the certification programs provide limited periods for the "grandfathering" of known experts.

While individually all of these programs have merit and definitely reflect the trend towards a recognized status in the purchasing field, collectively they tend to be somewhat divisive. The current proliferation of such certification programs is not unifying the public purchasing community.

It is time to consider the possibilities of consolidating existing certification programs into one national program receiving full faith and credit by all of the associations in the field. This development would reflect favorably in the eyes of the public, and public acceptance and confidence are paramount for the most effective public purchasing and its primary objective of serving the public interest.

If the education and, therefore, professional development of those immediately concerned with public purchasing remains somewhat unstructured, the orientation and education of those with whom public purchasers must interface is no better. There is a corresponding need, therefore, for public purchasers to develop better communication and interface with the public it serves.

INTERFACE WITH PURCHASING'S PUBLICS

As the practice of public purchasing has developed,

there has been a tendency (common among similar groups) for purchasing officials to view their efforts in an aura of great specialization, if not outright mysticism. Surrounding the practice in mystery and esoteric language does not contribute to good communication in government. An attempt to establish status by this approach is not prudent and not necessary. Government purchasers must communicate freely and fully and constantly with their constituent agencies, with prospective vendors, with contractors, and with the general public if the job of government procurement is to be performed effectively.

Communication

Purchasing professionals must communicate to the publics they serve a clear understanding of the level of knowledge, the personal and public discipline, and the range of responsibility and accountability which the purchasing activity requires. This report and the *Digest* which preceded it can and should be basic tools for promoting this kind of communication. A very specific methodology of communications lies in the proper construction of purchasing manuals, as will be developed in Chapters 17 and 18.

Absorbed in the day-to-day tasks of procurement, public purchasing officials frequently neglect upward reporting. A town chairman, a mayor, a county board chairman, or a Governor is receptive to reports of purchasing activity. It is a fascinating business, sometimes even an amusing business, and a good story can do a great deal to establish understanding and appreciation of the efforts of a central purchasing authority.

This study has emphasized the role of the purchasing official in government management. The greater the participation by public purchasers, the greater the opportunity for communication and a more effective role in management. Participation often pays dividends, as when a purchasing agent becomes a member of a building committee when the project is a gleam in everyone's eyes, rather than a nearly completed structure with impossible deadlines for obtaining and installing equipment.

Professionalism can be viewed as the hallmark carried by a profession, but that mark must be etched ever so carefully as the profession builds in structure. Public purchasing, like other professions in the making, is faced with a persistent challenge to encourage and instill public confidence. It recognizes that public confidence is earned by demonstrated performance of the highest quality and reliance. Public acceptance will come with increasing emphasis on accountability by the central purchasing authority at all levels within the procurement cycle.

Commitment of Resources

The instability of professionalism within public purchasing will be ameliorated when a total of comprehensive professional approach is applied. Governments must reassess their priorities to bring about a commitment to meeting the contemporary issues and concerns of public purchasing. This means, in part, that staffing resources beyond the level of buyer personnel must be made available to the central purchasing authority. Local governments, in general, seem to face a real void when it comes to the technical support and reinforcements necessary to assure effective and economical acquisition, management, and disposition of goods and services. Attracting needed staffing resources to the public purchasing profession requires salary levels which are commensurate with the skills required to meet both the expectations of the public and the legitimate objectives of the central purchasing authority. Crucial to the basic concept of professionalism in state and local government purchasing is a commitment to training and development programs for purchasing personnel. Refined skills directed toward economy, value, innovativeness, creativity, and increased productivity have their roots in continuing education programs. Revitalization within public purchasing is as indispensable as the quest for its hallmark, i.e., conformance to technical and ethical standards.

THE PROCESS OF EVALUATION: PROGRAMS AND PEOPLE

This discussion of the roles of people both in and out of the mainstream of state and local government purchasing has been, of necessity, somewhat abstract. There is, however, an opportunity inherent in the material presented in this study to permit the interested reader to make a purchasing program evaluation, which is also an evaluation of professional development.

The Pro-D Committee of the National Association of State Purchasing Officials submitted to the membership in September 1964 a *Recommendation for Criteria for Measuring the Effectiveness of State Purchasing Departments*. This paper identified seven areas of evaluation: legal basis, basic operating policies, organizational plans of the department, measures of the department's contribution to the "Total Supply Concept," personnel, physical area, and forms and detailed procedures. The reader can easily equate these subject areas to those considered in this study. There is a direct parallel except for the NASPO Pro-D Committee's concern with the physical environment of purchasing operations.

The committee suggested that each of these areas be rated on a scale of 100 and suggested that, because the actual efficiency of any one purchasing office is relative, it should be rated only by setting up specific rather than general objectives. In each of the seven areas, questions were proposed which would bring about the desired specificity.

A similar exercise can be derived from weighing actual performance against the essential elements identified in this study. Such an evaluation is largely subjective, but an honest appraisal reveals a great deal about the state-of-the-art and the state of professional development. Hopefully, repeating the exercise six to 12 months later will disclose a gratifying improvement.

Purchasing started out primarily as a buying function, but it is clear that it is no longer that limited in scope. The evolution of complex high-technology items subject to obsolescence in relatively short periods of time requires that public purchasing officials remain up-to-date in technical knowledge, related information systems, and new purchasing techniques. Also, a successful program must have the flexibility to adjust to varied and changing market conditions where supply and demand for different commodities are at times relatively in balance, and at other times quite unequal. Without this ongoing professional development, public purchasing cannot fulfill the government's needs.

16. Purchasing Manuals: Review and Evaluation

APPROACH TO THE REVIEW

This chapter presents an overview of purchasing manuals, instructional materials, and other written data used as a part of state purchasing systems. The essential elements of an effective purchasing system, which are discussed throughout the study, served as a baseline for this review. Specifically, the review was guided by the following objectives:

• Evaluation of the extent to which the States' manuals and other written materials address the pertinent subject areas of their purchasing systems;

• Identification of the methods used in developing detailed purchasing procedures and instructing using agencies; and

• Determination of those subject areas that require improvement.

The term "manual" is not uniformly defined in all States. Several of the documents provided in response to the request for manuals are, in fact, either compilations of rules and regulations, some of which carry the force and effect of law, or sets of procedural memoranda and instructions.

For purposes of the evaluation, "manual" was defined as a systematic and comprehensive guidebook of policy, procedures, and practices, which provides its users with detailed guidance in performing those tasks and functions associated with normally anticipated work situations.

Thirty-two States and territories responded to the request for purchasing manuals. (See the list of references at the end of this chapter.) Of the documents submitted, 20 fulfill this study's definition of manuals. Material submitted by the other 12 does not fall into the manual category and probably was not intended to. A number of instructional brochures for suppliers also were received, as were university and municipal purchasing manuals and other assorted materials.

After an initial review, 15 manuals were selected for in-depth review because in the aggregate they best represented overall subject coverage, geographical diversity, range of dollar volumes, and unique requirements. The remaining five manuals and the other materials were used for supplementary information.

The following criteria were established for evaluating the manuals:

• Coverage—Does the manual touch on all major subject areas?

• Completeness—Are the subject areas that are covered in the manuals discussed in enough detail to pro-

vide guidance on how particular tasks are to be performed?

• Utility and Clarity—Is the manual written clearly enough to be easily followed?

• Format and Content—Are the format and content developed in a fashion to permit easy, ready reference by users?

To structure the review, purchasing activities were grouped into four major subject areas:

• Principles, Policy, and Organization—the conceptual foundations and goals of state purchasing and its associated regulatory policies, and the organizational structure, duties, and responsibilities of central purchasing units.

• Requirements Planning, Specifications, and Standardization—the procedures for identifying using agency needs and planning for their acquisition by central purchasing; development and use of specifications and standard specifications.

• Requisitioning, Procurement, and Contracting—requisitioning procedures, competitive bidding procedures, types of purchases, contract administration, emergency procurement, and delegation of purchasing authority to using agencies.

• Receiving, Stores and Warehouses, and Quality Assurance.

None of the manuals reviewed, of course, is precisely organized in these four parts.

The review results are presented under three headings. The Summary of General Findings highlights the acceptable elements of a purchasing manual. The Evaluation of Manual Sections assesses the manuals against the four major subject areas described above. The third, Using Agency Manuals and Instructions to Prospective Vendors, is oriented toward assisting using agencies and suppliers in the procurement process.

SUMMARY OF GENERAL FINDINGS

Coverage

In nearly all cases, the manuals were written in an apparent attempt to serve both purchasing and using agencies and, in some cases, suppliers as well. Most of the manuals describe not only the procedures that the purchasing organization should follow in making awards, but also the responsibilities of using agencies and suppliers to comply with the requirements of the purchasing program. For example, several manuals devote sections to delegated authority and to defining the responsibilities of using agencies, with instructions for the treatment of requisitions, the use of term-contract purchase orders, and agency responsibilities for receipt and inspection of goods.

There appears to be general agreement among the States that using agency personnel and suppliers, as well as purchasing personnel, need guidance in purchasing procedures. Because of the relationship of purchasing and using agencies in acquiring goods and services, the purchasing manual could logically include all the necessary information for both activities. Although the purchasing manual should be readily available to suppliers and any others who may require it, a separate manual for suppliers seems desirable and has been prepared in some States.

Most of the manuals cover purchasing policies and goals by addressing specific subjects and, to a lesser degree, the procedures and constraints within which the policy is to be implemented. The extent to which the manuals deal with specific major subject areas varies significantly from one manual to another. It is unclear from reading them, especially those which fail to treat certain major subject areas at all, if or how purchasing personnel are expected to carry out each function. For example, one manual fails to discuss prequalification procedures, although that State has a prequalification program. In other words, a State may in fact perform certain activities even though its manual does not cover them.

Completeness

There is a lack of consistency among the manuals in the degree of coverage given to areas treated. Those manuals which come closest to being complete in describing the "how to" of a given task are those in which each procedure discussed is separately identified by title and number. In effect, such a manual represents a compendium of controlled procedures, each of which is the product of careful design and review by a purchasing official. Most of the manuals use a narrative approach to describe procedures. While this is necessary, the inclusion of checklists and flowcharts would be helpful to users of the manual.

Utility and Clarity

Clarity of writing and ease in locating subject matter are important features of good manuals. The usefulness of several of the manuals is impaired because they are unclear and because it is difficult to locate material about a specific subject. Some manuals have no table of contents at all, and others have tables of contents that are so abbreviated that they are virtually useless.

A common shortcoming of most of the manuals is

that they do not provide sufficient information for new personnel. Consequently, their usefulness for indoctrination and training purposes is questionable, especially for people having only limited knowledge and understanding of the purchasing procedures in a particular State.

Age, Updating, and Revisions

At the time of our review, six of the manuals were more than five years old, and only five were less than two years old. Some States are revising their manuals or developing new ones, which suggests that a similar updating process might be warranted in most other States. Several of the manuals use formats that facilitate continual updating. The most common technique is treating each main topic on a separate loose-leaf page, allowing for changes without a major overhaul of the entire manual.

EVALUATION OF MANUAL SECTIONS

Principles, Policy, and Organization

Nearly all of the manuals discuss the principles and goals of purchasing programs. These sections are generally well-written and should aid staff members in understanding their purchasing systems. One manual incorporates administrative rules and regulations, which serve not only as a link between the statutes and practice, but also as a general policy statement.

Only six of the manuals, however, cover ethics and standards of conduct. Such coverage is essential in establishing good purchasing practices.

Ten manuals contain organization charts; the others would benefit from such an inclusion. The office to which the purchasing unit reports is identified in two of the remaining five.

Job descriptions and job assignments of purchasing agents are frequently omitted from the manuals. From the eight manuals that indicate purchasing agent assignments, two dominant patterns emerged: assignment of purchasing agents by commodity specialties and assignment by agency or institutional specialty. One of the States using the agency/institutional orientation mentions in its manual that it is moving increasingly toward commodity orientation, although it is seeking to maintain a balance.

Nine manuals outline the duties and responsibilities of their purchasing units, basically by summarizing the statutes. Although it was sometimes difficult to evaluate the depth of coverage because of the organizational variation from State to State, few manuals appear to have fully identified and outlined all major purchasing duties and responsibilities applicable in their States.

Requirements Planning, Specifications, and Standardization

None of the manuals deals to any significant extent with requirements planning, even though that function undoubtedly is performed in varying degrees. Requirements planning involves determining the types of material and services needed and developing a plan to obtain the goods when needed. Several manuals touch on the need for central purchasing to have sufficient purchasing lead times, and some establish commodity buying schedules to ensure that such lead time is made available. In general, however, the manuals fail to treat either the importance of advance notification or the procedures by which using agencies are to convey their needs to central purchasing. The manuals provide little guidance to using agencies on how to plan for their purchases; this tends to result in "crisis" purchasing.

Specifications and standardization are covered in all but one of the manuals. In evaluating the treatment of this subject, the following aspects were considered:

- Definition and types of specifications;
- Responsibility for developing specifications;
- Procedures for developing specifications;
- Descriptions of how the specifications are to be used;
- Descriptions of how standard specifications are to be used; and
- Procedures for developing and controlling standard specifications.

Five of the manuals are especially effective in their treatment of specifications and standardization. The others are largely limited to naming the persons and departments responsible for developing the specifications, but there was little or no indication of how the specifications were developed or used. Most of the manuals fail to discuss the development of standards and standard specifications; most of the manuals urge the use of terms such as "or equal" and "or equivalent" when brand name specifications are used.

Apparently, a growing approach in developing specifications is the establishment of committees consisting of representatives of central purchasing and using agencies. These committees also assist in determining statewide commodity standards.

Requisitioning, Procurement, and Contracting

Procedures for advance planning of purchases generally are not well documented in the manuals. Most provide instructions to using agencies on preparing and submitting requisitions to purchasing, and some also cover commodity classifications and include sample requisition forms. But a number of important aspects of the requisitioning process are generally overlooked, particularly those pertaining to the interrelationship of the requisitioning activities with purchasing. For example, none of the manuals cover the following questions in any appreciable detail:

- How far in advance of the desired delivery date must a requisition be submitted to central purchasing by a using agency?
- How long should it take for central purchasing to get an order placed once a requisition is received?
- How are using agencies notified by central purchasing of a contract award and its terms?
- How are commodity catalogs, minimum standards, and standard specifications to be used in the requisitioning process?

Bidders Lists and Supplier Evaluation

Of the 11 manuals that discuss the use of bidders lists, the majority discuss this subject only briefly. Only two manuals supply details regarding the purpose and use of bidders lists, the procedure for adding suppliers to the bidders lists, and the maintenance of bidders lists.

Eight of the manuals discuss evaluating supplier performance. Using agency inspection reports provide the principal source of feedback to the purchasing organization. These eight manuals also cover suspension of suppliers from the bidders list because of nonperformance. None, however, fully describe the mechanics of the supplier evaluation programs. For example, it is unclear in all cases precisely what criteria are used as bases for suspending a supplier, how such criteria have been developed, and how they should be applied. Related subjects such as supplier appeals and reinstatement are neglected in all but three manuals.

Solicitation of Bids

Thirteen of the manuals provide instructions on formal, informal, and telephone solicitation of bids. The coverage for formal bids most commonly involves requirements relative to a stated dollar purchase amount, sealed bids, and other requirements tailored to individual governmental needs (e.g., bonding requirements). Informal solicitations generally do not require sealed submissions, although competition is still required. Telephone solicitations, normally for purchases of less than $100, usually require quotations from three suppliers.

Submission of Bids

Some of the more important aspects of bid submission are procedures for receiving and safeguarding bids, descriptions of what constitutes a properly executed bid, bid tabulations, bid bonds, samples, and certificates of noncollusion. Most of these subjects are not extensively covered in the manuals, though some are treated as parts of other subject areas. Several manuals note (especially in instructions to suppliers) the importance of submitting properly completed bids, including checking for extension errors, submission of samples, and adherence to designated bid deadlines.

In nearly every case, the manuals clearly state that bids are to be publicly opened, and two of the manuals point out that bids must be opened within a set period of time following submission. Eleven manuals discuss the tabulation and filing of bids and bid data for audit and record-keeping purposes.

Evaluation of Bids

With respect to the evaluation of bids and making awards, the coverage in most manuals is, at best, only cursory. Most manuals discuss the evaluation process, but usually without identifying the evaluation criteria or the guidelines for establishing such criteria. As a result, they make it appear that substantial latitude is allowed in the evaluation process.

Eight of the manuals mention procedures for resolving tie bids. Most procedures allow or require an in-state preference where tie bids involve both in-state and out-of-state bidders. However, the manuals generally do not define "in-state bidder," and supply very few details on the method for handling tie bids. The manuals generally leave unresolved such problems as:

• Tie bids in which collusion or illegal practices are suspected;

• Repeated patterns in bids from the same supplier(s);

• Procedures for resolving tie bids involving in-state suppliers;

• Procedures to discourage the incidence of identical bids;

• Situations, such as those involving fair-traded items, which often result in identical bids;

• Recommended procedures when no acceptable bids are received; and

• Definition of "lowest responsible bidder."

Eleven manuals, in various parts of their texts, refer to rights reserved to the State, such as rejection of any bid, all bids, or parts of bids; waiving of minor irregularities in bids; and cancelling or altering procurements.

Six of the manuals reviewed indicate that there is a procedure by which aggrieved bidders may protest awards. Generally, the procedures mentioned call for review by an authority higher than central purchasing, e.g., the director of administration or a board of review.

Contracts and Contract Administration

All of the manuals discuss the general procedures related to term contracts and contracts used for one-time purchases of standard items. The discussions of term contracts range from detailed to sparse, with most of the manuals providing relatively good coverage. Procedures to be followed by using agencies in monitoring technical performance of suppliers and providing feedback to central purchasing, however, are often overlooked. Only five of the manuals cover such contract administration activities as cancellations, terminations, contract changes, assignment of contracts, and supplier payments. Discussion of the techniques to be used in purchasing specialized services or complex technical equipment is also generally omitted.

Most of the manuals are unclear about the responsibilities of central purchasing vis-a-vis using agencies. Most are also unclear about precisely who has the authority to enter into contracts. Several manuals do include copies of the purchase order forms and purchase requisition forms, which are useful in acquainting suppliers and using agencies with the format and terms of the various purchase instruments.

Receiving, Stores and Warehouses, and Quality Assurance

Ten States refer to stores and warehouse operations, with the coverage generally including descriptions of the items carried, stores catalogs, and requisitioning procedures. The complete scope of warehouse operations, including inventory control, record-keeping, and the management and physical movement of goods, is not usually detailed. Such subjects may be beyond the intended scope of the purchasing manuals and may be covered elsewhere.

Most of the manuals reviewed indicate that using agencies have primary responsibility for inspecting shipments. An exception to this is the inspection of common items purchased in bulk for several agencies, in which case central purchasing is responsible for inspection.

Several manuals discuss the availability of supplementary inspection and testing assistance to the using agency, at its request. A few States mention the fact that inspection and test personnel also conduct programs of quality assurance which involve periodic random inspections of shipments and laboratory tests. The manuals generally relate tests and inspections to vendor performance evaluations, as well as to quality assurance in general. The coverage of inspection indicates a general acceptance of the need for proper inspection, but detailed procedures are frequently lacking.

All the manuals identify special or unique requirements applicable only to the particular State. Such special requirements are commonly concerned with such subjects as environmental quality standards and requirements, protecting state natural resources (e.g., oil, trees), handling dangerous drugs and medical supplies, and moving explosives and radioactive materials.

Several manuals include appendices which contain the forms used in purchasing, statutory authorities, administrative rules and regulations, procedures for procurement with federal funds, nonstandard procurement procedures, and glossaries.

Emergency Purchases

Twelve manuals discuss emergency purchases by using agencies, generally defining the circumstances which constitute emergencies and allowing for waiver of normal competitive bidding requirements. The procedures usually require advance notification, when circumstances permit, or documentation after-the-fact. Post-emergency reviews of circumstances and justification are required by most of the manuals.

Special Situations

Special situations, as used here, include such occurrences as rental, lease, and lease-purchase agreements; professional services; interagency transfers; negotiated purchases, both competitive and single-source; open-market purchases; multiple purchases under one procurement; printing purchases; insurance agreements; and trade-ins. The coverage of these subjects is generally spotty, and many are not covered at all. One notable exception is the purchase of printing services. Most States segregate the purchase of printing services and supplies into a separate procurement category and give it special attention in their manuals. The topic of interagency transfers, where it is considered at all, is usually associated with the disposition program.

In general, all of the manuals would benefit from more attention to these "special situations," to preclude their being handled informally or on an ad hoc basis as they arise.

Purchasing under Delegated Authority

A major objective of centralized purchasing is to locate both responsibility and control in one office. In state purchasing, the necessity to delegate purchasing authority can pose problems in terms of balancing the need for centralized management controls against the resources for implementing such controls. Therefore, purchasing manuals should clearly show the responsibilities of central purchasing and provide guidance on the controls which central purchasing units are to maintain over delegated activities.

All of the manuals discuss purchases by using agencies under delegated authority. Generally, using agencies are permitted to purchase under delegated authority according to predetermined conditions, e.g., purchases less than a specified dollar amount. Also, certain other types of purchases are sometimes excluded from central purchasing. Notable among such exemptions are purchases from "favored" industries (i.e., prison systems and industries for the handicapped) and the purchase of perishable foods. Further common delegations listed include emergency purchases, requisitions from stores, and credit card purchases. The coverage is incomplete in most cases because the manuals generally fail to relate the responsibilities of using agencies to those of central purchasing. For example, topics such as who is responsible for record-keeping, contract administration, and supplier evaluation are frequently omitted.

The most widely followed approach among the manuals to the delegation of purchasing authority is the establishment of dollar levels below which agencies are permitted to purchase, provided they follow the procedures and rules governing competitive bidding.

Another control mechanism mentioned is the establishment of purchasing rules which are applicable to specific circumstances rather than a general delegation of authority based on dollar amounts. One State, for example, delegates purchasing authority by means of "Direct Procurement Authorities," each of which sets out rules for specific types of transactions. Another manual describes the rules and procedures relative to delegations for gross amounts exceeding $500, as follows: "Each delegation shall be separate, and the authority shall be in writing," and it further specifies rules and procedures for such delegations. A third State delegates certain purchasing authority through "subpurchase orders," and the manual indicates what conditions and rules must be followed for various types of purchases.

USING AGENCY MANUALS AND INSTRUCTIONS TO PROSPECTIVE SUPPLIERS

Four States submitted manuals devoted exclusively to using agencies. The other manuals apparently are intended to serve using agencies as well as central purchasing. Some States have separate manuals for universities which are exempt from using central purchasing.

Several manuals include removable sections that are of particular interest to suppliers, and are intended to be distributed separately. Two States supply instructions to suppliers by means of instructional brochures. Most States also provide information and instructions to suppliers on their bid forms and in Invitations for Bids.

LIST OF REFERENCES

State	Documents	Date of publication
Alaska	Purchasing Regulations	August 1972
Arizona	Procurement Manual	June 10, 1968
Arkansas	Purchasing Manual	September 1, 1969
California	State Administrative Manual — Purchases	November 1972
	Department of General Services, Office of Procurement Manual, Vol. III, Part I	March 1969
Connecticut	Purchasing Manual	July 1972
Florida	Purchasing Manual	July 17, 1972
Illinois	Job Descriptions for Purchasing Personnel, Catalogue of Standard Specifications for Office Supplies	August 1, 1970
	"Selling to the State of Illinois"	July 1, 1972
Iowa	General Outline of Procedures, Agency Information General Outlines of Procedures, Vendor Information	....
Kansas	State Agency Guide for Procurement of Goods and Services	January 12, 1970
Kentucky	Purchasing Manual	April 7, 1966
Maine	Manual of Financial Procedures, Part III, Accounting	June 1, 1972
Maryland	Manual of Department of General Services, Requisitions and Invoices	August 1, 1970
Michigan	Administrative Manual, Purchasing Division	June 20, 1970
Minnesota	Manual of Standard Operation Procedures	June 1970
Missouri	Division of Procurement, Rules and Regulations	January 1954
Nevada	State Administrative Manual — Purchasing	....
New Hampshire	Division of Purchase and Property, Manual of Procedures	December 1972
New York	Printing Purchasing Guidelines Purchasing Manual	October 1971 December 1970
North Carolina	Purchasing Manual	1972
	Purchasing Manual, Addendum No. 1, Contractual Services: Management Consultants	September 28, 1972
	Purchasing Manual, University of North Carolina at Wilmington	....
North Dakota	Department of Accounts and Purchases, Purchasing Division Manual	October 1, 1966
Oklahoma	Purchasing Manual	July 1961
Oregon	Operating Procedures, Procurement Division	....
Pennsylvania	Central Purchasing Manual	June 12, 1972
	Field Purchasing Manual, City of Bethlehem Purchasing Procedures	March 15, 1971
	Department of Transportation, Bid Proposal Package	September 11, 1972
Rhode Island	Procurement Officer's Policy and Procedure Manual	March 1969
South Carolina	Manual for Planning and Execution of State Permanent Improvements	July 1, 1961
South Dakota	Purchasing Procedures and Instructions	July 1971
Texas	Purchasing Division Procedural Manual	November 30, 1962
Virgin Islands	Purchasing Manual of Procedure	....
Virginia	Centralized Purchasing Manual	1965
Washington	Department of General Administration, Rules and Regulations	January 20, 1966
Wisconsin	Administrative Practices, Purchasing Manual	January 1, 1962
	University of Wisconsin Purchasing Manual	April 1966
Wyoming	Purchasing Procedures	....

17. Purchasing Manuals: Purchasing Procedures Manual

INTRODUCTION

The previous chapter presented an evaluation of purchasing manuals reviewed during this study. The conclusions reached about the usefulness of the manuals were based on good management practices and on current trends in state purchasing as reflected in the statutes, rules and regulations, and other documents solicited and received from purchasing officials.

In this and the following chapter the same two bases have been used to develop guidelines for preparing purchasing manuals. This chapter addresses a purchasing manual for both using agencies and central purchasing. The detailed operational procedures of each government are necessarily unique in some ways and thus cannot be specified completely by a single, standard manual. Nonetheless, the basic principles and requirements of every purchasing organization are similar.

This chapter presents an expanded outline for a purchasing procedures manual. The sections of the manual generally coincide with the sequence of text material covered in the earlier chapters of this report. While this structure will facilitate reference to detailed report discussion, it is not intended as a required format for purchasing manuals.

Generally, the manual is keyed to the needs of all government officials and employees who participate in the purchasing process. The goal is to document procedures and practices required by statutes and regulations and to promote better coordination both among the using agencies and between using agencies as a group and central purchasing. The key to better coordination is understanding and agreement among all parties on the procedures to be followed. For that reason, suggestions for changes in those procedures should be referred to the central purchasing authority.

While the responsibility for and overall cognizance of the purchasing program lie with the central purchasing authority, using agencies are inextricably involved in the program. Consequently, it is essential that the authorities, responsibilities, and duties of both central purchasing and using agencies be clearly delineated, published, understood, and uniformly applied and adhered to by all concerned. Since the purchasing procedures manual must reflect applicable statutes and regulations, it is the one document which can define the joint effort of purchasing and using agencies in clear, unmistakable language.

While this section looks at purchasing from the government's viewpoints, the next chapter addresses the vendors manual, which is keyed to the needs of those doing, or wishing to do, business with state and local governments. Both manuals should be completely coordinated, consistent with each other, and fairly represent the realities of doing business with the government.

The purchasing manual is more detailed than the vendors manual and contains information needed specifically by government offices, central purchasing, and using agencies. Nevertheless, the purchasing manual should be available to all vendors who want to enhance their own understanding of the public purchasing system.

PURPOSE OF THE MANUAL

The purpose of the manual should be explained. Basically, the manual provides guidance and instructions to those people involved in the purchasing process. It presents the authorities and responsibilities of those participating in the system, outlines the requirements of pertinent statutes and regulations, and sets forth the policies and procedures established by the central purchasing authority. The statutory or regulatory authority for preparing the manual should be identified. Copies of pertinent laws and regulations should be appended to the manual. Important statutory requirements can be highlighted in bold type throughout the text, as is currently done by some state and local governments.

PURCHASING AIMS AND OBJECTIVES

The aims and objectives of the purchasing program should be clearly stated. Among these might be the spending of public funds prudently, making awards impartially, seeking to obtain maximum value, and providing effective service to using agencies. The principles of open competitive bidding, impartiality, and public record can be introduced in this section. The purchasing programs of California and Kentucky have adopted relatively formal statements of aims and objectives. See Exhibits 1 and 2 at the end of this chapter.

STANDARDS OF CONDUCT

This part of the manual is of paramount importance because it describes the ethics and professional conduct for the purchasing process and thereby ensures that all who participate in purchasing have a clear understanding of the professional behavior expected of them. These standards should apply not only to purchasing personnel but to using agency personnel as well. Vendors, too, must know what is expected of them in the way of ethics and professional behavior. By whatever means this information is conveyed (i.e., in a separate vendor's manual or in the purchasing manual), it should be distributed to bidders and vendors.

Statutory prohibitions against attempting to influence awards by offers of rewards, accepting such rewards, and the like, can be covered in this section. There should be some discussion of the prohibitions against circumventing the laws dealing with competitive bidding and engaging in "back-door selling." Similarly, conflict-of-interest provisions should be summarized or included verbatim here, including the penalties for violating them. The disciplinary actions which may be taken for violating the standards of conduct should also be set forth.

Organizations such as the National Association of Purchasing Managers (NAPM) and the National Institute of Governmental Purchasing (NIGP) have published codes of professional conduct which can be adopted for purchasing manuals. The illustration shown in Exhibit 3 is contained in the administrative manual of the Purchasing Division, State of Michigan, and was derived from the standards advocated by NAPM. Some States, such as Minnesota, have taken the approach of specifying forbidden practices. See Exhibit 4.

ORGANIZATION AND STAFFING

This section of the manual should present an overview of the purchasing organization and its position in the governmental structure. Perhaps the clearest way to show the placement and structure of purchasing is with organization charts. One chart might show purchasing's placement in government and the attendant chain of command, and another could depict the internal organization of purchasing, including branches, sections, and supervisory assignments. Information such as team-buying arrangements, commodity assignments, and staffing could also be shown. A third chart could present the programs, functions, and activities for which purchasing is responsible. This functional chart could be patterned after the one contained in the chapter on "Acquisition: Purchasing Structure" in this report.

The narrative accompanying the charts should set forth a declaration of policy, or quote the declaration of policy contained in the purchasing statute. The duties and responsibilities of the central purchasing authority should be clearly stated. Delegated authorities should also be identified, as well as the attendant

monitorship by central purchasing. It should be made clear that delegations carry with them the obligation to observe all statutory requirements and, also, that central purchasing will periodically review purchases made and procedures followed to assure that all statutory, regulatory, and written policies are being observed. The interface and coordination between purchasing and using agencies are frequently overlooked. Some coverage of these topics, perhaps by means of flow charts as well as text, can enhance mutual understanding of the purchasing process.

Some purchasing manuals contain brief summaries of the major functions for which central purchasing is responsible, such as vendor qualifications, maintaining the bidders list, approving Invitations for Bids, quality control, and disposition. These summaries can be a good means of illustrating to the reader the scope and breadth of the purchasing program.

For purposes of the purchasing procedures manual, staffing should refer to the delineation of the specific duties and responsibilities of the chief purchasing official and his professional staff. Departmental practices on the division of responsibility among buyers by commodity classification, for example, should be identified. The clear definition of the duties of administrative assistants to the chief purchasing official is also important. Such definition of the duties and responsibilities of the professional staff assists all readers in identifying key personnel and their responsibilities and duties.

ACQUISITION

Planning and Scheduling

This section should cover the detailed procedures which comprise the planning and scheduling functions at both the management and operating levels. Purchasing's role in top-level management planning and budgeting should be described, including the types of information normally provided by purchasing, the reviews conducted, and any other major functions which are assigned. Considerably more detail is needed to describe the planning and scheduling process at the operating level. The manual should define the procedures for both the initial compilation of future needs and the periodic revisions of these projections. As appropriate, general timetables can be established for these functions.

The workings of the purchasing information system should be described as it relates to planning and scheduling. Particularly important is an explanation of the types of data that are available in the system and how the system should be used by both purchasing and using agencies. The procedures should require using agencies to communicate their forecasted needs to purchasing in a systematic manner. If standard forms are used for this purpose, copies should be included with descriptive comments. Well-defined procedures in these areas can greatly assist in controlling the purchasing workload, obtaining goods and services when they are needed, and taking advantage of volume purchasing.

Commodity Catalogs

A commodity catalog is an orderly coded list of commodities which are commonly purchased. It is useful for identifying commodities, facilitating ordering, and providing a basis for statistical and other analyses. When correlated with a bidders list, it can be used to identify and select qualified bidders for mailing of Invitations for Bids. The commodity code listing can be included in the manual or distributed separately, whichever is more practical. In either case, the purchasing manual should describe the coding scheme and the manner in which the codes are used in purchase documents and reports.

Bidders List

Purchasing should be responsible for setting the policies for maintaining the bidders list. This section of the manual should identify who is responsible for maintaining the list and the procedures to be followed. Qualification requirements and procedures, use of the bidders list in soliciting bids, file maintenance, and suspension or debarment should be among the subjects treated here. If there is a prequalification program, the forms used and the information to be obtained should be described. More importantly, the standards, criteria, and procedures used in reviewing this information should be described. Any exceptions to the prequalification requirements should be identified and alternate procedures for these exceptions should be described.

Purchasing is responsible for assuring that there is an optimum base of qualified competitors available. The program for identifying new suppliers should, therefore, be detailed in the manual. Activities such as attending trade shows, reviewing trade publications, conducting market analyses, and exploratory advertising are among the techniques that can be discussed.

The system should also provide for evaluations of suppliers' performance. Normally, this is accomplished on an exception basis, i.e., a report is prepared only when there is unsatisfactory performance. The required procedures, forms, and standards of performance should be described. Responsibilities for preparing the reports and acting on them should also be covered. It usually is best to have only one contact point with suppliers for contract administration matters,

and this responsibility best rests in purchasing. The manual should delineate this authority and describe the procedures to be followed when performance problems arise. The procedures should include a requirement for feedback to the affected using agencies on decisions reached. Provisions should also be made for a central vendor file, within purchasing, for documentation on all such contacts with suppliers.

The conditions and circumstances under which suppliers can be deleted from the bidders list should be set forth. These procedures should provide for a written notice to the supplier advising him of the intended action and, as appropriate, what the supplier must do to remain on the list. In all cases, the central purchasing authority should approve deletions from the list. Reinstatement procedures, as well as suppliers' rights to administrative review, should be specified in the manual.

Types of Purchases

The manual should delineate the types of purchasing techniques used and the personnel authorized to enter into each type of purchase transaction. Purchases which can be made by using agencies on the open market, purchases which must come through central purchasing, and purchases which are defined as emergency purchases are among the topics that could be discussed. The manual should describe contracting procedures, as opposed to "spot purchases," and explain purchasing's role in each process. Instructions for the use of term or requirements contracts will undoubtedly be more extensive because of their more complex characteristics. Four types of such contracts should typically be addressed:

- Definite quantity over a definite period of time;
- Approximate quantity over a definite period;
- Indefinite quantity over a definite period; and
- Indefinite quantity over an indefinite period.

The key differences among these four types are quantity and time. The conditions under which each may be used should be described, and the manual should contain instructions on structuring the contract. Exhibit 5 presents excerpts on term contracting from the *Virginia Manual of Central Purchasing*.

The purchasing manual should also discuss purchase order procedures. A sample of the purchase order should be included here, or in an appendix to the manual. Responsibilities for preparing, reviewing, and approving purchase orders should be described. Filing, public record, and records retention should also be covered.

Requisitioning Procedures

For all purchases directed through or controlled by

central purchasing, the process begins with a requisition prepared by a using agency. The section of the manual which addresses requisitions should specify in detail:

- What a requisition is, how it should be prepared, and what information it should contain;
- Who may prepare or authorize a requisition;
- What the procedures are for filling out a requisition for the different types of purchases; and
- How and to whom requisitions should be sent for approval and processing.

A sample of the requisition form should be included in the manual, together with instructions on its preparation. The use of commodity catalogs and standard specifications to identify needed goods should be encouraged as a means of speeding the processing of requisitions.

Separate sections might be prepared to describe the requisitioning procedure in general terms for the benefit of all users of the manual, instruct using agencies in particular on the preparation of requisitions, and instruct purchasing personnel on processing requisitions when they are received. Where central stores and warehouses are maintained, the manual should cover the procedures for rquisitioning items from these facilities.

Competition

Competition is a fundamental principle of public purchasing. A section of the manual dealing with the statutory and regulatory requirements for competition will be highly useful. This section can summarize both the specific statutory requirements and the spirit of the law on this subject. Requirements for public notice and sealed bids should be included. Solicitation procedures for both formal sealed bids and informal bids should be presented in detail, including the documentation requirements. Where formal sealed bids are required, the general rule should be that all bidders on the bidders list for the item be solicited. Any exceptions to this rule should be explained, and the alternate procedures should be set forth.

There should be provisions for waiving the competitive bidding requirements. This is a very sensitive area and good instructions are needed. The conditions and circumstances under which competitive bidding may be waived should be spelled out. Review and approval procedures, as well as documentation requirements, should be covered. Terms such as "single-source" and "emergency purchases" should be defined as further guidance in this area.

Competitive negotiation techniques may be used in cases where the conventional sealed bidding process is determined to be inappropriate. The manual should provide guidance on the types of situations in which competitive negotiation may be more appropriate. Procedures for structuring Requests for Proposals should encompass preparing the statement of work and identifying the criteria to be used in evaluating proposals. The proposal evaluation process needs to be formalized and should provide for technical assistance as necessary, including cost or price analysis. The techniques of negotiation should also be covered in this section. Specific mention should be made of the fact that competition is required for negotiated awards, that impartiality in applying evaluation criteria must prevail, and that there must be complete documentation to support the award made.

Impediments to Competitive Bidding

Impediments to competitive bidding do arise. Some of the issues related to these impediments should be addressed in the statutes, but the purchasing manual should expand on the statutory coverage. Procedures should be developed, with the appropriate legislative body, for coordinating proposed legislation that directly or indirectly affects purchasing with the central purchasing authority. There should be a provision requiring bidders to submit statements of noncollusion with all bids. The subject of identical bids should be addressed, and procedures should be set for making awards under such conditions. The manual should provide that central purchasing maintain a bid-award history file, and describe the nature of the file and the analytical procedures for detecting apparent collusive bidding practices. In conjunction with the Attorney General, a procedure should be developed to report suspected collusion to the appropriate government element. Purchasing officials should be on the alert for situations which may indicate conspiracies or collusion, such as "customary" price changes made simultaneously by all or most suppliers of particular products. The manual should identify these situations.

If competitive bids cannot be obtained and the items are needed, central purchasing must have the authority to take alternative measures. These procedures and the documentation requirements supporting such purchases should be covered in this section of the manual.

The procedures for using option clauses and escalator clauses should be included. These procedures also pertain to structuring the Invitation for Bids but, if not properly handled, they may work to defeat the principle of competition. Similarly, the conditions under which suppliers may be granted relief under a contract should be covered. As a general rule, such relief should be granted only when holding a supplier to a contract would be patently inequitable.

The statutory provisions governing conflicts of interest should be included in the manual. Procedures for reporting conflicts of interest should be established, and the officials to whom they apply should be clearly identified. The penalties associated with violating the statutory provisions should also be specified.

The manual should prescribe the policies on back-door selling and other methods of circumventing the statutory requirements related to competitive bidding. Procedures for detecting such practices should also be defined and should provide for official reprimands for personnel who circumvent purchasing laws and regulations.

Fund Availability

Any responsibility central purchasing may have for the availability of funds for a given requisition or set of purchases usually is limited to verifying that funding has been approved by an appropriate accounting, budget, or finance function. The usual procedure is for the using agency to submit a requisition to purchasing and for the requisition to be honored and filled only after verification of fund availability. Procedures vary widely for accomplishing this verification, and the responsibility may even rest with the requisitioning agency. Purchasing may routinely send the requisition to finance, the using agency may send the requisition to both purchasing and finance simultaneously, or finance may have a representative at the using agency who verifies fund availability before the requisition is forwarded to purchasing. Whatever procedures are to be followed regarding fund availability should be explicitly defined in the purchasing manual.

Frequently overlooked in purchasing manuals is purchasing's additional responsibility for procurements made with federal funds. Federal Management Circular 74-7, Attachment O, dated September 13, 1974, provides standards for state and local governments for purchases made with federal grant funds. An effective purchasing system that meets a state or local government's needs will usually satisfy federal requirements.

Invitation for Bids

The preparation and distribution of the Invitation for Bids (IFB) or Request for Proposals (RFP), or Request for Quotations (RFQ) is a major step in the procurement process. The procedures for preparing the IFB, including authorities and responsibilities, should be covered. The central purchasing authority should be responsible for reviewing and approving all IFBs before they are issued. It is important that the IFB be complete and provide all the information needed by suppliers to prepare responsive bids in a competitive manner. Although the design of IFBs varies significantly among state and local governments,

the subject matter should generally include:

- Bid preparation instructions. Bids must be typed or prepared in ink, they must be signed in ink, all erasures or changes must be initialed, etc.
- Submission of bids. The date and time by which bids must be submitted; the location to which bids are to be delivered; and the date, time, and place of bid opening must be clearly stated.
- Changes and corrections. The procedures to be followed prior to bid opening should be delineated.
- Compliance requirements. Compliance with specifications and with contractual provisions in the event of an award should be set forth.
- Terms and conditions. Delivery, discounts, payment, inspection, and the right to reject unacceptable items should be clearly stated.
- Samples. Whether or not samples must be included and, if included, the policy regarding their return or destruction should be stated.
- Bid security. The terms of possible bid security requirements should be set forth.
- Certificate of Non-Collusion.
- Award criteria.

Guidance should be provided for reviewing IFBs before they are issued to assure that they are proper and complete. A checklist of items to be covered can be a useful tool for this review and can also serve as documentation that the review was made. In addition to the routine provisions in IFBs, purchasing must review the specifications and must also review any special provisions that may be needed. For example, if optional items are involved, the IFB should specify the expected needs and the manner in which the related bid prices will be considered in the evaluation process. If brand name specifications are being used, purchasing must assure that the accompanying specifications clearly indicate that the specification is not intended to be restrictive. The policies for bid security requirements should be covered in the manual and should specify that when bid security is requested it will be applied equally to all bidders.

In certain procurements, bidders' conferences may be advisable to ensure that prospective bidders understand the conditions and specifications for the procurement. The manual should identify the conditions which call for such a conference and the time and place for carrying it out. These should also be set forth in the IFB. Normally, bidders' conferences are held soon after bid invitations are sent out and as far in advance of the scheduled bid submission date as possible.

The manual should set forth the filing and records retention policies relative to IFBs. As a matter of course, a copy of the IFB and a list of suppliers to whom it was sent should be filed with a copy of the requisition.

Receipt, Opening, and Tabulation of Bids

Provision should be made for receiving, controlling, and safeguarding bids until they are opened. The individuals who are responsible for this function should be designated, and the procedures to be followed in assuring that bids are secured and unopened should be set forth. The central purchasing authority should be charged with monitoring this system.

The policies for bid openings should be covered, and they should provide for public bid openings. The bid tabulation procedures should also be described. These procedures should address the tabulation techniques or forms used, the time the tabulations will be made, and the necessity that all tabulations be public record. Informal bidding procedures should also be covered with a requirement that a record be made of all bidders solicited and all bids received. Records retention policies should be set for all documentation related to both formal and informal bids. The policies should describe the type of information in bid files that can be inspected by bidders or the public, either before or after award, and the type of information that remains confidential.

Bid Evaluation and Award

The concept of the "lowest responsible bidder who submits a responsive bid which is most advantageous to the government" places an obligation on purchasing officials to evaluate bids impartially. The evaluation process cannot be an informal one. Guidelines and procedures should be provided in the purchasing manual.

Standards of supplier responsibility should be set. Where prequalification is used, responsibility may have already been determined. In any event, the guidelines should present the factors to be considered in determining that the low bidder is capable of providing the required items or services. Although they are often routine, the guidelines for determining who is the low bidder should be listed. Factors such as discounts, treatment of options, alternate bids, and all or none bids should be covered. They should also be discussed in the IFB.

Responsiveness, substantial conformance, and minor irregularities in bids should also be covered in this section. The factors to consider, procedures to be used, and the documentation supporting these determinations should be described. If tests of samples are called for in the IFB, the procedures for documenting test results and using them in making an award should be specified. Provision should be made for obtaining technical assistance, as required, to determine conformance with specifications. The policies for mistakes or errors in bids should be included. Among the topics to be covered in this regard are extension errors, failure to sign bids, and failure to date bids. Policies for late bids should also be covered.

Central purchasing must have certain authorities in order to protect the government's interest and to act effectively in unusual circumstances. These include the authority to reject all bids or to reject bids in whole or in part. The conditions under which such action may be taken should be specified and the alternate courses of action for varying circumstances should be set forth. There should also be instructions on the procedures to be followed when one or no bids are received in response to a solicitation.

Bidders sometimes submit proprietary information, trade secrets, and the like with their bids. There should be procedures for identifying and safeguarding such material.

As mentioned before, purchasing officials must be on the alert for collusion, conspiracy, and suspected antitrust violations. Identical bids, particularly a pattern of such bids, call for special attention. The policies for making awards when identical bids are received should be designed to discourage the recurrence of tie bids. Collusion and conspiracy can exist without identical bidding, and there should be procedures for detecting such situations. A highly useful handbook on this subject is *Impediments to Competitive Bidding,* published by the Council of State Governments in 1963.

However well-managed a given procurement might be, the possibility exists that one or more bidders will think they have not been fairly dealt with and will want to protest the award. To be prepared for such actions, purchasing should have procedures covering:

- Protest. How and in what time frame should the protest be made, to whom should it be directed, and what information is required.
- Review. Who has primary review and decision authority; how is that authority to be exercised.
- Appeals. At least one level of appeal should be provided above that of the primary reviewer, if only to minimize the possibility of litigation. The point at which recourse to the courts is necessary to resolve the dispute should come only after all departmental resources have been exhausted.

Contract Administration

Central purchasing should be responsible for contract administration. Although not all contract administrations will necessarily be performed by its personnel, purchasing should develop the policies for carrying-out and monitoring these activities. The term "contract administration" refers to the post-award responsibilities of the government to:

- Ensure compliance by the supplier with contract provisions;
- Monitor deliveries, product quality, and schedules;
- Follow-up with suppliers on problems occurring during the period of performance;
- Receive and obtain approval of invoices and bills for payment, if this is a central purchasing responsibility;
- Negotiate contract modifications and administer terminations, where necessary and permissible; and
- Administer contract close-out and final payment.

Using agencies may often assist purchasing in certain facets of contract administration, such as in receiving, inspection, and technical evaluation of product quality. In cases where there is testing of products delivered, purchasing must coordinate with technical personnel at the test facility. Details of accomplishing contract administration in terms of authorities, responsibilities, and procedures should be clearly delineated in the manual. These procedures should provide that purchasing will be the contact point with suppliers on any problems. Conditions under which exceptions to this rule may be made should be specified. All correspondence, reports, and memoranda of contacts with suppliers should be sent to purchasing for inclusion in the vendor file.

QUALITY ASSURANCE

Specifications

The central purchasing authority should be responsible for establishing a specification program and a standardization program. This section of the manual should describe the program and should define the responsibilities and authorities for the various activities. If appropriate, a simple flow chart can be used to depict the preparation-review-approval process. Using agencies' participation, purchasing's role, and the final approval functions should be covered. The manual should make it clear that purchasing is responsible for reviewing specifications to assure that they do not call for features or a quality level which is not necessary for an item's intended use, and for seeing that the specifications are adequate to obtain competition.

The purchasing manual could also contain a section which describes the different types of specifications that may be used and, perhaps, the conditions under which each type might best be used. Brand names, design specifications, qualified products lists, calls for samples, and performance specifications are among those that should be covered.

Some of the more important principles relating to the specification process should be included in the manual. Among these are that:

- Specifications should set out the essential characteristics of the items being purchased;
- Specifications should call for the appropriate level of quality;
- Specifications should be prepared so as to obtain the maximum practicable competition; and
- Suppliers should not prepare or assist in preparing specifications.

This section should describe the procedures for using brand name specifications. There should be a requirement that, whenever brand name specifications are used, there be an accompanying explanation which clearly indicates that the specification is not intended to be restrictive. There should also be a requirement that several acceptable brand names be used wherever possible.

If testing is to be performed, the specifications should describe the nature and method of the tests and include guidelines for applying test results. The methods and responsibilities for developing this information should be covered in the manual.

This section of the manual should also describe the standardization program. The organization, objectives, and procedures to be followed should all be discussed. There should be provision for having using agency representation and for obtaining industry input when developing standard specifications. However, industry representatives should not be members of specification committees if there is the slightest possibility of conflict of interest. If standardization committees are used, their composition, responsibilities and authorities should be clearly established. The manual should encourage and discuss the use of existing information to the maximum extent possible. Potential sources of information include all state and local governments, the federal government, technical societies and organizations, and industry specifications. A format for standard specifications should be developed and presented in the manual. Such a format is set out in the *Standard Specifications Preparation Manual* which was published by the Council of State Governments in 1966. Once developed and approved, standard specifications should be indexed and filed, and procedures established for periodic review and updating.

Inspection and Testing

The policies and procedures for receiving, inspecting, and testing of goods received sometimes are included in the purchasing manual; in other cases, they are presented in a separate manual. In any event, the policies, responsibilities, and procedures should be in writing and should be part of central purchasing's stewardship.

In some cases, purchasing personnel inspect goods

received. In other cases, this function is delegated to using agencies, or to the warehouse, if applicable. The responsibility for inspection and the inspection procedures to be used should be set forth in this section of the manual. Verifying quantities received, identifying damaged goods, checking items against specifications, and noting late deliveries are all part of the inspection process and should be discussed in this section. The documentation to be used during receipt and inspection (e.g., receiving reports, specifications) should be identified. Provision should also be made for sending pertinent documentation to purchasing. This includes completed receiving reports, reports on damage, noncompliance with specifications, and other complaints. Copies of complaint and damage reports should be contained and described in the manual. As previously mentioned, purchasing should be responsible for contacting suppliers on any delivery problems and should maintain all pertinent documents and reports in the vendor file.

Central purchasing should develop a testing program, and the policies and procedures should be covered in the purchasing manual. The items to be tested, the nature of the tests, and available test facilities should be set forth. A valuable technique for this program is obtaining certificates of compliance or certified test results from suppliers. Procedures for this aspect of the program should also be covered. Some governments have test and inspection committees consisting of purchasing personnel, using agency personnel, and independent experts hired by the government. The committee develops and maintains a manual of procedures for testing various commodities. It also coordinates with the people who develop specifications and standard specifications. Where they are used, the committee's composition, objectives, duties, responsibilities, and authorities should all be defined in the purchasing manual.

DISPOSITION

The disposition of surplus and scrap is an integral part of the acquisition program and inventory management. Central purchasing's responsibilities for overall supervision over both the inventory and surplus programs should be covered in this section of the manual. The locations and functions of stores and warehouses should be described. Procedures governing inventory procedures should address the following topics:

• Quantities and Ordering Schedule. The concept of "forward purchasing" depends in large part on good working relationships with using agencies. Knowing their constant and variable needs requires a set of procedures for gathering such information on a periodic basis. These procedures should include consolidated

ordering and term contracting. Order and delivery schedules should be keyed to the maintenance of a minimum inventory, which in turn depends on a knowledge of using agency needs.

• Issue Procedures. Normally accomplished via standard requisitions, these procedures should include provision for screening requisitions against standard stores as they come into purchasing.

• Accounting and Billing. Procedures for accounting and billing of withdrawals can be tied in with purchasing's normal accounting of purchases from other sources, but should also be cross-indexed with stock records.

• Maintenance of Stock Records. Adequate recordkeeping of inventory is necessary to ensure that minimum but adequate stock is on hand at all times. Accounting and billing records, ordering and delivery records, and quantity levels all form part of this activity.

• Replenishment. Replenishment of items to maintain controlled inventory levels will be accomplished through the above procedures.

The purchasing manual should describe the procedures for identifying and reporting surplus items and scrap. Using agencies are a key to a successful disposition program. One way to enlist their support is to credit using agencies with the proceeds from disposition. Central purchasing, too, should review using agency inventory levels for excess stocks. Central purchasing should be responsible for determining the best disposition method. The manual should discuss the various methods (i.e., transfer, trade-in, sale). Want lists are an effective technique in the disposition program, and the procedures for using these lists should be described.

State statutes should make central purchasing responsible for keeping informed of items available under federal surplus programs, and give it the authority to operate programs related to federal surplus programs. This section of the manual should describe the activities and procedures for the federal surplus programs.

COOPERATIVE PURCHASING

The policies, requirements, and procedures governing cooperative purchasing arrangements should be set forth in the purchasing manual. This information is pertinent not only to the central purchasing unit, but also to participants in the cooperative purchasing program. Provision should be made for communicating to interested governmental units the items which can be purchased under the program. This may be accomplished by providing lists of contracts or copies of the contracts themselves. Surveys, questionnaires, seminars, and regular meetings can all be useful techniques in promoting and developing successful cooperative purchasing programs. Policies and procedures for these techniques should be presented in the manual.

Statutory requirements pertinent to the program should be set forth. The details on ordering from established contracts, contractual commitments, and routing of pertinent documentation should also be covered.

UNIQUE REQUIREMENTS

In recognition of the unique requirements embodied in statutes or regulations other than those directly associated with the purchasing functions, this section provides room for the inclusion of procedures and instructions covering such requirements. Examples of topics which may be addressed here include:

• The treatment of environmental quality and natural resources requirements, both federal and state;

• Special handling requirements for such commodities as explosives, dangerous drugs, and other medical supplies;

• Special exemptions from normal procedures, such as purchases from institutions for the blind, prison enterprises, and other units of government.

APPENDICES

The types of appendices to be included in the purchasing manual will depend on the format and organization of the body of the manual and, perhaps, on local conditions. If extensive use is made of exhibits in the body of the manual, there may be little or no need for appendices. Regardless of the technique used, the following types of material should be included in the purchasing procedures manual:

• Purchasing statutes, rules, and regulations.

• Guidelines on procurement with federal funds, particularly Federal Management Circular 74-7, Attachment O.

• Forms and reports, including Invitation for Bids, purchase requisitions, purchase orders, supplier qualification forms, supplier evaluation reports, complaint reports, and receiving reports. It usually is better to include a completed sample form rather than a blank form. The completed form shows exactly the type of information required and how it should be presented.

• A glossary of terms.

EXHIBIT 1

STATEMENT OF AIMS AND OBJECTIVES
EXCERPTED FROM THE CALIFORNIA OFFICE
OF PROCUREMENT PROCEDURES MANUAL

Aims and Objectives

The aims and objectives of the Office of Procurement, Department of General Services, are:

1. To buy the right material of the right quality in the proper quantity at the right time from the proper source.

2. To conserve public funds through reduction in cost and improvement in the quality of materials purchased.

3. To reduce the overhead cost of buying.

4. To reduce the volume and streamline the flow of paper work.

5. To promote a system of material simplification and standardization throughout the State in order that better materials at minimum cost may be secured for all agencies.

6. To improve the speed of delivery to agencies by predetermining through contracts or other appropriate means the sources of supply before an actual need for the particular material in question becomes known.

7. To bring the sources of supply as geographically close to the point of use of materials as is consistent with economical purchasing through contracts or other means. In short, to decentralize the sources of supply if decentralization does not command a price premium.

EXHIBIT 2

**STATEMENT OF AIMS AND OBJECTIVES
EXCERPTED FROM THE KENTUCKY DIVISION
OF PURCHASES PROCEDURES MANUAL**

Chapters 42, 45, and 57 of the Kentucky Revised Statutes govern the purchase of property and services for the various State agencies. In adopting the regulations on purchasing transactions, the Division of Purchases sought to establish practicable, efficient purchasing procedures based on statutory provisions so as to obtain:

1. The most value for each dollar spent by the State.

2. Prompt deliveries to the State.

3. Uniform enforcement of contractual obligations for all persons or firms having State contracts.

4. Interest in bidding by all responsible vendors who can furnish property and services meeting State specifications.

5. Fair and open competition among bidders.

6. Full opportunity for all bidders to compete for State business on an equal basis.

7. An understanding by State officials of State government's procurement policies and procedures.

8. An understanding by all bidders of State government's procurement policies and procedures.

9. An understanding by all interested persons of the basis for awarding any particular type of State contract.

EXHIBIT 3

THE PURCHASING PRACTICES CODE OF
ETHICS OF THE MICHIGAN PURCHASING DIVISION

Principles and Standards of Purchasing Practice

advocated by the

National Association of Purchasing Managers

Loyalty To His Company
Justice To Those With Whom He Deals
Faith In His Profession

From these principles are derived the N.A.P.M. standards of purchasing practice:

(1) To consider, first, the interests of his company in all transactions and to carry out and believe in its established policies.

(2) To be receptive to competent counsel from his colleagues and to be guided by such counsel without impairing the dignity and responsibility of his office.

(3) To buy without prejudice, seeking to obtain the maximum ultimate value for each dollar of expenditure.

(4) To strive consistently for knowledge of the materials and processes of manufacture, and to establish practical methods for the conduct of his office.

(5) To subscribe to and work for honesty and truth in buying and selling, and to denounce all forms and manifestations of commercial bribery.

(6) To accord a prompt and courteous reception, so far as conditions will permit, to all who call on a legitimate business mission.

(7) To respect his obligations and to require that obligations to him and to his concern be respected, consistent with good business practice.

(8) To avoid sharp practice.

(9) To counsel and assist fellow purchasing agents in the performance of their duties, whenever occasion permits.

(10) To cooperate with all organizations and individuals engaged in activities designed to enhance the development and standing of purchasing.

We Subscribe to These Standards

EXHIBIT 4

PURCHASING PRACTICES FORBIDDEN BY
THE MINNESOTA DIVISION OF PROCUREMENT

Practices Forbidden

No employee of the Division of Procurement shall be financially interested, or have any personal beneficial interest, directly or indirectly in any contract or purchase order for supplies, materials, equipment, or utility services used by or furnished to any department or agency of the state government; nor shall any employee accept or receive directly or indirectly from any person, firm or corporation to whom any contract or purchase order may be awarded, by rebate, gift or otherwise, any money or anything of value, or any promise, obligation or contract for future reward or compensation. A violation of this policy is a felony according to Law. Inexpensive advertising items, bearing the name of the firm, such as pens, pencils, paper weights, calendars, etc., are not considered articles of value or gifts in relation to this policy.

The following practices are also specifically forbidden:

1. Using information available to an employee solely because of his state position for personal profit, gain or advantage.

2. Directly or indirectly furnishing estimating services, or any other services or information not available to all prospective bidders, to any person bidding on, or who may reasonably be expected to bid on, a contract with the Department.

3. Providing confidential information to persons to whom issuance of such information has not been authorized.

4. Providing, or using, the names of persons from records of the department for a mailing list that has not been authorized.

5. Accepting, taking or converting to one's own use products of any kind in the course of or as the result of inspections of such products or the facilities of the owner or possessor.

6. Using a position or status in the department to solicit, directly or indirectly, business of any kind or to purchase supplies or equipment at special discounts or upon special concessions for private use from any person who sells or solicits sales to the state.

7. Serving, either as an officer, employee, member of the board of directors, or in any capacity for consideration, the interests of any organization which transacts or attempts to transact business with the State for profit when such employee holds a state position of review or control—even though remote—over such business transactions.

EXHIBIT 5

INSTRUCTIONS FOR TERM CONTRACTING EXCERPTED FROM
THE VIRGINIA MANUAL OF CENTRAL PURCHASING

Contracting, or forward buying for delivery as needed, offers the advantage of quantity price while spreading deliveries over a specified period of time. Price advantage is thus secured without over-burdening the capacity of storerooms, and there usually is an additional advantage of fresher stock by reason of the turnover of the supplier's inventory.

At times a contract price may not be as low as that available to an agency on a spot purchase, e.g., when a vendor is overstocked or under distress conditions, but "requirements" contracts usually are justified because they assure reliable sources of supply.

Always reduce term, sometimes called "open end," contracts to writing. They bind both buyer and seller. No verbal modifications are binding. In the written contract include all terms, conditions, and requirements applicable. Define clearly and specifically quantity, specifications, price, terms of payment, time, special conditions, inspections, guaranties, and deliveries of goods. In preparing contracts the following points are fundamental:

(a) Only contractual requirements specifically set forth or referred to above the signature are binding.
(b) Any additions or revisions to the original text of the contract must be signed by both parties.
(c) Include all necessary provisions in the contract. It represents the entire agreement between the two parties.
(d) Printed material in the body of the contract and above the signature, regardless of the size of the type, is binding.
(e) Make every clause of the contract susceptible to only one interpretation, thus avoiding misunderstanding.
(f) Clauses involving penalties and liquidated damages usually require legal advice. If there is any question as to the legality or interpretation of a proposed contract, submit it through channels to the Attorney General for opinion before signature.
(g) A contract for labor and materials, where the major portion of the contract is for labor or services, is construed as a contractual service within the interpretation of Section 2-260 of the 1950 Code of Virginia and procurement through the Department of Purchases and Supply is not mandatory. The Department, however, will function as agency's agent upon request. (Special law regarding public advertisement applies to capital improvement contracts. See Code Sections *11-17*)

Quantity may be expressed in either of the following forms:

1. Definite total quantity in tons, pounds, gallons, feet, or other units.
2. Buyer's requirements during the contract period.
3. Buyer's requirements during contract period not to exceed _____.
4. Estimated requirements (usually interpreted as 10 percent under to 10 percent over estimates).

Sometimes it is desirable to stipulate that the supplier shall maintain a specified minimum stock on hand to supply the needs of the State. Quantity also may be expressed as a maximum and a minimum. From the Commonwealth's viewpoint, the more latitude allowed on quantity the better the contract.

18. Purchasing Manuals: Vendors Manual

A vendors manual should provide guidance and instruction to prospective vendors. It should offer every vendor a fair chance in competing for business by providing the information needed to:

- Qualify for the bidders list;
- Respond properly to Invitations for Bids;
- Meet contractual requirements; and
- Conform to state and local laws, purchasing policies, and other standards of good purchasing.

In addition to providing information on government policies and requirements (as is common in texts on "How to Do Business with the State of . . ."), the manual should also advise vendors of what they are permitted, or even encouraged, to do to solicit business. Thus, a good vendors manual recognizes the essential partnership arrangement which exists between the state or local government as buyer and the vendor as seller, and which attributes rights and courtesies to each within an open, business framework.

There currently is a great disparity in the content, coverage, and size of vendors manuals. Their quality and treatment vary in similar fashion. Some are clear and simple, others far less so; and, noticeably, the tone and content range from a listing of punitive measures which may be taken against errant vendors to solicitations of vendors in a public relations manner calculated to encourage and stimulate them.

Vendors manuals reflect a wide spectrum of viewpoints about the material, the degree of detail, the treatment of the subject matter, and the tone of the instructional information. This chapter presents an expanded outline for a suggested manual, along with recommendations oriented toward providing guidelines to purchasing officials for preparing a vendors manual. The objective is to produce manuals which serve well the best interests of both the purchasing activities issuing them and the vendors for whom they are intended. The particular circumstances of volume of business, number of vendors, and many other considerations that vary from locality to locality require that each purchasing activity use appropriate selectivity and judgment in applying this outline and attendant recommendations to their own situation.

The central purchasing authority should prepare and publish the vendors manual. The requirement that it be maintained as a complete, accurate, and current document is inherent in this responsibility. As state and local government purchasing is becoming a more dynamic enterprise due to advances in the state-of-the-art, the need for monitoring revisions and updating is increasing.

ORGANIZATION OF THE MANUAL

Table of Contents

Purchasing officials must remember that vendors can choose to read or not read the manual; or some vendors may only skim through it for what specifically interests them. Many manuals, even some that are 20 or more pages long, do not have a table of contents. Obviously, a table of contents makes it easier to use a manual, and one which is appropriate to the volume of material presented should be included.

Introductory Material

A foreword inside the cover or flyleaf can set the tone for the entire manual. A vendor's reaction to a sentence or two in cryptic, bureaucratic (and sometimes autocratic) language which is unsigned differs greatly from his reaction to a well-written letter addressed to suppliers doing busines with the government. Some forewords are unsigned. Others consist of personal and sincere invitations to do business with the government, are signed by the chief executive, and state the purpose and objectives of the manual. Clearly, the former do not require periodic updating, but this can be disadvantageous; a built-in requirement for revision at the onset of a new chief executive's term has merit. Proper consideration of the foreword may help to establish a frame of mind and a climate in which the desired business relationships may thrive. The approach taken by the State of Tennessee in the foreword to its manual is shown in Figure 1.

FIGURE 1
SAMPLE FOREWORD

FOREWORD

The purpose of this guide is to inform prospective bidders of the procedures for selling to the State of Tennessee. To meet the State's expanding needs the Purchasing Division of the Department of General Services regularly purchases numerous types of commodities. To fulfill these needs in an efficient and cooperative manner, we encourage the bidders to follow these guidelines.

Prospective bidders should especially note the step-by-step procedures for submitting a bid and complying with bid requirements. These procedures include those required by State law and rules and regulations adopted by the State Board of

Standards. In addition to the procedural steps involved, related information concerning doing business with the State is provided.

We seek to achieve an effective procedural arrangement which will benefit both suppliers and the State of Tennessee. To accomplish this goal we invite all qualified suppliers to do business with the State. Therefore, this guide is presented to assist you in doing business with the State.

If you have any questions concerning procedures, please contact the Department of General Services, Purchasing Division, Nashville, Tennessee.

It is also good practice to include an introduction which provides visibility for at least the more important steps of the purchasing process. The narrative discussion can be supplemented with a flow chart of the process. The introduction can highlight or refer to major sections of the manual and their value to the vendor. This section could also indicate that while the manual is meant to explain the intricacies of the purchasing program, the best way to obtain a good understanding of the process is to visit the purchasing office.

Instructions to Vendors

The body of the manual should provide general information on standards of conduct and procedures for doing business with the government and should cover the specific subjects which affect the government-vendor relationship in the solicitation-award process. These subjects can be included in one section of the manual or separated into two sections as is done here. The remainder of this chapter discusses the subjects which should be included in the instructions to vendors. This is not meant to be the only outline, nor even an ideal model, because the needs of state and local governments vary too greatly. Rather, the outline should be viewed as a recommended guide to consider when preparing or revising a vendors manual.

GENERAL INSTRUCTIONS TO VENDORS

Statement of Aims

The chapter of this report which contains the purchasing procedures manual discusses the statement of aims and objectives of the purchasing activity. It is considered highly important that such a statement also be included in the vendors manual to provide a fundamental and sound framework upon which all of the policies and procedures enunciated throughout the manual are based.

A reference to these aims should be made in the introduction to the manual, thus directing readers to this section, which should contain a complete statement of aims. Exhibits concerning statements of aims are included at the end of Chapter 17.

Code of Ethics

A well-defined code of ethics for both purchasing personnel and vendors is essential. Consequently, the vendors manual should include the code promulgated by the purchasing authority so as to clearly delineate the relationship between purchasing personnel and vendor's representatives. In this way, all concerned will know the mode of behavior expected of them.

Prohibitions

The various practices that are prohibited by statute, regulation, or policy should be set forth in the manual. Among the subjects that may be covered are collusion and conspiracy; attempting to influence awards by offers of awards, giving gifts, and back-door selling; and the attendant penalties for such practices.

Selling Effectively

This section should include guidelines, suggestions, and hints which will assist vendors in doing a more successful and effective job in competing for contracts. Each state or local government's purchasing activity will apply its own judgments and preferences to this section regarding its importance and the particulars to be included. Figure 2 is an example from the manual published by the State of Illinois.

FIGURE 2*
SAMPLE SELECTION ON SELLING

How Can You Sell to the State Most Effectively?

There is no substitute for a personal call at the offices of buyers to find out which of the many state agencies may need your product. The buyers at these offices can advise you on where and to whom to show your products. By acquainting us with your products, you can be sure of an opportunity to quote in future bidding for the type of products you offer.

If you do not reply to several consecutive bid invitations, you may be removed from our bid lists.

Make your sales investment wisely. Sometimes a seller will expend considerable time and money in presenting his product to an individual state agency in the hope of making a sale. If you do this, remember that the purchase will eventually be made by competitive bid and what you spend for expensive designs, demonstrations, layouts, etc. does not guarantee you an order.

Agency-prepared specifications are carefully reviewed to weed out undue restrictions and other limitations, which unnecessarily reduce competition. The purchase will eventually be made from the lowest responsible bidder meeting these objective specifications. The help you gave the state agency in developing its purchase request cannot be considered when we make the purchase. We recommend, if you are called upon to provide expensive pre-purchase service, that (1) you consider contracting separately with the agency for this service, and (2) that you always ask the agency you assisted, to list you as a "reference vendor" on their requisition so we can send you a bid invitation.

---

*State of Illinois, Department of General Services, "Selling to the State of Illinois," issued July 1, 1972.

SPECIFIC INSTRUCTIONS TO VENDORS

This section of the manual should highlight the specific requirements associated with doing business with the state or local government. These requirements are summarized here under the headings:

- Bidders List
- Solicitation of Bids
- Preparation and Submission of Bids
- Receipt and Opening of Bids
- Awarding of Contracts
- Performance under Contracts.

This part of the manual will be of greatest initial interest to potential vendors. It should, therefore, present a comprehensive, clear, and concise statement of policies, procedures, and practices in each subject area.

Bidders List

This section should explain the process by which vendors may apply for inclusion on the bidders list. Application procedures and the prequalification process should be described. The application and/or prequalification forms should be appended to this section. There should also be some discussion of the structure of the bidders list including, if practicable, the commodity code breakdown. The policies related to conditions or circumstances under which vendors may be removed from the bidders list should be covered thoroughly. Provision should be made for written notice of removal, appeal by the vendor, and reinstatement.

Solicitation of Bids

The solicitation process should be explained to assure that vendors understand the system. This section should cover the following points:

- The requirements for competitive bidding;
- Waivers of competitive bidding (e.g., emergency purchases, purchases from imprest funds), as applicable;
- The requirement for sealed bids;
- Procedures for obtaining competition when formal sealed bids are not required;
- Policies (and any authorized exceptions to policy) for soliciting all vendors on the bidders list; and
- Requirements for public notice.

In addition, this section can cover general subjects and procedures, such as where bid forms may be obtained and methods of soliciting bids (i.e., mail, telegram, and telephone). A copy of the IFB form(s) used should be included in the manual. Supplementary narrative can discuss the major elements of IFBs and highlight some of the more important features.

Preparation and Submission of Bids

Potential vendors must understand that the government will award contracts only to responsible bidders who submit responsive bids which are most advantageous to the government. Specific directions on preparing and submitting bids should emphasize the importance of adhering to the following policies and procedures:

- Submission of a bid constitutes an offer to enter into a contract with the government and is binding.
- Capability to meet specifications must be demonstrated.
- Agreement on terms and conditions must be expressed.
- Unless otherwise specified in the IFB, items offered must be new and current.
- Designated formats which must be used for submission of bids (forms, special envelopes, etc.) along with identification and signature requirements must be described.
- Compliance with bid security requirements and/or surety company coverage must be evident, as required.

This section should also provide vendors with a clear and complete explanation of the rules regarding such issues as:

- Policies regarding the submission of changes or amendments to bids;
- Procedures for withdrawing bids;
- Procedures regarding late bids;
- Time options for government acceptance of bid prices or other terms and conditions; and
- If acceptable, conditions for submitting bids on an "all or none" basis.

The objective should be to provide vendors with the information that they require to prepare and submit responsive bids and, importantly, to present this information in a clear, simple, easily understood manner which encourages suppliers to participate with the state or local government in a mutually rewarding business relationship.

Receipt and Opening of Bids

While the policies and procedures for controlling bids need to be precisely delineated in purchasing manuals, such policies and procedures should be included in the vendors manual. In this way, vendors may be assured that there is a system for providing fair and equitable treatment to all.

The following points should be covered in this section:

- Procedures for recording and controlling incoming bids;
- Policies for safeguarding confidential or proprie-

tary information, such as trade secrets, formulas, or test data;

• Procedures for the opening of bids, and the right of bidders and the general public to be present;

• Procedures for tabulating bids, and advice that these are public records that are kept by the purchasing activity for a specified number of years; and

• Information concerning the availability of bid files as public records.

Including details such as these helps to ensure the integrity of the system and to assure vendors that such integrity, objectivity, and absence of favoritism are characteristic of the government purchasing activity with whom they wish to do business.

Awarding of Contracts

Vendors should be advised of the policies, procedures, and methodology used by the government in evaluating their bids and the rationale for award. The following list of subjects can serve as a checklist in preparing this section:

• Procedures for evaluation and review following bid opening;

• Guidelines used in determining responsibility and responsiveness to specifications, terms, and conditions of the IFB;

• Definition of the "lowest responsible bidder who submits a responsive bid which is most advantageous to the government";

• Delineation of persons authorized to make awards, their obligation to use judgment, and the structured framework of factors to be considered in exercising judgments during the evaluation;

• Provisions for making multiple awards;

• Specific policies governing consideration of discounts and the types of taxes which should be excluded from the bid prices because the government is exempt;

• Procedures or alternatives when identical bids are received;

• Policies governing the right to reject any or all bids in whole or in part;

• Procedures covering consideration of mistakes or errors in bids and procedures for modifying or correcting bids;

• Policies concerning consideration of alternate bids;

• Policies and procedures for establishing and maintaining public records of the evaluation of bids and the awards of all contracts, and for the timely provision of such information to concerned vendors both during evaluation and subsequent to award, as appropriate; and

• Policies and procedures governing appeals and/or administration of disputes arising out of awards.

While some of the information, policies, and guidance listed above may be included on each IFB and in the individual specifications, terms, and conditions of IFBs, it is recommended that these subjects be detailed in the vendors manual. This will provide a valuable reference in one document and will contribute to greater professionalism in the relationship between public purchasing and a more knowledgeable vendor public.

Performance under Contracts

The relationships among the purchasing activity, the using agency, and the vendor become more closely integrated after contract award. The vendors manual should cover the general and specific performance requirements of vendors in providing goods and services to the government.

Among the items that should be included in this section are:

• Policies governing performance bonds, amounts of bonds, surety requirements, and other aspects related to such bonds;

• Policies governing conformance and compliance with delivery schedules, places of delivery, freight charges and payments, degree of vendor responsibility, packaging and creating, and other such considerations;

• Policies governing assignments of contracts or purchase orders by successful bidders, subcontracting, and other related matters;

• Policies and procedures governing cancellation or termination of contracts, the actions necessary to obtain compensation for damages, and the additional costs to the government resulting from cancellation or termination of contracts;

• Policies and procedures concerning appeal procedures and/or administrative reviews available to vendors when cancellations of contracts are anticipated or executed; and

• Policies governing status of vendors and eligibility for future contracts, etc., as a result of contract cancellations.

This section should also discuss the policies, procedures, and forms related to processing and payment of vendor invoices. Information should be provided to vendors concerning where and when to bill, the average payment cycle, and conditions and circumstances for partial payment.

APPENDICES

Those governmental forms that affect vendors, such as applications, IFBs, and purchase orders, should be included in the manual, and can be placed in an appendix. The purchasing statute can also be included so that vendors can see the basic law on which policies are based. Within the text of the manual, appropriate references can be made to the statute. As a further means of assisting vendors, it is suggested that a listing of agencies served by purchasing be included as a separate appendix. An index of commodities and/or services commonly required and purchased should be included or, alternatively, a separate manual or booklet may be preferred when the list is lengthy or when it needs frequent revision.

Appendix A

Profile of State Government
Purchasing and Contracting

PROFILE OF STATE GOVERNMENT
PURCHASING AND CONTRACTING

(As of March 1973)

Purchasing	Alabama	Alaska	Arizona
A. Organization			
1. Organizational placement of purchasing	Dept. of Fin.	Dept. of Admin.	Dept. of Fin.
2. Total cost of purchasing operations, FY 72	$235,636	$429,000	$173,676
3. Dollar value of contracts awarded by purchasing department, FY 72	$48,000,000	$51,000,000	$14,608,036
4. Number of budget positions in purchasing dept.:			
Administrative	2	3	1
Buyers	7	11	8
Standards engineers	0	0	0
Inspectors	0	0	0
Other	2	0	6
Total	11	14	15
5. Basis for selecting state purchasing official	Civil service	Commissioner, Dept. of Admin.	Civil service
6. Basis for determining purchasing official's term of office	Merit system	Discretion of appointor	Merit system
7. Are experience and/or educational qualifications required of the purchasing official?	Yes (a)	No	Yes
8. Basis for hiring the professional staff	Civil service	Civil service	Civil service
9. Number of years management & prof. staff served in respective positions:			
State purchasing official	12	3	5
Assistant purchasing official	12	10	0
Professional staff (avg. years)	8	7	4
10. Is there bonding coverage for purchasing personnel?			
Officials	Yes	Yes	Yes
Employees	No	Yes	Yes
B. Specifications			
11. Is there a standardization/specification committee?	No	No	Yes
12. How is standardization/specification committee membership determined?	N/A	N/A	Dir. of Purch.
13. What other bodies prepare specifications?	Using agencies	Buyers	Purch. Dept.
14. Is the use of brand or trade names permitted?	Yes (a)	Yes	Yes (a)
C. Management of bidders list			
15. Must bidders meet prequalification requirements to be included on the bidders list?	No	Yes (a)	Yes (a)
16. Does the State have a procedure for suspending vendors from selling to the State?	No	Yes	Yes
D. Bidding and contract award			
17. Competitive bidding requirements:			
Informal	N/C	>$100–<$1,000	N/C
Formal	>$500	>$1,000	>$1,000
18. Advertising (legal notice) required when purchase exceeds:	$500	$1,000	Not required
19. Is there a procedure for breaking tie bids?	Yes	Yes	Yes
20. Are late bids considered in making awards?	If transmitted prior to bid opening (a)	If transmitted prior to bid opening	No
21. Is the purchasing dept. authorized to act in any manner to discourage collusive bidding practices?	No	Yes (a)	Yes
22. Is there a procedure to be followed if none of the bidders bid to specifications?	Yes (a)	Yes	Yes
23. Is there provision for in-state preference?	Q/P	5%	5% for supplies & materials only
24. Are bid openings open to the public?	Yes	Yes	Yes
25. Bid bond requirements	Discretionary	Discretionary	Discretionary
26. Performance bond requirements	Discretionary	Discretionary	Discretionary

N/A = Not applicable.
N/C = Not covered.
(a) = Unwritten.
(b) = State verification response not received.
(c) = Incomplete data—unverified.

> = More than.
< = Less than.
≧ = Equal to or more than.
≦ = Equal to or less than.
Q/P = No loss of quality or price.

Arkansas	California	Colorado	Connecticut	Delaware
Dept. of Fin. & Admin.	Dept. of Gen. Serv.	Dept. of Admin.	Dept. of Fin.	Dept. of Adm. Serv.
$182,453	$1,307,000	$182,000	$419,000	$70,600
$30,000,000	$182,696,000	$36,000,000	$56,000,000	Not available
4	5	2	2	1
4	31	6	8	4
2	12	0	3	0
2	0	0	2	0
5	0	0	8	2
17	48	8	23	7
Dir., Dept. of Fin. & Admin.	Governor	Civil service	Civil service	Civil service
Discretion of appointor	Discretion of appointor	Merit system	Merit system	Merit system
Yes	No	Yes	Yes	Yes
Dir. of Purch.	Civil service	Civil service	Civil service	Civil service
1	Vacant	<1	10	3
5	5	3	10	Not available
2	12	10	14	4
Yes	No	Yes	No	Yes
Yes	No	Yes	No	Yes
No	Yes	Yes (inactive)	Yes	No
N/A	Dir. of Purch.	Dir. of Purch.	Governor	N/A
Using agencies & Purch. Dept.	N/C	Buyers using agencies and Purch. Dept.	N/C	Using agencies, buyers and Purch. Dept. (a)
Yes	Yes	Yes	Yes	Yes
Yes	Yes	Yes	Discretionary	Discretionary
Yes	Yes	Yes	Yes	No
≧$250–<$500	N/C	$50–$200	≦$2,000	N/C
≧$500	≧$1,000	>$200	>$2,000	>$2,000—Material; >$5,000—Service
$500	Not required	Not required	$2,000	$5,000
Yes	Yes	Yes	Yes	Yes
No	No	No	No	No
Yes	Yes	No	Yes	Yes
Yes	Yes	Yes	Yes (a)	Yes
5%	Q/P	No	Q/P	No
Yes	Yes	Yes	Yes	Yes
Discretionary	Discretionary	Discretionary	Discretionary	Mandatory >$2,000
Mandatory ≧$3,000	Discretionary	Discretionary	Discretionary	Mandatory >$2,000

PROFILE OF STATE GOVERNMENT
PURCHASING AND CONTRACTING
(As of March 1973)

Purchasing	Florida	Georgia	Hawaii
A. Organization			
1. Organizational placement of purchasing	Dept. of Gen. Serv.	Dept. of Adm. Serv.	Dept. of Acctg. & Gen. Serv.
2. Total cost of purchasing operations, FY 72	$570,000	Not available	$135,000
3. Dollar value of contracts awarded by purchasing department, FY 72	$45,650,100	Not available	$11,000,000
4. Number of budget positions in purchasing dept.:			
Administrative	10	4	2
Buyers	17	7	5
Standards engineers	1	6	2
Inspectors	0	0	0
Other	0	0	4
Total	28	17	13
5. Basis for selecting state purchasing official	Governor & 6 bd. members	Governor	Civil service
6. Basis for determining purchasing official's term of office	Discretion of appointor	Discretion of appointor	Merit system
7. Are experience and/or educational qualifications required of the purchasing official?	Yes (a)	No	Yes
8. Basis for hiring the professional staff	Civil service	Civil service	Civil service
9. Number of years management & prof. staff served in respective positions:			
State purchasing official	2	2	6
Assistant purchasing official	18	2	7
Professional staff (avg. years)	6	5	6
10. Is there bonding coverage for purchasing personnel?			
Officials	Yes	Yes	Yes
Employees	Yes	No	Yes
B. Specifications			
11. Is there a standardization/specification committee?	Yes	No	No
12. How is standardization/specification committee membership determined?	Dir. of Purch.	N/A	N/A
13. What other bodies prepare specifications?	N/C	Purch. Dept.	Purch. Dept. (a)
14. Is the use of brand or trade names permitted?	Yes	Yes (a)	Yes (a)
C. Management of bidders list			
15. Must bidders meet prequalification requirements to be included on the bidders list?	Yes (a)	Yes	Yes (a)
16. Does the State have a procedure for suspending vendors from selling to the State?	Yes	No	Yes
D. Bidding and contract award			
17. Competitive bidding requirements:			
Informal	N/C	$\leq$$1,000	>$4,000–<$8,000
Formal	>$1,000	>$1,000	$\geq$$8,000
18. Advertising (legal notice) required when purchase exceeds:	$2,000	$1,000	$4,000
19. Is there a procedure for breaking tie bids?	Yes	No	Yes (a)
20. Are late bids considered in making awards?	No	No	No
21. Is the purchasing dept. authorized to act in any manner to discourage collusive bidding practices?	Yes	No	Yes
22. Is there a procedure to be followed if none of the bidders bid to specifications?	Yes	No	Yes
23. Is there provision for in-state preference?	Q/P	Q/P	3%—Class I Products 5%—Class II Products 10%—Class III Products
24. Are bid openings open to the public?	Yes	Yes	Yes
25. Bid bond requirements	Discretionary	Discretionary	Mandatory >$8,000
26. Performance bond requirements	Discretionary	Discretionary	Mandatory >$8,000

N/A = Not applicable.
N/C = Not covered.
(a) = Unwritten.
(b) = State verification response not received.
(c) = Incomplete data—unverified.

$>$ = More than.
$<$ = Less than.
$\geq$ = Equal to or more than.
$\leq$ = Equal to or less than.
Q/P = No loss of quality or price.

Idaho	Illinois	Indiana (b)	Iowa	Kansas	Kentucky
State Purch. Agent	Dept. of Gen. Serv.		Dept. of Gen. Serv.	Dept. of Admin.	Dept. of Fin.
$113,000	$610,000		$160,000	$426,470	$631,000
$13,000,000	$85,000,000		$17,000,000	$78,340,410	$123,125,000
3	5		2	1	5
4	10		4	13	11
0	0		1	1	1
0	3		0	0	2
3	0		3	20	0
10	18		10	35	19
Governor	Civil service		Dir. of Gen. Serv.	Civil service	Commissioner, Dept. of Fin.
Discretion of appointor	Merit system		Discretion of appointor	Merit system	Discretion of appointor
No	Yes		No	Yes	Yes
Civil service	Civil service		Civil service	Civil service	Civil service
2	9		20	16	1
19	4		12	16	16
12	7		8	12	5
Yes	Yes		No	Yes	Yes
No	No		No	Yes	Yes
No	No		No	Specific commodities	Specific commodities
N/A	N/A		N/A	Dir. of Purch. and using agencies	Dir. of Purch.
Using agencies (a)	Purch. Dept.		Dir. of Gen. Serv. & Using Agencies	Purch. Dept. w/using agencies	Buyers and using agencies
Yes (a)	Yes		Yes (a)	Yes (a)	Yes
No	Yes		Yes	No	Yes
No	Yes		Yes	Yes	Yes
$100–$1,000	≦$1,500	≦$500	<$2,500	≦$1,000	≦$1,000—Repairs; ≦$500—Others
>$1,000	>$1,500	>$500	>$2,500	>$1,000	>$1,000—Repairs; >$500— Others
$1,000	$1,500		$15,000	$2,000	>$1,000—Repairs; >$500—Others
Yes (a)	Yes		Yes	Yes	Yes (a)
No	No		No	No	Yes—only if no other acceptable bids received
Yes	Yes		Yes	Yes	Yes
Yes (a)	Yes		Yes	Yes	Yes
Q/P	Q/P		Q/P	Reciprocal treatment	No
Yes	Yes		Yes	Yes	Yes
Mandatory	Discretionary		Mandatory	Mandatory >$1,000	Discretionary
Discretionary	Discretionary		Discretionary	Mandatory >$1,000	Discretionary

PROFILE OF STATE GOVERNMENT
PURCHASING AND CONTRACTING
(As of March 1973)

Purchasing	Louisiana	Maine	Maryland
A. Organization			
1. Organizational placement of purchasing	Div. of Admin.	Dept. of Fin. & Admin.	Dept. of Gen. Serv.
2. Total cost of purchasing operations, FY 72	$408,000	$172,000	$401,000
3. Dollar value of contracts awarded by purchasing department, FY 72	$75,000,000	$25,000,000	$56,548,000
4. Number of budget positions in purchasing dept.:			
Administrative	4	3	2
Buyers	13	6	12
Standards engineers	0	1	0
Inspectors	0	1	0
Other	49	7	0
Total	66	18	14
5. Basis for selecting state purchasing official	Civil service	Dir. of Admin.	Civil service
6. Basis for determining purchasing official's term of office	Merit system	Discretion of appointor	Merit system
7. Are experience and/or educational qualifications required of the purchasing official?	Yes	No	Yes (a)
8. Basis for hiring the professional staff	Civil service	Civil service	Civil service
9. Number of years management & prof. staff served in respective positions:			
State purchasing official	3	5	1
Assistant purchasing official	1	15	Vacant
Professional staff (avg. years)	7	14	4
10. Is there bonding coverage for purchasing personnel?			
Officials	Yes	No	Yes
Employees	Yes	No	Yes
B. Specifications			
11. Is there a standardization/specification committee?	No	Yes	No
12. How is standardization/specification committee membership determined?	N/A	Governor	N/A
13. What other bodies prepare specifications?	Using agencies	N/C	Buyers
14. Is the use of brand or trade names permitted?	Yes	Yes	Yes (a)
C. Management of bidders list			
15. Must bidders meet prequalification requirements to be included on the bidders list?	Yes	No	Yes
16. Does the State have a procedure for suspending vendors from selling to the State?	Yes	Yes	Yes
D. Bidding and contract award			
17. Competitive bidding requirements:			
Informal	$<$1,000	$\leqq$$7,500	"Competitive bidding" required $>$$100
Formal	$>$$1,000	$>$$7,500	
18. Advertising (legal notice) required when purchase exceeds:	$1,000	Not required	Not required
19. Is there a procedure for breaking tie bids?	Yes (a)	Yes	Yes
20. Are late bids considered in making awards?	No	No	No
21. Is the purchasing dept. authorized to act in any manner to discourage collusive bidding practices?	Yes	Yes	Yes (a)
22. Is there a procedure to be followed if none of the bidders bid to specifications?	Yes	No	Yes
23. Is there provision for in-state preference?	3%	Q/P	Q/P (a)
24. Are bid openings open to the public?	Only those under legal notice	Yes (a)	Yes
25. Bid bond requirements	Discretionary	Discretionary	Discretionary
26. Performance bond requirements	Discretionary	Discretionary	Discretionary

N/A = Not applicable.
N/C = Not covered.
(a) = Unwritten.
(b) = State verification response not received.
(c) = Incomplete data—unverified.

$>$ = More than.
$<$ = Less than.
$\geqq$ = Equal to or more than.
$\leqq$ = Equal to or less than.
Q/P = No loss of quality or price.

Massachusetts	Michigan	Minnesota	Mississippi	Missouri	Montana
Dept. of Admin.	Dept. of Admin.	Dept. of Admin.	Comm. on Budg. & Acctg.	Office of Admin.	Dept. of Admin.
$849,000	$631,000	$421,500	$44,000	Not available	$148,138
$64,097,000	$69,266,000	$65,000,000	Not available	$40,667,000	$20,000,000
2	2	2	Not available	3	2
6	16	12	Not available	7	5
2	3	1	Not available	0	1
2	0	1	Not available	3	0
79	4	35	Not available	2	7
91	25	51		15	15
Governor	Civil service	Civil service	Dir., Comm. on Budg. & Acctg.	Civil service	Dir. of Admin.
Discretion of appointor	Merit system	Merit system	Merit system	Merit system	Discretion of appointor
Yes (a)	Yes	Yes	No	Yes	Yes (a)
Competitive examination	Civil service	Civil service	Competitive examination	Civil service	Selected by state purch. official
13	6	14	2	3 Months	7
2	2	14	Not available	1 Month	5
20	4	6	Not available	7	4
Yes	Yes	No	No	Yes	Yes
No	Yes	No	No	No	Yes
No	Yes	No	No	Yes	No
N/A	Dir. of Purch.	N/A	N/A	Governor	N/A
Purch. Dept.	Using agencies	Purch. Dept. & using agencies	Using agencies (a)	Using agencies	Using agencies & buyers (a)
Yes (a)	Yes	Yes	N/C	No	Yes (a)
Yes (a)	Yes	Yes	No	Yes	Yes (a)
No	Yes (a)	Yes	No	Yes	Yes (a)
N/C	≦$2,000	≦$5,000	$500–$1,500	"Competitive bidding" required >$200	>$100–<$2,000
>$500	>$2,000	>$5,000	>$1,500		≧$2,000
$500	Not required	$500	$1,500	$10,000	$2,000
Yes	Yes (a)	Yes	No	Yes (a)	Yes (a)
No	No	No	No	Yes	No
Yes	Yes (a)	Yes	No	Yes	Yes
Yes (a)	Yes (a)	Yes	No	Yes	Yes
Q/P	Q/P	Reciprocal treatment	Q/P	Q/P	3%
Yes	Yes	Yes	Yes	Yes	Yes
Mandatory >$10,000 (a)	Discretionary	Mandatory >$2,000	Discretionary (a)	Discretionary	Discretionary
Mandatory >$10,000 (a)	Discretionary	Discretionary	Discretionary (a)	Discretionary	Discretionary

PROFILE OF STATE GOVERNMENT
PURCHASING AND CONTRACTING
(As of March 1973)

Purchasing	Nebraska	Nevada	New Hampshire
A. Organization			
1. Organizational placement of purchasing	Dept. of Adm. Serv.	Dept. of Adm. Serv.	Dept. of Admin.
2. Total cost of purchasing operations, FY 72	$93,000	Not available	$129,000
3. Dollar value of contracts awarded by purchasing department, FY 72	$14,461,000	$9,000,000	$15,000,000
4. Number of budget positions in purchasing dept.:			
Administrative	1	2	1
Buyers	5	3	4
Standards engineers	0	0	0
Inspectors	0	0	1
Other	0	0	0
Total	6	5	6
5. Basis for selecting state purchasing official	Dir. of Adm. Serv.	Governor	Comptroller and exec. officer of Dept. of Admin.
6. Basis for determining purchasing official's term of office	Discretion of appointor	Discretion of appointor	"Shall hold office during good behavior"
7. Are experience and/or educational qualifications required of the purchasing official?	Yes	Yes	Yes
8. Basis for hiring the professional staff	Selected by State Purch. Official	Civil service	Civil service
9. Number of years management & prof. staff served in respective positions:			
State purchasing official	1	1	16
Assistant purchasing official	8	6	0
Professional staff (avg. years)	5	3	10
10. Is there bonding coverage for purchasing personnel?			
Officials	Yes	Yes	No
Employees	Yes	No	No
B. Specifications			
11. Is there a standardization/specification committee?	Yes	No	No
12. How is standardization/specification committee membership determined?	Dir. of Purch.	N/A	N/A
13. What other bodies prepare specifications?	Using agencies & buyers	Purch. Dept.	Purch. Dept.
14. Is the use of brand or trade names permitted?	Yes	Yes	Yes
C. Management of bidders list			
15. Must bidders meet prequalification requirements to be included on the bidders list?	No	No	Yes
16. Does the State have a procedure for suspending vendors from selling to the State?	Yes (a)	Yes	Yes (a)
D. Bidding and contract award			
17. Competitive bidding requirements:			
Informal	$\geqq$$100–<$1,000	N/C	"Minor purchases"
Formal	$\geqq$$1,000	>$500	>$500
18. Advertising (legal notice) required when purchase exceeds:	$1,000	$500	Not required
19. Is there a procedure for breaking tie bids?	Yes (a)	Yes (a)	Yes
20. Are late bids considered in making awards?	No	No	No
21. Is the purchasing dept. authorized to act in any manner to discourage collusive bidding practices?	Yes (a)	Yes (a)	Yes (a)
22. Is there a procedure to be followed if none of the bidders bid to specifications?	Yes (a)	Yes (a)	Yes (a)
23. Is there provision for in-state preference?	Q/P	5% <$50,000 2½% $50,000–$500,000 1½% >$500,000	Q/P (a)
24. Are bid openings open to the public?	Yes	Yes	Yes (a)
25. Bid bond requirements	Discretionary	No	No
26. Performance bond requirements	Discretionary	Discretionary	No

N/A = Not applicable.	> = More than.
N/C = Not covered.	< = Less than.
(a) = Unwritten.	$\geqq$ = Equal to or more than.
(b) = State verification response not received.	$\leqq$ = Equal to or less than.
(c) = Incomplete data—unverified.	Q/P = No loss of quality or price.

New Jersey	New Mexico	New York	North Carolina	North Dakota	Ohio
Dept. of Treas.	Office of State Purch. Agent	Office of Gen. Serv.	Dept. of Admin.	Dept. of Accts. & Purch.	Dept. of Fin.
$1,192,776	$162,000	$1,513,000	$400,000	Not available	$312,000
$146,393,000	$18,000,000	$350,000,000	$155,000,000	$28,000,000	$60,000,000
3	2	8	2	1	3
20	3	48	22	5	4
7	0	17	6	0	4
5	0	8	3	0	3
38	4	64	4	0	15
73	9	145	37	6	29
Governor	Governor	Civil service	Sec'y. of Admin.	Cabinet official	Civil service
4 Years	Discretion of appointor	Merit system	Discretion of appointor	Discretion of appointor	Merit system
No	Yes (a)	Yes	Yes (a)	No	Yes
Civil service	Civil service	Civil service	Appointed by State Purch. Official	Selected by State Purch. Official	Appointed by State Purch. Director
2	2	29	3	12	8
18	1	18	14	1	2
15	4	9	9	7	4
Yes	Yes	No	No	Yes	Yes
Yes	Yes	No	No	No	No
Yes	Yes	Yes	Yes	No	No
Dir. of Purch. & using agencies (a)	Governor	Commissioner of Gen. Serv.	Governor	N/A	N/A
Buyers (a)	Using agencies	N/C	Buyers, using agencies & Purch. Dept.	Purch. Dept.	Using agencies
Yes (a)	Yes	Yes	Yes (a)	Yes (a)	Yes
Yes	Discretionary (a)	Yes (a)	Yes	Yes (a)	No
Yes	Yes	Yes	Yes	Yes (a)	Yes
≦$300	<$1,250	"Competitive bidding" required >$1,000	≦$2,000	Discretionary	N/C
>$300	≧$1,250		>$2,000	Discretionary	>$2,000
$2,500	$1,250	Not required	$2,500	Not required	2,000
Yes	Yes	Yes	Yes	No	Yes (a)
No	No	No	No	If transmitted prior to bid opening (a)	No
Yes	Yes	No	Yes	Yes (a)	Yes (a)
Yes	Yes	Yes (a)	Yes	Yes (a)	Yes (a)
No	5%	Q/P (a)	Q/P	Q/P (a)	No
Yes	Yes	Yes (a)	Yes	Yes (a)	Yes
Mandatory >$2,500	Discretionary	Discretionary	Discretionary	No (a)	Discretionary
Mandatory >$2,500	Discretionary	Discretionary	Discretionary	No (a)	Discretionary

PROFILE OF STATE GOVERNMENT
PURCHASING AND CONTRACTING
(As of March 1973)

Purchasing	Oklahoma	Oregon	Pennsylvania
A. Organization			
1. Organizational placement of purchasing	State Board of Public Affairs	Dept. of Gen. Serv.	Dept. of Prop. & Supplies
2. Total cost of purchasing operations, FY 72	$418,108	$612,000	$2,195,000
3. Dollar value of contracts awarded by purchasing department, FY 72	$150,000,000	$71,206,000	$141,651,000
4. Number of budget positions in purchasing dept.:			
Administrative	2	2	14
Buyers	12	10	23
Standards engineers	0	4	13
Inspectors	0	0	11
Other	25	0	9
Total	39	16	70
5. Basis for selecting state purchasing official	State Board of Public Affairs	Civil service	Governor
6. Basis for determining purchasing official's term of office	Discretion of appointor	Merit system	Discretion of appointor
7. Are experience and/or educational qualifications required of the purchasing official?	Yes	Yes (a)	Yes
8. Basis for hiring the professional staff	Merit system through competitive examination	Civil service	Civil service
9. Number of years management & prof. staff served in respective positions:			
State purchasing official	½	20	4
Assistant purchasing official	11	Vacant	5
Professional staff (avg. years)	10	5	7
10. Is there bonding coverage for purchasing personnel?			
Officials	Yes	Yes	Yes
Employees	Yes	Yes	Yes
B. Specifications			
11. Is there a standardization/specification committee?	No	Yes	Yes (a)
12. How is standardization/specification committee membership determined?	N/A	Dir. of Purch. (a)	Civil service
13. What other bodies prepare specifications?	Using agencies	Purch. Dept.	N/C
14. Is the use of brand or trade names permitted?	Yes	Yes	Yes
C. Management of bidders list			
15. Must bidders meet prequalification requirements to be included on the bidders list?	Yes	Yes (a)	Yes
16. Does the State have a procedure for suspending vendors from selling to the State?	Yes	Yes (a)	Yes
D. Bidding and contract award			
17. Competitive bidding requirements:			
Informal	N/C	$\leqq$$2,500	$50–$300
Formal	>$500	>$2,500	>$300
18. Advertising (legal notice) required when purchase exceeds:	Not required	$2,500	$1,000
19. Is there a procedure for breaking tie bids?	Yes	Yes	Yes
20. Are late bids considered in making awards?	No	No	No
21. Is the purchasing dept. authorized to act in any manner to discourage collusive bidding practices?	Yes	Yes (a)	No
22. Is there a procedure to be followed if none of the bidders bid to specifications?	Yes (a)	No	Yes
23. Is there provision for in-state preference?	Reciprocal treatment	5%	No
24. Are bid openings open to the public?	Yes (when requested)	Yes	Yes
25. Bid bond requirements	Discretionary	Discretionary	Mandatory
26. Performance bond requirements	Discretionary	Discretionary	Mandatory

N/A = Not applicable.		$>$ = More than.	
N/C = Not covered.		$<$ = Less than.	
(a) = Unwritten.		$\geqq$ = Equal to or more than.	
(b) = State verification response not received.		$\leqq$ = Equal to or less than.	
(c) = Incomplete data—unverified.		Q/P = No loss of quality or price.	

Rhode Island	South Carolina	South Dakota	Tennessee	Texas	Utah
Dept. of Admin.	Div. of Gen. Serv.	Dept. of Admin.	Dept. of Gen. Serv.	State Board of Control	Dept. of Fin.
$412,000	$152,000	$101,000	$435,000	$943,536	$134,000
$83,000,000	$35,000,000	$30,000,000	$120,000,000	$196,025,909	$28,808,000
3	2	1	3	6	2
7	6	4	14	17	5
3	Not available	0	3	3	0
2	Not available	0	2	2	1
25	Not available	0	0	19	6
40	5	0	22	47	14
Civil service	Budg. & Control Board	Commr., Dept. of Admin.	Commr., Dept. of Gen. Serv.	Official board	Dir. of Fin.
Merit system	Merit system	Merit system	Discretion of appointor	Discretion of appointor	Discretion of appointor
Yes	Yes	No	No	Yes	No
Civil service	Selected by head of State Purch.	At pleasure of State Purch. Director	Appointed by State Purch. Official	Hired by Asst. Dir. of Purch.	Civil service
4	1	2	1	2	7
2	1	0	1	4	24
15	4	5	1	10	10
Yes	No	Yes	Yes	Yes	Yes
Yes	No	Yes	Yes	Yes	Yes
Yes	No	Yes	No	Yes	Yes
Prescribed by law	N/A	Dir. of Purch.	N/A	Ass't. Dir. of Purch.	Prescribed by law
N/C	Using agencies (a)	Buyers & using agencies	Using agencies	Using agencies	Buyers & using agencies
Yes	Yes	No	Yes	Yes (a)	Yes
Yes	No	Yes	Yes	Yes (a)	No
Yes	Yes	Yes (a)	No	Yes	Yes
$100–$500	N/C	N/C	≦$200	≦$100	Discretionary
>$500	Always required	≧$1,500	>$200	>$100	>$1,000
Not required	$500	$1,500	Not required	Required only on all annual contracts	$1,000
Yes	Yes (a)	Yes (a)	Yes (a)	Yes	Yes
No	No	Yes (a)	No	No	No
Yes	Yes (a)	Yes	Yes	No	Yes
Yes	Yes (a)	Yes (a)	Yes	Yes	Yes
No	Q/P (a)	Q/P	No	No	Q/P
Yes	Yes	Yes	Yes (a)	Yes	Yes
Discretionary	No	Mandatory >$2,000	Discretionary	Discretionary	Mandatory
Discretionary	No	Mandatory >$2,000	Discretionary	Discretionary	Mandatory

PROFILE OF STATE GOVERNMENT
PURCHASING AND CONTRACTING
(As of March 1973)

Purchasing	Vermont	Virginia	Washington
A. Organization			
1. Organizational placement of purchasing	Dept. of Admin.	Dept. of Purch.	Dept. of Gen. Admin.
2. Total cost of purchasing operations, FY 72	$179,000	$570,000	$530,933
3. Dollar value of contracts awarded by purchasing department, FY 72	$35,000,000	$50,000,000	$43,746,000
4. Number of budget positions in purchasing dept.:			
Administrative	15	5	1
Buyers	5	11	8
Standards engineers	0	0	2
Inspectors	0	0	0
Other	0	2	7
Total	20	18	18
5. Basis for selecting state purchasing official	Governor or Sec'y. of Admin.	Governor	Dir. of Gen. Admin.
6. Basis for determining purchasing official's term of office	2 Years	Discretion of appointor	Discretion of appointor
7. Are experience and/or educational qualifications required of the purchasing official?	No	No	No
8. Basis for hiring the professional staff	Civil service	Selected by State Purch. Official	Civil service & competitive exam
9. Number of years management & prof. staff served in respective positions:			
State purchasing official	12	3	3
Assistant purchasing official	Not available	3	0
Professional staff (avg. years)	14	5	8
10. Is there bonding coverage for purchasing personnel?			
Officials	Yes	Yes	Yes
Employees	Yes	Yes	Yes
B. Specifications			
11. Is there a standardization/specification committee?	No	No	Yes
12. How is standardization/specification committee membership determined?	N/A	N/A	Purch. Advisory Comm.
13. What other bodies prepare specifications?	Buyers & using agencies	Advisory comm. (a)	Using agencies & Purch. Dept.
14. Is the use of brand or trade names permitted?	Yes	Yes	Yes
C. Management of bidders list			
15. Must bidders meet prequalification requirements to be included on the bidders list?	No	Yes	Discretionary
16. Does the State have a procedure for suspending vendors from selling to the State?	Yes (a)	No	Yes
D. Bidding and contract award			
17. Competitive bidding requirements:			
Informal	>$100	$100–$500	≦$500
Formal	>$2,000	>$500	>$500
18. Advertising (legal notice) required when purchase exceeds:	Not required	$500	Not required
19. Is there a procedure for breaking tie bids?	No	Yes (a)	Yes (a)
20. Are late bids considered in making awards?	No	No	No
21. Is the purchasing dept. authorized to act in any manner to discourage collusive bidding practices?	Yes (a)	No	Yes (a)
22. Is there a procedure to be followed if none of the bidders bid to specifications?	Yes (a)	Yes (a)	Yes (a)
23. Is there provision for in-state preference?	No	Q/P	No
24. Are bid openings open to the public?	Yes (if over $2,000) (a)	Yes	Yes
25. Bid bond requirements	Discretionary (a)	Discretionary	Discretionary
26. Performance bond requirements	Discretionary (a)	Discretionary	Discretionary

N/A = Not applicable.
N/C = Not covered.
(a) = Unwritten.
(b) = State verification response not received.
(c) = Incomplete data—unverified.

> = More than.
< = Less than.
≧ = Equal to or more than.
≦ = Equal to or less than.
Q/P = No loss of quality or price.

West Virginia	Wisconsin	Wyoming	Guam	Puerto Rico (c)	Virgin Islands
Dept. of Fin. & Admin.	Dept. of Admin.	Dept. of Admin.	Dept. of Admin.	Dept. of Treas.	Dept. of Prop. & Procurement
$232,000	$302,000	$54,000	$236,000		$210,000
$125,000,000	$99,557,000	$320,800	$7,000,000		$17,994,000
1	1	1	4		8
9	8	2	8		6
0	2	0	0		1
3	0	0	3		2
2	1	0	0		0
15	12	3	15		17
Civil service	Civil service	Dir. of Admin.	Civil service		Governor
Merit system	Merit system	Discretion of appointor	Merit system		Discretion of appointor
Yes	No	Yes (a)	No		Yes
Civil service	Civil service	Competitive examination	Competitive examination		Civil service
3	5	7	10		3
6	12	Vacant	7		11
4	6	7	4		7
Yes	Yes	Yes	No		Yes
Yes	No	Yes	No		Yes
Specific commodities	Specific commodities	No	Yes	Yes	Yes
N/C	Dir. of Purch.	N/A	Governor	Sec'y. of Treas.	Prescribed by law
Purch. Dept.	Purch. Dept.	Purch. Dept. (a)	Purch. Dept.		Purch. Dept.
Yes (a)	Yes (a)	Yes (a)	Yes		Yes
Yes	Discretionary (a)	Yes (a)	No	Yes	Yes
Yes	Yes	Yes (a)	Yes	Yes	No
≤$2,000	N/C	"Competitive bidding" required >$200	"Competitive bidding" >$2,500	≤$2,000	N/C
>$2,000	>$3,000			>$2,000	Always required
$2,000	$3,000	$2,500	$2,500		$1,000
Yes (a)	Yes	Yes (a)	Yes	Yes	Yes
No	No	Yes (a)	If transmitted prior to bid opening	No	If transmitted prior to bid opening (a)
Yes	Yes (a)	Yes (a)	Yes		Yes
Yes	Yes	Yes (a)	No		Yes (a)
Q/P	Q/P	5%	10%	Yes	15%
Yes	Yes	Yes	Yes		Yes
Discretionary	Discretionary	Mandatory	Mandatory	Discretionary	Discretionary
Discretionary	Discretionary	Discretionary	Mandatory		Discretionary

Appendix B

Cities and Counties

Cities and Counties

This appendix of the study addresses the nature of city and county purchasing and the attendant structure surrounding its operation. It also discusses the nature of safeguards and controls and the extent to which they are exercised through specified sources of authority or documented policy. A questionnaire was used for surveying all cities and counties having a population of 10,000 and over. (A copy of the questionnaire is included as Attachment 1.) In addition to their appearing here, the survey results are also being published in the International City Management Association's (ICMA) *Municipal Yearbook for Cities and Counties, 1974,* and its *Urban Data Services Report, July 1974.*

Tables B-1 and B-2 summarize the responses to the survey by population size, geographic region, form of government, and metropolitan status. The geographic regions are those used by the Bureau of the Census and are illustrated in Figure B-1. Of 2,290 cities surveyed,

1,169 (51 percent) responded; of 2,203 counties surveyed, 696 (32 percent) responded.

PURCHASING AUTHORITY

Public purchasing is a vital element of government operations. It touches vast sections of the marketplace in providing services and goods to public recipients. The dynamics of this interaction are further sensitized by the spending of public monies. The use of public monies generally requires full accountability which is subject to constant public scrutiny. Therefore, authority for carrying out the purchasing function is likely to be found in one or more governing sources. An objective of the survey in addressing this subject was to determine the impact of the specified sources of authority on local government purchasing and the degree of restrictiveness of such authority. Given certain broad

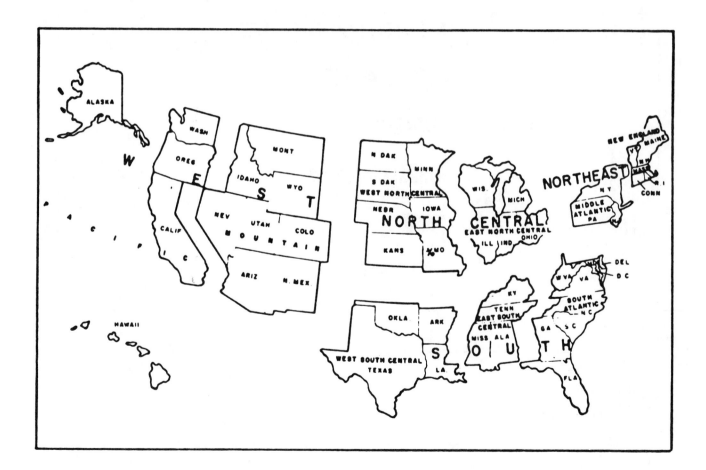

FIGURE B-1: GEOGRAPHIC REGIONS USED BY THE BUREAU OF THE CENSUS

sources of authority, a further objective was to determine the extent to which local ordinances governing purchasing have been adopted.

Respondents were asked to indicate the source of their authority to operate, i.e., state statute, charter, administrative code, local ordinance, legislative resolution, or administrative edict. Figure B-2 graphically illustrates the responses. Approximately 80 percent of the reporting counties and almost 60 percent of the cities indicated that state statutes are the dominant source from which they derive their purchasing authority. As anticipated, cities with a great deal of autonomy through home rule and similar legislation showed that the major source of their purchasing authority is in the charter, local ordinance, or administrative code. Approximately 90 percent of the cities and counties responding indicated that such sources of authority also apply to purchases made under federal and state grants. This demonstrates the recognition by local governments

that across-the-board consistency in the application of purchasing policies is needed for grant compliance and management.

More than 20 years ago the National Institute of Municipal Law Officers (NIMLO), in cooperation with the National Institute of Governmental Purchasing (NIGP), developed a Model Purchasing Ordinance to assist municipalities in efficiently running their purchasing programs. The purpose of the model was to provide a guide that could be used by local governments to adopt volume-buying practices by applying centralized purchasing techniques and related principles. The model ordinance deals with creating the office of purchasing agent, setting forth the powers and duties of the purchasing agent, establishing a committee on standardization and specifications, establishing and documenting purchasing procedures, and prescribing penalties for violating the provisions of the ordinance.

However, the survey results indicate that only 14

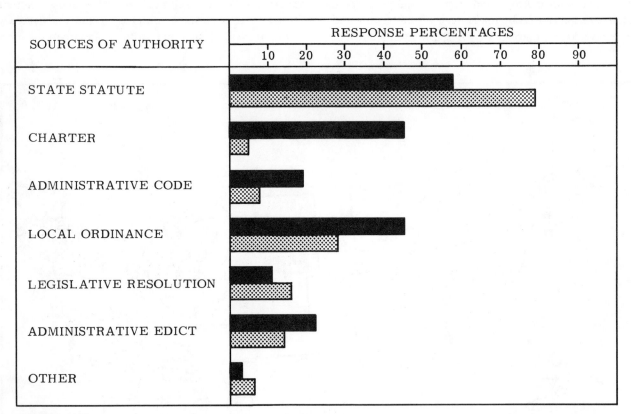

RESPONSE

■ CITIES - 1,139

▨ COUNTIES - 646

*Percentages, when totaled, exceed 100 percent because many respondents indicated more than one source.

FIGURE B-2: SOURCE OF PURCHASING AUTHORITY

percent of the counties and 21 percent of the cities have adopted any or all of the features of the NIMLO Model Purchasing Ordinance. This disuse may be attributed to insufficient communication between the purchasing community and local government management officials on one level, and between the management officials and the law-makers on another level. Survey correspondence indicated that many of the respondents were not even aware of the Model Purchasing Ordinance.

Similarly, the survey results indicate that cities (Table B-3) and counties (Table B-4) have been rather reluctant to adopt local purchasing ordinances or to modify existing ordinances to reflect current needs. Only 22 percent of the responding counties report that they have local ordinances governing purchasing. The impact of this figure is somewhat tempered because more than 51 percent of the counties with populations of 250,000 and over have adopted a local purchasing ordinance. This suggests that smaller counties are relying more on state statutes for direction. Cities have been a little more aggressive than counties in adopting purchasing ordinances. As shown in Table B-3, 55 percent of the responding cities have adopted local purchasing ordinances. A majority of respondents indicated that purchasing ordinances have been in effect since 1950. Several of the larger cities adopted ordinances as early as from 1900 to 1920; in fact, 50 percent of the largest cities fall in this category. One city reported that it adopted an ordinance in the late 1800s.

The data in Tables B-5 and B-6 show the authorities used to govern construction contracting. For 58 percent of the cities and 76 percent of the counties, the state statute governs construction contracting. As might be expected, the charter is also a significant source of construction contracting authority for the cities. Thirty-five percent of all cities reporting, and more than 60 percent of the cities with populations of 250,000 and over, use the charter. The use of a separate purchasing ordinance as a source of authority for construction contracting is limited (28 percent for the cities and 10 percent for the counties).

NATURE OF THE PURCHASING FUNCTION

To explore the nature of the purchasing function in local government, a series of questions was structured to discern the state-of-the-art with respect to the extent to which centralized purchasing is practiced, the types of cooperative purchasing permitted, and the scope of purchasing activities authorized.

Many public purchasing officials recognize that there are benefits to volume buying through centralized efforts. Centralization substantially reduces duplication of effort and, therefore, results in more efficient

and economical purchasing operations. As shown in Tables B-7 and B-8, 64 percent of the cities and 40 percent of the counties responding have central purchasing. Cities, even those with populations of 10,000 to 24,999, seem to be well entrenched in the concept of centralization. More than 90 percent of the counties with populations of 250,000 and over have central purchasing.

Tradition, circumstances, or alleged uniqueness are some of the reasons why many cities and counties legally exempt certain departments, agencies, or bureaus from central purchasing. Nearly 20 percent of the cities and more than 30 percent of the counties provide legal exemptions. These unwarranted exclusions tend to weaken the fiber of centralization and diminish the full benefits that might otherwise be obtainable. To the chief local government administrator or manager in search of efficiency and economy in purchasing, investigation here should prove fruitful.

The pooling of purchasing with neighboring jurisdictions is another way of multiplying the volume-buying leverage for local governments. When successfully combined with centralization, cooperative purchasing can become a significant resource to management. Evidence of the effectiveness of this resource dates back to the Cincinnati Plan developed in 1931. For purposes of this survey, cooperative purchasing means making purchases under contracts established by another governmental jurisdiction, establishing contracts under which other governmental jurisdictions may purchase, or combining requirements with another governmental jurisdiction under the same contract.

As shown in Tables B-9 and B-10, 85 percent of the cities reporting and 68 percent of the counties are permitted to engage in cooperative purchasing. However, smaller counties (50,000 and under) do not seem to utilize cooperative purchasing resources as vigorously as larger counties do (72 to 97 percent, respectively).

Suitable state laws seem to be the basic stimulus for many of the cooperative measures at the local level. Yet, in practice, the leadership in establishing effective cooperative programs seems to lie with the large cities and counties. While the data indicate that 67 percent of both the responding cities and counties may purchase cooperatively under state contracts, a large proportion interact with other cities and counties as well.

The functions provided by local governments are, by nature, service-oriented and responsive to the needs of the citizenry. The functions range from maintaining health, welfare, and education delivery programs to public protection programs; from supplying local utilities to enhancing the quality of life. To perform these functions, various activities must be carried out in the purchasing of needed goods and services. These activities are listed in Tables B-11 and B-12. Local governments were asked to indicate the approximate number and dollar volume of contracts awarded for selected purchasing activities for the latest fiscal year. The low number of responses in this area and their wide range of disparity precluded making any meaningful measures and interpretations of the data.

While authorized purchasing policies are usually delineated in the basic purchasing authority, and purchasing manuals communicate operating procedures, rules and regulations often are at an intermediate level. Eighty-two percent (926 of 1,126) of the cities and 79 percent of the counties (491 of 623) reported that they operate under purchasing rules and regulations which are legally binding.

ORGANIZATIONAL PATTERNS

The placement of the purchasing function within an administering organization often reflects the status relegated to local government purchasing and indicates which of two management styles, custodial (guardian) or participatory, is being practiced.

A custodial style tends to stress management rein-

forcement for purchasing. Adherents to this style maintain that purchasing can discharge its function more efficiently under another department, such as finance or administration. A participatory style establishes that purchasing be handled through a separate department with the autonomy to participate more fully in the procurement management process. The purchasing function in cities and counties may be located in any of several organizational units, which generally may be classified under the management styles indicated.

Figure B-3 depicts the various organizational structures through which the purchasing activity is handled. Approximately 60 percent of the city purchasing functions are a part of either the finance department or the administration department. Thirty-two percent of the responding counties handle purchasing on a decentralized basis; that is, each department does its own purchasing. Only 14 percent of both city and county respondents indicated that purchasing is handled through a separate purchasing department.

Local government purchasing, with its impact on the process of distributing public funds within the com-

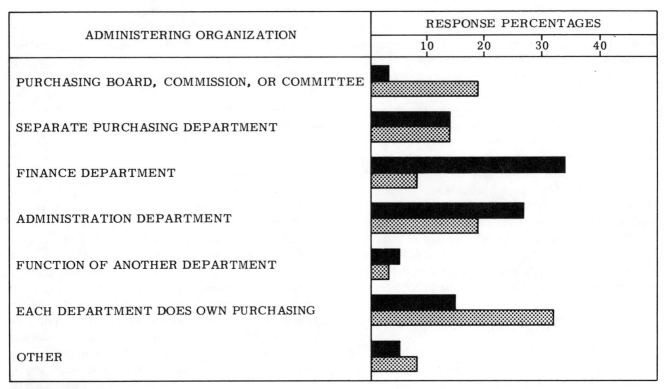

RESPONSE

■ CITIES - 1,135

▨ COUNTIES - 624

FIGURE B-3: ORGANIZATIONAL ENTITY RESPONSIBLE FOR PURCHASING

munity, has high economic visibility. Accordingly, it attracts the attention of legislators, elected officials, and municipal administrators. Certainly, one measure of the importance of purchasing is the office to which the purchasing officer directly reports.

The cities responding indicated that the purchasing officer generally reports directly to the manager or chief administrative officer, the finance director, and/or a legislative body (Table B-13). Since respondents could check all applicable officials or offices to which they reported, an indication of the influence shared by officials or offices is revealed in the pattern of multiple responses. More than 60 percent of the cities with populations of 50,000 and under have purchasing officers reporting to the legislative body or the chief executive. Forty-five percent of the responding counties indicated that the purchasing officer reports directly to the legislative body (Table B-14). This is particularly common in counties with populations of 10,000 to 49,999. In counties of 50,000 and over, the purchasing officer is most likely to report directly to the manager or chief administrative officer.

The data in Tables B-15 and B-16 indicate that only 37 percent of the responding cities and 22 percent of the responding counties have a full-time purchasing officer. However, more than 90 percent of the cities with populations of 100,000 and over and more than 90 percent of the counties of 250,000 and over have a full-time purchasing officer. But a considerable number of the cities and counties with populations under 100,000 do not have full-time purchasing officers.

The data in Table B-17 identify the official assigned to the purchasing function where no full-time purchasing officer exists and relate him to the administering organization through which purchasing functions. More than 65 percent of the cities responding indicated that the manager, chief administrative officer, or assistant manager is the official assigned to the purchasing function when purchasing is handled through part of the administration department. More than 50 percent of the counties indicated that the manager or chief administrative officer is the official assigned to the purchasing function when purchasing is handled through part of the administration department. Seventy-five percent of the counties and 60 percent of the cities reported that the department head is the official assigned to the purchasing function when each department does its own purchasing.

PURCHASING OPERATIONS AND MANAGEMENT

The character of purchasing operations and management becomes more visible if documented procedures exist, if an effective method of communication with using agencies exists, or if the purchasing system is integrated with the basic management functions of budgeting and accounting. When these are further evidenced by financial or performance audits, the level of confidence in the character of purchasing is significantly enhanced.

A manual of procedures may be among the most helpful tools available to aid purchasing managers in implementing and ensuring the continued existence of uniform purchasing practices. Yet the results of this survey, as shown in Tables B-18 and B-19, indicate that only 33 percent of the 1,139 reporting cities, and 14 percent of the 650 reporting counties, have prepared or issued purchasing manuals. The large cities (100,000 population and over) and large counties (500,000 population and over) are more likely to have purchasing manuals than are the smaller ones.

As shown in Tables B-20 and B-21, 59 percent of the cities and 44 percent of the counties reported that their purchasing systems regularly supply pricing information to using agencies. The type and extent of data furnished or the degree of formality of this process were not identified in the survey. As a general observation, it appeared that local governments did not have formal programs for accumulating pricing data as a means of input to the budget process. Historical data, as well as prospective pricing information, are valuable to budget formulation. Appropriate interaction with purchasing officials at this stage in planning is necessary to meaningful budgets.

During the authorization and execution process, the purchasing official, together with the budget official, may exert influence by applying internal checks and controls, such as comparing selected acquisition requests against available fund and item authorizations. Significant changes in operational information such as current inventory status and market conditions will (or should) necessitate a replanning and adjustment cycle in the budget process. The data in Tables B-22 and B-23 show that the purchasing system is substantially integrated with the budgeting process in both cities and counties. A purchasing system which is completely integrated with budgeting on all fronts strengthens the need for concomitant management information systems development.

Similarly, the accounting interface with purchasing is essentially concerned with accounting for availability of funds, commitment of requisitions, encumbrance and liquidation of orders, recognition of expenditures, processing of payments, and asset accounting and disposal of assets (including stores inventory and equipment). It was in this context that the concept of complete integration of accounting with purchasing was contemplated. The survey results indicate a strong degree of accounting integration with purchasing. These results were somewhat expected, since most local government legislatures exact some measure of statutory accountability and control in the initiation and disposition of purchasing transactions.

A total management information system involving effective procurement management would necessitate that purchasing be an integral subsystem which interacts with other subsystems such as budgeting, accounting, and inventory management. A concept of this system-subsystem interrelationship is illustrated in Figure B-4.

Local government officials often regard the audit as an opportunity to corroborate and attest to the character of their fiscal accountability and management performance. It is purchasing's job to translate the requests from authorities into firm fiscal commitments against which acquisitions are made. It is here, within purchasing, where most fiscal transactions are formally consummated, and this consummation point is where most audit examinations are directed. The need for audit as a control is evidenced by the concerns of the public and purchasing officials to adequately and fairly discharge the local government purchasing function. This was reflected in the survey results as shown in Tables B-24 and B-25. Of the 1,014 cities and 495 counties responding, 74 percent and 79 percent, respectively, indicated that the purchasing department is subject to audit. Both the cities and counties responding are more frequently subject to a financial audit than to a performance/management audit.

The authority by which purchasing departments are audited largely rests with state statutes. Fifty-one percent (383 of 752) of the cities and 81 percent (317 of 389) of the counties responding indicated that the state statute is the dominant authority. Other authority sources for cities are, local ordinances (23 percent), charters (32 percent), and administrative codes (14 percent). The sources of audit authority for a particular administering organization pattern are seen in Table B-26.

PERSONNEL PRACTICES AND SALARIES

The wave of public concern about purchasing is beginning to crest, causing public professional organizations, purchasing officials, top public officials, and academicians, to mention a few, to become more involved. Much of this concern is occasioned by the state of the economy and a deepening resistance to perennial tax increases. With existing personnel practices and salary remunerations in mind, the survey addressed hiring methods, minimum education and experience requirements, titles of purchasing officials, employee training programs, fidelity bonding policy, and salaries for purchasing officials.

Although salary data are quickly outdated by inflationary pressures, a survey of annual salary ranges (i.e., beginning and ending salaries) for selected classifications of purchasing personnel was considered vital to assessing the state-of-the-art. The survey data cover

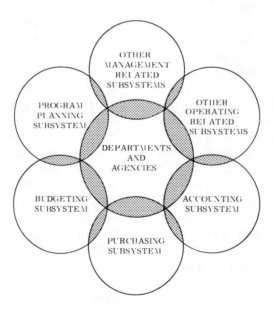

FIGURE B-4: CONCEPTUAL MANAGEMENT INFORMATION SYSTEM
WITH INTERFACING SUBSYSTEMS EMPHASIZING
PURCHASING MANAGEMENT

full-time purchasing positions for the latest available fiscal year, i.e., ideally, fiscal year 1973. Contained in Tables B-27 and B-28 are mean salary range values for such purchasing personnel.

There were relatively few responses to questions regarding the method of hiring, titles of purchasing officials, and minimum requirements of education and experience. However, a few general conclusions may be drawn as perhaps rough indications of current practices. The principal methods of hiring most purchasing officials are by civil service and appointment. According to the responses by 50 percent of the cities and counties, most purchasing officials are appointed for an indefinite term. This process may not attract the most competent purchasing officials. Under such arrangements (i.e., in the absence of suitable contractual coverage or other augmenting legislation), appointed purchasing officials may be more sensitive to political pressures. Moreover, they are more receptive to the problems caused by the lack of tenure. Tenure is frequently necessary to reinforce purchasing continuity within and between local government administrations. To a lesser degree, purchasing officials are hired by civil service. Nearly one third of the responding cities and counties use civil service examinations as a means of selecting purchasing officials.

The remaining respondents indicated that purchasing professionals are hired either by civil service without examinations, or by appointment for a specified term. Of the very few respondents indicating that hiring is done by appointment for a fixed term, the average term for all professionals is two to three years. Overall, counties seem to rely somewhat more heavily on a civil service examination for selecting purchasing professionals than do cities.

Responses to the question of title or name for the position were relatively low. A review of individual responses revealed such titles as: Commissioner, Director, Purchasing Agent, Clerk-Treasurer, Buyer, and so forth. The most commonly used titles were Purchasing Agent and Assistant Purchasing Agent.

TRAINING

The importance of training is evidenced by the fact that nearly 80 percent of the counties and over 90 percent of the cities responded to these questions. However, the survey responses show that only 13 percent of the cities and 9 percent of the counties have ongoing training programs. Tables B-29 and B-30 show that the most impact on professional training is attributable to cities and counties with populations of 250,000 and over. Most of the training which is available to professional purchasing staff members (over 60 percent) is provided by the purchasing departments

themselves. The responses in this area suggest that the in-house training is primarily on-the-job training.

Traditionally, the public has caused to be legislated or demanded the institution of certain protective devices that minimize improprieties which may be initiated by public officials. Eighty-three percent of all respondents reported that they use fidelity and surety bonds or position bonds to cover purchasing officials. Other employees with purchasing authority are bonded in 71 percent of the responding cities and 65 percent of the counties.

Public purchasing management and operations appear to be severely stressed if the reported data are representative of the personnel resources available. A look at the paucity of inspectors, researchers, and standards engineers suggests weakness in these areas. There is also an indication that a significant number of cities and counties are perhaps without the in-house skills to handle the areas of total cost purchasing and value analysis. If any of these skills or resources are present, they are most likely found in cities and counties with a population in excess of 100,000.

Reasonable employee turnover and employee upgrading usually exact professional expansion and retraining, which would indicate a need for an intern program of junior buyers. The survey results show, however, that the use of junior buyers is not widespread. Overall, salary survey statistics for the cities reveal an overlapping salary cluster of beginning and ending salaries between purchasing management and supervisory buyer classifications. This pertains especially to assistant chief purchasing officers, purchasing agent-managers, supervisory buyers, and senior buyers. The salary ranges for specialists (e.g., standards engineers, value analysts, research market analysts) appear to have affected the salary ceilings of chief purchasing officers, as well as the salary stratification of other purchasing personnel. Counties appear to have restricted the salary levels of such specialists to a level just below that for buyers. Maintenance of this posture among the counties can contribute significantly to deterioration within purchasing management. The incremental salary differential between population groups for both cities and counties suggests that pyramiding duplications could be significantly decreased and substantial economic efficiency increased if personnel pooling arrangements were effected among the cities and counties.

DEGREE OF RESPONDENTS' SATISFACTION WITH PURCHASING MANAGEMENT INFORMATION AVAILABLE

The local governments surveyed were asked to indicate whether they are very satisfied, satisfied, or not satisfied with the management information in various purchasing areas available to them through the purchasing system. The tabulation of responses appears in Tables B-31 and B-32. Purchasing operation and management encompass a wide variety of organizational patterns and functions, usually performed under differing sources of authority. Faced with varying levels of operational sophistication, many respondents found certain areas to be unrelated to their own purchasing operation. These cases are indicated in the column headed "Number responding 'not applicable.' "

The data indicate that both cities and counties are generally very satisfied with the purchasing management information available in the areas of bid solicitation, bid processing, contract award, contract administration, and funds authorization and availability. At least 40 percent of the cities responded that they were dissatisfied with purchasing management information available in research and development studies; commodity cataloging; quality control; storage, warehousing, and distribution; inventory management; value analysis; economic market analysis; and statistical data accumulations. At least 40 percent of the counties responding indicated that they were dissatisfied with the purchasing management information available in the areas of quality control, economic market analysis, and statistical data accumulations.

COMPOSITE PROFILE OF EXISTING PURCHASING PRACTICES FOR CITIES AND COUNTIES

A composite profile of existing purchasing practices for cities and counties was generated for inclusion in the *ICMA Urban Data Service Report, July 1974.* It represents a synthesis of responses from selected survey questions. The profile, entitled "Characteristics of the Purchasing Function in Cities and Counties with 10,000 and Over Population," highlights by population group the following survey features for each responding city or county:

• Types of purchasing activities authorized;

• Existence of full-time purchasing officers;

• Approximate annual purchasing dollar volume for the latest available fiscal year, ending before January 1, 1974;

• Annual cost of operating the purchasing department for the latest available fiscal year ending before January 1, 1974;

• Existence of centralized purchasing;

• Existence of cooperative purchasing, and the extent practiced; and

• Preparation and issuance of a purchasing manual.

This composite profile provides a significant reference point and can serve as a communication link among public purchasing officials.

SELECTED PURCHASING PRACTICES AND RELATED SOURCES OF AUTHORITY

Among cities and counties there are a variety of commonly accepted purchasing practices for soliciting, opening, and reviewing bids which serve to emphasize and safeguard the competitive bidding process. The emphasis placed on each of these practices by the citizenry, legislators, and public officials can be related to the degree of coverage provided through governing sources of authority.

Tables B-33 and B-34 show for responding cities and counties, respectively, the specific sources of authority which govern each purchasing practice concerned with soliciting, opening, and reviewing bids. The tables list percentages of the total number reporting for each source of authority indicated, even though several sources may be applicable. For both cities and counties, the strongest responses were on the following practices or functions: competitive bidding requirements; exceptions, exemptions, and waivers of competitive bidding; legal notice requirements; sealed bid requirements and processing; and requirements for public opening of bids. For cities, the dominant sources of authority for the above practices are state statutes or local purchasing ordinances, with the larger cities showing a greater likelihood to derive this authority from local ordinances and the smaller cities relying more on state statutes. For counties, regardless of size, the tendency is to derive authority from state statutes. However, the more populated counties are also governed by local ordinances. Response statistics also show that Western cities and counties are more likely to derive authority from local ordinances for those areas listed in the tables than are localities in other parts of the country.

In order to ensure consistency and continuity, it is necessary to set forth by formal written policy the rules and guidelines which govern various established purchasing practices. But, contrary to this view, many of the local governments are without formally documented sources of authority for such practices as resolving tie bids, considering late bids, and making awards in a manner to discourage identical or collusive bidding. Unwritten policy appears to be the extent of coverage, if any, for a significant number of the responding cities and counties. Over half of the 15 cities and one third of the 27 counties responding in the over 500,000 population category indicated that no stipulated policy covers the practice of making awards to avoid collusive bidding. Interestingly enough, the large cities and counties are less likely to be governed by any written policy than are small ones.

The procuring of insurance coverage by cities and counties is a universal function. Yet the survey results reveal that a significant number of the cities with populations below 250,000 have no laws, regulations, or documented policy covering insurance purchases; the same conditions pertain to counties of all population groups. Underlying the procuring of insurance is the basic question of whether this activity belongs under the direction of central purchasing. Most public purchasing professionals feel it does.

The survey results show that 52 percent of the responding cities and 47 percent of the responding counties are authorized to procure outside professional services through central purchasing. However, as shown in Tables B-33 and B-34, more than 30 percent of the responding cities are without appropriate laws, regulations, or documented policy covering the solicitation, opening, and reviewing of bids for the purchase of professional services. Where appropriate coverage does exist for cities and counties, it can usually be found in the state statute or local purchasing ordinance.

Within public purchasing circles, the use of local preferences or "buy locally" has long been among the considerations used to award contracts. Realizing the existence of this practice, the survey sought to determine the extent to which local preferences are used and the authorizing sources supporting their use. For cities, such practices seem to rest mostly in unwritten policy. While some coverage for local preferences exists among state statutes, local purchasing ordinances, and other written policy, more than 30 percent of the responding cities are without any documented coverage for local preferences. In a similar fashion, counties show that this practice is provided for by unwritten policy. But they differ from cities in that the practice of local preference appears to be somewhat more heavily supported by state statute or local purchasing ordinance, even though 26 percent of the responding counties are without documented procedures for local preferences.

Somewhat at variance with the competitive bidding process is the notion of such purchasing practices as minority set aside, small business set aside, and affirmative action programs. This is because at one end of the spectrum is the cry for absoluteness and rigidity with respect to the "lowest responsible bidder." At the opposite end is the social commitment for enlargement and enrichment of the competitive process. Toward this end, such practices existed rather sparsely on the basis of unwritten policy for both cities and counties. An interesting observation about counties is that there is noticeable concern toward a focus on increased social commitment. With counties, the emphasis emanating from state statutes and local purchasing ordinances is significantly more evident than with cities.

SAFEGUARDS AND CONTROLS

Safeguards and controls in public purchasing operate through practices and procedures which reasonably assure that purchasing programs are conducted openly and fairly to both the procuring body and the vendor. The more commonly accepted practices are listed in Tables B-35 and B-36.

Bidder prequalification presupposes the existence of predictable aspects of vendor responsibility and performance. The survey results show that 43 percent of the responding cities do not provide for bidder prequalification, nor does statutory or local legislation seem to require it. Although it is not dominant in counties, bidder prequalification is supported through state statutes.

Establishing and maintaining a bidders list may be so generally accepted that it does not warrant a written policy or other documented coverage. Both cities and counties show that unwritten policy or no coverage is most prevalent in establishing and maintaining a bidders list.

Among cities and counties there is widespread acceptance that bids submitted competitively should be certified against collusion. State and local legislation, legal opinions, and other forms of written policy strongly endorse this posture. However, 18 percent of the responding cities operate with unwritten policies, and 32 percent do not cover this subject. Counties show 15 percent operating without written policies and 29 percent not covering the subject.

State and local legislation, legal opinions, and other forms of written policy overwhelmingly support safeguards and controls dealing with the establishment of provisions for conflict of interest; prohibitions against corrupt vendors; and prohibitions against the acceptance of gifts, promises, or bribes. Noticeably absent from the safeguards and control practices are agency complaint procedures, bidder or vendor protest procedures, and suspension of vendor measures.

BIDDING PRACTICES

The nature of the competitive bidding process is largely determined by the bidding practices followed. Since the bidding practices followed by most local governments tend to be rather specific, they are generally set forth in state or local laws. Those selected bidding practices with legal emphasis were reviewed to disclose the state-of-the-art for: dollar values required for competitive bidding; dollar amounts requiring legal bid notices; extent of exceptions, exemptions, and waivers of competitive bidding permitted by law; and types of surety required to accompany bids submitted.

With inflationary pressures continuing to soar, public

purchasing officials are even more concerned with the procurement problems caused by established floors requiring competitive bidding. Tables B-37 and B-38 present the dollar value requirements for competitive bidding for cities and counties. Since the responses contained several very high dollar values, the median statistics are used as a measure of central tendency rather than the mean. Overall, the median range of dollar values of bids which require competitive bidding are shown below.

	City range	County range
Informal verbal quotes	$50-500	$100-500
Informal written quotes	$325-2,000	$500-1,500
Formal sealed bids	$1,500 and over	$1,500 and over

The overlap in the ranges of values indicates the use of various quotation/bid methods. This probably occurred because some respondents reported that the same range applies to both types of informal quotes, while others reported that a different range applies. For example, the tables show that the number of respondents at the top of each classification range is significantly greater than at the base reference point within that classification range.

Tables B-39 and B-40 show the dollar amount at which legal notices are required. The dollar amount in this category for larger cities is somewhat higher than the dollar amounts required for smaller cities. For instance, the median range of values is from $1,500 for the cities with populations of under 25,000, to $4,000 for the cities with populations of 500,000 and over. For counties, the median range of values is from $1,500 for the counties with populations of 500,000 and over, to $2,000 for the counties with populations of under 25,000. For cities, the overall mean value of $2,353 is approximated by the median value of $2,000, probably because of infrequent responses at those values. Therefore, it appears that smaller counties have considerably more flexibility in obtaining bids without legal notice than smaller cities. This also holds true for other county and city population categories, but to a somewhat lesser extent.

Although most cities and counties have a documented source of authority which describes their competitive bidding requirements, the capability to provide an exception, exemption, or waiver of the competitive bidding practice in case of emergency is necessary. As a practical matter, the application of exemptions or waivers of competitive bidding should focus on the conditions giving rise to the departure from the competitive bidding and award process rather than a specific commodity or service.

Most responding cities and counties regard emergencies as a permissive waiver of competitive bidding. Figure B-5 depicts this response in summary fashion, as well as responses on exemptions and waivers for single sources, professional services, and others. Most cities are somewhat less enthusiastic about exemptions or waivers on the basis of single-source procurements. Many cities and counties also recognize a need for exemptions or waivers for professional services. Presumably, the responses applicable to "other" are concerned with "where in the best interest of the city or county."

The type of surety most required by cities and counties when bids are submitted is bid bonds. Figure B-6 shows overall that 87 percent of the responding cities and 76 percent of the responding counties require bid bonds to accompany all bids above a certain amount. Interestingly, the percentages for the individual population groups parallel the consolidated percentages for both the cities and counties.

For both cities and counties, the use of bid deposits is considerably less frequent than the use of bid bonds. This should not imply that bid bonds are used instead of bid deposits. Often local governments include the option to use either, depending upon the sensitivity of purchasing management. Nevertheless, the survey results reveal that cities with populations of 50,000 to 99,999 employ both bid bonds and bid deposits fairly evenly. The results also show that the use of other forms of surety is minimal. Although only 9 percent of all responding cities indicate that no bond or deposit is required, larger cities require such protection less often than smaller cities. For counties, the distribution of those not requiring the protection of a bond or deposit (18 percent of the 593 reporting) is fairly even regardless of the population.

Tables B-41 and B-42 summarize the current practice in the use of bid bonds or bid deposits and performance bonds. Although about half of the cities and counties require bid bonds or bid deposits, their discretionary use is more prevalent in cities and counties with populations greater than 500,000. The overall median dollar amount requirement is the same for cities and counties, but larger cities have a higher limit than smaller cities and smaller counties have a higher limit than larger counties. The limits are highest in the Western cities and North Central counties.

In addition to the use of bid bonds or bid deposits, slightly over one half of the responding cities and counties require performance bonds. The larger localities have a greater tendency toward performance bond requirements than the smaller ones. The distribution of responses is about the same geographically for both cities and counties.

TYPES OF EXEMPTIONS AND WAIVERS PERMITTED	NUMBER RESPONDING	RESPONSE PERCENTATES

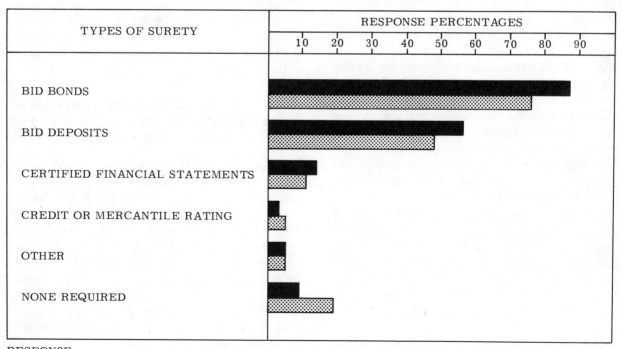

RESPONSE

■ CITIES

▨ COUNTIES

FIGURE B-5: EXCEPTIONS, EXEMPTIONS, AND WAIVERS OF
COMPETITIVE BIDDING PERMITTED BY LAW

RESPONSE

■ CITIES = 1,116

▨ COUNTIES = 593

FIGURE B-6: SURETY REQUIRED WHEN BIDS SUBMITTED

PURCHASING SPECIFICATION PRACTICES

The survey addressed the drafting and approval of specifications that accompany the Invitation for Bids and the nature and content of the specifications. The results indicate that the responsibility for drafting specifications is held by either the using agency or the purchasing department (Figure B-7). Eighty-two percent of the cities with populations greater than 500,000 and 51 percent of the cities with populations less than 500,000 place the responsibility for drafting specifications with the using agencies. The distribution for counties indicates that this responsibility is fairly evenly split between the using agencies and the purchasing department. However, the larger counties tend to place the specification drafting authority in the purchasing department. Cities with a town meeting form of government rely more heavily than others on the using agencies' drafting specifications for purchasing.

Figure B-8 shows where the cities and counties place the authority for approving purchasing specifications. Cities are likely to have specifications approved by a city manager or a purchasing agent (38 and 22 percent, respectively), while counties would choose a council or purchasing agent (44 and 18 percent, respectively). The data indicate that larger cities and counties (over 100,000 population) prefer to locate final approval authority in the purchasing department, probably because they usually have separate purchasing departments. Smaller cities usually place this authority with the city manager, while the smaller counties place it with a county board.

Table B-43 relates the entity responsible for drafting specifications to the entity responsible for final approval of such specifications. For cities, the city manager is most likely to have the authority for final specification approval, regardless of where the drafting responsibility may rest. The only possible exception to this is where a separate committee is responsible for drafting the specifications, which is the case for 83 percent of the cities with less than 25,000 population.

In counties, the specifications are usually approved by a county board regardless of where the responsibility for drafting such specifications lies. Although this may be desirable for smaller counties, it hardly appears suitable for the larger counties. Practice shows that the larger counties place the authority for specification approval with the using agency or purchasing department.

Tables B-44 and B-45 show the current practices for using of brand or trade name specifications, the constraints on restrictive specifications, and the drafting of standard specifications for common use by all using agencies. The following listing summarizes the practices shown.

	Cities (percent)	Counties (percent)
Permit use of brand or trade names	64	52
Legally constrain the writing of restrictive specifications	40	47
Use standard specifications	51	36

All three of the practices listed above occur more often in larger cities and counties. For example, 84 percent of the cities and 72 percent of the counties with populations over 100,000 permit the use of brand and trade names, versus 62 percent of the cities and 46 percent of the counties with populations less than 100,000.

Less than one half of all cities and counties responding have legal requirements which constrain the writing of restrictive specifications. More cities and counties in the Northeast than anywhere else place constraints on writing restrictive specifications.

Standardization relates to a program of examining needs and specifications to determine whether or not it is appropriate and feasible to adopt a common specification for a particular item. As shown in Tables B-44 and B-45, the larger cities and counties (over 250,000 population) are more likely to use standard specifications—87 percent of the cities and 74 percent of the counties. The localities with populations less than 250,000 are less apt to use standard specifications—50 percent and 31 percent for the small cities and counties, respectively. Cities and counties in the West use standard specifications more often than those in other parts of the country.

COMPOSITE PROFILE OF PURCHASING SPECIFICATIONS AND STANDARDS FOR CITIES AND COUNTIES

A composite profile of purchasing practices relating to specifications and standards for cities and counties was prepared for inclusion in the ICMA *Municipal Yearbook, 1974*. It represents a synthesis of responses from selected survey questions. The profile, entitled "Purchasing Specifications and Standards in Cities and Counties with 10,000 and Over Population," highlights, by population group, the following survey features for each responding city or county:

• Existence of centralized purchasing;
• Responsible entity for drafting specifications that accompany Invitations for Bids;
• Final authority for approving specifications;
• Allowance of brand or trade names in specifications;
• Existence of legal requirements constraining the writing of restrictive specifications;

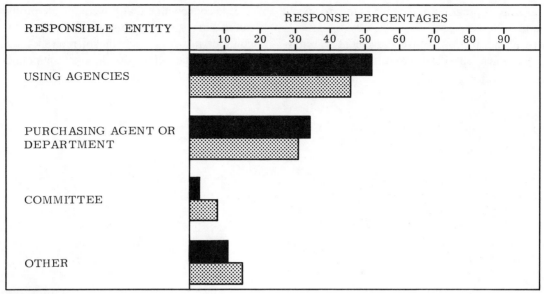

RESPONSE

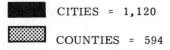

FIGURE B-7: RESPONSIBILITY FOR DRAFTING PURCHASING SPECIFICATIONS

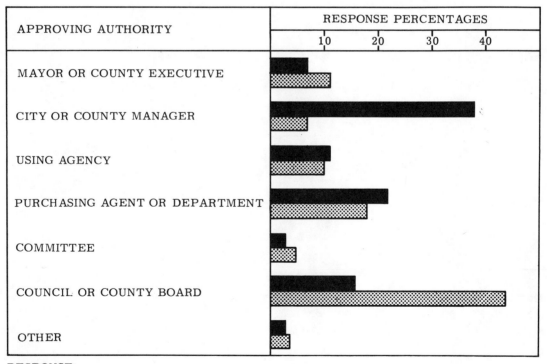

RESPONSE

CITIES = 1,120

COUNTIES = 594

FIGURE B-8: FINAL AUTHORITY FOR APPROVING PURCHASING SPECIFICATIONS

• Existence of a program to develop standard specifications; and

• Degree of satisfaction with management information received when specifications and standards are used.

It is conceivable that the composite profile of existing purchasing specifications and standards for cities and counties provides a significant reference point and can serve as a communication link among public purchasing officials.

TABLES

TABLE B-1

RESPONSE TABLE FOR CITIES

Classification	Cities Surveyed (A)	Cities Responding Number	% of A
Total, All Cities	2,290	1,169	51
Population Group			
Over 500,000	26	17	65
250,000 - 500,000	30	22	73
100,000 - 249,999	98	65	66
50,000 - 99,999	256	163	64
25,000 - 49,999	520	288	55
10,000 - 24,999	1,360	614	45
Geographic Region			
Northeast	707	284	40
North Central	673	344	51
South	541	276	51
West	369	265	72
Metro/City Type			
Mayor-Council	920	340	37
Council-Manager	1,127	749	66
Commission	120	45	38
Town Meeting	80	23	29
Rep. Town Meeting	43	12	28
Form of Government			
Central	360	225	63
Suburban	1,301	643	49
Independent	629	301	48

TABLE B-2

RESPONSE TABLE FOR COUNTIES

Classification	Counties Surveyed (A)	Counties Responding	
		Number	% of A
Total, All Counties	2,203	696	32
Population Group			
Over 500,000	58	30	52
250,000 - 500,000	70	37	53
100,000 - 249,999	185	78	42
50,000 - 99,999	326	109	33
25,000 - 49,999	566	161	28
10,000 - 24,999	998	281	28
Geographic Region			
Northeast	189	66	35
North Central	734	233	32
South	1,037	286	28
West	243	111	46
Metro Status			
Metro	573	221	39
Nonmetro	1,630	475	29
Form of Government			
Without Administrator	624	251	40
With Administrator	271	146	54
Unknown	1,308	299	23

Table B-3 CITIES WITH LOCAL ORDINANCES GOVERNING PURCHASING

Classification	No. of cities reporting (A)	Cities with local purchasing ordinance		Year purchasing ordinance first adopted											
				1900-1920		1921-1940		1941-1950		1951-1960		1961-1970		1971 and after	
		No. (B)	% of (A)	No.	% of (B)	No.	% of (B)	No.	% of (B)	No.	% of (B)	No.	% of (B)	No.	% of (B)
Total, all cities	1,112	613	55	18	3	48	8	55	9	151	25	198	32	46	8
Population group															
Over 500,000	16	12	75	6	50	2	17	1	8	2	17	1	8	0	0
250,000-500,000	19	15	79	0	0	4	27	2	13	1	7	5	33	1	7
100,000-249,999	64	47	73	4	9	8	17	9	19	10	21	7	15	3	6
50,000- 99,999	160	108	68	2	2	11	10	15	14	33	31	36	33	3	3
25,000- 49,999	274	159	58	3	2	8	5	7	4	40	25	53	33	19	12
10,000- 24,999	579	272	47	3	1	15	6	21	8	65	24	96	35	20	7
Geographic region															
Northeast	267	117	44	2	2	10	9	15	13	24	21	38	32	10	9
North Central	329	176	53	9	5	21	12	12	7	34	19	52	30	12	7
South	259	141	54	3	2	10	7	19	13	35	25	38	27	13	9
West	257	179	70	4	2	7	4	9	5	58	32	70	39	11	6
Metro/city type															
Central	216	144	67	13	9	23	16	21	15	25	17	41	28	7	5
Suburban	614	345	56	2	1	17	5	19	6	96	28	133	39	28	8
Independent	282	124	44	3	2	8	6	15	12	30	24	24	19	11	9
Form of government															
Mayor-council	322	162	50	12	7	15	9	13	8	26	16	47	29	14	9
Council-manager	715	415	58	5	1	29	7	38	9	120	29	145	35	27	7
Commission	43	19	44	1	5	2	11	1	5	2	11	3	16	5	26
Town meeting	22	13	59	0	0	2	15	1	8	3	23	2	15	0	0
Rep. town meeting	10	4	40	0	0	0	0	2	50	0	0	1	25	0	0

TABLE B-3 (continued)

Classification	Cities with local purchasing ordinance (B)	Year purchasing ordinance last changed											
		1900-1920		1921-1940		1941-1950		1951-1960		1961-1970		1971 and after	
		No.	% of (B)	No.	% of (B)	No.	% of (B)	No.	% of (B)	No.	% of (B)	No.	% of (B)
Total, all cities	613	1	0	3	0	6	1	43	7	180	29	162	26
Population group													
Over 500,000	12	1	8	0	0	1	8	2	17	3	25	4	33
250,000-500,000	15	0	0	0	0	1	7	1	7	7	47	4	27
100,000-249,999	47	0	0	0	0	0	0	3	6	15	32	20	43
50,000- 99,999	108	0	0	1	1	2	2	5	5	45	42	28	26
25,000- 49,999	159	0	0	0	0	1	1	15	9	45	28	45	28
10,000- 24,999	272	0	0	2	1	1	0	17	6	65	24	61	22
Geographic region													
Northeast	117	0	0	0	0	1	1	5	4	28	24	35	30
North Central	176	0	0	2	1	1	1	13	7	48	27	42	24
South	141	1	1	1	1	4	3	8	6	45	32	29	21
West	179	0	0	0	0	0	0	17	9	59	33	56	31
Metro/city type													
Central	144	1	1	0	0	4	3	12	8	49	34	47	33
Suburban	345	0	0	2	1	1	0	19	6	106	31	89	26
Independent	124	0	0	1	1	1	1	12	10	25	20	26	21
Form of government													
Mayor-council	162	1	1	0	0	2	1	9	6	46	28	43	27
Council-manager	415	0	0	3	1	4	1	33	8	125	30	113	27
Commission	19	0	0	0	0	0	0	0	0	5	26	2	11
Town meeting	13	0	0	0	0	0	0	0	0	2	15	4	31
Rep. town meeting	4	0	0	0	0	0	0	1	25	2	50	0	0

Table B-4 COUNTIES WITH LOCAL ORDINANCE GOVERNING PURCHASING

Classification	No. of counties reporting (A)	Counties with local purchasing ordinance No. (B)	Counties with local purchasing ordinance % of (A)	Year purchasing ordinance first adopted 1900-1920 No.	1900-1920 % of (B)	1921-1940 No.	1921-1940 % of (B)	1941-1950 No.	1941-1950 % of (B)	1951-1960 No.	1951-1960 % of (B)	1961-1970 No.	1961-1970 % of (B)	1971 and after No.	1971 and after % of (B)
Total, all counties	635	140	22	1	1	12	9	3	2	28	20	40	29	23	16
Population group															
Over 500,000	28	17	61	1	6	5	29	1	6	4	24	1	6	3	18
250,000-500,000	37	19	51	0	0	2	11	0	0	4	21	7	37	4	21
100,000-249,999	74	26	35	0	0	0	0	1	4	6	23	6	23	8	31
50,000- 99,999	99	27	27	0	0	2	7	0	0	6	22	11	41	4	15
25,000- 49,999	140	23	16	0	0	2	9	0	0	3	13	9	39	2	9
10,000- 24,999	257	28	11	0	0	1	4	1	4	5	18	6	21	2	7
Geographic region															
Northeast	59	11	19	0	0	1	9	0	0	0	0	1	9	3	27
North Central	211	34	16	0	0	3	9	1	3	4	12	6	18	7	21
South	263	54	21	0	0	4	7	1	2	9	17	20	37	11	20
West	102	41	40	1	2	4	10	1	2	15	37	13	32	2	5
Metro status															
Metro	206	76	37	1	1	7	9	3	4	15	20	21	28	17	22
Nonmetro	429	64	15	0	0	5	8	0	0	13	20	19	30	6	9
Form of government															
Without administrator	226	31	14	0	0	3	10	1	3	1	3	8	26	5	16
With administrator	142	65	46	1	2	6	9	1	2	19	29	23	35	9	14
Unknown	267	44	16	0	0	3	7	1	2	8	18	9	20	9	20

Table B-4 (continued)

Classification	Counties with local purchasing ordinance (B)	Year purchasing ordinance last changed											
		1900-1920		1921-1940		1941-1950		1951-1960		1961-1970		1971 and after	
		No.	% of (B)	No.	% of (B)	No.	% of (B)	No.	% of (B)	No.	% of (B)	No.	% of (B)
Total, all counties	140	0	0	1	1	0	0	3	2	31	22	50	36
Population group													
Over 500,000	17	0	0	0	0	0	0	0	0	8	47	9	53
250,000-500,000	19	0	0	0	0	0	0	1	5	9	47	5	26
100,000-249,999	26	0	0	0	0	0	0	1	4	2	8	13	50
50,000- 99,999	27	0	0	0	0	0	0	0	0	5	19	14	52
25,000- 49,999	23	0	0	0	0	0	0	1	4	3	13	5	22
10,000- 24,999	28	0	0	1	4	0	0	0	0	4	14	4	14
Geographic region													
Northeast	11	0	0	0	0	0	0	0	0	2	18	1	9
North Central	34	0	0	1	3	0	0	0	0	6	18	10	29
South	54	0	0	0	0	0	0	1	2	11	20	20	37
West	41	0	0	0	0	0	0	2	5	12	29	19	46
Metro status													
Metro	76	0	0	0	0	0	0	1	1	23	30	34	45
Nonmetro	64	0	0	1	2	0	0	2	3	8	13	16	25
Form of government													
Without administrator	31	0	0	1	3	0	0	0	0	3	10	10	32
With administrator	65	0	0	0	0	0	0	2	3	20	31	29	45
Unknown	44	0	0	0	0	0	0	1	2	8	18	11	25

B.23

Table B-5   SOURCES OF AUTHORITY FOR GOVERNING CONSTRUCTION IN CITIES

Classification	No. of cities reporting (A)	Purchasing ordinance		Construction contracting ordinance		State statute		Charter		Administrative code		Legislative resolution		Other	
		No.	% of (A)	No.	% of (A)	No.	% of (A)	No.	% of (A)	No.	% of (A)	No.	% of (A)	No.	% of (A)
Total, all cities	1,110	307	28	145	13	644	58	384	35	163	15	174	16	55	5
Population group															
Over 500,000	17	4	24	5	29	6	35	11	65	1	6	0	0	4	24
250,000-500,000 . .	21	8	38	5	24	14	67	13	62	10	48	3	14	2	10
100,000-249,999 . .	62	27	44	11	18	30	48	30	48	13	21	7	11	3	5
50,000- 99,999 . .	157	55	35	18	11	100	64	72	46	24	15	26	17	5	3
25,000- 49,999 . .	276	78	28	34	12	174	63	86	31	37	13	38	14	11	4
10,000- 24,999 . .	577	135	23	72	12	320	55	172	30	78	14	100	17	30	5
Geographic region															
Northeast	262	47	18	38	15	166	63	69	26	28	11	41	16	14	5
North Central	331	87	26	53	16	189	57	98	30	52	16	67	20	12	4
South	257	69	27	34	13	122	47	134	52	43	17	35	14	15	6
West	260	104	40	20	8	167	64	83	32	40	15	31	12	14	5
Metro/city type															
Central	216	75	35	36	17	121	56	106	49	51	24	25	12	12	6
Suburban	614	173	28	82	13	359	58	189	31	75	12	112	18	26	4
Independent	280	59	21	27	10	164	59	89	32	37	13	37	13	17	6
Form of government															
Mayor-council	316	62	20	69	22	189	60	72	23	41	13	74	23	18	6
Council-manager . . .	723	229	32	68	9	404	56	302	42	111	15	91	13	34	5
Commission	43	10	23	8	19	31	72	5	12	9	21	6	14	2	5
Town meeting	19	4	21	0	0	16	84	2	11	1	5	3	16	1	5
Rep. town meeting . .	9	2	22	0	0	4	44	3	33	1	11	0	0	0	0

1/ Percentages, when totaled, exceed 100%, because many respondents indicated more than one source.

B.24

TABLE B-6 SOURCES OF AUTHORITY OF GOVERNING CONSTRUCTION

Classification	No. of counties reporting (A)	Purchasing ordinance		Construction contracting ordinance		State statute		Charter		Administrative code		Legislative resolution		Other	
		No.	% of (A)	No.	% of (A)	No.	% of (A)	No.	% of (A)	No.	% of (A)	No.	% of (A)	No.	% of (A)
Total, all counties	610	61	10	42	7	462	76	18	3	55	9	94	15	59	10
Population group															
Over 500,000	29	7	24	4	14	26	90	7	24	7	24	3	10	2	7
250,000-500,000 ...	35	10	29	1	3	24	69	4	11	5	14	5	14	3	9
100,000-249,999 ...	71	16	23	2	3	51	72	4	6	9	13	17	24	9	13
50,000- 99,999 ...	99	12	12	4	4	78	79	2	2	6	6	18	18	7	7
25,000- 49,999 ...	138	12	9	16	12	101	73	1	1	16	12	19	14	13	9
10,000- 24,999 ...	238	4	2	15	6	182	76	0	0	12	5	32	13	25	11
Geographic region															
Northeast	55	3	5	3	5	36	65	6	11	9	16	17	31	7	13
North Central	204	9	4	21	10	149	73	0	0	13	6	36	18	28	14
South	252	22	9	12	5	189	75	7	3	23	9	35	14	19	8
West	99	27	27	6	6	88	89	5	5	10	10	6	6	5	5
Metro status															
Metro	205	35	17	12	6	152	74	15	7	30	15	38	19	19	9
Nonmetro	405	26	6	30	7	310	77	3	1	25	6	56	14	40	10
Form of government															
Without administrator ..	216	8	4	14	6	162	75	0	0	17	8	30	14	25	12
With administrator	136	37	27	9	7	100	74	17	13	17	13	25	18	13	10
Unknown	258	16	6	19	7	200	78	1	0	21	8	39	15	21	8

1/ Percentages, when totaled, exceed 100%, because many
respondents indicated more than one source.

B.25

Table B-7 CITIES HAVING CENTRAL PURCHASING

| Classification | No. of cities reporting (A) | Cities having central purchasing | | Average number of years central purchasing has been in use | | Cities having departments, agencies, or bureaus legally exempted from central purchasing | |
		No. (B)	% of (A)	No.	Mean years	No.	% of (B)
Total, all cities	1,143	732	64	699	13	142	19
Population group							
Over 500,000	17	16	94	16	36	6	38
250,000-500,000	22	22	100	21	30	4	18
100,000-249,999	65	58	89	58	23	17	29
50,000- 99,999	159	133	84	130	15	24	18
25,000- 49,999	282	198	70	190	11	34	17
10,000- 24,999	598	305	51	284	9	57	19
Geographic region							
Northeast	277	165	60	160	12	49	30
North Central	335	181	54	168	13	39	22
South	269	191	71	187	14	32	17
West	262	195	74	184	13	22	11
Metro/city type							
Central	222	189	85	186	21	39	21
Suburban	627	394	63	372	10	70	18
Independent	294	149	51	141	10	33	22
Form of government							
Mayor-council	327	165	50	161	14	47	28
Council-manager	741	532	72	508	13	85	16
Commission	44	25	57	22	15	6	24
Town meeting	21	6	29	5	8	3	50
Rep. town meeting	10	4	40	3	14	1	25

Table B-8 COUNTIES HAVING CENTRAL PURCHASING

Classification	No. of counties reporting (A)	Counties having central purchasing		Average number of years central purchasing has been in use		Counties having departments, agencies, or bureaus legally exempted from central purchasing	
		No. (B)	% of (A)	No.	Mean years	No.	% of (B)
Total, all counties	651	262	40	226	14	85	32
Population group							
Over 500,000	29	27	93	27	26	10	37
250,000-500,000	36	33	92	32	17	12	36
100,000-249,999	75	47	63	41	12	15	32
50,000- 99,999	105	52	50	43	9	16	31
25,000- 49,999	148	48	32	39	14	14	29
10,000- 24,999	258	55	21	44	9	18	33
Geographic region							
Northeast	61	29	48	26	15	8	28
North Central	214	55	26	45	12	26	47
South	268	119	44	99	12	35	29
West	108	59	55	56	17	16	27
Metro status							
Metro	214	145	68	130	15	52	36
Nonmetro	437	117	27	96	11	33	28
Form of government							
Without administrator	230	77	33	60	15	31	40
With administrator	142	102	72	96	16	29	28
Unknown	279	83	30	70	10	25	30

Table B-9 COOPERATIVE PURCHASING IN CITIES

Classification	No. of cities reporting (A)	Cities permitted to conduct cooperative purchasing No. (B)	Cities permitted to conduct cooperative purchasing % of (A)	State No.	State % of (B)	Other municipalities/counties No.	Other municipalities/counties % of (B)	Hospitals No.	Hospitals % of (B)	Authorities/districts (sewer, water, housing) No.	Authorities/districts (sewer, water, housing) % of (B)
Total, all cities	1,119	947	85	635	57	565	60	43	5	128	14
Population group											
Over 500,000	17	11	65	7	64	9	82	2	18	6	55
250,000-500,000	22	18	82	13	72	14	78	5	28	7	39
100,000-249,999	65	56	86	37	66	34	61	5	9	10	18
50,000- 99,999	157	142	90	94	66	98	69	7	5	21	15
25,000- 49,999	277	245	88	178	73	151	62	13	5	36	15
10,000- 24,999	581	475	82	306	64	259	55	11	2	48	10
Geographic region											
Northeast	267	241	90	198	82	135	56	2	1	23	10
North Central	329	241	73	125	52	145	60	15	6	33	14
South	262	212	81	134	63	95	45	16	8	39	18
West	261	253	97	178	70	190	75	10	4	33	13
Metro/city type											
Central	219	185	84	123	66	111	60	16	9	40	22
Suburban	615	529	86	366	69	367	69	18	3	61	12
Independent	285	233	82	146	53	87	37	9	4	27	12
Form of government											
Mayor-council	321	236	74	159	67	121	51	10	4	25	11
Council-manager	728	662	91	438	66	422	64	31	5	99	15
Commission	43	29	67	21	72	8	28	2	7	3	10
Town meeting	18	14	78	12	36	11	79	0	0	1	7
Rep. town meeting	9	6	67	5	33	3	50	0	0	0	0

Types of organizations involved in cooperative purchasing[1]

Table B-9 (continued)

Classification	Cities permitted to conduct cooperative purchasing No. (B)	Types of organizations involved in cooperative purchasing[1]											
		School districts		Colleges and universities		Grantee organizations (state and federal sources)		Regional councils or bodies		State leagues		Other	
		No.	% of (B)	No.	% of (B)	No.	% of (B)	No.	% of (B)	No.	% of (B)	No.	% of (B)
Total, all cities	947	257	27	45	5	52	5	85	9	20	2	31	3
Population group													
Over 500,000	11	6	55	0	0	5	45	4	36	1	9	0	0
250,000-500,000	18	13	72	5	28	3	17	1	6	0	0	0	0
100,000-249,999	56	17	30	4	7	7	13	5	9	1	2	1	2
50,000- 99,999	142	47	33	9	6	10	7	10	7	2	1	6	4
25,000- 49,999	245	70	29	11	4	10	4	23	9	7	3	11	4
10,000- 24,999	475	104	22	16	3	17	4	42	9	9	2	13	3
Geographic region													
Northeast	241	58	24	2	1	10	4	22	9	2	1	7	3
North Central	241	75	31	16	7	12	5	11	5	3	1	9	4
South	212	40	19	10	5	16	8	37	17	4	2	4	2
West	253	84	33	17	7	14	6	15	6	11	4	11	4
Metro/city type													
Central	185	62	34	17	9	18	10	20	11	6	3	4	2
Suburban	529	142	27	17	3	22	4	47	9	4	1	20	4
Independent	233	53	23	11	5	12	5	18	8	10	4	7	3
Form of government													
Mayor-council	236	47	20	10	4	14	6	16	7	1	0	4	2
Council-manager	662	201	30	34	5	36	5	68	10	19	3	27	4
Commission	29	4	14	1	3	1	3	1	3	0	0	0	0
Town meeting	14	3	21	0	0	1	7	0	0	0	0	0	0
Rep. town meeting	6	2	33	0	0	0	0	0	0	0	0	0	0

[1] Percentages, when totaled, exceed 100%, since many respondents indicated more than one type of participating organization.

B.29

Table B-10 COOPERATIVE PURCHASING IN COUNTIES

Classification	No. of counties reporting (A)	Counties permitted to conduct cooperative purchasing No. (B)	% of (A)	Types of organizations involved in cooperative purchasing[1] State No.	% of (B)	Other municipalities/counties No.	% of (B)	Hospitals No.	% of (B)	Authorities/districts (sewers, water, housing) No.	% of (B)
Total, all counties	616	417	68	281	67	192	46	47	11	71	17
Population group											
Over 500,000	29	28	97	25	89	23	82	9	32	10	36
250,000-500,000	36	34	94	22	65	24	71	6	18	7	21
100,000-249,999	75	60	80	38	63	34	57	6	10	12	20
50,000- 99,999	101	73	72	47	64	32	44	7	10	14	19
25,000- 49,999	132	86	65	61	71	34	40	7	8	15	17
10,000- 24,999	243	136	56	88	65	45	33	12	9	13	10
Geographic region											
Northeast	60	43	72	33	77	20	47	4	9	3	7
North Central	192	96	50	45	47	52	54	10	10	8	8
South	259	193	75	142	74	68	35	18	9	27	14
West	105	85	81	61	72	52	61	15	18	33	39
Metro status											
Metro	208	167	80	110	66	104	62	23	14	35	21
Nonmetro	408	250	61	171	68	88	35	24	10	36	14
Form of government											
Without administrator	214	137	64	93	68	58	42	18	13	14	10
With administrator	139	120	86	82	68	77	64	17	14	37	31
Unknown	263	160	61	106	66	57	36	12	8	20	13

B.30

Table B-10 (continued)

Classification	Counties permitted to conduct cooperative purchasing (B)	Types of organizations involved in cooperative purchasing[1]											
		School districts		Colleges and universities		Grantee organizations (state and federal sources)		Regional councils or bodies		State leagues		Other	
		No.	% of (B)	No.	% of (B)	No.	% of (B)	No.	% of (B)	No.	% of (B)	No.	% of (B)
Total, all counties	417	99	24	33	8	33	8	55	13	2	0	20	5
Population group													
Over 500,000	28	14	50	6	21	3	11	5	18	1	4	4	14
250,000-500,000	34	9	26	6	18	2	6	2	6	0	0	3	9
100,000-249,999	60	21	35	9	15	5	8	8	13	0	0	5	8
50,000- 99,999	73	23	32	5	7	3	4	11	15	1	1	1	1
25,000- 49,999	86	17	20	5	6	7	8	13	15	0	0	3	3
10,000- 24,999	136	15	11	2	1	13	10	16	12	0	0	4	3
Geographic region													
Northeast	43	3	7	2	5	0	0	3	7	0	0	1	2
North Central	96	15	16	4	4	9	9	8	8	1	1	10	10
South	193	33	17	6	3	14	7	36	19	0	0	8	4
West	85	48	56	21	25	10	12	8	9	1	1	1	1
Metro status													
Metro	167	49	29	21	13	13	8	23	14	1	1	13	8
Nonmetro	250	50	20	12	5	20	8	32	13	1	0	7	3
Form of government													
Without administrator	137	23	17	5	4	12	9	24	18	1	1	5	4
With administrator	120	46	38	20	17	8	7	20	17	1	1	9	8
Unknown	160	30	19	8	5	13	8	11	7	0	0	6	4

[1] Percentages, when totaled, exceed 100%, since many respondents indicated more than one type of participating organization.

Table B-11 TYPES OF PURCHASING ACTIVITIES AUTHORIZED TO BE PERFORMED BY PURCHASING DEPARTMENT IN CITIES[1]

Classification	No. of cities reporting (A)	Material and Supply purchases		Equipment purchases		Equipment Leases/ renting		Outside Personal services		Outside Professional services	
		No.	% of (A)	No.	% of (A)	No.	% of (A)	No.	% of (A)	No.	% of (A)
Total, all cities	992	979	99	925	93	748	75	514	52	514	52
Population group											
Over 500,000	17	17	100	17	100	15	88	7	41	6	35
250,000-500,000	22	22	100	22	100	21	95	14	64	9	41
100,000-249,999 . . .	62	62	100	61	98	55	89	33	53	29	47
50,000- 99,999 . . .	152	152	100	151	99	130	86	97	64	81	53
25,000- 49,999 . . .	251	248	99	238	95	200	80	132	53	137	55
10,000- 24,999 . . .	488	478	98	436	89	327	67	231	47	252	52
Geographic region											
Northeast	229	226	99	210	92	164	72	125	55	124	54
North Central	275	268	97	252	92	202	73	130	47	143	52
South	243	242	100	230	95	180	74	129	53	109	45
West	245	243	99	233	95	202	82	130	53	138	56
Metro/city type											
Central	212	211	100	209	99	185	87	128	60	106	50
Suburban	543	537	99	506	93	415	76	272	50	282	52
Independent	237	231	97	210	89	148	62	114	48	126	53
Form of government											
Mayor-council	255	247	97	230	90	173	68	113	44	120	47
Council-manager	691	686	99	652	94	539	78	380	55	369	53
Commission	32	32	100	30	94	26	81	15	47	19	59
Town meeting	10	10	100	10	100	7	70	5	50	5	50
Rep. town meeting . . .	4	4	100	3	75	3	75	1	25	1	25

Table B-11 (continued)

Classification	No. of cities reporting (A)	Construction contracts		Real property purchases		Real property leases/renting		Surplus/ excess sales		Inter-department agency transfers		Other	
		No.	% of (A)	No.	% of (A)	No.	% of (A)	No.	% of (A)	No.	% of (A)	No.	% of (A)
Total, all cities	992	608	61	243	24	229	23	583	59	403	41	33	3
Population group													
Over 500,000	17	9	53	0	0	0	0	15	88	10	59	1	6
250,000-500,000	22	11	50	2	9	6	27	22	100	16	73	3	14
100,000-249,999	62	43	69	7	11	13	21	47	76	35	56	1	2
50,000- 99,999	152	95	63	36	24	39	26	120	79	85	56	5	3
25,000- 49,999	251	167	67	60	24	52	21	150	60	105	42	8	3
10,000- 24,999	488	283	58	138	28	119	24	229	47	152	31	15	3
Geographic region													
Northeast	229	158	69	48	21	51	22	113	49	73	32	7	3
North Central	275	155	56	82	30	65	24	135	49	105	38	13	5
South	243	150	62	51	21	48	20	150	62	93	38	5	2
West	245	145	59	62	25	65	27	185	76	132	54	8	3
Metro/city type													
Central	212	141	67	35	17	42	20	162	76	119	56	11	5
Suburban	543	323	59	124	23	121	22	303	56	190	35	9	2
Independent	237	144	61	84	35	66	28	118	50	94	40	13	5
Form of government													
Mayor-council	255	161	63	60	24	50	20	116	45	90	35	10	4
Council-manager	691	417	60	169	24	163	24	438	63	296	43	23	3
Commission	32	21	66	9	28	11	34	20	63	10	31	0	0
Town meeting	10	7	70	4	40	4	40	7	70	5	50	0	0
Rep. town meeting	4	2	50	1	25	1	25	2	50	2	50	0	0

[1]Percentages, when totaled, exceed 100%, since many respondents indicated more than one type of activity.

B.33

Table B-12 TYPES OF PURCHASING ACTIVITIES AUTHORIZED TO BE PERFORMED BY PURCHASING DEPARTMENT IN COUNTIES[1]

Classification	No. of counties reporting (A)	Material and supply purchases		Equipment purchases		Equipment Leases/ renting		Outside Personal services		Outside Professional services	
		No.	% of (A)	No.	% of (A)	No.	% of (A)	No.	% of (A)	No.	% of (A)
Total, all counties	471	447	95	435	92	321	68	200	42	221	47
Population group											
Over 500,000	28	28	100	28	100	26	93	18	64	20	71
250,000-500,000	36	35	97	36	100	33	92	21	58	20	56
100,000-249,999	55	53	96	55	100	42	76	26	47	23	42
50,000- 99,999	76	73	96	74	97	53	70	37	49	34	45
25,000- 49,999	101	99	98	88	87	65	64	40	40	46	46
10,000- 24,999	175	159	91	154	88	102	58	58	33	78	45
Geographic region											
Northeast	39	36	92	36	92	27	69	17	44	20	51
North Central	143	134	94	128	90	86	60	47	33	62	43
South	204	196	96	192	94	152	75	94	46	99	49
West	85	81	95	79	93	56	66	42	49	40	47
Metro status											
Metro	177	172	97	174	98	143	81	91	51	91	51
Nonmetro	294	275	94	261	89	178	61	109	37	130	44
Form of government											
Without administrator	171	160	94	151	88	108	63	58	34	74	43
With administrator	125	124	99	122	98	97	78	70	56	65	52
Unknown	175	163	93	162	93	116	66	72	41	82	47

B.34

Table B-12 (continued)

Classification	No. of counties reporting (A)	Construction contracts		Real property purchases		Real property leases/renting		Surplus/ excess sales		Inter-department agency transfers		Other	
		No.	% of (A)	No.	% of (A)	No.	% of (A)	No.	% of (A)	No.	% of (A)	No.	% of (A)
Total, all counties	471	298	63	155	33	146	31	216	46	177	38	10	2
Population group													
Over 500,000	28	20	71	6	21	10	36	22	79	19	68	0	0
250,000-500,000	36	29	81	9	25	11	31	27	75	19	53	2	6
100,000-249,999	55	42	76	10	18	18	33	34	62	27	49	0	0
50,000- 99,999	76	46	61	22	29	27	36	37	49	37	49	3	4
25,000- 49,999	101	62	61	47	47	32	32	40	40	36	36	2	2
10,000- 24,999	175	99	57	61	35	48	27	56	32	39	22	3	2
Geographic region													
Northeast	39	25	64	10	26	12	31	18	46	17	44	3	8
North Central	143	85	59	41	29	32	22	41	29	36	25	2	1
South	204	132	65	77	38	72	35	104	51	79	39	1	0
West	85	56	66	27	32	30	35	53	62	45	53	4	5
Metro status													
Metro	177	125	71	48	27	61	34	108	61	87	49	3	2
Nonmetro	294	173	59	107	36	85	29	108	37	90	31	7	2
Form of government													
Without administrator . . .	171	112	65	65	38	57	33	64	37	50	29	3	2
With administrator	125	83	66	30	24	37	30	88	70	76	61	2	2
Unknown	175	103	59	60	34	52	30	64	37	51	29	5	3

[1] Percentages, when totaled, exceed 100%, since many respondents indicated more than one type of activity.

B.35

Table B-13 OFFICIAL OR OFFICE TO WHICH PURCHASING OFFICER DIRECTLY REPORTS IN CITIES[1]

Classification	No. of cities reporting (A)	Legislative body No.	Legislative body % of (A)	Mayor or chief elected official No.	Mayor or chief elected official % of (A)	Manager/chief administrative officer No.	Manager/chief administrative officer % of (A)	Finance director No.	Finance director % of (A)	Controller/comptroller No.	Controller/comptroller % of (A)	Other No.	Other % of (A)
Total, all cities	943	213	23	127	13	394	42	268	28	22	2	57	6
Population group													
Over 500,000	17	3	18	7	41	5	29	4	24	0	0	1	6
250,000-500,000	21	0	0	2	10	7	33	12	57	0	0	2	10
100,000-249,999	61	0	0	10	16	17	28	29	48	6	10	7	11
50,000- 99,999	148	14	9	16	11	55	37	72	49	6	4	16	11
25,000- 49,999	244	35	14	30	12	113	46	87	36	6	2	12	5
10,000- 24,999	452	161	36	62	14	197	44	64	14	4	1	19	4
Geographic region													
Northeast	203	63	31	37	18	81	40	32	16	6	3	11	5
North Central	265	75	28	54	20	100	38	63	24	7	3	19	7
South	240	37	15	29	12	103	43	81	34	8	3	13	5
West	235	38	16	7	3	110	47	92	39	1	0	14	6
Metro/city type													
Central	210	16	8	34	16	73	35	98	47	9	4	19	9
Suburban	509	134	26	65	13	219	43	119	23	8	2	33	6
Independent	224	63	28	28	13	102	46	51	23	5	2	5	2
Form of government													
Mayor-council	240	84	35	103	43	34	14	43	18	14	6	20	8
Council-manager	660	118	18	15	2	355	54	210	32	7	1	32	5
Commission	32	7	22	6	19	3	9	14	44	1	3	4	13
Town meeting	6	4	67	1	17	1	17	0	0	0	0	0	0
Rep. town meeting	5	0	0	2	40	1	20	1	20	0	0	1	20

[1] Percentages, when totaled, exceed 100%, since many respondents indicated more than one official or office.

B.36

Table B-14 OFFICIAL OR OFFICE TO WHICH PURCHASING OFFICER DIRECTLY REPORTS IN COUNTIES[1]

Classification	No. of counties reporting (A)	Legislative body		Mayor or chief elected official		Manager/chief administrative officer		Finance director		Controller/ comptroller		Other	
		No.	% of (A)	No.	% of (A)	No.	% of (A)	No.	% of (A)	No.	% of (A)	No.	% of (A)
Total, all counties	375	169	45	55	15	85	23	30	8	11	3	64	17
Population group													
Over 500,000	26	6	23	4	15	8	31	2	8	3	12	8	31
250,000-500,000	32	6	19	2	6	16	50	2	6	1	3	8	25
100,000-249,999	52	16	31	5	10	18	35	8	15	3	6	13	25
50,000- 99,999	62	24	39	10	16	22	35	5	8	1	2	4	6
25,000- 49,999	75	39	52	11	15	13	17	8	11	1	1	10	13
10,000- 24,999	128	78	61	23	18	8	6	5	4	2	2	21	16
Geographic region													
Northeast	35	13	37	12	34	6	17	3	9	2	6	4	11
North Central	102	54	53	16	16	10	10	4	4	4	4	24	24
South	169	79	47	22	13	38	22	17	10	3	2	24	14
West	69	23	33	5	7	31	45	6	9	2	3	12	17
Metro status													
Metro	150	44	29	22	15	52	35	15	10	7	5	33	22
Nonmetro	225	125	56	33	15	33	15	15	7	4	2	31	14
Form of government													
Without administrator	109	65	60	24	22	8	7	3	3	3	3	15	14
With administrator	118	32	27	7	6	50	42	15	13	3	3	21	18
Unknown	148	72	49	24	16	27	18	12	8	5	3	28	19

[1] Percentages, when totaled, exceed 100%, since many respondents indicated more than one official or office.

Table B-15 **CITIES WITH FULL-TIME PURCHASING OFFICER**

Classification	No. of cities reporting (A)	Have a full-time purchasing officer	
		No.	% of (A)
Total, all cities	1,149	422	37
Population group			
Over 500,000	17	17	100
250,000-500,000	22	22	100
100,000-249,999	64	59	92
50,000- 99,999	161	125	78
25,000- 49,999	284	119	42
10,000- 24,999	601	80	13
Geographic region			
Northeast	278	73	26
North Central	335	92	27
South	273	136	50
West	263	121	46
Metro/city type			
Central	222	172	77
Suburban	628	178	28
Independent	299	72	24
Form of government			
Mayor-council	332	108	33
Council-manager	742	293	39
Commission	44	18	41
Town meeting	21	1	5
Rep. town meeting . . .	10	2	20

Table B-16 COUNTIES WITH FULL-TIME PURCHASING OFFICER

Classification	No. of counties reporting (A)	Have full-time purchasing officer	
		No.	% of (A)
Total, all counties	652	143	22
Population group			
Over 500,000	29	27	93
250,000-500,000	36	33	92
100,000-249,999	76	37	49
50,000- 99,999	104	26	25
25,000- 49,999	146	9	6
10,000- 24,999	261	11	4
Geographic region			
Northeast	60	20	33
North Central	216	24	11
South	269	54	20
West	107	45	42
Metro status			
Metro	212	105	50
Nonmetro	440	38	9
Form of government			
Without administrator .	230	32	14
With administrator . . .	143	74	52
Unknown	279	37	13

Table B-17 ORGANIZATIONAL STRUCTURE OF PURCHASING, AND OFFICIAL ASSIGNED THE PURCHASING FUNCTION WHERE NO FULL-TIME PURCHASING OFFICER EXISTS (CITIES AND COUNTIES UNDER 100,000)

Official assigned purchasing function (percent reporting)

Administering organization	No. of respondents		Mayor or chief elected official		Manager/chief administrative officer		Assistant manager/chief administrative officer		Finance director	
	City	County	City	County	City	County	City	County	City	County
Purchasing board or committee	30	116	17	12	10	9	0	12	0	3
Separate purchasing department	154	86	1	0	3	0	1	1	1	0
Part of finance department	390	49	2	2	10	20	2	0	23	8
Part of administration department	306	118	4	11	54	40	12	3	1	3
Part of another department	59	19	3	5	14	5	5	0	2	0
Each department does its own purchasing	169	202	6	5	18	4	1	0	7	1
Other	27	34	0	6	30	9	4	3	0	0

Table B-17 (continued)

Official assigned purchasing function (percent reporting)

Administering organization	No. of respondents		Controller/comptroller		City/county clerk		Each department head		Other	
	City	County	City	County	City	County	City	County	City	County
Purchasing board or committee	30	116	0	0	13	15	7	22	3	17
Separate purchasing department	154	86	1	0	1	0	1	5	4	3
Part of finance department	390	49	3	4	3	12	3	4	7	10
Part of administration department	306	118	0	1	5	12	2	8	5	5
Part of another department	59	19	0	11	17	5	0	11	24	21
Each department does its own purchasing	169	202	1	0	4	5	60	75	1	4
Other	27	34	0	6	4	6	7	24	30	32

B.40

Table B-18 **CITIES WHICH HAVE PREPARED OR ISSUED A PURCHASING MANUAL**

Classification	No. of cities reporting (A)	Cities with manual	
		No.	% of (A)
Total, all cities	1,139	372	33
Population group			
Over 500,000	17	12	71
250,000-500,000	22	16	73
100,000-249,999	65	40	62
50,000- 99,999	158	81	51
25,000- 49,999	278	115	41
10,000- 24,999	599	108	18
Geographic region			
Northeast	272	54	20
North Central	337	100	30
South	269	107	40
West	261	111	43
Metro/city type			
Central	221	132	60
Suburban	623	181	29
Independent	295	59	20
Form of government			
Mayor-council	329	70	21
Council-manager	736	287	39
Commission	43	11	26
Town meeting	21	4	19
Rep. town meeting . . .	10	0	0

Table B-19 **COUNTIES WHICH HAVE PREPARED OR ISSUED A PURCHASING MANUAL**

Classification	No. of counties reporting (A)	Counties with manual	
		No.	% of (A)
Total, all counties	650	93	14
Population group			
Over 500,000	29	17	59
250,000-500,000	36	16	44
100,000-249,999	74	22	30
50,000- 99,999	106	17	16
25,000- 49,999	146	13	9
10,000- 24,999	259	8	3
Geographic region			
Northeast	62	9	15
North Central	214	12	6
South	267	43	16
West	107	29	27
Metro status			
Metro	213	66	31
Nonmetro	437	27	6
Form of government			
Without administrator .	231	14	6
With administrator . . .	142	58	41
Unknown	277	21	8

Table B-20   CITIES IN WHICH PURCHASING
SYSTEM REGULARLY SUPPLIES
PRICING INFORMATION TO USING
AGENCIES IN THE BUDGET
FORMULATION PROCESS

Classification	No. of cities reporting (A)	Purchasing system supplies information	
		No.	% of (A)
Total, all cities	1,048	621	59
Population group			
Over 500,000	16	10	63
250,000-500,000	20	18	90
100,000-249,999	60	53	88
50,000- 99,999	154	126	82
25,000- 49,999	265	165	62
10,000- 24,999	533	249	47
Geographic region			
Northeast	242	128	53
North Central	308	156	51
South	250	168	67
West	248	169	68
Metro/city type			
Central	208	163	78
Suburban	581	324	56
Independent	259	134	52
Form of government			
Mayor-council	282	140	50
Council-manager	707	453	64
Commission	37	20	54
Town meeting	14	3	21
Rep. town meeting . . .	8	5	63

Table B-21   COUNTIES IN WHICH
PURCHASING SYSTEM
REGULARLY SUPPLIES
PRICING INFORMATION
TO USING AGENCIES IN THE
BUDGET FORMULATION
PROCESS

| Classification | No. of counties reporting (A) | Purchasing system supplies information | |
		No.	% of (A)
Total, all counties	504	224	44
Population group			
Over 500,000	27	22	81
250,000-500,000	35	32	91
100,000-249,999	66	38	58
50,000- 99,999	85	47	55
25,000- 49,999	106	32	30
10,000- 24,999	185	53	29
Geographic region			
Northeast	44	23	52
North Central	154	47	31
South	223	97	43
West	83	57	69
Metro status			
Metro	183	113	62
Nonmetro	321	111	35
Form of government			
Without administrator .	165	68	41
With administrator . . .	132	87	66
Unknown	207	69	33

Table B-22 EXTENT TO WHICH PURCHASING SYSTEM IN CITIES IS INTEGRATED WITH MANAGEMENT FUNCTIONS IN VARIOUS AREAS

balance of table →

Classification	No. of cities reporting (A)	Budgeting							
		Completely integrated		Partially integrated		Not integrated		Not applicable	
		No.	% of (A)	No.	% of (A)	No.	% of (A)	No.	% of (A)
Total, all cities	1,049	550	52	397	38	67	6	35	3
Population group									
Over 500,000	15	6	40	7	47	2	13	0	0
250,000-500,000	18	7	39	9	50	2	11	0	0
100,000-249,999	61	32	52	21	34	6	10	2	3
50,000- 99,999	156	71	46	69	44	10	6	6	4
25,000- 49,999	266	143	54	103	39	15	6	5	2
10,000- 24,999	533	291	55	188	35	32	6	22	4
Geographic region									
Northeast	244	123	50	97	40	17	7	7	3
North Central	304	157	52	127	42	9	3	11	4
South	251	134	53	85	34	24	10	8	3
West	250	136	54	88	35	17	7	9	4
Metro/city type									
Central	207	99	48	85	41	17	8	6	3
Suburban	583	310	53	221	38	31	5	21	4
Independent	259	141	54	91	35	19	7	8	3
Form of government									
Mayor-council	278	145	52	104	37	15	5	14	5
Council-manager	708	377	53	270	38	42	6	19	3
Commission	38	17	45	15	39	4	11	2	5
Town meeting	17	7	41	6	35	4	24	0	0
Rep. town meeting	8	4	50	2	25	2	25	0	0

Table B-22 (continued)

| | | Accounting | | | | | | | |
| Classification | No. of cities reporting (B) | Completely integrated | | Partially integrated | | Not integrated | | Not applicable | |
		No.	% of (B)	No.	% of (B)	No.	% of (B)	No.	% of (B)
Total, all cities	1,030	569	55	364	35	67	7	30	3
Population group									
Over 500,000	16	7	44	9	56	0	0	0	0
250,000-500,000	19	10	53	8	42	1	5	0	0
100,000-249,999	62	36	58	20	32	4	6	2	3
50,000- 99,999	156	89	57	59	38	4	3	4	3
25,000- 49,999	258	150	58	88	34	17	7	3	1
10,000- 24,999	519	277	53	180	35	41	8	21	4
Geographic region									
Northeast	234	133	57	76	32	16	7	9	4
North Central	297	151	51	118	40	19	6	9	3
South	249	127	51	96	39	21	8	5	2
West	250	158	63	74	30	11	4	7	3
Metro/city type									
Central	209	112	54	84	40	9	4	4	2
Suburban	566	327	58	191	34	30	5	18	3
Independent	255	130	51	89	35	28	11	8	3
Form of government									
Mayor-council	266	138	52	99	37	16	6	13	5
Council-manager	701	402	57	241	34	43	6	15	2
Commission	38	16	42	17	45	4	11	1	3
Town meeting	17	8	47	7	41	1	6	1	6
Rep. town meeting ...	8	5	63	0	0	3	38	0	0

B.46

Table B-22 (continued)

Classification	No. of cities reporting (C)	Management information system							
		Completely integrated		Partially integrated		Not integrated		Not applicable	
		No.	% of (C)	No.	% of (C)	No.	% of (C)	No.	% of (C)
Total, all cities	968	352	36	342	35	120	12	154	16
Population group									
Over 500,000	13	3	23	4	31	5	38	1	8
250,000-500,000	19	5	26	9	47	2	11	3	16
100,000-249,999	60	22	37	24	40	8	13	6	10
50,000- 99,999	150	54	36	59	39	13	9	24	16
25,000- 49,999	250	88	35	94	38	26	10	42	17
10,000- 24,999	476	180	38	152	32	66	14	78	16
Geographic region									
Northeast	212	79	37	72	34	28	13	33	16
North Central	278	87	31	102	37	39	14	50	18
South	237	91	38	85	36	32	14	29	12
West	241	95	39	83	34	21	9	42	17
Metro/city type									
Central	199	65	33	79	40	24	12	31	16
Suburban	532	200	38	185	35	60	11	87	16
Independent	237	87	37	78	33	36	15	36	15
Form of government									
Mayor-council	244	88	36	85	35	30	12	41	17
Council-manager	672	251	37	238	35	79	12	104	15
Commission	33	6	18	14	42	7	21	6	18
Town meeting	12	5	42	4	33	1	8	2	17
Rep. town meeting	7	2	29	1	14	3	43	1	14

Table B-23 EXTENT TO WHICH PURCHASING SYSTEM IN COUNTIES IS INTEGRATED WITH MANAGEMENT FUNCTIONS IN VARIOUS AREAS

Classification	No. of counties reporting (A)	Budgeting							
		Completely integrated		Partially integrated		Not integrated		Not applicable	
		No.	% of (A)	No.	% of (A)	No.	% of (A)	No.	% of (A)
Total, all counties	488	247	51	158	32	26	5	57	12
Population group									
Over 500,000	27	13	48	11	41	1	4	2	7
250,000-500,000	33	16	48	15	45	1	3	1	3
100,000-249,999	60	23	38	25	42	6	10	6	10
50,000- 99,999	78	37	47	30	38	6	8	5	6
25,000- 49,999	104	61	59	28	27	3	3	12	12
10,000- 24,999	186	97	52	49	26	9	5	31	17
Geographic region									
Northeast	41	18	44	12	29	2	5	9	22
North Central	148	75	51	43	29	9	6	21	14
South	217	112	52	73	34	10	5	22	10
West	82	42	51	30	37	5	6	5	6
Metro status									
Metro	175	83	47	68	39	10	6	14	8
Nonmetro	313	164	52	90	29	16	5	43	14
Form of government									
Without administrator	157	79	50	44	28	7	4	27	17
With administrator	123	59	46	57	45	5	4	7	5
Unknown	203	109	54	57	28	14	7	23	11

Table B-23 (continued)

Classification	No. of counties reporting (B)	Accounting							
		Completely integrated		Partially integrated		Not integrated		Not applicable	
		No.	% of (B)	No.	% of (B)	No.	% of (B)	No.	% of (B)
Total, all counties	452	246	54	133	29	22	5	51	11
Population group									
Over 500,000	28	17	61	7	25	2	7	2	7
250,000-500,000	33	17	52	12	36	3	9	1	3
100,000-249,999	55	24	44	19	35	7	13	5	9
50,000- 99,999	79	42	53	29	37	3	4	5	6
25,000- 49,999	92	57	62	22	24	2	2	11	12
10,000- 24,999	165	89	54	44	27	5	3	27	16
Geographic region									
Northeast	39	16	41	13	33	1	3	9	23
North Central	131	72	55	31	24	10	8	18	14
South	205	114	56	66	32	7	3	18	9
West	77	44	57	23	30	4	5	6	8
Metro status									
Metro	172	93	54	52	30	14	8	13	8
Nonmetro	280	153	55	81	29	8	3	38	14
Form of government									
Without administrator	144	73	51	43	30	5	3	23	16
With administrator	125	70	56	46	37	4	3	5	4
Unknown	183	103	56	44	24	13	7	23	13

balance of table below →

B.49

Table B-23 (continued)

Classification	No. of counties reporting (C)	Management information system							
		Completely integrated		Partially integrated		Not integrated		Not applicable	
		No.	% of (C)	No.	% of (C)	No.	% of (C)	No.	% of (C)
Total, all counties	428	144	34	131	31	38	9	115	27
Population group									
Over 500,000	27	7	26	9	33	4	15	7	26
250,000-500,000	32	14	44	16	50	0	0	2	6
100,000-249,999	56	15	27	16	29	11	20	14	25
50,000- 99,999	72	24	33	22	31	8	11	18	25
25,000- 49,999	90	34	38	28	31	6	7	22	24
10,000- 24,999	151	50	33	40	26	9	6	52	34
Geographic region									
Northeast	38	6	16	8	21	5	13	19	50
North Central	126	43	34	31	25	13	10	39	31
South	187	68	36	62	33	12	6	45	24
West	77	27	35	30	39	8	10	12	16
Metro status									
Metro	162	49	30	54	33	20	12	39	24
Nonmetro	266	95	36	77	29	18	7	76	29
Form of government									
Without administrator	139	47	34	33	24	8	6	51	37
With administrator	118	33	28	55	47	7	6	23	19
Unknown	171	64	37	43	25	23	13	41	24

Table B-24 AUDITING IN CITIES

Classification	No. of cities reporting (A)	Purchasing department required to be audited		Auditing methods for each type of audit											
		No. (B)	% of (A)	Financial audit						Performance/management audit					
				Internal		External (public)		External (private)		Internal		External (public)		External (private)	
				No.	% of (B)	No.	% of (B)	No.	% of (B)	No.	% of (B)	No.	% of (B)	No.	% of (B)
Total, all cities	1,014	752	74	275	37	388	52	326	43	166	22	71	9	63	8
Population group															
Over 500,000	17	15	88	3	53	10	67	1	7	7	47	8	53	0	0
250,000-500,000	22	19	86	13	68	7	37	7	37	7	37	3	16	1	5
100,000-249,999	59	48	81	26	54	21	44	24	50	7	15	5	10	5	10
50,000- 99,999	149	113	76	45	40	54	48	56	50	29	26	10	9	12	11
25,000- 49,999	253	195	77	65	33	90	46	92	47	44	23	16	8	22	11
10,000- 24,999	514	362	70	118	33	206	57	146	40	72	20	29	8	23	6
Geographic region															
Northeast	234	161	69	59	37	94	58	57	35	26	16	14	9	12	7
North Central	289	221	76	77	35	134	61	78	35	46	21	31	14	11	5
South	245	189	77	77	41	86	46	86	46	48	25	14	7	20	11
West	246	181	74	62	34	74	41	105	58	46	25	12	7	20	11
Metro/city type															
Central	210	173	82	77	45	83	48	73	42	40	23	23	13	20	12
Suburban	563	408	72	142	35	214	52	181	44	93	23	39	10	34	8
Independent	241	171	71	56	33	91	53	72	42	33	19	9	5	9	5
Form of government															
Mayor-council	278	188	68	69	37	110	59	61	32	37	20	30	16	14	7
Council-manager	682	522	77	192	37	255	49	252	48	122	23	35	7	45	9
Commission	34	26	76	9	35	14	54	10	38	6	23	6	23	4	15
Town meeting	14	11	79	5	45	6	55	1	9	0	0	0	0	0	0
Rep. town meeting	6	5	83	0	0	3	60	2	40	1	20	0	0	0	0

B.51

Table B-25 AUDITING IN COUNTIES

Classification	No. of counties reporting (A)	Purchasing department required to be audited		Auditing methods for each type of audit											
		No. (B)	% of (A)	Financial audit						Performance/management audit					
				Internal		External (public)		External (private)		Internal		External (public)		External (private)	
				No.	% of (B)	No.	% of (B)	No.	% of (B)	No.	% of (B)	No.	% of (B)	No.	% of (B)
Total, all counties	495	389	79	173	44	232	60	76	20	75	19	67	17	18	5
Population group															
Over 500,000	28	23	82	13	57	12	52	8	35	12	52	4	17	1	4
250,000-500,000	36	30	83	18	60	15	50	7	23	8	27	5	17	4	13
100,000-249,999	62	49	79	24	49	33	67	15	31	15	31	10	20	4	8
50,000- 99,999	80	60	75	30	50	36	60	14	23	9	15	10	17	2	3
25,000- 49,999	103	84	82	33	39	55	65	14	17	13	15	16	19	4	5
10,000- 24,999	186	143	77	55	38	81	57	18	13	18	13	22	15	3	2
Geographic region															
Northeast	46	32	70	15	47	19	59	7	22	6	19	4	13	2	6
North Central	160	120	75	53	44	71	59	14	12	27	23	23	19	4	3
South	211	171	81	72	42	104	61	37	22	23	13	26	15	8	5
West	78	66	85	33	50	38	58	18	27	19	29	14	21	4	6
Metro status															
Metro	180	147	82	75	51	84	57	40	27	40	27	23	16	11	7
Nonmetro	315	242	77	98	40	148	61	36	15	35	14	44	18	7	3
Form of government															
Without administrator	172	130	76	51	39	77	59	23	18	22	17	22	17	5	4
With administrator	129	107	83	59	55	60	56	31	29	31	29	17	16	8	7
Unknown	194	152	78	63	41	95	63	22	14	22	14	28	18	5	3

Table B-26 SOURCES OF AUDIT AUTHORITY FOR ADMINISTERING ORGANIZATIONS

| Administering organization | No. of respondents | | Sources of audit authority (% reporting)[1] | | | | | | | | | |
| | City | County | State statute | | Local ordinance | | Charter | | Administrative code | | Other | |
			City	County	City	County	City	County	City	County	City	County
Purchasing board or committee	30	116	57	60	20	3	10	0	7	3	0	2
Separate purchasing department	154	86	32	62	19	9	36	6	12	13	1	6
Part of finance department	390	49	36	65	18	8	28	4	10	6	7	6
Part of administration department	306	118	35	49	14	7	15	1	11	8	5	4
Part of another department	59	19	32	47	15	16	19	16	10	21	5	0
Each department does its own purchasing . . .	169	202	24	34	5	2	7	0	1	2	2	0
Other	27	34	22	50	7	3	15	3	4	3	11	6

[1] Percentages, when totaled, exceed 100%, since many respondents noted more than one source.

B.53

Table B-27 MEAN ANNUAL SALARY RANGE FOR PURCHASING PERSONNEL
IN CITIES

| | Chief purchasing officer | | | | Assistant purchasing officer | | | |
Classification	No. of cities reporting	Beginning (entrance step)	No. of cities reporting	Ending (last step)	No. of cities reporting	Beginning (entrance step)	No. of cities reporting	Ending (last step)
Total, all cities	295	12,156	303	15,173	98	10,514	105	12,619
Population group								
Over 500,000	16	18,411	16	22,881	12	15,529	13	19,649
250,000-500,000	18	16,839	18	20,614	14	12,887	13	16,650
100,000-249,999	43	13,528	47	17,410	21	10,281	24	11,856
50,000- 99,999	91	12,357	97	14,939	28	9,212	30	11,508
25,000- 49,999	80	10,290	82	13,132	10	6,813	12	8,882
10,000- 24,999	47	9,769	43	12,002	13	9,354	13	8,978
Geographic region								
Northeast	54	11,145	55	13,690	12	11,246	16	10,816
North Central	70	13,421	73	15,684	28	11,168	29	13,295
South	89	10,658	90	13,821	35	8,869	37	11,413
West	82	13,369	85	17,125	23	11,838	23	14,959
Metro/city type								
Central	124	13,376	131	16,842	62	11,270	66	13,908
Suburban	125	12,117	129	14,600	28	9,997	32	10,923
Independent	46	8,976	43	11,806	8	6,460	7	8,218
Form of government								
Mayor-council	81	12,752	74	15,476	31	12,265	33	13,853
Council-manager	203	11,947	218	15,038	61	9,744	66	12,178
Commission	10	11,451	9	15,680	5	8,580	5	10,093
Town meeting	0	0	1	17,250	1	12,841	1	13,624
Rep. town meeting . . .	1	13,545	1	15,570	0	0	0	0

Table B-27 (continued)

table continued →

Classification	Purchasing agent/manager				Supervisory buyers			
	No. of cities reporting	Beginning (entrance step)	No. of cities reporting	Ending (last step)	No. of cities reporting	Beginning (entrance step)	No. of cities reporting	Ending (last step)
Total, all cities	42	11,478	43	14,267	44	10,077	43	12,689
Population group								
Over 500,000 . . .	4	13,187	4	17,163	11	11,987	11	14,971
250,000-500,000 .	3	13,026	3	15,636	6	10,661	6	13,782
100,000-249,999 .	3	13,652	4	14,269	12	9,873	12	11,960
50,000- 99,999 .	10	12,114	11	14,917	6	8,551	5	10,762
25,000- 49,999 .	10	10,415	12	13,118	7	9,001	7	11,639
10,000- 24,999 .	12	10,333	9	13,260	2	7,389	2	9,716
Geographic region								
Northeast	6	11,105	6	14,556	5	10,398	4	13,011
North Central . . .	9	10,394	10	13,487	10	11,254	10	13,897
South	12	9,805	13	11,981	14	8,479	14	11,046
West	15	13,615	14	16,822	15	10,676	15	13,330
Metro/city type								
Central	21	12,199	23	14,741	32	10,624	31	13,400
Suburban	15	10,867	15	13,976	9	8,899	9	11,041
Independent	6	10,479	5	12,955	3	7,770	3	10,285
Form of government								
Mayor-council . . .	10	10,646	10	13,461	14	11,237	13	14,410
Council-manager . .	30	11,823	31	14,637	28	9,615	28	12,014
Commission	2	10,458	2	12,558	2	8,418	2	10,953
Town meeting . . .	0	0	0	0	0	0	0	0
Rep. town meeting .	0	0	0	0	0	0	0	0

Table B-27 (continued)

Classification	Senior buyers				Junior buyers			
	No. of cities reporting	Beginning (entrance step)	No. of cities reporting	Ending (last step)	No. of cities reporting	Beginning (entrance step)	No. of cities reporting	Ending (last step)
Total, all cities	90	10,037	92	11,370	65	7,971	66	9,920
Population group								
Over 500,000	16	10,126	16	12,653	10	9,002	10	10,935
250,000-500,000	16	14,984	15	12,502	12	8,119	12	10,167
100,000-249,999	16	8,603	20	10,664	17	7,973	17	10,223
50,000- 99,999	25	9,135	25	11,246	16	7,289	17	8,909
25,000- 49,999	10	8,468	9	10,907	10	7,848	10	9,813
10,000- 24,999	7	7,271	7	9,064	0	0	0	0
Geographic region								
Northeast	8	8,357	9	9,956	6	7,506	7	8,716
North Central	17	9,308	18	11,248	10	8,918	10	10,612
South	28	10,923	28	10,504	23	6,689	23	8,827
West	37	10,065	37	12,428	26	8,848	26	10,945
Metro/city type								
Central	59	10,680	63	11,550	48	7,969	49	9,954
Suburban	27	8,941	25	11,043	16	8,014	16	9,688
Independent	4	7,949	4	10,579	1	7,344	1	11,952
Form of government								
Mayor-council	29	11,758	29	11,025	20	7,732	19	10,226
Council-manager	59	9,217	60	11,546	42	8,137	43	9,882
Commission	2	9,273	3	11,170	3	7,229	4	8,880
Town meeting	0	0	0	0	0	0	0	0
Rep. town meeting	0	0	0	0	0	0	0	0

Table B-27 (continued)

Classification	Standards engineers				Value analysts			
	No. of cities reporting	Beginning (entrance step)	No. of cities reporting	Ending (last step)	No. of cities reporting	Beginning (entrance step)	No. of cities reporting	Ending (last step)
Total, all cities	9	11,427	9	13,694	5	9,894	5	13,092
Population group								
Over 500,000	5	12,911	5	15,791	2	12,801	2	16,577
250,000-500,000	1	13,153	1	14,459	1	9,840	1	15,264
100,000-249,999	2	9,094	2	10,699	1	8,964	1	10,564
50,000- 99,999	0	0	0	0	0	0	0	0
25,000- 49,999	1	6,948	1	8,436	1	5,064	1	6,480
10,000- 24,999	0	0	0	0	0	0	0	0
Geographic region								
Northeast	2	11,364	2	13,267	1	12,690	1	14,998
North Central	4	12,394	4	15,029	2	10,938	2	14,360
South	1	12,372	1	15,036	0	0	0	0
West	2	9,084	2	10,782	2	7,452	2	10,872
Metro/city type								
Central	8	11,987	8	14,352	4	11,101	4	14,745
Suburban	1	6,948	1	8,436	0	0	0	0
Independent	0	0	0	0	1	5,064	1	6,480
Form of government								
Mayor-council	6	12,090	6	14,727	3	11,814	3	16,139
Council-manager	3	10,101	3	11,630	2	7,014	2	8,522
Commission	0	0	0	0	0	0	0	0
Town meeting	0	0	0	0	0	0	0	0
Rep. town meeting	0	0	0	0	0	0	0	0

table continued →

Table B-27 (continued)

Classification	Researchers (market analysts)[1]				Inspectors			
	No. of cities reporting	Beginning (entrance step)	No. of cities reporting	Ending (last step)	No. of cities reporting	Beginning (entrance step)	No. of cities reporting	Ending (last step)
Total, all cities	3	10,688	3	13,904	7	7,308	7	8,886
Population group								
Over 500,000	2	11,768	2	15,849	1	9,206	1	10,045
250,000-500,000	0	0	0	0	2	8,420	2	10,695
100,000-249,999	1	8,530	1	10,015	2	7,072	2	8,376
50,000- 99,999	0	0	0	0	1	5,904	1	7,536
25,000- 49,999	0	0	0	0	0	0	0	0
10,000- 24,999	0	0	0	0	1	5,064	1	6,480
Geographic region								
Northeast	1	10,696	1	11,767	2	7,920	2	9,024
North Central	2	10,685	2	14,973	3	6,945	3	8,742
South	0	0	0	0	1	9,420	1	11,448
West	0	0	0	0	1	5,064	1	6,480
Metro/city type								
Central	3	10,688	3	13,904	6	7,682	6	9,287
Suburban	0	0	0	0	0	0	0	0
Independent	0	0	0	0	1	5,064	1	6,480
Form of government								
Mayor-council	2	11,768	2	15,849	3	8,420	3	9,832
Council-manager	1	8,530	1	10,015	3	6,665	3	8,390
Commission	0	0	0	0	1	5,904	1	7,536
Town meeting	0	0	0	0	0	0	0	0
Rep. town meeting	0	0	0	0	0	0	0	0

Table B-27 (continued)

Classification	Other professionals				Nonprofessionals (clerical)			
	No. of cities reporting	Beginning (entrance step)	No. of cities reporting	Ending (last step)	No. of cities reporting	Beginning (entrance step)	No. of cities reporting	Ending (last step)
Total, all cities	37	8,162	37	10,037	262	5,927	270	7,746
Population group								
Over 500,000	6	11,647	6	13,422	10	6,225	10	9,205
250,000-500,000 . .	5	8,120	5	11,352	17	5,683	16	7,906
100,000-249,999 . .	4	8,325	4	10,013	42	5,823	46	8,029
50,000- 99,999 . .	12	7,188	13	9,086	87	6,285	94	7,966
25,000- 49,999 . .	6	7,109	5	7,564	70	5,730	71	7,389
10,000- 24,999 . .	4	7,329	4	9,517	36	5,602	33	6,973
Geographic region								
Northeast	3	9,279	4	11,091	43	6,025	47	7,805
North Central . . .	5	7,009	5	8,889	54	6,188	56	7,640
South	11	7,870	11	8,883	83	5,105	85	7,201
West	18	8,475	17	10,872	82	6,537	82	8,349
Metro/city type								
Central	25	8,482	25	10,452	126	5,695	132	7,582
Suburban	10	7,434	9	9,463	103	6,472	107	8,273
Independent	2	7,806	3	8,293	33	5,115	31	6,624
Form of government								
Mayor-council . . .	9	9,766	10	12,468	63	5,972	65	7,656
Council-manager . .	28	7,647	27	9,136	189	5,963	195	7,840
Commission	0	0	0	0	9	4,808	9	6,342
Town meeting . . .	0	0	0	0	1	6,368	1	7,934
Rep. town meeting . .	0	0	0	0	0	0	0	0

Table B-28 MEAN ANNUAL SALARY RANGE FOR PURCHASING PERSONNEL IN COUNTIES

Classification	Chief purchasing officer				Assistant purchasing officer			
	No. of counties reporting	Beginning (entrance step)	No. of counties reporting	Ending (last step)	No. of counties reporting	Beginning (entrance step)	No. of counties reporting	Ending (last step)
Total, all counties	98	14,183	81	17,852	47	10,875	41	19,397
Population group								
Over 500,000	20	21,243	17	24,060	16	14,805	15	23,029
250,000-500,000	26	13,852	26	17,766	19	9,714	17	17,610
100,000-249,999	28	12,436	23	16,090	6	7,434	6	19,769
50,000- 99,999	18	10,508	13	13,259	5	7,517	3	10,622
25,000- 49,999	3	8,500	0	0	1	7,500	0	0
10,000- 24,999	3	14,028	2	16,311	0	0	0	0
Geographic region								
Northeast	16	16,932	14	18,528	11	12,634	9	21,217
North Central	15	12,934	13	16,610	4	7,958	4	33,197
South	37	11,894	24	16,703	13	9,090	9	13,260
West	30	16,164	30	18,993	19	11,692	19	18,537
Metro status								
Metro	80	14,701	68	18,447	42	11,074	37	20,228
Nonmetro	18	11,880	13	14,740	5	9,204	4	11,706
Form of government								
Without administrator	19	12,057	16	15,506	7	8,385	5	10,330
With administrator	58	15,996	53	19,550	36	11,937	34	18,985
Unknown	21	11,099	12	13,481	4	5,677	2	49,068

Table B-28 (continued)

Classification	Purchasing agent/manager				Supervisory buyers			
	No. of counties reporting	Beginning (entrance step)	No. of counties reporting	Ending (last step)	No. of counties reporting	Beginning (entrance step)	No. of counties reporting	Ending (last step)
Total, all counties	18	11,250	18	13,285	24	9,966	23	12,444
Population group								
Over 500,000	6	12,845	6	14,341	13	11,432	13	13,854
250,000-500,000	3	10,306	3	13,113	6	8,370	6	10,578
100,000-249,999	2	10,233	3	12,109	4	8,834	3	11,809
50,000- 99,999	4	8,350	4	9,930	1	5,000	1	7,224
25,000- 49,999	2	13,573	2	18,850	0	0	0	0
10,000- 24,999	1	13,500	0	0	0	0	0	0
Geographic region								
Northeast	0	0	0	0	3	10,527	3	11,484
North Central	2	10,196	2	13,076	5	9,990	5	12,514
South	7	11,735	6	12,556	6	8,424	5	11,164
West	9	11,107	10	13,764	10	10,710	10	13,338
Metro status								
Metro	12	11,393	13	13,157	22	10,293	21	12,838
Nonmetro	6	10,964	3	13,618	2	6,364	2	8,304
Form of government								
Without administrator	3	9,716	4	11,763	5	8,508	5	9,668
With administrator	10	12,009	10	14,308	16	10,843	16	13,578
Unknown	5	10,652	4	12,249	3	7,714	2	10,316

table continued →

Table B-28 (continued)

Classification	Senior buyers				Junior buyers			
	No. of counties reporting	Beginning (entrance step)	No. of counties reporting	Ending (last step)	No. of counties reporting	Beginning (entrance step)	No. of counties reporting	Ending (last step)
Total, all counties	51	9,205	52	14,596	35	7,650	33	9,966
Population group								
Over 500,000	17	10,731	17	13,695	16	8,355	16	11,122
250,000-500,000	15	8,625	17	14,584	10	7,099	12	8,716
100,000-249,999	12	8,705	11	11,756	7	7,215	4	8,843
50,000- 99,999	5	7,067	6	23,149	1	5,500	0	0
25,000- 49,999	1	10,956	0	0	1	7,068	1	10,956
10,000- 24,999	1	6,905	1	10,025	0	0	0	0
Geographic region								
Northeast	8	7,995	10	17,182	4	7,119	6	8,959
North Central	4	10,235	4	12,341	4	8,398	4	10,446
South	15	8,338	15	11,452	16	6,510	13	8,883
West	24	9,979	23	15,914	11	9,228	10	11,785
Metro status								
Metro	43	9,457	45	13,523	34	7,667	32	9,935
Nonmetro	8	7,851	7	21,490	1	7,068	1	10,956
Form of government								
Without administrator	6	7,479	8	17,635	4	6,726	6	8,341
With administrator	42	9,684	42	12,412	28	7,913	26	10,397
Unknown	3	5,950	2	48,300	3	6,420	1	8,500

Table B-28 (continued)

Classification	Standards engineers				Value analysts			
	No. of counties reporting	Beginning (entrance step)	No. of counties reporting	Ending (last step)	No. of counties reporting	Beginning (entrance step)	No. of counties reporting	Ending (last step)
Total, all counties	6	10,105	8	10,741	4	6,471	4	8,433
Population group								
Over 500,000	5	10,455	6	12,581	3	6,890	3	9,070
250,000-500,000	1	8,355	1	10,445	1	5,215	1	6,520
100,000-249,999	0	0	0	0	0	0	0	0
50,000- 99,999	0	0	0	0	0	0	0	0
25,000- 49,999	0	0	0	0	0	0	0	0
10,000- 24,999	0	0	1	1	0	0	0	0
Geographic region								
Northeast	1	8,355	2	9,607	2	5,857	2	7,260
North Central	1	11,665	2	6,722	0	0	0	0
South	1	13,749	1	18,450	1	9,048	1	12,984
West	3	8,954	3	11,608	1	5,124	1	6,228
Metro status								
Metro	6	10,105	7	12,276	4	6,471	4	8,433
Nonmetro	0	0	1	1	0	0	0	0
Form of government								
Without administrator	0	0	1	8,770	1	6,500	1	8,000
With administrator	6	10,105	6	12,860	3	6,462	3	8,577
Unknown	0	0	1	1	0	0	0	0

table continued →

Table B-28 (continued)

Classification	Researchers (market analysts)				Inspectors			
	No. of counties reporting	Beginning (entrance step)	No. of counties reporting	Ending (last step)	No. of counties reporting	Beginning (entrance step)	No. of counties reporting	Ending (last step)
Total, all counties	4	5,895	2	8,093	5	7,624	5	8,291
Population group								
Over 500,000	1	6,708	0	0	3	7,705	2	8,450
250,000-500,000	2	6,049	2	8,093	2	7,502	3	8,185
100,000-249,999	1	4,775	0	0	0	0	0	0
50,000- 99,999	0	0	0	0	0	0	0	0
25,000- 49,999	0	0	0	0	0	0	0	0
10,000- 24,999	0	0	0	0	0	0	0	0
Geographic region								
Northeast	1	5,942	1	7,427	4	7,493	4	7,888
North Central	0	0	0	0	0	0	0	0
South	1	4,775	0	0	0	0	0	0
West	2	6,432	1	8,760	1	8,148	1	9,900
Metro status								
Metro	4	5,895	2	8,093	5	7,624	5	8,291
Nonmetro	0	0	0	0	0	0	0	0
Form of government								
Without administrator ...	0	0	0	0	3	7,656	3	7,600
With administrator	3	6,268	2	8,093	2	7,576	2	9,327
Unknown	1	4,775	0	0	0	0	0	0

Table B-28 (continued)

Classification	Other professionals				Nonprofessionals (clerical)			
	No. of counties reporting	Beginning (entrance step)	No. of counties reporting	Ending (last step)	No. of counties reporting	Beginning (entrance step)	No. of counties reporting	Ending (last step)
Total, all counties	20	7,642	21	10,058	84	5,536	81	7,602
Population group								
Over 500,000	10	8,159	9	11,944	22	5,734	21	8,732
250,000-500,000	3	6,332	6	7,219	19	5,612	21	7,178
100,000-249,999	5	6,713	4	10,271	25	5,504	24	7,585
50,000- 99,999	1	6,684	2	9,666	12	5,120	11	6,574
25,000- 49,999	1	12,010	0	0	2	5,349	2	7,114
10,000- 24,999	0	0	0	0	4	5,630	2	6,560
Geographic region								
Northeast	5	8,342	5	9,831	15	5,357	15	7,425
North Central	1	6,198	2	7,555	12	5,839	13	7,344
South	6	6,934	5	10,654	28	5,180	24	7,153
West	8	7,917	9	10,411	29	5,847	29	8,182
Metro status								
Metro	17	7,468	19	10,062	66	5,595	65	7,798
Nonmetro	3	8,631	2	10,026	18	5,320	16	6,807
Form of government								
Without administrator	2	6,570	3	7,215	16	5,334	18	6,709
With administrator	12	8,125	14	11,267	50	5,670	49	8,104
Unknown	6	7,034	4	7,962	18	5,344	14	6,996

TABLE B-29

TRAINING OF PURCHASING PERSONNEL FOR CITIES

	No. of Cities Reporting (A)	With Ongoing Training Program		Without Ongoing Training Program		Inhouse: Within Dept.				Inhouse: Another Dept.				Outside Sources			
		No. (B)	% of (A)	No.	% of (A)	Staff No.	% of (B)	Entry Level No.	% of (B)	Staff No.	% of (B)	Entry Level No.	% of (B)	Staff No.	% of (B)	Entry Level No.	% of (B)
Total, All Cities	1,067	135	13	932	87	61	45	25	19	24	18	4	3	74	55	12	9
Population Group																	
Over 500,000	15	7	47	8	53	4	57	1	14	2	29	0	0	3	43	0	0
250,000–500,000	21	9	43	12	57	7	78	3	33	1	11	0	0	2	22	1	11
100,000–249,999	62	12	19	50	81	10	83	4	33	4	33	0	0	2	17	1	8
50,000– 99,999	155	33	25	118	77	11	31	6	17	7	20	1	3	25	71	3	9
25,000– 49,999	267	30	11	237	89	12	40	6	20	6	20	2	7	18	60	2	7
10,000– 24,999	549	42	8	507	92	17	40	5	12	4	10	1	2	24	57	5	12

TABLE B-30

TRAINING OF PURCHASING PERSONNEL FOR COUNTIES

	No. of Counties Reporting	With Ongoing Training Program		Without Ongoing Training Program		Source Of Training							
						Inhouse: Within Dept.				Inhouse: Another Dept.				Outside Sources			
						Staff		Entry Level		Staff		Entry Level		Staff		Entry Level	
	(A)	No. (B)	% of (A)	No.	% of (A)	No.	% of (B)	No.	% of (B)	No.	% of (B)	No.	% of (B)	No.	% of (B)	No.	% of (B)
Total, All Counties	545	47	9	498	91	35	74	11	23	9	19	4	9	16	34	6	13
Population Group																	
Over 500,000	28	13	46	15	54	12	92	4	31	3	23	2	15	5	38	3	23
250,000-500,000	34	12	35	22	65	9	75	3	25	2	17	0	0	3	25	1	8
100,000-249,999	66	9	14	57	86	7	78	3	33	0	0	1	11	1	11	1	11
50,000- 99,999	85	6	7	79	93	3	50	1	17	1	17	1	17	4	67	1	17
25,000- 49,999	115	4	3	111	97	2	50	0	0	2	50	0	0	1	25	0	0
10,000- 24,999	217	3	1	214	99	2	67	0	0	1	35	0	0	2	67	0	0

Table B-31 LEVEL OF SATISFACTION WITH AVAILABLE MANAGEMENT INFORMATION IN CITIES

Purchasing areas	No. responding	Very satisfied		Satisfied		Not satisfied		No. responding not applicable	Weighted mean
		No.	%	No.	%	No.	%	No.	
Research and development studies	501	40	8	244	49	217	43	278	2.3
Specifications and standards	765	120	16	489	64	155	20	52	2.0
Economic order quantities	718	95	13	398	55	225	32	70	2.1
Delivery scheduling	710	55	8	452	64	203	28	87	2.2
Commodity cataloging	575	50	8	298	52	227	40	196	2.3
Commodity buying schedules	572	52	9	330	58	190	33	192	2.2
Cooperative buying	671	135	20	356	53	180	27	117	2.0
Qualification of vendors	711	86	12	504	71	121	17	80	2.0
Bid solicitation	775	196	25	519	67	60	8	35	1.8
Bid processing	778	212	27	524	68	42	5	33	1.7
Contract award	766	216	28	515	67	35	5	45	1.7
Contract administration	717	138	20	499	69	80	11	75	1.9
Receiving	732	71	8	490	69	171	23	60	2.1
Quality control (inspection, testing, etc.)	634	38	6	322	51	274	43	144	2.3
Vendor performance evaluation	669	30	5	352	57	237	38	161	2.3
Storage, warehousing, distribution	587	63	9	285	50	239	41	196	2.3
Interdepartment surplus transfer	584	65	12	365	62	154	26	193	2.1
Funds authorization and availability	696	133	20	476	68	87	12	86	1.9
Inventory management	682	72	11	337	49	273	40	105	2.2
Value analysis	535	32	6	269	50	234	44	225	2.3
Economic market analysis	436	24	6	224	51	188	43	317	2.3
Statistical data accumulations	438	27	6	204	47	207	47	288	2.4
Salvaged goods disposal	651	85	13	444	68	122	19	131	2.0

Table B-32 LEVEL OF SATISFACTION WITH AVAILABLE
MANAGEMENT INFORMATION IN COUNTIES

Purchasing areas	No. responding	Very satisfied		Satisfied		Not satisfied		No. responding 'not applicable'	Weighted mean
		No.	%	No.	%	No.	%	No.	
Research and development studies	180	26	14	88	49	66	37	114	2.2
Specifications and standards	277	49	18	164	59	64	23	41	2.0
Economic order quantities	264	43	16	140	53	81	31	45	2.1
Delivery scheduling	263	33	13	150	57	80	30	45	2.1
Commodity cataloging	192	18	9	115	60	59	31	89	2.2
Commodity buying schedules	189	24	13	106	56	59	31	92	2.1
Cooperative buying	232	42	18	119	51	71	31	67	2.1
Qualification of vendors	251	38	15	165	66	48	19	49	2.0
Bid solicitation	295	86	29	171	58	38	13	28	1.8
Bid processing	294	90	31	174	59	30	10	26	1.8
Contract award	297	87	29	186	63	24	8	26	1.7
Contract administration	258	57	22	158	61	43	17	41	1.9
Receiving	247	26	10	150	61	71	29	50	2.1
Quality control (inspection, testing, etc.)	209	20	9	98	47	91	44	85	2.3
Vendor performance evaluation	206	20	10	108	52	78	38	83	2.2
Storage, warehousing, distribution	182	21	12	93	51	68	37	102	2.2
Interdepartment surplus transfer		28	14	129	60	56	26	80	
Funds authorization and availability	258	53	20	159	62	46	18	46	1.9
Inventory management	234	35	15	124	53	75	32	68	2.1
Value analysis	194	25	13	97	50	72	37	99	2.2
Economic market analysis	160	20	13	76	47	64	40	120	2.2
Statistical data accumulations	157	24	15	70	45	63	40	116	2.2
Salvaged goods disposal	218	46	21	118	54	54	25	70	2.0

B.69

TABLE B-33

SOURCE OF AUTHORITY IN CITIES FOR SOLICITING, OPENING, AND REVIEWING BIDS

Selected Purchasing Practices	Number Reporting	Sources of Authority* (%)					
		Local			Other		
		State Statute	Purchasing Ordinance	Legal Opinions	Written Policy	Unwritten Policy	Not Covered
Competitive Bidding Requirements	1,111	63	53	13	13	0	0
Exemptions from Competitive Bidding	1,015	42	41	22	18	10	6
Legal Solicitation Notices	1,020	53	45	13	16	7	5
Sealed Bid Processing	1,102	55	49	11	19	10	1
Public Opening of Bids	1,102	54	48	10	18	10	2
Resolution of Tie Bids	1,016	23	28	21	11	20	20
Consideration of Late Bids	998	23	21	26	10	20	20
Avoidance of Collusion	980	26	23	16	10	20	29
Disposal of Surplus and Scrap	1,031	27	43	9	18	18	9
Purchasing of Insurance	1,066	22	29	12	16	24	18
Professional Services Contracts	1,008	23	32	13	16	21	16
Local Preferences	930	12	17	5	10	31	36
Minority Set-Aside	817	9	7	5	5	10	72
Small Business Set-Aside	809	7	6	4	3	10	76
Affirmative Action Program	821	10	12	5	12	11	60

*Percentages, when totaled, exceed 100 percent, because respondents could indicate more than one practice.

TABLE B-34

SOURCE OF AUTHORITY IN COUNTIES FOR SOLICITING, OPENING, AND REVIEWING BIDS

| Selected Purchasing Practices | Number Reporting | Sources of Authority* (%) | | | | | |
| | | Local | | | Other | | |
		State Statute	Purchasing Ordinance	Legal Opinions	Written Policy	Unwritten Policy	Not Covered
Competitive Bidding Requirements	597	82	21	12	10	12	1
Exemptions for Competitive Bidding	483	61	19	19	8	10	7
Legal Solicitation Notices	495	77	16	9	6	9	5
Sealed Bid Processing	569	77	19	9	9	10	1
Public Opening of Bids	566	75	17	9	8	11	2
Resolution of Tie Bids	462	40	12	20	5	16	21
Consideration of Late Bids	466	37	9	23	6	15	23
Avoidance of Collusion	446	44	10	13	7	18	24
Disposal of Surplus and Scrap	488	55	18	10	9	19	11
Purchasing of Insurance	494	40	17	11	10	25	14
Professional Services Contracts	479	42	17	14	11	20	16
Local Preferences	416	25	15	7	6	30	26
Minority Set-Aside	359	20	4	6	4	12	60
Small Business Set-Aside	355	18	4	5	2	12	65
Affirmative Action Program	342	19	6	8	6	13	55

*Percentages, when totaled, exceed 100 percent, because respondents could indicate more than one practice.

TABLE B-35

SOURCES OF AUTHORITY IN CITIES FOR
SAFEGUARD AND CONTROL PRACTICES

| Safeguard and Control Practices | Number Reporting | Sources of Authority* (%) | | | | | |
| | | Local | | | Other | | |
		State Statute	Purchasing Ordinance	Legal Opinions	Written Policy	Unwritten Policy	Not Covered
Bidder prequalification	1,049	18	14	7	9	25	43
Bidders list	1,066	7	19	2	10	42	28
Certification of non-collusion by bidder	1,034	26	17	10	15	18	32
Conflict of interest	1,062	45	26	15	16	14	14
Prohibition of corrupt vendors	1,034	39	18	14	11	17	24
Prohibition of the acceptance of gifts, promises, or bribes	1,057	40	25	9	25	23	10
Procedures for agency complaints	1,007	7	8	6	10	32	45
Procedures for bidder or vendor protest	1,007	14	10	15	6	26	41
Suspension of bidder measures	1,008	9	12	11	7	28	43
Prior legal review of purchasing contracts	1,019	12	17	27	12	28	20
Authorized purchase order pre-existent to acknowledgement of vendor invoices	1,038	11	32	5	32	25	11

*Percentages, when totaled, exceed 100 percent, because respondents could indicate more than one practice.

TABLE B-36

SOURCES OF AUTHORITY IN COUNTIES FOR SAFEGUARD AND CONTROL PRACTICES

| | | Sources of Authority*
(%) | | | | | |
| | | Local | | | Other | | |
	Number Reporting	State Statute	Purchasing Ordinance	Legal Opinions	Written Policy	Unwritten Policy	Not Covered
Safeguard and Control Practices							
Bidder prequalification	514	36	10	9	6	19	36
Bidders list	488	22	13	4	8	30	33
Certification of non-collusion by bidder	502	44	11	10	7	15	29
Conflict of interest	503	67	10	12	7	11	14
Prohibition of corrupt vendors	498	59	10	12	4	13	19
Prohibition of the acceptance of gifts, promises, or bribes	511	66	12	11	10	20	8
Procedures for agency complaints	461	21	6	6	6	25	41
Procedures for bidder or vendor protests	458	29	6	16	4	21	33
Suspension of bidder measures	456	22	8	12	6	23	40
Prior legal review of purchasing contracts	463	31	10	25	7	23	19
Authorized purchase order pre-existent to acknowledgement of vendor invoices	479	28	19	6	16	22	21

*Percentages, when totaled, exceed 100 percent because respondents could indicate more than one practice.

TABLE B-37

DOLLAR VALUES REQUIRING COMPETITIVE BIDDING BY CITIES (Median Values)

| | Informal Verbal Quotes | | | | Informal Written Quotes | | | | Formal Sealed Bids | |
| | From | | To | | From | | To | | From | |
	No. Responding	Median*	No. Responding	Median*	No. Responding	Median*	No. Responding	Median*	No. Responding	Median*
Total, All Cities	414	50	702	500	626	325	699	2,000	962	1,500
Population Groups										
Over 500,000	6	13	12	750	14	500	14	2,000	15	2,500
250,000–500,000	14	3	20	874	15	300	18	2,000	21	2,500
100,000–249,999	24	25	44	500	34	275	45	2,000	55	2,000
50,000– 99,999	77	50	127	500	106	300	128	2,000	144	2,000
25,000– 49,999	110	50	187	500	171	500	186	2,000	247	1,800
10,000– 24,999	183	100	312	500	286	300	308	1,500	480	1,500
Geographic Region										
Northeast	91	75	142	500	138	250	144	1,500	231	1,500
North Central	101	50	192	750	161	500	198	1,500	275	1,500
South	121	50	180	500	159	300	167	1,000	229	1,000
West	101	100	188	750	168	450	190	2,500	227	2,500
Metro/City Type										
Central	102	25	164	500	145	200	163	1,999	193	2,000
Surburban	216	100	386	500	336	451	388	2,000	546	2,000
Independent	96	50	152	500	145	300	148	1,500	223	1,500
Form of Government										
Mayor-Council	105	75	166	500	153	500	159	1,500	259	1,500
Council-Manager	292	50	506	500	441	400	504	2,000	643	1,000
Commission	10	1	18	500	18	100	24	1,500	33	1,500
Town Meeting	5	10	7	250	9	300	7	1,000	19	1,000
Rep. Town Meeting	2	0	5	500	5	250	5	1,000	8	1,000

*The presence of low median values indicates that 50 percent of the response values range between zero and the low median values shown; a few of the remaining 50 percent of response values were exceptionally higher.

B.74

TABLE B-38

DOLLAR VALUES REQUIRING COMPETITIVE
BIDDING BY COUNTIES (Median Values)

| | Informal Verbal Quotes | | | | Informal Written Quotes | | | | Formal Sealed Bids | |
| | From | | To | | From | | To | | From | |
	No. Responding	Median*	No. Responding	Median*	No. Responding	Median*	No. Responding	Median*	No. Responding	Median*
Total, All Counties	146	100	235	500	227	500	248	1,500	401	1,500
Population Group										
Over 500,000	12	10	19	500	18	300	21	1,000	24	1,000
250,000-500,000	11	10	22	875	23	500	24	1,500	30	1,500
100,000-249,999	18	38	44	500	32	500	47	1,500	60	1,500
50,000-99,999	29	50	50	500	45	500	50	1,750	70	1,750
25,000-49,999	33	100	44	500	46	500	48	1,500	86	1,375
10,000-24,999	43	300	56	625	63	500	58	1,250	131	1,500
Geographic Region										
Northeast	16	38	21	999	18	250	26	1,500	40	1,500
North Central	38	500	63	500	66	500	71	2,000	120	2,000
South	65	100	101	500	98	500	102	1,500	177	1,000
West	27	50	50	750	45	500	49	1,250	64	2,500
Metro Status										
Metro	58	50	115	500	101	500	119	1,500	161	1,500
Non-Metro	88	200	120	625	126	500	129	1,500	240	1,500
Form of Government										
Without Administrator	48	100	69	999	64	500	69	1,500	129	1,500
With Administrator	45	50	86	625	78	500	88	2,000	108	2,000
Unknown	53	100	80	500	85	500	91	1,000	164	1,126

*The presence of low median values indicates that 50 percent of the response
values range between zero and the low median values shown; a few of the remaining 50 percent of response values were exceptionally higher.

TABLE B-39

DOLLAR AMOUNT REQUIRING LEGAL NOTICE FOR CITIES

Classification	No. Responding	Mean	Quartile 1	Median	Quartile 3
Total, All Cities	920	2,353	1,000	2,000	2,500
Population Group					
Over 500,000	17	3,500	1,250	4,000	5,000
250,000-500,000	21	2,654	1,125	2,500	3,500
100,000-249,999	50	2,950	1,125	2,250	3,750
50,000- 99,999	135	2,650	1,500	2,000	3,000
25,000- 49,999	238	2,184	1,000	2,000	2,500
10,000- 24,999	459	2,232	1,000	1,500	2,500
Geographic Region					
Northeast	236	1,818	1,500	1,500	2,500
North Central	257	2,267	1,000	1,500	2,875
South	202	2,079	1,000	1,000	2,500
West	225	3,257	2,000	2,500	3,500
Metro/City Type					
Central	174	2,413	1,000	2,000	3,000
Surburban	534	2,403	1,000	2,000	2,500
Independent	212	2,177	1,000	1,500	2,500
Form of Government					
Mayor-Council	266	2,084	1,000	1,500	2,500
Council-Manager	602	2,540	1,000	2,000	3,000
Commission	31	1,819	1,000	1,500	2,500
Town Meeting	14	1,250	750	1,000	2,000
Rep. Town Meeting	7	1,071	675	1,000	1,000

TABLE B-40

DOLLAR AMOUNT REQUIRING LEGAL NOTICE FOR COUNTIES

Classification	No. Responding	Mean	Quartile 1	Median	Quartile 3
Total, All Counties	403	3,007	1,000	2,000	3,000
Population Group					
Over 500,000	25	2,504	1,000	1,500	3,000
250,000-500,000	27	2,361	1,188	2,000	2,500
100,000-249,999	46	3,126	1,000	1,500	2,500
50,000- 99,999	69	2,361	1,000	2,000	2,500
25,000- 49,999	82	2,826	1,000	2,000	4,000
10,000- 24,999	154	3,552	1,000	2,000	3,000
Geographic Region					
Northeast	44	1,936	1,500	1,500	2,500
North Central	128	5,000	1,000	2,000	5,000
South	170	1,821	500	1,500	2,500
West	61	2,900	1,000	2,500	4,000
Metro Status					
Metro	145	2,501	1,000	2,000	2,875
Non-Metro	258	3,291	1,000	2,000	3,000
Form of Government					
Without Administrator	145	3,054	1,000	2,000	3,000
With Administrator	95	3,337	1,000	2,000	3,000
Unknown	163	2,773	1,000	1,501	2,626

BID BONDS OR DEPOSITS AND PERFORMANCE BONDS FOR CITIES

Classification	Bid Bonds					Minimum Amount Requiring Bid Bonds				Performance Bonds				
	No. Reporting (A)	Discretionary		Mandatory		No. Responding	Mean	Median	Highest	No. Reporting (B)	Required		Not Required	
		No.	% of (A)	No.	% of (A)						No.	% of (B)	No.	% of (B)
Total, All Cities	989	493	50	496	50	220	2,871	2,500	25,000	1,023	551	54	472	46
Population Group														
Over 500,000	16	12	75	4	25	3	3,333	4,000	5,000	15	11	73	4	27
250,000-500,000	20	11	55	9	45	6	2,750	3,000	5,000	19	15	79	4	21
100,000-249,999	53	29	55	24	45	17	4,323	3,000	20,000	56	26	46	30	54
50,000- 99,999	146	79	54	67	46	34	3,522	2,500	20,000	144	91	63	53	37
25,000- 49,999	248	122	49	126	51	54	2,879	2,500	25,000	255	140	55	115	45
10,000- 24,999	506	240	47	266	53	106	2,420	2,000	10,000	534	268	50	266	50
Geographic Region														
Northeast	253	106	42	147	58	69	2,425	1,500	20,000	253	179	71	74	29
North Central	290	130	45	160	55	53	2,438	1,500	10,000	301	160	53	141	47
South	218	129	59	89	41	38	3,197	2,500	25,000	236	95	40	141	60
West	228	128	56	100	44	55	3,663	3,000	30,000	233	117	50	116	50

TABLE B-42

BID BONDS OR DEPOSITS AND PERFORMANCE BONDS FOR COUNTIES

Classification	No. Reporting (A)	Bid Bonds Discretionary No.	% of (A)	Mandatory No.	% of (A)	Minimum Amount Requiring Bid Bonds No. Responding	Mean	Median	Highest	No. Reporting (B)	Performance Bonds Required No.	% of (B)	Not Required No.	% of (B)
Total, All Counties	464	217	47	247	53	94	3,837	2,500	50,000	552	286	52	266	48
Population Group														
Over 500,000	25	15	60	10	40	6	1,691	1,250	5,000	27	23	85	4	15
250,000-500,000	30	16	53	14	47	7	2,715	2,500	6,000	34	20	59	14	41
100,000-249,000	56	35	63	21	38	7	3,114	3,000	6,000	67	29	43	38	57
50,000- 99,999	83	29	35	54	65	26	2,394	2,500	6,000	89	35	39	54	61
25,000- 49,999	94	45	48	49	52	17	5,265	3,000	30,000	121	69	57	52	43
10,000- 24,999	176	77	44	99	56	31	5,096	2,500	50,000	214	110	51	104	49
Geographic Region														
Northeast	47	22	47	25	53	9	1,251	1,500	2,500	49	35	71	14	29
North Central	159	51	32	108	68	37	3,540	4,000	6,000	179	103	58	76	42
South	181	96	53	85	47	34	5,495	2,500	50,000	236	101	43	135	57
West	77	48	62	29	38	14	2,257	2,500	5,000	88	47	53	41	47

TABLE B-43

RESPONSIBILITY FOR DRAFTING AND AUTHORITY FOR
FOR FINAL APPROVAL OF PURCHASING SPECIFICATIONS

Responsible Entity for Drafting	Number	Responsible Entity for Final Approval (%)						
		Mayor or County Executive	City or County Manager	Using Agency	Purchasing Agent or Department	Committee	Council or County Board	Other
Cities								
Using Agency	564	5	38	17	22	2	13	2
Committee	30	30	7	-	7	37	20	-
Purchasing Department	375	6.	39	5	30	2	15	2
Other Department	119	8	39	4	6	4	24	9
Counties								
Using Agency	250	9	7	20	15	2	40	4
Committee	44	14	-	-	11	39	34	-
Purchasing Department	169	12	9	4	34	1	37	1
Other Department	81	7	5	-	4	5	59	15

TABLE B-44

PURCHASING SPECIFICATION PRACTICES FOR CITIES

	Number Reporting (A)	Brand or Trade Names Permitted		Brand Names Not Permitted		Number Reporting (B)	Constraints on Restrictive Specs		No Constraints On Specs		Number Reporting (C)	Has Standard Specs		No Number Standard Specs	
		Number	% of (A)	Number	% of (A)		Number	% of (B)	Number	% of (B)		Number (C)	% of (C)	Number	% of (C)
Total, All Cities	1,097	699	64	398	36	1,051	423	40	628	60	1,081	549	51	532	49
Population Group															
Over 500,000	16	13	81	3	19	16	5	31	11	69	16	14	88	2	13
250,000-500,000	22	20	91	2	9	21	13	62	8	38	22	19	86	3	14
100,000-249,999	61	50	82	11	18	58	32	55	26	45	60	39	65	21	35
50,000- 99,999	157	117	75	40	25	154	75	49	79	51	156	96	62	60	38
25,000- 49,999	274	163	59	111	41	263	98	37	165	63	268	148	55	120	45
10,000- 24,999	567	336	59	231	41	539	200	37	339	63	559	233	42	326	58
Geographic Region															
Northeast	262	169	65	93	35	254	132	52	122	48	263	125	48	138	52
North Central	321	185	58	136	42	306	112	37	194	63	311	151	49	160	51
South	259	174	67	85	33	249	80	32	169	68	256	136	53	120	47
West	255	171	67	84	33	242	99	41	143	59	251	137	55	114	45

TABLE B-45

PURCHASING SPECIFICATION PRACTICES FOR COUNTIES

	Number Reporting (A)	Brand or Trade Names Permitted		Brand Names Not Permitted		Number Reporting (B)	Constraints on Restrictive Specs		No Constraints On Specs		Number Reporting (C)	Has Standard Specs		No Standard Specs	
		Number	% of (A)	Number	% of (A)		Number	% of (B)	Number	% of (B)		Number (C)	% of (C)	Number	% of (C)
Total, All Cities	582	303	52	279	48	518	246	47	272	53	541	196	36	345	64
Population Group															
Over 500,000	29	25	86	4	14	29	18	62	11	38	28	22	79	6	21
250,000-500,000	35	28	80	7	20	34	26	76	8	24	34	24	71	10	29
100,000-249,999	72	45	63	27	38	65	31	48	34	52	68	32	47	36	53
50,000- 99,999	93	50	54	43	46	85	40	47	45	53	86	28	33	58	67
25,000- 49,999	123	59	48	64	52	107	56	52	51	48	116	34	29	82	71
10,000- 24,999	230	96	42	134	58	198	75	38	123	62	209	56	27	153	73
Geographic Region															
Northeast	52	29	56	23	44	49	31	63	18	37	47	16	34	31	66
North Central	194	84	43	110	57	165	70	42	95	58	171	56	33	115	67
South	242	135	56	107	44	220	107	49	113	51	235	76	32	159	68
West	94	55	59	39	41	84	38	45	46	55	88	48	55	40	45

Municipal Year Book

Urban Data Service

1140
Connecticut
Avenue
Northwest
Washington DC
20036

International City Management Association

CITY/COUNTY GOVERNMENT PURCHASING PRACTICES

DEFINITION: Purchasing Practices includes functions concerned with Materiel Management i.e., the acquisition and disposition aspects of materials, equipment and services.

I. AUTHORITY

1. From what sources is your purchasing authority derived? Indicate whether the sources are restrictive.

Sources of Authority (Check all applicable)   Restrictive

7-_____ a. State statute . . . .   YES ( )   NO ( ) 14
8-_____ b. Charter . . . .   YES ( )   NO ( ) 15
9-_____ c. Administrative code . . . .   YES ( )   NO ( ) 16
10-_____ d. County/city ordinance . . . .   YES ( )   NO ( ) 17
11-_____ e. Legislative resolution . . . .   YES ( )   NO ( ) 18
12-_____ f. Administrative edict . . . .   YES ( )   NO ( ) 19
13-_____ g. Other (specify) _____ . . . .   YES ( )   NO ( ) 20

2. Do the above checked sources of authority apply to purchases made under:

a. Federal grants? . . . .   YES ( )   NO ( ) 21
b. State grants? . . . .   YES ( )   NO ( ) 22

3. Is there a local ordinance which governs purchasing? . . . .   YES ( )   NO ( ) 23

IF "YES,"

A. When was the purchasing ordinance first adopted and last changed?

a. Year adopted . . . .   19_____ 24-25
b. Year last changed . . . .   19_____ 26-27

B. Have you adopted all or any features of the National Institute of Municipal Law Officers Model Purchasing Ordinance? . . . .   YES ( )   NO ( ) 28

4. How is construction contracting governed? (Check all applicable)

29-_____ a. Purchasing ordinance   32-_____ d. Charter
30-_____ b. Construction contracting ordinance   33-_____ e. Administrative code
31-_____ c. State statute   34-_____ f. Legislative resolution
                                           35-_____ g. Other (specify) _____

5. Do you operate under prescribed purchasing rules and regulations which are
   legally binding? . . . .   YES ( )   NO ( ) 36

6. Have you prepared or issued a purchasing manual? . . . .   YES ( )   NO ( ) 37

7. Do you have central purchasing? . . . .   YES ( )   NO ( ) 38

   IF "YES,"

      A. How many years has central purchasing been used? . . . .   _____ years
                                                                                              (39-40)
      B. Are any departments, agencies, or bureaus legally exempted from
         central purchasing? . . . .   YES ( )   NO ( ) 41

8. Under your purchasing policies or procedures are you permitted to conduct cooperative purchasing? *(Cooperative purchasing means: (1) making purchases under
   contracts established by another governmental jurisdiction; (2) establishing contracts under which other governmental jurisdictions may purchase; or (3) combining requirements with another governmental jurisdiction under the same
   contract.)* . . . .   YES ( )   NO ( ) 42

   IF "YES," what types of participating organizations are currently involved in your cooperative purchasing?
   (Check all applicable.)

43-_____ a. State   48-_____ f. Colleges and universities
44-_____ b. Other municipalities/counties   49-_____ g. Grantee organizations (state and
45-_____ c. Hospitals   federal sources)
46-_____ d. Authorities/Districts (sewer, water,   50-_____ h. Regional councils or bodies
             housing)   51-_____ i. State leagues
47-_____ e. School districts   52-_____ j. Other (specify)_____

9. Please indicate under (A) the types of purchasing activities authorized to be performed by the purchasing department and under (B) for such purchases the approximate number of contracts or purchase orders awarded with the
   approximate dollar volume for the latest ended fiscal year.

   A. Types of Purchasing Activities Authorized (Check all applicable)

53-_____ a. Material and supply purchase   59-_____ g. Real property purchases
54-_____ b. Equipment purchases   60-_____ h. Real property leases/renting
55-_____ c. Equipment leases/renting   61-_____ i. Surplus/excess sales
56-_____ d. Outside personal services   62-_____ j. Inter-department/agency transfers
57-_____ e. Outside professional services   63-_____ k. Other (specify)_____
58-_____ f. Construction contracts

   B. Number and Dollar Volume

      a. Total number of contracts awarded . . . .   _____ 64-68
      b. Total dollar volume of contracts awarded . . . . $_____ 69-74

B.84

II. ORGANIZATION

10. Please indicate the organizational structure through which the purchasing activity is handled. (Check one)

7-_____ 1. Purchasing Board, Commission, or Committee
_____ 2. Separate department, concerned exclusively with the purchasing function
_____ 3. Part of the Finance Department
_____ 4. Part of the Administration Department
_____ 5. Part of another department (specify department)_____
_____ 6. Each department does its own purchasing
_____ 7. Other (specify) _____

11. Do you have a full-time purchasing officer? . . . .   YES ( )   NO ( ) 8

IF "NO,"

A. Who is assigned the purchasing function? (Check one)

9-_____ 1. Mayor or chief elected official
_____ 2. Manager or chief administrative officer
_____ 3. Assistant manager or assistant chief administrative officer
_____ 4. Finance director
_____ 5. Controller/comptroller
_____ 6. City clerk/county clerk
_____ 7. Each department head
_____ 8. Other (specify) _____

B. What percentage of his time is devoted exclusively to purchasing matters? . . . . . _____ %
(10-11)

IF "YES,"

A. What was the total actual cost of operating the purchasing department
(materiel management) for the latest ended fiscal year? . . . . $ _____ 12-17

B. For the classification levels shown below, what was the actual number of
full-time employees working in the purchasing department as of the latest ended
fiscal year? Show the annual salary range paid each classification.

Classification levels	Actual number of full-time positions (as of latest ended FY)	Annual salary ranges	
		Beginning (entrance step) ($)	Ending (last step) ($)
a. Chief purchasing officer (specify title) _____ . . .	(18)	(19-23)	(24-28)
b. Assistant purchasing officer	(29-30)	(31-36)	(36-40)
c. Purchasing agent-manager	(41-42)	(43-47)	(48-52)
d. Supervisory buyers	(53-54)	(55-59)	(60-64)
e. Senior buyers	(65-66)	(67-71)	(72-76)
f. Junior buyers	(7-8)	(9-13)	(14-18)
g. Standards engineers	(19-20)	(21-25)	(26-30)
h. Value analysts	(31-32)	(33-37)	(38-42)
i. Researchers (market analysts)	(43-44)	(45-49)	(50-54)
j. Inspectors	(55-56)	(57-61)	(62-66)
k. Other professionals	(67-68)	(69-73)	(7-11)
l. Non-professionals (clerical)	(12-13)	(14-18)	(19-23)

B.85

12. To what official or office does the purchasing officer directly report? (Check all applicable.)

24-_____a. Legislative body   27-_____d. Finance director
25-_____b. Mayor or chief elected official   28-_____e. Controller/comptroller
26-_____c. Manager or chief administrative officer   29-_____f. No one
     30-_____g. Other (specify)_____

13. A. How are the following officials and professional staff hired?

Official/Staff	Hired by civil service:		Appointed by:			
	Without exam (1)	Competitive exam (2)	For specified term (3)	For non-specified term (4)		Title (specify) (5)
Purchasing officer ...					(31)	(34)
Assistant purchasing officer					(32)	(35)
Other professional purchasing staff					(33)	(36)

B. If they are appointed for a specified term please indicate the number of years for the official or staff.

a. Purchasing officer .... _____years
(37)

b. Assistant purchasing officer .... _____years
(38)

c. Other professional purchasing staff .... _____years
(39)

14. What constitutes the minimum (A) education, (B) experience, and/or (C) professional designation requirements for selecting and hiring purchasing officers and other professional purchasing staff?

Minimum requirements	Purchasing officer (Check)	Assistant purchasing officer (Check)	Other professional purchasing staff (Check)
NO MINIMUM REQUIREMENTS..............	(40)	(41)	(42)
(A) Education:			
1. Some high school.................	(43)	(44)	(45)
2. High school diploma	(46)	(47)	(48)
3. 1-2 years college	(49)	(50)	(51)
4. Over 2 years college, but no degree	(52)	(53)	(54)
5. Bachelor of Arts or Science	(55)	(56)	(57)
6. Law degree.....................	(58)	(59)	(60)
7. Masters degree...................	(61)	(62)	(63)
8. Other (specify) ———————	(64)	(65)	(66)
(B) Previous purchasing experience .... _____yrs. (67-68)	_____yrs. (69)	_____yrs. (70)	
(C) Professional designation:			
1. CPPO	(71)	(72)	(73)
2. Other (specify) ———————	(74)	(75)	(76)

15. Are officials and other employees having purchasing authority covered by either fidelity, surety, or position bond?

A. Officials .... YES ( ) NO ( ) 77
B. Other employees .... YES ( ) NO ( ) 78

B.86

III. SOLICITATION, OPENING AND REVIEWING OF BIDS (exclude construction contracting)

16. By what sources of authority are the following practices or functions covered? (Check all applicable.)

Practices/Functions	State statute	Local purchasing ordinance	Legal opinions	Other written policy	Unwritten policy	Not covered
a. Competitive bidding requirements	(7)	(8)	(9)	(10)	(11)	(12)
b. Exceptions, exemptions, and waivers of competitive bidding	(13)	(14)	(15)	(16)	(17)	(18)
c. Legal solicitation notices requirements	(19)	(20)	(21)	(22)	(23)	(24)
d. Sealed bid requirements and processing	(25)	(26)	(27)	(28)	(29)	(30)
e. Public opening of bid requirements	(31)	(32)	(33)	(34)	(35)	(36)
f. Resolution of tie bids	(37)	(38)	(39)	(40)	(41)	(42)
g. Consideration of late bids .	(43)	(44)	(45)	(46)	(47)	(48)
h. Making awards in a manner to discourage identical or collusive bidding	(49)	(50)	(51)	(52)	(53)	(54)
i. Disposal of surplus and scrap	(55)	(56)	(57)	(58)	(59)	(60)
j. Insurance purchase	(61)	(62)	(63)	(64)	(65)	(66)
k. Professional services contracts	(67)	(68)	(69)	(70)	(71)	(72)
l. Local preferences	(73)	(74)	(75)	(76)	(77)	(78)
m. Minority set-aside	(7)	(8)	(9)	(10)	(11)	(12)
n. Small business set-aside ...	(13)	(14)	(15)	(16)	(17)	(18)
o. Affirmative action program	(19)	(20)	(21)	(22)	(23)	(24)

17. Please indicate the dollar values requiring competitive bidding:

a. Informal quotations (verbal) .... From $ _____(25-29)_____ to $ _____(30-34)_____

b. Informal quotations (written)............................. From $ _____(35-39)_____ to $ _____(40-44)_____

c. Formal (sealed bids) .... From $ _____(45-49)_____

18. At what dollar amount are legal notices for bids required? .... $ _____(50-54)_____

19. Are there exceptions, exemptions, and waivers of competitive bidding permitted by law (statute, charter, ordinance) for the following conditions?

a. Emergencies .... YES ( ) NO ( ) 55
b. Only one source .... YES ( ) NO ( ) 56
c. Professional services .... YES ( ) NO ( ) 57
d. Other (specify)_____ .... YES ( ) NO ( ) 58

20. Who is responsible for drafting the specifications that accompany the invitation to bid? (Check one)

59-_____ 1. User agencies
_____ 2. Committee
_____ 3. Purchasing agent or department
_____ 4. Other (specify)_____

21. Who has final authority for approving specifications before they are issued with the invitation to bid? (Check one)

60-_____ 1. Mayor or county executive   _____ 5. Committee
_____ 2. City/county manager   _____ 6. Council or County Board
_____ 3. User agency   _____ 7. Other (specify) _____
_____ 4. Purchasing agent or department

22. Is the use of brand or trade names permitted in specifications? . . . . YES (   )   NO (   ) 61

23. Is there a legal requirement which constrains the writing of restrictive specifications? YES (   )   NO (   ) 62

24. Do you have a program to develop standard specifications for common use by all user agencies? . . . . YES (   )   NO (   ) 63

IV. SAFEGUARDS AND CONTROLS

25. By what sources of authority are the following practices or functions covered? (Check all applicable.)

Practices/Functions	State statute	Local purchasing ordinance	Legal opinions	Other written policy	Unwritten policy	Not covered
a. Bidder meeting prequalification requirements prior to being included on the bidder's list	(64)	(65)	(66)	(67)	(68)	(69)
b. Establishing a bidder's list . .	(70)	(71)	(72)	(73)	(74)	(75)
c. Bidder certification that the bids are submitted competitively and without collusion, either in the terms of the invitation to bid or as a separate certification . . .	(7)	(8)	(9)	(10)	(11)	(12)
d. Conflict of interest provision	(13)	(14)	(15)	(16)	(17)	(18)
e. Prohibition against corrupt bidder or vendor combinations, collusions or conspiracies	(19)	(20)	(21)	(22)	(23)	(24)
f. Prohibition against the acceptance of gifts. promises or bribes	(25)	(26)	(27)	(28)	(29)	(30)
g. Procedures for using agencies to register complaints about vendors to the purchasing department.	(31)	(32)	(33)	(34)	(35)	(36)
h. Bidder or vendor protest/appeals procedures	(37)	(38)	(39)	(40)	(41)	(42)
i. Suspension of vendors from selling to the county/city	(43)	(44)	(45)	(46)	(47)	(48)
j. Purchasing contracts having prior legal review and approval before execution.	(49)	(50)	(51)	(52)	(53)	(54)
k. Having an authorized purchase order in existence before acknowledging vendor invoices	(55)	(56)	(57)	(58)	(59)	(60)

B.88

26. What type of surety or other information is required when bids are submitted? (Check all applicable)

61-_____ a. Bid bonds   64-_____ d. Credit or mercantile ratings
62-_____ b. Bid deposits   65-_____ e. Other (specify)_____
63-_____ c. Certified financial statements   66-_____ f. NONE required

27. If bid bonds or bid deposits are required (excluding construction) are they: (Check one)

-67_____1. Discretionary
    _____2. Mandatory (If mandatory, beyond what bid amount? . . . . $_____ 68-72

                                                    and/or %_____ 73-74

28. Are performance bonds required (excluding construction)? . . . . YES ( ) NO ( ) 7

V. PURCHASING MANAGEMENT

29. Does the purchasing system regularly supply pricing information to user departments
    in the budget formulation process? . . . . YES ( ) NO ( ) 8

30. To what extent is the existing purchasing system integrated with management functions in the following
    areas? (Check one for each segment applicable.)

	Completely integrated (1)	Partially integrated (2)	Not integrated (3)	Not applicable (4)	
a. Budgeting	_____	_____	_____	_____	9
b. Accounting	_____	_____	_____	_____	10
c. Management information system	_____	_____	_____	_____	11

31. Is there an on-going training program for professional purchasing personnel
    (excluding attendance at 2 or 3 day conferences)? . . . . YES ( ) NO ( ) 12

    IF "YES," who provides such training to what professionals? (Check all applicable)

	Professionals	
	Staff (1)	Entry level (3)
Provides training		
a. In-house — within department or division	_____	_____ 13
b. In-house — by another department of division	_____	_____ 14
c. By outside sources	_____	_____ 15

32. Is the purchasing department required to be audited? . . . . YES (   ) NO (   ) 16

IF "YES,"

A. By what authority? (Check all applicable.)

17-_____a. State statute   20-_____d. Administrative code
18-_____b. Local ordinance   21-_____e. Other (specify)_____
19-_____c. Charter

B. Indicate for each type of audit the auditing method(s) and the frequency of the audits.

Methods of auditing	Financial audit		Performance/Management Audit	
	Check method(s) applicable	Frequency	Check method(s) applicable	Frequency
a. Internal	____ (22)	every ___(23-24) year(s)	____ (25)	every ___(26-27) year(s)
b. External (public)	____ (28)	every ___(29-30) year(s)	____ (31)	every ___(32-33) year(s)
c. External (private)	____ (34)	every ___(35-36) year(s)	____ (37)	every ___(38-39) year(s)

33. How satisfied are you with the management information in the following areas available to you through the purchasing system? (Circle appropriate response.)

Purchasing areas	Very satisfied (1)	Satisfied (2)	Not satisfied (3)	Not applicable (4)	
a. Research & development studies	1	2	3	4	40
b. Specifications & standards	1	2	3	4	41
c. Economic ordering quantities	1	2	3	4	42
d. Delivery scheduling	1	2	3	4	43
e. Commodity cataloguing.	1	2	3	4	44
f. Commodity buying schedules	1	2	3	4	45
g. Cooperative buying	1	2	3	4	46
h. Qualification of vendors	1	2	3	4	47
i. Bid solicitation	1	2	3	4	48
j. Bid processing	1	2	3	4	49
k. Contract award	1	2	3	4	50
l. Contract administration.	1	2	3	4	51
m. Receiving	1	2	3	4	52
n. Quality control (inspection, testing, etc.)	1	2	3	4	53
o. Vendor performance evaluations	1	2	3	4	54
p. Storage warehousing and distribution	1	2	3	4	55
q. Inter-department surplus transfers	1	2	3	4	56
r. Funds authorization and availability	1	2	3	4	57
s. Inventory management	1	2	3	4	58
t. Value analysis	1	2	3	4	59
u. Economic market analysis	1	2	3	4	60
v. Statistical accumulation and analysis (quantitative, qualitative)	1	2	3	4	61
w. Salvaged goods disposal	1	2	3	4	62
x. Other (specify) _____ . . .	1	2	3	4	63
y. Other (specify) _____ . . .	1	2	3	4	64

Name_____ Title _____ Telephone number _____

THANK YOU!

Appendix C

Scope and Methodology

SCOPE AND METHODOLOGY

Scope and Methodology

SCOPE

The scope of public purchasing, in terms of authority, is frequently confusing. To some, this particular function is understood to encompass responsibility for the entire spectrum of acquisitions made by government; for others, it is more narrowly defined as the acquisition of the supplies, equipment, and services that are necessary to maintain the daily operations of government. Since nearly all state and local government purchasing laws specifically address the scope and authority of purchasing from this latter viewpoint, the major thrust of this study has been to examine the laws, regulations, policies, practices, and procedures used by state and local governments for acquiring personal property and services. Accordingly, laws, policies, practices, and procedures governing public works and construction contracting, and real property are not included in this report. However, because purchasing authorities do become involved in construction contracting and because construction does come under the umbrella of the acquisition function, an analysis was made of the construction statutes of 32 States. The resulting data and comments were delivered separately to the Law Enforcement Assistance Administration in June 1973. They can provide the basis for a separate and subsequent inquiry.

Information concerning purchasing laws, policies, practices, and procedures was gathered from the 50 States, three territories, and 1,865 cities and counties. Although quasigovernmental organizations such as boards, commissions, and authorities are frequently active in governmental purchasing, they generally operate independently and were, therefore, not included in this study.

METHODOLOGY

To accomplish the study objectives, it was first necessary to determine what is being done and, from this body of knowledge, to arrive at recommendations for enhancing the effectiveness of all public purchasing programs. The latter effort was essentially one of comparative evaluation and entailed measuring the results achieved against the desired objectives. Examining the state-of-the-art was a fact-finding process which entailed an extensive review of statutes, ordinances, regulations, case law, Attorneys General's opinions, and procedural manuals.

The study was divided into two phases. The first was devoted primarily to collecting pertinent written materials governing the field of public purchasing, developing a method of analysis, and applying it to the data. The second phase consisted of field trips to selected States, cities, and counties. The purpose of these visits was to determine whether actual procedures and practices conformed with written requirements, and to identify effective implementing procedures and practices.

Analysis of Statutes and Regulations

Statutes and regulations were obtained by mail from the 50 States and three territories. Where the information received was incomplete or outdated, it was supplemented with additional research at university law libraries. Purchasing ordinances of several cities and counties were obtained from the National Institute of Governmental Purchasing (NIGP). A checklist was developed to assure that all major areas of interest in the statutes and regulations were reviewed in a consistent manner.

These areas were identified by initially analyzing the purchasing laws from several States having notably comprehensive coverage. Various law review articles were also used in focusing on problem areas in statutory coverage. Considering these data, 44 checklist questions were formulated in the following categories:

- Purchasing function;
- Bidders lists;
- Specifications;
- Bidding and contract award;
- Safeguards and controls; and
- Miscellaneous.

The checklist questions were applied to the laws and regulations. A listing was made of those questions for which statutory and regulatory provisions were either silent or too general to provide specific answers. These questions were sent to each State involved for further information. The States were asked to provide information to answer specific designated questions and to support their responses with either a copy of or a reference to the appropriate authoritative source. These replies were merged with the answers previously obtained in the original checklist and the final data were sent to the purchasing officials of each State for verification. The data gathered during this phase of research are presented in matrix fashion in Appendix A of this report. When using Appendix A, the reader should keep in mind that the data were accumulated as of March 1973. Changes which may have been made subsequent to this date are not reflected in the matrix. Nevertheless, the information provides a comprehensive profile of purchasing as generally covered in statutes and regulations.

Evaluation of Purchasing Manuals

In order to determine how well public purchasing organizations provide procedural instructions to their staffs, purchasing manuals were reviewed. Thirty-two States and territories responded to requests for purchasing manuals and other instructional materials. Fifteen of the manuals were selected for in-depth review because, in the aggregate, they represented the best overall subject coverage.

Based on a preliminary review of all manuals received, published articles, and other studies, evaluation criteria were established in the form of a checklist which encompassed the following major subjects:
* Principles, policy, and organization;
* Requirements planning, specifications, and standards;
* Requisitioning, procurement, and contracting; and
* Receiving, stores and warehouses, quality control, and disposal.

The review results and corresponding recommendations are presented in the chapters of this report entitled "Purchasing Manuals."

Bibliography

To ensure that purchasing was covered from every vantage point, the span of research included professional, technical, scholarly, and legal sources of information. The Bibliography, Appendix E, was divided into two listings—List of General References and List of Legal-Citations—to facilitate ease in using by the reader. The *Index to Legal Periodicals* and the *Index of Business Periodicals* were used as bases to identify pertinent articles. These indices provided a launching point for isolating articles and reviews that concern the public purchasing field. Information was also obtained from a variety of published and unpublished papers received from state and local purchasing officials, professional organizations, and members of the academic community. Once the reference materials were collected, they were arranged according to 14 subject headings which paralleled the statutory and regulatory research. The material gathered is presented in the List of General References portion of the Bibliography.

For a more specific view of the sensitive issues and problems associated with public purchasing, pertinent court decisions and Attorneys General's opinions were collected. This material provided a composite view of which issues are important, how such issues have been approached, and various degrees of latitude allowed purchasing officials in resolving these issues.

The gathering of this material encompassed a review of many sources that treated public purchasing not as a distinct topic but as a part of larger subjects such as general discussions of state and municipal law. Assistance was initially provided by the National Association of Attorneys General, whose members identified relevant Attorneys General's opinions and leading cases in the purchasing field. As the study progressed, additional court decisions and Attorneys General's opinions were identified, read, and, where deemed leading, added to the research base. The sources that were consulted to identify additional court decisions include *American Jurisprudence, Corpus Juris Secundum, American Law Reports,* and West's *Decennial Digest.* Additional Attorneys General's opinions were identified by consulting annotations to the state statutory codes, Shepard's state citations, state digests, and indices to bound volumes of State Attorneys General's opinions. The information gathered is arranged according to topic areas of the purchasing function within the List of Legal Citations portion of the Bibliography.

Purchasing Procedures in Cities and Counties

Another phase of the study included the research and review of city and county purchasing laws, policies, procedures, and practices. Although some of this information was made available from the ordinances obtained during other facets of the study, sufficient information was not received to make an accurate appraisal of city and county purchasing operations. Because of the sheer number of cities and counties, a complete review of all ordinances, administrative regulations, and manuals, as was conducted in the review of state procedures, was neither practicable nor feasible. It was, therefore, decided to conduct a nationwide survey of cities and counties. The assistance of the International City Management Association (ICMA) was sought because it is expert in surveying techniques and well-known to local governments.

With over 10,000 cities and counties from which to choose, it was necessary to reduce the number to a manageable and meaningful level and to focus on those collective purchasing practices which gave rise to purchasing systems. It was determined that the sample should consist of cities and counties with populations of 10,000 and over. This resulted in a survey population of 4,493 local governments.

As an initial step in developing the survey questionnaire, the following subjects were selected as major areas of interest: authorities, organization, bidding procedures, contract award, safeguards and controls, and purchasing management. Within each of these sections, a series of questions was developed which indicated the extent to which purchasing functions were covered by state statute, local ordinance, rules and regulations, manuals, and unwritten purchasing policies or practices. The synthesizing process involved developing a series of iterative drafts which were reviewed in depth with selected purchasing authorities and with ICMA. County and city purchasing authorities were visited and contacted by letter to obtain their reaction and input to the questionnaire.

To ensure that the questionnaire was clear and meaningful, and to elicit comments for improvement, a field test was conducted by sending the questionnaire to 150 cities and counties. Suggestions for improving the questionnaire were also obtained from representatives of various professional organizations, including the National Institute of Governmental Purchasing, the National League of Cities, the National Association of Counties, and the National Association of Purchasing Managers. Upon completing all aspects of the field test, the questionnaire was modified, finalized, and sent to all cities and counties included in the sample.

Over the course of several months, three successive mailings were made by ICMA. Survey responses were collected until the specified cut-off date. In order to facilitate the analysis of the tremendous volume of information received, responses were keypunched and tabulated according to prescribed formats and classifications. Extensive analyses were subsequently made, the results of which are presented in Appendix B, Cities and Counties. In accordance with a pre-arranged agreement, the results and observations of this survey are available to ICMA for publication in its *Urban Data Service Report* and *Municipal Yearbook*.

Field Visits

To augment the information obtained from researching statutes, regulations, and manuals, and from the local government survey, field visits were made to various state and local governments. These visits were particularly valuable in identifying exceptional and unique practices. A field visit program was developed for these visits to assure that the major areas of interest were covered. Although somewhat different programs were used for state and for local government field visits, both programs were essentially designed to:

- Clarify ambiguities resulting from prior research;
- Determine whether current practices are in compliance with written requirements;
- Examine what practices are in effect to implement statutory and regulatory purchasing requirements; and

- Identify practices which promote efficient purchasing operations.

Twelve States were selected for field visits. In an effort to obtain a representative cross section of all levels of practice, the selection process considered factors such as:

- Statutory and regulatory coverage;
- Geographic location;
- Centralized operations; and
- Size of purchasing operations.

The following States were visited:

California	New Mexico
Florida	New York
Kansas	Ohio
Kentucky	Pennsylvania
New Hampshire	Texas
New Jersey	Washington

Purchasing officials from Illinois, North Carolina, and Wisconsin were deeply involved in the study and provided considerable information on their purchasing operations to the study group. Consequently, visits to these States were not considered necessary.

The selection of cities and counties to be visited was even more difficult. A listing of proposed locations was circulated among study group participants, professional purchasing associations, and leaders in local government purchasing. The following locations were selected:

Cincinnati, Ohio
Fort Lauderdale, Florida
Long Beach, California
Philadelphia, Pennsylvania
St. Joseph, Missouri
Hennepin County, Minnesota
Nashville-Davison County, Tennessee
Prince Georges County, Maryland

Professional Services

During the course of the study, it became increasingly evident that contracting for professional services rarely came under the umbrella of the central purchasing authority but was handled by the using agencies. Coupling this observation with the increasing concern over the need for control and guidance of the very large amount of monies spent in this area, it was decided to increase the scope of the inquiry to include contracting for professional services. Consequently, a brief questionnaire was developed requesting information regarding practices and procedures for procuring professional services. The questionnaire was sent to the purchasing officials of all 50 States, and 34 replied. Because the laws and regulations governing this area usually are scattered throughout the statutes and are sparse and loosely structured, many of the responses were ambiguous and frequently contradicted other responses to the questionnaire. It was, therefore, necessary to conduct additional inquiries and research through personal interviews with various state purchasing officials.

Reports

This report represents the final product of the study. In June 1973, about midway through the study, an interim report was prepared. The interim report contained information on data collected, as well as tentative observations, conclusions, and recommendations. Its purpose was to provide a basis for reviewing the results to date and to provide direction for the remainder of the study. As such, it was a working tool for the study group and was not distributed.

Because of the intense interest in the study, and in response to numerous inquiries, *State and Local Government Purchasing, A Digest* was prepared and distributed to state and local governments in June 1974. The *Digest* highlights in capsule fashion many of the subjects presented in this final report.

Appendix D

Glossary of Public Purchasing Terms

Glossary of Public Purchasing Terms

INTRODUCTION

This glossary contains selected terms and definitions related to state and local government purchasing that, in many cases, cannot be found in standard, general-purpose dictionaries. The selected definitions are intended to make the terms understandable and usable by public purchasing representatives; thus, practical rather than legally perfect definitions are included.

Some of the definitions have appeared in specialized and technical glossaries and dictionaries. Some of these definitions have been borrowed exactly as earlier used; others have been modified. The sources from which definitions have been borrowed, either in whole or in part, include:

A Dictionary for Accountants. Eric L. Kohler. Prentice-Hall, Inc., Englewood Cliffs, New Jersey, 1970.

Dictionary of Purchasing Terms. National Institute of Governmental Purchasing, Inc., Washington, D.C., 1970.

Purchasing Handbook, second edition. George W. Aljian, Editor-in-Chief, McGraw-Hill Book Co., Inc., 1966.

The definitions for the following words and phrases may be found in the *Uniform Commercial Code* and, to conserve space, are not reproduced here except for the very few having additional definitions peculiar to public procurement.

Definitions Contained in the *Uniform Commercial Code*

Accept	Contract	Insolvency proceedings	Properly payable
Acceptance	Contract for sale	Insolvent	Protest
Action	Contract right	Installment contract	Purchase
Aggrieved party	Customer	Instrument	Purchaser
Agreement	Debtor	Inventory	Receipt
Alteration	Defendant	Issue	Remedy
Bailee	Definite time	Issuer	Rights
Bearer	Delivery	Item	Sale
Bearer form	Delivery order	Lot	Sale on approval
Bill of lading	Document	Merchant	Sale or return
Bona fide purchaser	Document of title	Negotiation	Secondary party
Buyer	Equipment	Note	Secured party
Buyer in ordinary course	Fault	Notice	Security
of business	Fungible	On demand	Seller
Cancellation	Genuine	Order	Surety
Certificate of deposit	Gives	Party	Term
Certification	Good faith	Presumed	Termination
Conforming to contract	Goods	Presumption	Third party
Consignee	Holder	Proceeds	Unauthorized
Consignor	Holder in due course	Promise	Value
Consumer goods			Warehouse receipt

GLOSSARY

Acknowledgement—A form used by a vendor to advise a purchaser that his order has been received. It usually implies acceptance of the order.

Act of God—A danger that could not be avoided by human power; any natural cause of damage which is irresistible (e.g., hurricane, flood, lightning), and which is in no way connected with negligence.

Advertising—*See,* Formal advertising; Legal notice.

Advice of shipment—A notice sent to a purchaser advising that shipment has gone forward and usually containing details of packing, routing, etc.

Agency—(1) A relationship between two parties by which one, the agent, is authorized to perform or transact certain business for the other, the principal; also, the office of the agent. (2) An administrative division of a government.

Agent—A person authorized by another, called a principal, to act for him.

All-or-none bid—A bid for a number of different items, services, etc., in which the bidder states that he will not accept a partial award, but will only accept an award for all the items, services, etc., included in the bid. Such bids are acceptable only if provided for in the Invitation for Bids or if the bidder quoted prices for all items, services, etc., and is actually the low bidder for every one.

Alternate bid—(1) A response to a call for alternate bids. *See,* Alternate bid, call for. (2) A bid submitted in knowing variance from the specifications. Such a bid is only acceptable when the variance is deemed to be immaterial.

Alternate bid, call for—An Invitation for Bids for a single need that can be filled by commodities of varying materials, dimensions, or styles. Bidders may submit one or more bids for each material, style, etc., and only one award will be made based on an assessment of what is best for the government, taking price as only one factor involved.

Antitrust legislation—Laws that attempt to prevent or eliminate monopolies or oligopolies and to prevent noncompetitive practices.

Authorized price list—A price list of the products and/or services covered in a contract which contains minimum essential information needed by users for placing orders.

Appropriation—Legislative sanction to use public funds for a specific purpose. Money set apart for a specific use.

Approved brands list—*See,* Qualified products list.

Arbitrary and capricious action—A willful and unreasoning action, without consideration of, and in disregard of, the facts and circumstances, without rational basis; grounds for a court to overrule or remand a discretionary decision or action by an administrative authority of the government.

Arbitration—A process by which a dispute between two contending parties is presented to one or more disinterested parties for a decision.

Architect and Engineer (A&E)—All professional services associated with the research, design, and construction of facilities.

Arrival notice—A notice sent by a carrier to a consignee advising of the arrival of a shipment.

As is—A term indicating that goods offered for sale are without warranty or guarantee, and that the purchaser takes the goods at his own risk without recourse against the seller for the quality or condition of the goods.

Award—The presentation of a purchase agreement or contract to a bidder; the acceptance of a bid or proposal.

Back-door buying—Making a purchase without going through the central purchasing authority.

Back order—That portion of an order which a vendor cannot deliver at the scheduled time and which he has re-entered for shipment at a later date.

Best interests of the State (city, county)—A term frequently used in granting a purchasing official the authority to use his discretion to take whatever action he feels is most advantageous to the government. The term is used when it is impossible to anticipate adequately the circumstances that may arise so that more specific directions could be delineated by the law or regulation.

Bid—An offer, as a price, whether for payment or acceptance. A quotation specifically given to a prospective purchaser upon his request, usually in competition with other offerors. Also, an offer by a buyer to a seller, as at an auction.

Bid-award file—A file that is divided into commodity and item sections each of which contains listings of who was solicited for individual bids, what each response was, and other information. The bid-award file is used to compare past bids for award patterns that might reveal collusive agreements or to make other comparisons of data.

Bid bond—An insurance agreement in which a third party agrees to be liable to pay a certain amount of money in the event that a specific bidder, if his bid is accepted, fails to sign the contract as bid. *See,* Bid deposit; Bid security.

Bid deposit—A sum of money or check, deposited with and at the request of the government, in order to guarantee that the bidder (depositor) will, if selected, sign the contract as bid. If the bidder does not sign the contract, he forfeits the amount of the deposit. *See,* Bid bond; Bid security. *See also,* Forfeiture of deposit or bond.

Bid opening—The process through which the contents of bids are revealed for the first time to the government, to the other bidders, and usually to the public. *See,* Public bid opening.

Bid sample—A sample required by the Invitation for Bids to be furnished by bidders as part of their bids to establish a quality level for the products being offered.

Bid security—A guarantee, in the form of a bond or deposit, that the bidder, if selected, will sign the contract as bid; otherwise, the bidder (in the case of a deposit) or the bidder or his guarantor (in the case of a bond) will be liable for the amount of the bond or deposit. *See,* Bid bond; Bid deposit.

Bidder—Any person who makes a bid.

Bidders list—A list maintained by the purchasing authority setting out the names and addresses of suppliers of various goods and services from whom bids, proposals, and quotations can be solicited. *See,* Prequalification of bidders; Qualified bidder.

Bill—A list of charges or costs presented by a vendor to a purchaser, usually enumerating the items furnished, their unit and total costs, and a statement of the terms of sale; an invoice.

Bill of materials—A list specifying the quantity and character of materials and parts required to produce or assemble a stated quantity of a particular product.

Blanket order—A purchase arrangement in which the purchaser contracts with a vendor to provide the purchaser's requirements for an item(s) or a service, on an as-required and often over-the-counter basis. Such arrangements set a limit on the period of time they are to be valid and the maximum amount of money which may be spent at one time or within a period of time. *See,* Open-end contract; Price agreement; Requirements contract.

Blanket purchase—*See,* Blanket order.

Bona fide—In good faith.

Bond—An obligation in writing, binding one or more parties as surety for another.

Brand name—A product name which serves to identify that product as having been made by a particular manufacturer. A trade name.

Brand name specification—A specification that cites a brand name, model number, or some other designation that identifies a specific product as an example of the quality level desired. *See,* Equal, Or equal.

Breach of contract—A failure without legal excuse to perform any promise which forms a whole or part of a contract. *See,* Forfeiture of deposit or bond.

Breach of warranty—Infraction of an express or implied agreement as to the title, quality, content, or condition of a thing sold.

Bulk purchasing—Purchasing in large quantities in order to reduce the price per unit; volume purchasing.

Buyer—*See,* Purchasing agent. *See also, Uniform Commercial Code.*

Buyer's market—Market conditions in which goods can easily be secured and economic forces of business tend to cause goods to be priced at the purchaser's estimate of value.

Cash discount—A discount from the purchase price allowed to the purchaser if he pays within a specified period. *See,* Discount.

Cash on delivery (COD)—Payment due and payable upon delivery of goods.

Catalog—A listing of item identifications arranged systematically.

Caveat emptor—"Let the buyer beware." A maxim that stands for the rule that the buyer should be careful in making a purchase because the burden of defective goods rests with him. The vendor can be made to take the responsibility for some defects through specifications and warranties.

Caveat venditor—"Let the seller beware." A maxim relating to situations where the vendor bears the responsibility for defects in the goods he sells.

Central purchasing authority—The administrative unit in a centralized purchasing system with the authority, responsibility, and control of purchasing activities.

Centralized purchasing—A system of purchasing in which the authority, responsibility, and control of purchasing activities is concentrated in one administrative unit.

Certificate of compliance—A supplier's certification that the supplies or services in question meet certain specified requirements.

Certificate of non-collusion—A statement signed by a bidder and submitted with his bid to affirm that his bid is made freely without consultation with any other bidder.

Claim—The aggregate of the operative facts which serve as a basis for a demand for payment, reimbursement, or compensation for injury or damage under law or contract; the assertion of such a demand.

Code of ethics—A written set of guidelines within which judgements and considerations of professional ethics and behavior should be made. *See,* Purchasing ethics.

Collusion—A secret agreement or cooperation between two or more persons to accomplish a fraudulent, deceitful, or unlawful purpose.

Collusive bidding—The response to bid invitations by two or more vendors who have secretly agreed to circumvent laws and rules regarding independent and competitive bidding. *See,* Corrupt combination, collusion, or conspiracy in restraint of trade; Price fixing.

Commercial law—That branch of the law that designates the rules that determine the rights and duties of persons engaged in trade and commerce.

Commodity—An article of trade, a moveable article of value, something that is bought or sold; any moveable or tangible thing that is produced or used as the subject of barter or sale.

Competition—The process by which two or more vendors vie to secure the business of a purchaser by offering the most favorable terms as to price, quality, and service.

Competitive bidding—The offer of prices by individuals or firms competing for a contract, privilege, or right to supply specified services or merchandise.

Competitive negotiation—A technique for purchasing goods and services, usually of a technical nature, whereby qualified suppliers are solicited, negotiations are carried on with each bidder, and the best offer (in terms of performance, quality of items, price, etc.), as judged against proposal evaluation criteria, is accepted; negotiated award.

Confirming order—A purchase order issued to a vendor, listing the goods or services and terms of an order placed verbally, or otherwise, in advance of the issuance of the usual purchase document.

Conflict of interest—A situation wherein an individual as part of his duties must make a decision or take action that will affect his personal interests.

Consideration—Acts, promises, or things of value exchanged by two parties and serving as the basis for a contract between them.

Consultants and experts—Those persons who are exceptionally qualified, by education or by experience, in a particular field to perform some specialized service.

Contingency—A possible future event or condition arising from presently known or unknown causes, the outcome of which is indeterminate at the present time.

Contract—A deliberate verbal or written agreement between two or more competent persons to perform or not to perform a specific act or acts. *See, Uniform Commercial Code.*

Contract administration—The management of all facets of contracts to assure that the contractor's total performance is in accordance with his contractual commitments and that the obligations of the purchaser are fulfilled. In government, this management is conducted within the framework of delegated responsibility and authority and includes the support of using agencies.

Contract modification—An alteration that introduces new details or cancels details but leaves the general purpose and effect of the contract intact.

Contract record—A record providing full particulars regarding the orders placed for delivery of goods in a contract so that the volume of purchases against the contact can be determined.

Contractor—One who contracts to perform work or furnish materials in accordance with a contract.

Contractual services—Services furnished under a contract in which charges, effective periods, and extent of work are defined.

Convenience termination clause—A contract clause which permits the government to terminate, at its own discretion, the performance of work in whole or in part, and to make settlement of the vendor's claims in accordance with appropriate regulations.

Cooperative purchasing—The combining of requirements of two or more political entities in order to obtain the benefits of volume purchases and/or reduction in administrative expenses.

Corrupt combination, collusion, or conspiracy in restraint of trade—A phrase referring to an agreement between two or more businesses to stifle, control, or otherwise inhibit free competition in violation of state and/or federal antitrust statutes. *See,* Collusive bidding; Price fixing.

Damages—Compensation, usually in money, for injury to goods, persons, or property.

Debarment—A shutting out or exclusion for cause (as a bidder from the list of qualified bidders).

Debt—Any obligation to pay money. Ordinarily the term debt means a sum of money due by reason of a contract expressed or implied. Broadly, the word may include obligations other than to pay money, such as the duty to render services or deliver goods.

Default—Failure by a party to a contract to comply with contractual requirements; vendor failure.

Defect—A noncomformance of an item with specified requirements.

Delivery schedule—The required or agreed time or rate of delivery of goods or services purchased for a future period.

Delivery terms—Conditions in a contract relating to freight charges, place of delivery, time of delivery, and method of transportation.

Descriptive literature—Information, such as charts, illustrations, drawings, and brochures which show the characteristics or construction of a product or explain its operation, furnished by a bidder as a part of his bid to describe the products offered in his bid. The term includes only information required to determine acceptability of the product, and excludes other information, such as that furnished in connection with the qualifications of a bidder or for use in operating or maintaining equipment.

Design specification—A purchase specification delineating the essential characteristics that an item bid must possess to be considered for award and so detailed as to describe how the product is to be manufactured; generic specification.

Designation of special purpose—A technique used when purchasing items for a special use for which no items of that kind are produced (e.g., sewing machines for teaching blind people to sew), accomplished by sending out the specification that is used for the basic item with a description of the special purpose for which the item will be used, and a questionnaire asking what modifications bidders are willing to make in their standard products to meet the particular needs.

Discount—An allowance or deduction granted by the seller to the buyer, usually when certain stipulated conditions are met by the buyer, which reduces the cost of the goods purchased. However, discounts may be granted by the seller without reference to stipulated conditions. An example of such use of discount is the application of discount to a nominal or "list" price to establish the "net" or actual price. *See,* Cash discount; Quantity discount; Standard package discount; Trade discount.

Discount schedule—The list of discounts applying to varying quantities of goods or applicable to differing classifications of purchasers.

Disposition—Acting to remove from the premises and control of a using agency goods that are surplus or scrap.

Disposition can be accomplished by transferring, selling, or destroying the goods.

Emergency purchase—A purchase made without following the normal purchasing procedure in order to obtain goods or services quickly to meet an emergency.

Equal, Or equal—A phrase(s) used to indicate the substitutability of products of similar or superior function, purpose, design, and/or performance characteristics. *See,* Brand name specification.

Equal Employment Opportunity Program—A plan to include minority groups or other disadvantaged persons in the work force of businesses affected by the plan.

Equipment—Personal property of a durable nature which retains its identity throughout its useful life. *See, Uniform Commercial Code.*

Escalation clause—A clause in a purchase contract providing for upward adjustment of the contract price if specified contingencies occur; price escalation clause.

Ethics—*See,* Code of ethics; Purchasing ethics.

Evaluation of bid—The process of examining a bid after opening to determine the bidder's responsibility, responsiveness to requirements, and other characteristics of the bid relating to the selection of the winning bid.

Exhaustion of administrative remedies—A legal doctrine to the effect that where an administrative remedy is provided by statute, relief must be first sought from the administrative body, and all attempts to obtain such administrative relief must be used up before the complaining party may look to the courts for relief.

Expedite—To hasten or to assure delivery of goods purchased in accordance with a time schedule, usually by contact by the purchaser with the vendor.

Express warranty—Any affirmation of fact or promise made by a seller to a buyer which relates to the goods and becomes part of the basis of the bargain.

Extend, option to—A part of a contract which contemplates a continuance of the original contract for a further time upon compliance with the conditions for the exercise of the option.

Fair market value—A price that would induce a willing purchaser to purchase or a willing seller to sell in an open market transaction; the price a property would bring at a fair sale between parties dealing on equal terms.

Fair-trade statute—A state law providing that a manufacturer may legally set a minimum resale price for his products and that retailers and distributors must observe that minimum.

Fidelity bond—A bond which secures an employer up to an amount stated in the bond for losses caused by dishonesty or infidelity on the part of an employee.

Field purchase order—A limited and specific purchase order used in situations where authority to make the type of purchase involved has been delegated to using agencies.

Firm bid—A bid that binds the bidder until a stipulated time of expiration.

Fiscal year—A period of 12 consecutive months selected as a basis for annual financial reporting, planning, or budgeting.

Fixed price contract—A contract which provides for a firm price under which the contractor bears the full responsibility for profit or loss.

Forfeiture of deposit or bond—A loss by omission, negligence, or misconduct for the performing of or the failure to perform a particular act, (e.g., not accepting a contract when an award is made); breach of contract. *See,* Bid bond; Bid deposit; Fidelity bond; Performance bond.

Formal advertising—The placement of a notice in a newspaper or other publication according to legal requirements to inform the public that the government is requesting bids on specific purchases that it intends to make. *See,* Legal notice.

Formal bid or offer—A bid which must be forwarded in a sealed envelope and in conformance with a prescribed format to be opened at a specified time.

Forward purchasing—The purchasing of quantities exceeding immediate needs, e.g., in anticipation of a price increase or a future shortage.

Forward supply contract—A contract for future supply of definite quantities of materials or services over a fixed period. May be drawn off by "draw-off orders," or delivered at a fixed and predetermined rate set out in the contract.

Fraud—A positive act resulting from a willful intent to deceive another with the purpose of depriving him of his rights or property.

Full cost recovery funding—*See,* Industrial funding.

General provisions—The mandatory (by law or regulation) clauses for all contracts by type of purchase or contract. Clauses devised especially for a given purchase are called special provisions.

Generic name—Relating to or characteristic of a whole group or class; not protected by trademark registration.

Generic specification—*See,* Design specification.

Goods—Anything purchased other than services or real property. *See, Uniform Commercial Code.*

Gross negligence—The degree of lack of care that shows a reckless disregard for life or safety, or that indicates a conscious indifference to the rights of others.

Guarantee—To warrant, stand behind, or ensure performance or quality, as a supplier in relation to his product.

Identical bid—A bid that agrees in all respects with another bid.

Imprest funds—Funds set aside as a cash reserve for expenditures made in accordance with established policies and controls; petty cash.

Improper influence—Domination by the actions of one person over the actions of another so as to prevent the proper exercise of the latter's discretion.

Industrial funding—Full financing of program activities out of sale of goods or services furnished; full cost recovery funding.

Ineligible bidder—A supplier who, by reason of financial instability, unsatisfactory reputation, poor history of performance, or other similar reasons, cannot meet the qualifications for placement on the bidders list or for award.

Informal bid—An unsealed competitive offer conveyed by letter, telephone, telegram, or other means.

Inspection—Critical examination and/or testing of items to determine whether they have been received in the proper quantity and in the proper condition, and to verify that they conform to the applicable specifications.

Inspection report—A report to inform the purchasing authority of the quality or condition of the items delivered.

In-state preference—*See,* Preference.

Invitation for Bids—A request, verbal or written, which is made to prospective suppliers requesting the submission of a bid on commodities or services.

Item—Any product, material, or service.

Labor surplus area—A geographical section of concentrated unemployment or underemployment, as designated by the U.S. Department of Labor.

Late bid or proposal—A bid or proposal which is received at the place designated in the Invitation for Bids after the hour established by the invitation as the time by which all bids or proposals must be received.

Latent defect—A defect which could not be discovered by ordinary and reasonable inspection.

Lead time—The period of time from date of ordering to date of delivery which the buyer must reasonably allow the vendor to prepare goods for shipment.

Lease—A contract conveying from one person (lessor) to another (lessee) real estate or personal property for a term in return for a specified rent or other compensation.

Lease-purchase agreement—A rental contract in which the renting party's periodic payments or parts thereof are applied both to fulfill the rental obligation and as installments for eventual ownership of the commodity upon completion of the agreement.

Legal notice—The notice that is required by law. Legal notice for some purchases may be the posting of an announcement of the purchase in a public place, the notification of the appropriate bidders from the bidders list, a formal advertisement in a newspaper or newspapers, or a combination of these methods. *See,* Formal advertising.

License—A non-transferable permission granted by a government or other authority to perform an act or to engage in an enterprise that is restricted or regulated by law.

Life-cycle costing—A procurement technique which considers operating, maintenance, acquisition price, and other costs of ownership in the award of contracts to ensure that the item acquired will result in the lowest total ownership cost during the time the item's function is required.

Line item—A procurement item specified in the Invitation for Bids for which the bidder is asked to give individual pricing information and which, under the terms of the invitation, is usually susceptible to a separate contract award.

Liquidated damages—A specific sum of money, set as part of a contract, to be paid by one party to the other if he should default on the contract.

List price—The published price for an item that a vendor uses for informing customers and potential customers.

Local preference—*See,* Preference.

Local purchase—A purchase by an agency for its own use or for the use of another agency logistically supported by it.

Lowest and best bid—*See,* Lowest responsible bidder.

Lowest responsible bidder—That bidder who is awarded a contract because his bid in unit price, total cost of operation, or value per dollar is lower than any of the bidders whose reputation, past performance, and business and financial capabilities are such that they would be judged by the appropriate government authority to be capable of satisfying the government's needs for the specific contract. Virtually the same as "lowest and best bid," "lowest responsive and responsible bidder," and "most advantageous bid, price and other factors considered."

Lump sum—A price agreed upon between vendor and purchaser for a group of items without breakdown of individual values; a lot price.

Manual—*See,* Purchasing manual.

Manufacturer—One who (1) controls the design and production of an item, or (2) produces an item from crude or fabricated materials, or (3) assembles materials or components, with or without modification, into more complex items.

Market (noun)—The aggregate of forces that determine the prices and amount of trade in the exchange of goods.

Market (verb)—To carry out all activities intended to sell a product or service. Includes advertising, packaging, surveying the potential market, etc.

Material(s)—Supplies required to perform a function or manufacture an item, particularly that which is incorporated into an end item or consumed in its manufacture.

Merit system—A system of selecting and promoting civil servants on the basis of competitive examination or other comparable objective evaluation of their abilities rather than by political appointment.

Misrepresentation—A manifestation by words or other conduct that, under the circumstances, amounts to an assertion not in accordance with the facts.

Mistake in bid—A miscalculation in composing a bid resulting in an incorrect price or other term which may affect the bidder's eligibility to be awarded the contract.

Mock-up—A model, usually full size and constructed of inexpensive material, made for the purpose of studying the construction and use of an article or mechanical device. *See,* Pilot model; Prototype.

Modification—Any formal revision of the terms of a contract.

Monopoly—(1) An exclusive right or power to carry on a particular activity. (2) The ownership or control of enough of the supply of or market for a product or service to stifle competition, control prices, or otherwise restrict trade.

Multiple award—The award of separate contracts to two or more bidders for the same commodities in situations where the award of a single contract would be impossible or impractical.

Mutual assent—The state where the parties to a contract agree to all the terms and conditions in the same sense and with the same meaning.

Negligence—The failure to do that which an ordinary, reasonable, prudent man would do, or the doing of some act which an ordinary, prudent man would not do. Reference must always be made to the situation, the circumstances, and the knowledge of the parties.

Negotiated award—*See,* Competitive negotiation.

Net price—Price after all discounts, rebates, etc., have been allowed.

Net terms—*See,* Discount.

No bid—A response to an Invitation for Bids stating that the respondent does not wish to submit a bid. It usually operates as a procedural device to prevent debarment from the bidders list for failure to submit bids.

Nonresponsive bid—A bid that does not conform to the essential requirements of the Invitation for Bids; nonconforming bid, unresponsive bid.

Obsolescent—Becoming obsolete, due usually to technological development.

Obsolete—Out of date; no longer in use.

Offer—The act of one person that gives another person the legal power to create a contract to which both of them are parties; to perform such an act.

Oligopoly—A market situation in which a few companies control or dominate the market for a product or service.

Open-account purchase—A purchase made by a buyer who has established credit with the seller. Payment terms are usually stated to require payment of invoice on or before a specific date or dates; also, to require payment of invoice in full, or less a certain percentage for prompt payment. Such terms are agreed upon between buyer and seller at the time of placing the order, or before.

Open-end contract—A contract in which quantity or duration is not specified, such as a requirements contract. *See,* Blanket order; Price agreement; Requirements contract; Term contracting.

Open-market purchase—A purchase, usually of a limited dollar amount, which is made by buying from any available source, as opposed to buying from a bidder who has responded to an Invitation for Bids.

Option—The right, acquired for consideration, to buy or sell something at a fixed price within a specified time.

Option to extend—*See,* Extend, option to.

Option to renew—A contract clause that allows a party to elect to reinstitute the contract for an additional term.

Or equal—*See,* Equal, Or equal.

Order—A request or command issued to a supplier for goods or services at a specified price. *See, Uniform Commercial Code.*

Order form—A form by which a supplier is informed of an order.

Order level—The level of stock of any item at which an order is initiated for more supplies of that item.

Order record—A central numerical register of orders issued.

Packing list—A document which itemizes in detail the contents of a particular package or shipment.

Partnership—An agreement under which two or more persons agree to carry on a business for profit, sharing in the profits and losses by an agreed to proportion, but each being liable for losses to the extent of all of his personal assets.

Patent—A grant made by a government to an inventor, which gives the inventor the exclusive right to make, use, and sell the invention for a period of years.

Patent clearance—A letter or other formal communication stating that the reporting requirements of the patent rights clause contained in a contract have been complied with by the contractor.

Penalty clause—A clause in a contract specifying the sum of money to be paid if the contractor defaults on the terms of his contract, particularly in respect to time.

Performance bond—A contract of guaranty executed subsequent to award by a successful bidder to protect the government from loss due to his inability to complete the contract as agreed. *See,* Forfeiture of deposit or bond.

Performance record—Record to indicate a supplier's ability to keep delivery promises and reliability, together with consistency of quality of the product.

Performance specification—A specification setting out performance requirements that have been determined to be necessary for the item involved to perform and last as required.

Perishable goods—Goods which are subject to spoilage within a relatively short time.

Personal property—Everything which is not real property, which is subject to ownership, and which has exchangeable value.

Petty cash—*See,* Imprest funds.

Pilot model—A model, usually handmade, used in production planning for production engineering studies. *See,* Mock-up; Prototype.

Political subdivision—A subdivision of a State which has been delegated certain functions of local government, and which can include counties, cities, towns, villages, hamlets, boroughs, and parishes.

Preference—An advantage in consideration for award of a contract granted to a vendor by reason of the vendor's residence, business location, or business classification (e.g., small business).

Prepaid—A term denoting that transportation charges have been or are to be paid at the point of shipment.

Prequalification of bidders—The screening of potential vendors in which a government considers such factors as financial capability, reputation, management, etc., in order to develop a list of bidders qualified to bid on government contracts. *See,* Bidders list; Qualified bidder.

Price—The amount of money that will purchase a definite quantity, weight, or other measure of a commodity.

Price agreement—A contractual agreement in which a purchaser contracts with a vendor to provide the purchaser's requirements at a predetermined price. Usually it involves a minimum number of units, orders placed directly with the vendor by the purchaser, and a limited duration of the contract (usually one year). *See,* Blanket order; Open-end contract; Requirements contract; Term contracting.

Price at the time of delivery—A term used in sales contracts when market prices are so volatile that a vendor will not give a firm price or use an escalator clause but will only agree to charge the price that he is charging all customers for similar purchases on the day he ships or delivers the goods in question.

Price competition—The selection of a contractor, from two or more competing firms, based either solely on prices submitted, or on the final prices resulting from negotiation with all competing contractors within a range.

Price control—The fixing or restricting of prices especially by a governmental agency.

Price escalation clause—*See,* Escalation clause.

Price fixing—Agreements among competitors to sell at the same price, to adopt formulas for the computation of selling prices, to maintain specified discounts, to establish lower prices without prior notification to others, or to maintain predetermined price differentials between different quantities, types, or sizes of products. *See,* Collusive bidding; Corrupt combination, collusion, or conspiracy in restraint of trade.

Price maintenance—The establishment by a manufacturer or wholesaler of a price for an item below which he will not sell or permit his product to be sold by others.

Price protection—An agreement by a vendor with a purchaser to grant the purchaser any reduction in price which the vendor may establish on his goods prior to shipment of the purchaser's order. Price protection is sometimes extended for an additional period beyond the date of shipment.

Price rebate—An allowance on price, usually given after the completion of the contract and most frequently based on some relationship with the business turnover.

Price schedule—The list of prices applying to varying quantities or kinds of goods.

Principal—One who employs an agent; a person who has authorized another to act on his account and subject to his control.

Priority—The degree of precedence given to a particular requisition, order, or contract to obtain completion, delivery, or performance on a particular date at the expense, if necessary, of competing demands to the same supplier or facility.

Procurement—The process of obtaining goods or services, including all activities from the preparation and processing of a requisition, through receipt and approval of the final invoice for payment. The acts of preparing specifications, making the purchase, and administering the contract are involved. *See,* Purchasing cycle.

Professional behavior—*See,* Code of ethics; Purchasing ethics.

Program—A scheme of action to accomplish a definitive objective covering a major area of an organization's responsibility.

Proprietary article—An item made and marketed by a person or persons having the exclusive right to manufacture and sell it.

Proprietary information—Information or data describing technical processes, tools, or mechanisms that a business wishes to keep from general public view in order to maintain its competitive position in the market. *See,* Trade secret.

Proposal—An offer made by one party to another as a basis for negotiations for entering into a contract.

Proposal evaluation criteria—Weighted standards, relating to management capability, technical capability, approach in meeting performance requirements, price, and other important factors that are used for evaluating which bidder in a competitive negotiation has made the most advantageous offer.

Protest—A complaint about a governmental administrative action or decision brought by a bidder or vendor to the appropriate administrative section with the intention of achieving a remedial result.

Prototype—A model suitable for evaluation of design, performance, and production potential of a system, subsystem, or component. *See,* Mock-up; Pilot model.

Public—The people of an area.

Public bid opening—The process of opening and reading bids, conducted at the time and place specified in the Invitation for Bids and/or the advertisement, and in the view of anyone who wishes to attend. *See,* Bid opening.

Public policy—That which is deemed by courts to be general and well-settled public opinion relating to the duties of men and government.

Public record—All information about government activities that is available for public inspection.

Purchase order—A purchaser's document used to formalize a purchase transaction with a vendor. A purchase order, when given to a vendor, should contain statements as to the quantity, description, and price of the goods or services ordered; agreed terms as to payment, discounts, date of performance, transportation terms, and all other agreements pertinent to the purchase and its execution by the vendor. Acceptance of a purchase order constitutes a contract.

Purchase requisition—A form used to request the purchasing department to purchase goods or services from vendors.

Purchasing agent—An administrator whose job includes soliciting bids for purchases and making awards of purchase contracts; buyer.

Purchasing cycle—The cycle of activities carried out by a purchasing department in the acquisition of goods and services. *See,* Procurement.

Purchasing ethics—Moral principles that apply to the personnel of the purchasing department and all people who are involved in the purchasing process, particularly with respect to the use of government funds and relationships between buyers and sellers. *See,* Code of ethics.

Purchasing manual—A formal collection of instructions relative to procedures to be followed by all parties when making use of or dealing with the purchasing department in procurement actions.

Purchasing official—The administrative official who most directly oversees the activities of purchasing agents and those other aspects of property management that are joined as separate or subordinate sections under individual administrative control.

Purchasing, public—The process of obtaining goods and services for public purposes following procedures implemented to protect public funds from being expended extravagantly or capriciously.

Qualified bidder—A bidder determined by the government to meet minimum set standards of business competence, reputation, financial ability, and product quality for placement on the bidders list. *See,* Bidders list; Prequalification of bidders.

Qualified products list—A specification which is developed by evaluating various brands and models of an item and listing those that are determined to be acceptable as the only ones for which bids may be submitted; an approved brands list.

Quality assurance—A planned and systematic series of actions considered necessary to provide adequate confidence that a product that has been purchased will perform satisfactorily in service.

Quality control—The procedures and policies used to ensure adequate quality of goods produced or received.

Quantity discount—An allowance determined by the quantity or value of a purchase. *See,* Discount.

Quotation—A statement of price, terms of sale, and description of goods or services offered by a vendor to a prospective purchaser; the stating of the current price of a commodity; the price so stated.

Receiving report—A form used by a receiving function to inform others, such as the purchasing and accounting departments, of the receipt of goods purchased.

Renegotiation—Deliberation, discussion, or conference to change or amend the terms of an existing agreement.

Renew, option to—*See,* Option to renew.

Reordering level—The stock level at which a requisition for the replenishment of the stock should be initiated.

Repudiation of contract—A positive and unequivocal refusal to perform a contract.

Requirements contract—A contract in which the vendor agrees to supply all the purchaser's requirements that arise for an item or items within a specified period. *See,* Blanket order; Open-end contract; Price Agreement; Term contracting.

Requisition—An internal document by which a using agency requests the purchasing department to initiate a procurement.

Research and development (R&D)—The process by which new products or new product forms are created; precedes production.

Responsible bidder—A bidder whose reputation, past performance, and business and financial capabilities are such that he would be judged by the appropriate government authority to be capable of satisfying the government's needs for a specific contract.

Responsive bidder—A bidder whose bid does not vary from the specifications and terms set out by the government in the Invitation for Bids.

Restraint of trade—The effect of contracts or combinations which eliminate or stifle competition, effect a monopoly, artificially maintain prices, or otherwise hamper or obstruct the course of trade and commerce as it would be carried on if left to the control of natural and economic forces.

Restrictive specifications—Specifications that unnecessarily limit competition by eliminating items that would be capable of satisfactorily meeting actual needs.

Rules and regulations—Governing precepts and procedures made by an administrative body or agency under legislative authority that sometimes have the force and effect of law.

Salvage—Property that is no longer useful as a unit in its present condition but has some value in addition to its value as scrap, usually because parts from it may be recovered and reused.

Sample—*See,* Bid sample.

Scheduled purchase—A purchase for which a bid opening date is prescheduled so that using agencies' requirements for the period covered by the contract can be gathered and combined for the Invitation for Bids.

Scrap—Property that has no value except for its basic material content.

Sealed bid—A bid which has been submitted in a sealed envelope to prevent dissemination of its contents before the deadline for the submission of all bids; usually required by the purchasing authority on major procurements to ensure fair competition among bidders.

Seasonal—Depending upon the seasons, either climatic or economic, and usually cyclic on an annual basis.

Seasonal rate—A rate instituted for specified articles or commodities and effective only for certain periods of the year.

Seller's market—A market condition where demand is greater than supply; sellers can set prices and terms of sale, and prices are high or rising.

Service—Work performed to meet a demand, especially work that is not connected with manufacturing a product.

Service contract—A contract that calls for a contractor's time and effort rather than for a concrete end product.

Shipping list—A memorandum listing all items shipped at one time on a given order.

Single-source procurement—An award for a commodity which can only be purchased from one supplier, usually because of its technological, specialized, or unique character.

Small business—A designation for certain statutory purposes referring to a firm, corporation, or establishment having a small number of employees, low volume of sales, small amount of assets, or limited impact on the market.

Small Business Administration—A federal agency created to foster and protect the interests of small business concerns.

Solicitation—The process of notifying prospective bidders that the government wishes to receive bids on a set of requirements to provide goods or services. The process might consist of public advertising, the mailing of Invitations for Bids, the posting of notices, or telephone calls to prospective bidders.

Sovereign immunity—The principle which absolves the sovereign (State, city, county) from responding in damages for past injuries to another party.

Specification—A description of what the purchaser requires and, consequently, what a bidder must offer to be considered for an award.

Specifications committee—A committee whose purpose is to advise and assist the central purchasing authority in establishing specifications. This committee may also offer advice and assistance in developing standards. *See,* Standards committee.

Spot purchase—A one-time purchase made in the open market out of necessity or to take advantage of a bargain price.

Standard—A characteristic or set of characteristics for an item that, for reasons of quality level, compatibility with other products, etc., is generally accepted by the manufacturers and users of that item as a required characteristic for all items of that sort.

Standard commercial supplies—Articles which, in the normal course of business, are customarily maintained in stock by a manufacturer or any dealer, distributor, or other commercial dealer for the marketing of such articles.

Standard package discount—An allowance applied to goods supplied in the vendor's regular package. *See,* Discount.

Standard specification—A specification established through a standardization process to be used for all or most purchases of the item involved.

Standardization (of specifications)—The process of examining specifications and needs for items of similar end usage and drawing up one specification that will meet the needs for most or all purchases of that item.

Standards committee—A committee whose purpose is to advise and assist the central purchasing authority in establishing standards and, in some cases, specifications. *See,* Specifications committee.

Standing order—*See,* Blanket order.

Stock—A supply of goods maintained on hand in a supply system to meet anticipated demands.

Stock control—Control of the level of stock by control over the movement of goods into and out of stores.

Stock record—A record kept of items of materials in stock, usually located at a central point and showing stock level position.

Storage—The holding of goods in a designated place for safekeeping; a space or a place for the safekeeping of goods.

Supplemental agreement—Any contract modification which is accomplished by the mutual action of the parties.

Supplier—A firm that regularly furnishes needed items to a business or government; a vendor.

Supplies—Items which are consumed or expended in the course of being used.

Surplus property—Inventory not required by one using agency or all using agencies at the present time or in the foreseeable future.

Tabulation of bids—The recording of bids and bidding data that was submitted in response to a specific invitation for the purposes of comparison, analysis, and record-keeping.

Term contracting—A technique in which a source or sources of supply are established for a specified period of time, usually characterized by an estimated or definite minimum quantity, with the possibility of additional requirements beyond the minimum, all at a predetermined unit price. *See,* Blanket order; Open-end contract; Price agreement; Requirements contract.

Terms and conditions—A phrase generally applied to the rules under which all bids must be submitted and the terms that are included in most purchase contracts which are often published by purchasing authorities for the information of all potential bidders.

Terms of payment—All purchase transactions require a payment for the goods or services received and, excepting an unusual exchange or barter agreement, payment is made in negotiable funds in accordance with the terms agreed between the buyer and seller. There are three basic payment terms: cash, open account, and secured account.

Testing—A phase of inspection involving the determination by technical means of the physical and chemical properties of items, or compounds thereof, requiring not so much the element of personal judgment as the application of recognized and established scientific principles and procedures.

Title—The means whereby a person's ownership of property is established.

Token bid—A perfunctory offer submitted by a bidder with no serious intent of being the lowest bid; usually submitted when the bidder wishes to maintain eligibility for the bidders list or as a collusive device.

Total supply—A concept of purchasing, the objective of which is to plan in advance and provide for the broadest scope of purchasing and purchasing-related activities as possible in order to minimize costs, increase managerial effectiveness, and improve operational efficiency. Total supply is not only concerned with ordering but also with requirements planning, logistics, and general procurement management.

Trade discount—A deduction from an established price for items or services, often varying in percentage with volume of transactions, made by the seller to those engaged in certain businesses and allowed irrespective of the time when payment is made. *See,* Discount.

Trade name—*See,* Brand name.

Trade secret—Any aspect of a business or its operations which is known only to the manufacturer. *See,* Proprietary information.

Trademark—Generally, any sign, symbol, mark, word, or arrangement of words in the form of a label adopted and used by a manufacturer or distributor to designate his particular goods, and which no other person has the legal right to use.

Trade-off analysis—The process of determining the "best" course of action by weighing the advantages and disadvantages associated with available alternatives. The selected course will usually involve a compromise with some resources (e.g., time) traded-off for another (e.g., money).

Ultra vires action—An action which is beyond the power or purpose of a corporation, city, county, or other body, but not an action which is merely performed in an unauthorized manner or without authority.

Unit price—The price of a selected unit of a good or service (e.g., price per ton, labor hour, foot).

Unit price extension—The calculation of the total price of goods by multiplying the price per unit by the number of units purchased.

Unresponsive bid—*See,* Nonresponsive bid.

Unsuccessful bidder—An offeror whose bid is not accepted for reasons of price, quality, failure to comply with specifications, etc.

Using agency—A unit of government that requisitions items through central purchasing.

Value—Intrinsic worth. The amount of money for which goods or services can be exchanged. *See, Uniform Commercial Code.*

Value analysis—An organized effort directed at analyzing the function of systems, products, specifications and standards, and practices and procedures for the purpose of satisfying the required functions at the lowest total cost of ownership.

Vendor—A supplier.

Vendor failure—*See,* Default.

Vendor file—The accumulated record maintained by the central purchasing authority of information relevant to his business relationship with the government, including application for inclusion on the bidders list, record of performance under contracts, correspondence, and the results of special-purpose analyses.

Void—Without legal effect; unenforceable.

Volume purchasing—*See,* Bulk purchasing.

Waiver of bid(s)—A process, usually statutory, whereby a government purchasing office may procure items without formal bidding procedures because of uniqueness of circumstances related to that procurement action.

Waiver of mistake or informality—The act of disregarding errors or technical nonconformities in the bid which do not go to the substance of the bid and will not adversely affect the competition between bidders.

Appendix E

Bibliography

This Bibliography is divided into two major parts—List of General References and List of Legal Citations—and includes material that was used during the study. The Bibliography is presented in the hope that others will find it a useful reference when researching technical and legal aspects of public purchasing.

LIST OF GENERAL REFERENCES

METHODOLOGY

The majority of the articles in the List of General References was identified by consulting the *Index to Legal Periodicals* and the *Index to Business Periodicals*. The articles selected address contemporary purchasing subjects and provide views on purchasing from various vantage points—professional, scholarly, legal, and technical—that were desired. Since these indices have such a wide range of subject headings, from "government contracts" to "public administration," only extremely relevant headings were traced from the most recent issues back to 1951 for the legal periodicals and 1941 for the business periodicals. A representative sample of articles listed under the various headings was selected and reviewed to determine the sources of the most pertinent articles. Additional published and unpublished papers were furnished by state and local officials, professional organizations, and the academic community.

STRUCTURE

The List of General References is subdivided into 14 topic areas. Some are narrowly drawn, while others are broader in scope. The breadth of any one subject heading is dependent on the topic's relative importance in the field of purchasing, the number of references located, and the divisibility of any potential topic into distinct subtopics. Certain technical subjects (e.g., specifications and competitive bidding) lend themselves well to being grouped under a single topic heading, while less technical subjects (e.g., preferential treatment) require individual topic headings because of the amount of pertinent information that was collected.

Because the study spans the entire purchasing spectrum, the List of General References is long. It seeks to structure the purchasing field from the rudiments of setting up a purchasing office through the intricacies of contract administration. Consequently, each of the 14 subject headings represents a significant component in the purchasing spectrum.

In order to facilitate using the List of General References for finding material relating to any specific topic, the material that relates closely to more than one topic is listed under each topic to which it applies. For example, the article "Municipal Contracts" by Louis Ancel is listed under the topic headings "Contract Disputes" and "Conflict of Interests" because its contents are germane to both.

The following brief descriptions should afford the reader insight into each topic heading.

• *Purchasing Organization and Operations* — a broad category which includes information on the authority and organization of a purchasing office, pros and cons of centralized and cooperative purchasing, and reports on intergovernmental purchasing.

• *State and Local Government Purchasing Methods* — a broad category which surveys purchasing procedures and limitations in most States and includes general references concerning problems at the local government level.

• *Specifications* — includes references to a manual on specifications, as well as to a number of informative articles.

• *Standardization* — includes references to a number of articles and to a standardization manual.

• *Ordering* — includes references to articles on blanket orders, comprehensive quota requests, and pre-pricing considerations.

• *Preferential Treatment* — concerns in-state preference and Buy American practices.

• *Competitive Bidding* — contains references to articles ranging from bidder prequalification to the lowest and best bid; also references articles on the analysis of competitive bidding practices.

• *Processing of Bids* — covers problems from acceptance to surety rights.

• *Mistakes and Misrepresentations* — a narrow classification containing references to articles on changed conditions as misrepresentation, bidding errors, and relief from mistakes.

• *Contract Administration* — a broad category which deals with the administration of contracts, including referenced articles on substantial compliance, changes clauses, equal employment, methods of accounting, and waivers of delivery schedules.

• *Contract Disputes* — references articles on the causes of contract disputes, the liability of the parties, and the types of relief available.

• *Conflict of Interest* — focuses on self-interest of local governments and public officials.

• *Local Government Purchasing* — includes references to annual purchasing reports, purchasing manuals, selected local ordinances, and general articles highlighting local purchasing practices.

• *Federal Government Contracts* — a general listing of articles on federal government contracts, including a comparison of the differences between government and private contracts and a guide to government contracts.

PURCHASING ORGANIZATION AND OPERATIONS

"The Authority for and Organization of a Purchasing Department." Unpublished paper by O. H. Gartman, Purchasing Agent. Oshkosh, Wisconsin.

"The Case for Cooperative or Centralized Purchasing." National Association of County Officials. Washington, D.C., 1968.

"Centralized — Decentralized Purchasing in the Academic Institution." P. Bacon. *Journal of Purchasing* 7:56, August 1971.

"Centralized Purchasing: A Sentry at the Tax Exit Gate." R. Forbes. National Association of Purchasing Agents, New York, New York, 1941.

"Check List on Ways and Means to Improve Operation of Intergovernmental Purchasing Plans." Allegheny Council for Intergovernmental Action. University of Pittsburgh, Pittsburgh, Pennsylvania, March 1969.

"Contracting Officer: Authority to Act and Duty to Act Independently." C. Hanes and S. Smith. *Dickinson Law Review* 70:333, Spring 1966.

"Cooperative Purchasing." H. P. Cannon. *Golden West Purchaser.* March 1969.

"Cooperative Purchasing — An Introduction." Unpublished paper by W. G. Boland, Coordinator of Purchasing. Ottawa, Canada.

"Cooperative Purchasing in Rhode Island." Unpublished paper by E. S. Crossman, Purchasing Agent. State of Rhode Island.

"The Cooperative Purchasing Story." *Civic Newsletter.* San Antonio, Texas, May 10, 1968.

"Feasibility Study of Centralized Purchasing for Public Universities." State of Illinois, May 1972.

"Five Years of Joint Purchasing Saves $25,000 for Communities in Sussex." J. P. Braun. *New Jersey Municipalities,* February 1962.

"How Governmental Units Can Share in Centralized Purchasing Through Joint Procurement with State of Illinois." State of Illinois, April 1970.

"How Uncle Sam Can Help Your City Buy Better." *Nation's Cities* 41, June 1971.

"IGCP: The Wave of the Future." R. F. Steinbauer. *Journal of Purchasing* 8:34, August 1972.

Joint Purchasing for Local Governments. Community Research, Inc. Dayton, Ohio, 1968.

A Model Intergovernmental Purchasing Agreement. Allegheny Council for Intergovernmental Action. Pittsburgh, Pennsylvania, March 1969.

The Organization and Administration of a Governmental Purchasing Office. R. Forbes. National Association of Purchasing Agents, New York, New York, 1941.

Policy on Use of Consultants in State Government. Michigan Senate Governmental Efficiency Committee. Council of State Governments, Lexington, Kentucky, 1965.

"Principles and Authority of Contracting Officers in Administration of Government Contracts." J. P. Shedd. *Public Contract Law Journal* 5:88, April 1972.

Purchasing Laws for State, County and City Government. R. Forbes. National Association of Purchasing Agents, New York, New York, 1941.

"Purchasing Through Intergovernmental Agreements. *Management Information Service* 3:S-6. International City Management Association, June 1971.

"Regional Purchasing: A Study in Governmental Cooperative Buying." C. T. Hardwick. *Journal of Purchasing,* November 1969.

A Report on Voluntary Intergovernmental Purchasing Programs. Allegheny Seminar. Pittsburgh, Pennsylvania, February 1967.

"The Salem Plan of Cooperative Purchasing." Paper presented by C. C. Ward at the Oregon Finance Officers Association. Eugene, Oregon, March 1961.

Standardization Manual: A Book of Principles and Practices for Purchasing Personnel. Value Techniques Committee, National Association of Purchasing Agents, New York, New York, 1964.

State Purchasing — The Essentials of a Modern Service for Modern Government. G. W. Jennings. Council of State Governments, Lexington, Kentucky, 1969.

"A Systems Approach to Purchasing." J. E. Fleming. *Journal of Purchasing* 5:45, February 1969.

Uniform Administrative Requirements for Grants-in-Aid to State and Local Governments. Federal Management Circular 74-7, Attachment O. Washington, D.C. September 13, 1974. (Formerly OMB Circular A-102).

"Voluntary Joint Public Bidding." R. Belmonte. *The American City,* October 1969.

STATE AND LOCAL GOVERNMENT PURCHASING METHODS

"Bonanza for Florida Lawyers." W. F. Beemer. *Florida Bar Journal* 42:99, February 1968.

"Boulder Takes the Long View." *Purchasing Magazine,* April 21, 1966.

"Buying Shortcuts Help Sales Soar." S. Dowst. *Purchasing Magazine,* January 27, 1966.

"California's Buy-American Policy: Conflict with GATT and the Constitution." Student Note, *Stanford Law Review* 17:119, November 1964.

California Public Contract Law Conference. Public Contract Section, American Bar Association. Los Angeles, California, October 1970.

"The Challenge to Municipal Purchasing." C. N. Luizzo. *Journal of Purchasing,* February 1967.

County Purchasing. J. W. Nicholson. National Association of Purchasing Agents, New York, New York, 1940.

Data Processing Resources. J. W. Hawes. Standards Committee, National Association of State Purchasing Officials. Council of State Governments, Lexington, Kentucky, August 1969.

"The Function of Purchasing." J. C. Denton. *Journal of Purchasing* 1:5, August 1965.

"Government by Procurement." P. F. Hannah. *The Business Lawyer* 18:997, July 1963.

Government Contracting and Purchasing. State of Hawaii. March 1962.

Governor's Management Study. Commonwealth of Virginia. November 1970.

Grant Manager Handbook. Law Enforcement Assistance Administration. Washington, D.C., February 1973.

Guide to Governmental Purchasing. J. W. Nicholson, T. J. Nammacher, and K. L. Smith. Lakewood Publications, Minneapolis, Minnesota, 1965.

"Is Your Purchasing Department a Good Buy?" O. S. Ammer. *Harvard Business Review* 52:36, March-April 1974.

"Managing in a Shortage Economy." *Business Week,* November 10, 1973.

Modernizing State Government. Committee for Economic Development. July 1967.

"Pennsylvania Government Contract Procedures." P. C. Hamilton. *Pennsylvania Bar Association Quarterly* 39:497, June 1968.

"Problems and Procedure in Highway and Building Contracts with the State of New York." H. E. Peters. *Fordham Law Review* 26:628, 1957.

"Problems in State and Local Contracting." R. S. Mitchell. *Briefing Papers,* No. 72-2, April 1972.

"Procedural Fairness in Public Contracts: The Procurement Regulations." J. J. Grossman. *Virginia Law Review* 57:171, March 1971.

Procurement Handbook. Law Enforcement Assistance Administration. Washington, D.C., January 1973.

"Professionalization of the Public Buyers." J. H. Holland. *Purchasing Magazine,* June 13, 1968.

"Public Relations in Public Purchasing." P. Boney. *Purchasing Magazine,* June 1, 1964.

"Purchaser of Supplies." *Administrative Code,* City of San Francisco, January 1972.

Purchasing and Leasing Study. State of Vermont. December 1970.

Purchasing by the States, 3rd Edition. Committee to Revise, National Association of State Purchasing Officials. Council of State Governments, Lexington, Kentucky, September 1964.

Purchasing Handbook, 2nd Edition. G. W. Aljian. McGraw-Hill, New York, New York, 1966.

Purchasing Study of Local Government in the Southeast Michigan Metropolitan Six-County Region. C. T. Hardwick. Metropolitan Fund Inc., Detroit, Michigan, 1965.

"Standards and Specifications, Form and Substance." H. S. Schenker. Paper presented at the 21st annual conference and products exhibit of the National Institute of Governmental Purchasing, October 1966.

"Status of Computer Development Activity in Purchasing." M. J. Timbers. *Journal of Purchasing* 6:45, November 1970.

Summary of the Report of the Commission on Governmental Procurement. Government Printing Office, Washington, D.C., December 1972.

"Survey of State and Municipal Public Contracts." P. M. Gantt. *Public Contract Law Journal* 1:41, July 1967.

Survey of States: Facts and Functions. National Association of State Purchasing Officials. Council of State Governments, Lexington, Kentucky, October, 1970.

"Symposium: Contracting with the State of Texas." M. E. Grossberg and B. E. O'Neill. *University of Texas Law Review* 44:56, November 1965.

"The Systems Era: Its Impact on Purchasing." F. F. Mauser. *Journal of Purchasing* 4:5, November 1968.

"Systems Management Means a New Kind of Purchasing." J. Van de Water. *Purchasing Magazine,* January 9, 1969.

"Time Shared Information Systems for Purchasing and Materials Management." R. M. Monozka. *Journal of Purchasing* 7:15, May 1971.

Total Cost Purchasing, Vol. 3, No. S-4. Management Information Service. International City Management Association, April 1971.

"What Constitutes a Good Purchasing Manager?" H. Crystal. Paper presented to the 27th Annual Meeting of the National Association of State Purchasing Officials at Oklahoma City, Oklahoma, September 11, 1972.

SPECIFICATIONS

"A Federal Spur to Product Development." *Business Week,* August 25, 1973.

National Traffic and Motor Vehicle Safety Act of 1966: Its Implementation and Proposed Future Standards and Standard Revisions. National Association of State Purchasing Officials. Council of State Governments, Lexington, Kentucky, June 1968.

The National Traffic and Motor Vehicle Safety Act of 1966. Committee on Standards, National Association of State Purchasing Officials. Council of State Governments, Lexington, Kentucky, 1968.

"Problems Relating to Changes and Changed Conditions on Public Contracts." M. E. Greenberg. *Public Contract Law Journal* 3:135, 1970.

"Specification for Public Contracts — A Critique of Competitive Bidding." D. R. Mandelker. *Washington Law Quarterly,* 1951:513, 1951.

Standard Specifications Preparation Manual. Standards Committee, National Association of State Purchasing Officials. Council of State Governments, Lexington, Kentucky, 1966.

"The Validity of a Municipal Contract Award where the Bid Specifications Call for Both Design and Construction of the Contract Subject Matter." J. A. Miller. *University of Pittsburgh Law Review* 33:231, 1971.

"What Constitutes a Good Specification?" H. Crystal. Paper presented to the 25th Annual Meeting of the National Association of State Purchasing Officials at Myrtle Beach, South Carolina, October 14, 1970.

STANDARDIZATION

"Standardization: Focus on Cooperation." J. J. Simpson. *Purchasing Magazine,* March 7, 1968.

"Standardization . . . Focus on Planning." J. Van de Water. *Purchasing Magazine,* March 7, 1967.

Standardization Manual: A Book of Principles and Practices for Purchasing Personnel. Value Techniques Committee, National Association of Purchasing Agents. New York, New York, 1964.

"Where You Can Go Wrong on Value Analysis." T. Mataxas. *Purchasing Magazine,* January 27, 1964.

ORDERING

"Blanket Orders, Cash Buying Save Three Ways." *Purchasing Magazine,* October 7, 1965.

"Blanket Orders Makes Buying Easier." L. M. Head. *Purchasing Magazine,* October 8, 1962.

"Comprehensive Quota Requests." *Purchasing Magazine,* July 11, 1968.

"How to Build a Better Contract." *Chemical Week* 27, April 1, 1967.

Information Systems Technology in State Governments. National Association for State Information Systems. Council of State Governments, Lexington, Kentucky, 1970.

"Pre-pricing Strengthens the Buyer's Hand." *Purchasing Magazine,* October 7, 1965.

"Selection of Rules of Thumb in Inventory Control." R. R. Mayer. *Journal of Purchasing* 8:19, May 1971.

PREFERENTIAL TREATMENT

The Buy American Act: A Survey and Analysis. H. Ficker. Library of Congress Legislative Reference Service, April 1964.

"Buy American Policies." M. S. Baram. *Boston College Industrial and Commercial Law Review* 7:269, Spring 1966.

"California's Buy American Policy: Conflict with GATT and the Constitution." Student Note, *Stanford Law Review* 17:119, November 1964.

Foreign Made Products — A Survey Report. National Association of State Purchasing Officials. Council of State Governments, Lexington, Kentucky, July 1965.

In-State Preference in Public Purchasing. National Association of State Purchasing Officials. Council of State Governments, Lexington, Kentucky, July 1965.

"State 'Buy American' Policies — One Vice, Many Voices." H. A. Berliner, *George Washington Law Review* 32:584, 1963.

Survey of In-State Preference Policy and Practice 1970. Committee on Competition in Governmental Purchasing, National Association of State Purchasing Officials. Council of State Governments, Lexington, Kentucky, 1970.

Survey on In-State Preference Practices 1963. National Association of State Purchasing Officials. Council of State Governments, Lexington, Kentucky, 1963.

COMPETITIVE BIDDING

"American Casualty Company v. Town of Shattuck, A Statutory Payment Bond Problem and Speculations Engendered Thereby." M. H. Merril and E. A. Klem. *Oklahoma Law Review* 20:135, 1967.

"An Analysis of Competitive Bidding Strategy." R. G. Newman. *Journal of Purchasing* 5:73, May 1969.

"Analysis of Competitive Bids." W. N. Smith and J. R. McCreight, *Management Services Magazine,* May-June 1968.

"Anti-Trust — What Every Good PM Should Know." *Purchasing World,* 12, March 1974.

"Bidder Pre-Qualification: Theory in Search of Practice." R. E. Lieblich. *Public Contracts Law Journal* 5:32, April 1972.

"Competitive Advantage." M. L. Glass. *Oklahoma Law Review* 19:386, November 1966.

"Competitive Bidding: A Comprehensive Bibliography." R. M. Stark. *Operations Research,* March-April 1971.

"Competitive Bidding and the Option to Renew or Extend a State Purchase Contract." Student Note, *Dickinson Law Review* 74:166, Fall 1969.

"Competitive Bidding in New York." Student Note, *Syracuse Law Review* 10:271, 1959.

"Competitive Bidding: Public Construction Contracts in the State of Washington." Student Note, *Washington Law Review* 39:796, October 1964.

"Consideration Reconsidered — The Problem of the Withdrawn Bid." Student Note, *Stanford Law Review* 10:441, June 1958.

"Fact and Fancy on Identical Bids." P. W. Cook, Jr. *Harvard Business Review* 41:67, January 1963.

"The Federal Government's Program on Identical Bids." R. A. Bicks. *Antitrust Bulletin* 5:617, November-December 1960.

"FPC Studies Bidding." *Engineering News-Record,* September 26, 1968.

"Forfeiture of Construction Bid Bond Denied Because of Unilateral Mistake." Student Note, *Utah Law Review,* Fall 1959.

"Government's Obligation to Disclose Under the Truth in Negotiations Act." W. F. Pettit and J. J. Allen. *William and Mary Law Review* 10:18, Fall 1968.

"Identical Bid Cools Off." *Business Week,* August 25, 1962.

Identical Bids and How to Combat Them. J. Nicholson. National Institute of Government Purchasing, Washington, D.C., October 5, 1968.

Impediments to Competitive Bidding — How to Detect and Combat Them. Antitrust Committee, National Association of Attorneys General and the Committee on Competition in Governmental Purchasing, National Association of State Purchasing Officials. Council of State Governments, Lexington, Kentucky, October 1963.

"Lowest and Best Bid and Bidding Errors." Unpublished paper by E. H. Campbell. University of Washington, Bureau of Governmental Research.

"Market Segmentation for Better Purchasing Results." C. E. Kiser. *Journal of Purchasing,* November 1969.

"The Necessity of Competitive Bidding in Municipal Contracts." Student Note, *Pittsburgh Law Review* 27:117, October 1965.

"New York Acts to Boost Bid Competition." *Engineering News-Record,* October 30, 1969.

"A Note on Competitive Bidding." R. G. Newman. *Journal of Purchasing,* May 1967.

"Notice Requirement under Government Construction Contracts." J. J. Buford. *Minnesota Law Review* 44:275, 1959.

"Primer of Procurement by Formal Advertising and Relief for Mistakes in Bids." R. L. Owens. *New York State Bar Journal* 42:428, August 1970.

"Purchasing and Vendor Evaluation." *Purchasing Magazine,* February 9, 1967.

"Segregated Bids Save Money." *Air Conditioning, Heating and Refrigeration News,* September 10, 1962.

"Specifications for Public Contracts: A Critique of Competitive Bidding." D. R. Mandelker. *Washington University Law Quarterly* 1951:513, 1951.

"States Jar Contracting Systems." *Engineering News-Record,* October 21, 1965.

A Study of Formally Advertised Procurement. S. S. Handel and R. M. Paulson. Rand Corporation, Santa Monica, California, 1968.

"What Constitutes the Lowest Responsible Bidder?" H. Crystal. Paper presented to the 22nd Annual Meeting of the National Association of State Purchasing Officials at Mackinac Island, Michigan, August 22, 1967.

PROCESSING OF BIDS

"American Casualty Company v. Town of Shattuck: A Statutory Payment Bond Problem and Speculations Engendered Thereby." M. H. Merril and E. A. Clem. *Oklahoma Law Review* 20:135, May 1967.

"Anticipatory Repudiation — Contracting Officers' Dilemma." R. N. Fairbanks and R. E. Speidel. *Military Law Review* 6:129, October 1959.

"The Corporate Surety and Public Construction Bonds." T. H. Haas. *George Washington Law Review* 25:206, 1957.

"Disappointed Low Bidder on Public Contract has Cause of Action Against State Officials and Successful High Bidder for Malicious Interference with Prospective Advantage." Student Note, *Columbia Law Review* 59:935, 1959.

"The Finality of Acceptance Under Government Supply Contracts." P. C. Hill. *Public Contract Law Journal* 3:97, 1970.

"Government Contracts and the Commercial Code." T. M. Kostos. *Pennsylvania Bar Association Quarterly* 41:165, January 1970.

"Liability of the Surety When Contractor Withdraws Bid."

J. W. Callahan. *Federation of Insurance Counsel* 17:80, Summer 1967.

"Life Cycle Costing: Decision Making Tool for Capital Equipment Acquisition." R. J. Kaufman. *Journal of Purchasing,* August 1969.

"The Material and Workmanship Clause in Standard Government Construction Contracts." Student Note, *George Washington Law Review* 35:998, June 1967.

The Miller Act in New Mexico — Materialman's Right to Recover on Prime Surety Bond in Public Works Contracts — Notice as a Condition Precedent to Action." Student Note, *Natural Resources Journal* 9:295, 1969.

"New Developments in Statutory Bond Law." G. Ashe. *Commercial Law Journal* 74:114, May-June 1969.

"Performance Bond Servicing of Government Contracts." J. R. Rudolf. *Insurance Counsel Journal* 19:145, 1952.

"Pitfalls in Purchasing Under the Uniform Commercial Code." T. L. Lartny and J. D. McConahay. *Journal of Purchasing* 4:43, November 1968.

"Rights of the Unsuccessful Low Bidder on Government Contracts." Student Note, *Western Law Review* 15:208, December 1963.

"Specification for Public Contracts: A Critique of Competitive Bidding." D. R. Mandelker. *Washington Law Quarterly* 1951:513, 1951.

"State and Local Contracts and Subcontracts." J. E. Conway. *Buffalo Law Review* 14:130, 1965.

"State Printing Statute — Rejection of Sole Bid — Application of Rules of Construction." Student Note, *Wisconsin Law Review* 1964:141, 1964.

"State Public Works Contract Bond Problems." R. L. Ager. *The Forum* 1:23, April 1966.

State Purchasing Preference Laws. Research Department, Arkansas Legislative Council. October 1966.

"Suretyship and Guaranty: Coverage of Oklahoma Public Works Bond." Student Note, *Oklahoma Law Review,* 15:205, 1962.

"The Surety's Rights to Money Retained from Payments Made on a Public Contract." Student Note, *Fordham Law Review,* 31:161, 1962.

"What Constitutes Adequate Security?" H. Crystal. Paper presented to the 26th Annual Meeting of the National Association of State Purchasing Officials, Chicago, Illinois, August 23, 1971.

MISTAKES AND MISREPRESENTATION

"Changed Conditions as Misrepresentation in Government Construction Contracts." Student Note, *George Washington Law Review* 35:972, June 1967.

"Forfeiture of Construction Bid Bond Denied Because of Unilateral Mistake." Student Note, *Utah Law Review* 6:578, Fall 1959.

"Lowest and Best Bid and Bidding Errors." Unpublished paper by E. H. Campbell. University of Washington, Bureau of Government Research.

"Misrepresentation in Public Contracts: Allocating the Risk of Loss." Student Note, *Syracuse Law Review* 21:1004, 1970.

"Mistake In Government Contracts." Student Note, *Southwestern Law Journal* 18:1, March 1964.

"Primer of Procurement by Formal Advertising and Relief from Mistakes in Bids." R. L. Owens. *New York State Bar Journal* 42:428, August 1970.

CONTRACT ADMINISTRATION

"Accounting Practices in State Agencies." E. L. Kohler. *Journal of Accountancy* 108:52, August 1959.

"Administrative Resolution of Breaches; Service Contract Developments, Incentive Contract Changes; Application of Freedom of Information Act to Procurement." P. A. Barron. *Federal Bar Journal* 28:161, 1968.

"Changed Conditions as Misrepresentation in Government Construction Contracts." Student Note, *George Washington Law Review* 35:972, June 1967.

"Changes Clause in Federal Construction Contracts." R. Nash and J. Cibinic, Jr. *George Washington Law Review* 35:908, June 1967.

"Changes Clause in Incentive Contracting." E. Parry. 28 *Federal Bar Journal,* Summer 1968.

"Contracting Officer: Authority to Act and Duty to Act Independently." C. Hanes and S. Smith. *Dickinson Law Review* 70:333, Spring 1966.

"The Doctrine of Substantial Compliance in Federal Government Contracts." P. H. Gantt and R. C. Burg. *Public Contract Law Journal* 2:313, July 1969.

"Doctrine of Substantial Compliance Applicable to Supply Contracts." Student Note, *Boston University Law Review* 47:441, Summer 1967.

"Enforcement of Nondiscrimination Requirements for Government Contract Work." W. H. Speck. *Columbia Law Review* 63:243, 1963.

"Equal Employment in the Construction Industry." H. F. Blasky. *William and Mary Law Review* 10:3, Fall 1968.

"Evaluating Governmental Purchasing Performance." Unpublished paper by H. Cannon, Purchasing Department, Orange, California.

Governmental Accounting, Auditing and Financial Reporting. National Committee on Governmental Accounts, Municipal Finance Officers Association. Chicago, Illinois, 1968.

An Informational Guide for Rules and Procedures in Contract Maintenance. American Association of State Highway Officials. Washington, D.C., 1964.

"Liquidated Damages in Government Contracts: A Comment on Defenses." G. K. Gleason. *Southwestern Law Journal* 25:264, May 1971.

"The Non-Discrimination Clause in Government Contracts." R. S. Pasley. *Virginia Law Review* 43:837, 1957.

"Practical Aspects of Changed Conditions Clause Under Government Construction Contracts." J. W. Gaskins. *Boston College Industrial and Commercial Law Review* 5:79, January 1963.

"A Primer on the Standard Form Changes Clause." E. H. Crowell and W. Stanfield Johnson. *William and Mary Law Review* 8:550, Summer 1967.

"Principles and Authority of Contracting Officers in Administration of Government Contracts." J. P. Shedd. *Public Contract Law Journal* 5:88, April 1972.

"Problems Relating to Changes and Changed Conditions in Public Contracts." M. E. Greenberg. *Public Contract Law Journal* 3:135, August 1970.

"Purse Strings, Payment and Procurement." J. W. Whelan. *Public Law* 322, Winter 1964.

"Reasonable Compensation Deductability for Income Tax Purposes — Three Case Studies." F. W. Rogers. *William and Mary Law Review* 10:118, Fall 1968.

"Reform of the Renegotiation Process in Government Contracting." Student Note, *George Washington Law Review* 39:1141, July 1971.

Renegotiation Practiced Procedure. C. R. Aurzen. New Fairfield, Connecticut, 1962.

"Risk Allocation in Government Contracts." R. C. Nash. *George Washington Law Review* 34:693, 1966.

Study of the Need for a Materials Management System. State of California. May 1970.

"The Surety's Rights to Money Retained from Payments Made On a Public Contract." Student Note, *Fordham Law Review* 31:161, 1962.

"Technical Data in Government Contracts." J. B. Farmakides. *William and Mary Law Review* 8:573, Summer 1967.

"Uniform Accounting Standards for Government Contractors." S. Richardson. *Management Accounting,* January 1969.

"Validity of a Municipal Contract Award Where Bid Specifications Call for Both Design and Construction of the Contract Subject Matter." J. A. Miller. *University of Pittsburgh Law Review* 33:231, Winter 1971.

CONTRACT DISPUTES

"Administration of Claims Against the Sovereign — A Survey of State Techniques." Student Note, *Harvard Law Review* 68:506, January 1955.

"Administration of Government Contracts: Disputes and Claims Procedures." H. K. Lidstone and R. D. Witte. *Virginia Law Review* 46:252, 1960.

"Administrative Resolution of Breaches; Service Contract Developments, Incentive Contract Changes; Application of Freedom of Information Act to Procurement." P. A. Barron. *Federal Bar Journal* 28:161, 1968.

"Administrative Resolution of Government Breaches — The Case for an All-Breach Clause." J. Lane, Jr. *Federal Bar Journal* 28:199, Summer 1968.

"Administrative Resolution of Government Breaches—A Problem." R. D. White. *Federal Bar Journal* 28:234, Summer 1968.

"Ambiguity in the Law of Government Construction Contracts." Student Note, *Santa Clara Lawyer* 7:256, 1966-1967.

"The Application of Quasi-Contractual Liability Against a Public Entity." Student Note, *Hasting Law Journal* 23:874, March 1972.

"Arbitration in Government Contracts." S. Katzman. *Arbitration Journal* 24:133, 1969.

"The Contractual and Quasi-Contractual Liability of Arkansas Local Government Units." M. Gitelman. *Arkansas Law Review* 20:292, 1966-1967.

"Disappointed Low Bidder on Public Contract Has Cause of Action Against State Official — and Successful High Bidder for Malicious Interference with Prospective Advantage." Student Note, *Columbia Law Review* 59:953, 1959.

"Discovery Before the Contract Appeals Board." G. A. Cuneo and T. H. Truitt. *William and Mary Law Review* 8:505, Summer 1967.

"An Expanded Cause of Action Under the Tucker Act for an Unsuccessful Bidder." Student Note, *Temple Law Quarterly* 44:552, Summer 1971.

"Fragmentation of Remedies — The 'All Disputes' Solution." J. P. Shedd, Jr. *Federal Bar Journal* 28:185, Summer 1968.

"Are Government Bodies Bound by Arbitration Agreements?" J. P. Cogan, Jr. *Arbitration Journal* 22:151, 1967.

"Government Contracts: Subcontractors and Privity." J. W. Whelan and G. Gnoss. *William and Mary Law Review* 10:80, Fall 1968.

"Liability of the Surety When Contractor Withdraws Bid." J. W. Callahan. *Federation of Insurance Counsel* 17:80, Summer 1967.

"Liquidated Damages in Governmental Contracts: A Comment on Defenses." G. K. Gleason. *Southwestern Law Journal* 25:264, May 1971.

"Mandatory Administrative Proceedings and Statute of Limitations in Government Contracts." Student Note, *Virginia Law Review* 53:150, January 1967.

"Misrepresentation in Public Contracts: Allocating the Risk of Loss." Student Note, *Syracuse Law Review* 21:1004, 1970.

"Mistake in Government Contracts." Student Note, *Southwestern Law Journal,* March 1964.

"Municipal Conflicts of Interest: Rights and Remedies Under an Invalid Contract." R. B. Lillich. *Fordham Law Review* 27:31, Spring 1958.

"Municipal Contracts." L. Ancel. *University of Illinois Law Forum* 1961:357, 1961.

"Municipal Corporations: Remedies of the Private Contractor Against a Wisconsin Municipality Where the Contract is Ultra Vires or Defective." Student Note, *Marquette Law Review* 48:228, 1964.

"Municipal Liability Upon Improperly Executed Contracts." Student Note, *Duquesne Law Review* 1:221, Spring 1963.

"A New Concept of Mitigation in Government Contracts." Student Note, *George Washington Law Review* 38:463, March 1970.

"A New Liability for Government Contractors." Student Note, *Southwestern Law Journal* 24:852, December 1970.

"Problem of Defective Public Contracts in New York." A. W. Haight. *Syracuse Law Review* 14:426, Spring 1963.

"Public Contract Claims Procedure — A Perspective." L. Spector. *Federal Bar Journal* 30:1, Winter 1971.

"Reform of the Renegotiation Process in Government Contracting." Student Note, *George Washington Law Review* 39:1141, July 1971.

"Relief Under a Defective Municipal Contract in Ohio." G. D. Vaubel. *Akron Law Review* 2:20, Fall 1968.

"Remedies of Contractors with the Government." F. T. Vom Baur. *William and Mary Law Review* 8:469, Summer 1967.

Renegotiation Practice and Procedure. C. R. Aurzen. New Fairfield, Connecticut, 1962.

"Resolving Ambiguities in Interpretation of Government Contracts." J. P. Shedd. *George Washington Law Review* 36:555, October 1967.

"Rights of Unsuccessful Low Bidders on Government Contracts." Student Note, *Western Reserve Law Review* 15:208, December 1963.

"Settlement of Government Contract Disputes — A Comparative Study." A. Mewett. *Catholic Law Review* 9:65, May 1960.

"State Contractors' Remedies in Pennsylvania." J. M. March. *Public Contracts Law Journal* 3:207, August 1970.

Survey of State Procurement and Protest Procedures. American Bar Association. Chicago, Illinois, June 1970.

"Validity of a Municipal Contract Award Where Bid Specifications Call for Both Design and Construction of the Contract Subject Matter." J. A. Miller. *University of Pittsburgh Law Review* 33:231, Winter 1971.

"What Constitutes Adequate Security?" H. Crystal. Paper presented to the 26th Annual Meeting of the National Association of State Purchasing Officials. Chicago, Illinois. August 23, 1971.

CONFLICT OF INTEREST

"Case Commentary — On Conflict of Interest Where Government Expert's Principal Employment Insufficient to Void Contract on Grounds of Public Policy." Student Note, *Vanderbilt Law Review* 13:787, June 1960.

"Interest of Public Officers in Contracts Prohibited by Law." H. W. Kennedy and J. B. Beck. *Southern California Law Review* 28:335, July 1955.

"Municipal Conflicts of Interest: Inconsistencies and Patchwork Prohibitions." M. Kaplan and R. B. Lillich. *Columbia Law Review* 58:157, 1958.

"Municipal Conflicts of Interest, Rights and Remedies Under an Invalid Contract." R. B. Lillich. *Fordham Law Review* 27:31, Spring 1958.

"Municipal Contracts." L. Ancel. *University of Illinois Forum* 1961:357, 1961.

"Municipal Purchasing and Self-Interest: An Up-date." R. P. Sentell. *Georgia State Bar Journal* 7:431, May 1971.

"Self-Dealing by School Board Members." J. Kinley. *Illinois Bar Journal* 45:168, November 1956.

LOCAL GOVERNMENT PURCHASING

"The Challenge to Municipal Purchasing." C. N. Liuzzo. *Journal of Purchasing,* February 1967.

"Contracts of Political Subdivision in Iowa — Procedure, Defects, Recovery." J. Knox. *Drake Law Review* 10:53, 1960.

"Contractual and Quasi-Contractual Liability of Arkansas Local Government Units." M. Gitelman. *Arkansas Law Review* 20:292, 1966-1967.

County Purchasing. J. W. Nicholson. National Association of Purchasing Agents, New York, New York, 1940.

"Determinants of State and Local Expenditures." Student Note, *National Tax Journal* 17:75, March 1964.

"Effective Purchasing in Urban 'New County, USA'." R. M. Belmonte. Presented to 35th Annual Conference of the National Association of Counties, Atlanta, Georgia, July 26-29, 1970.

A Handbook for Interlocal Agreements and Contracts. Advisory Commission on Intergovernmental Relations. Washington, D.C., March 1967.

"Inter-Municipal Cooperation." M. H. Merrill. *Oklahoma Law Review* 23:349, November 1970.

"Local Governments and Contracts that Bind." R. P. Sentell. *Georgia Law Review* 3:546, Spring 1969.

Modernizing State Government. Committee for Economic Development. July 1967.

"The Need for a Model Code on Purchasing by State and Local Government." N. W. Keyes. *Pennsylvania Bar Quarterly,* October 1971.

Purchasing Laws for State, County, and City Governments. National Association of Purchasing Agents. New York, New York, 1941.

"An Outline of Statutory Provisions Controlling Purchasing by Local Governments in North Carolina." Unpublished paper by W. J. Wicker. Institute of Government, University of North Carolina, Chapel Hill, North Carolina.

"Price Index for Municipal Purchases." N. Walzer. *National Tax Journal* 23:441, December 1970.

"Problems and Opportunities in Purchasing for Local Subdivisions." G. L. Nunnally. Presented at 20th Convention of National Association of State Purchasing Officials, Las Vegas, Nevada, November 1965.

"Reasonable Compensation in Municipal Contracts Under Missouri Statutes." Student Note, *Missouri Law Review* 26:87, 1961.

"Relief Under a Defective Municipal Contract in Ohio." G. D. Vaubel. *Akron Law Review* 2:20, Fall 1968.

"Some Legal Aspects of Local Government Purchasing in Georgia." R. P. Sentell. *Mercer Law Review* 16:371, Spring 1965.

"Supplements to Direct Enforcement of State and Local Contracts and Subcontracts." E. J. Conway. *Buffalo Law Review* 14:130, 1965.

"The Trouble With Municipal Purchasing Agents." B. H. Cruce. *The American City,* November 1969.

Uniform Administrative Requirements for Grants-in-Aid to State and Local Governments. Federal Management Circular 74-7, Attachment O. Washington, D.C. September 13, 1974. (Formerly OMB Circular A-102).

FEDERAL GOVERNMENT CONTRACTS

"Administrative Contracts in the United States." D. Frenzen. *George Washington Law Review* 37:270, December 1968.

From America's Counties Today. New County USA Center. National Association of Counties, Washington, D.C., 1973.

"The Consequences of an Improper Award." Student Note, *William and Mary Law Review* 11:706, Spring 1970.

Construction Contracting Systems. Public Building Service. General Services Administration, March 1970.

"Differences Between Commercial Contracts and Government Contracts." Doke, Jenkins, Perlman, and F. T. Vom Baur. *Public Contract Law Journal* 2:33, October 1969.

"Federal Contractor: A Survey of Government Contract Law." R. B. Bowytz. *Commercial Law Journal* 76:239, July-September 1971.

"Federal Procurement and the Freedom of Information Act." A. Caron, Jr. *Federal Bar Journal* 28:271, Summer 1968.

"Fifty Years of Government Contract Law." F. T. Vom Baur. *Federal Bar Journal* 29:305, Fall 1970.

"Formal and Doctrinal Differences Between Government and Private Contracts." Student Note, *San Diego Law Review* 1:88, January 1964.

"Formalities in Government Contracts." Student Note, *Wayne Law Review* 5:503, Summer 1959.

"Fundamental Differences Which Characterize Public Contracts." F. T. Vom Baur. *Pennsylvania Bar Association Quarterly* 39:505, June 1968.

"Waiver of the Delivery Schedule in Government Contracts — A Review of the 1967 BCA Decisions." E. K. Gubin. *William and Mary Law Review* 10:58, Fall 1968.

"Government Contracts Today: Turning Square Corners in a One-Way Street?" Student Note, *Indiana Legal Forum* 4:489, 1971.

"Government Contracts: The Role of the Comptroller General." O. Binnbaum. *American Bar Association Journal* 433, May 1956.

1972 Government Contracts Guide. Commerce Clearing House, Chicago, Illinois, 1972.

"Government Option Contracts." Student Note, *Tennessee Law Review* 31:230, Winter 1964.

"A New Era in Government Construction Contracts." O. S. Hiestand, Jr. *Federal Bar Journal* 28:165, Summer 1968.

"New 'Law' of Government Service Contracts." D. D. Korneich and R. S. Schwartz. *Federal Bar Journal* 28:239, Summer 1968.

"Patent Infringement in Government Procurement: GAO's Role." J. E. Welch. *William and Mary Law Review* 10:39, Fall 1968.

"The Rice Doctrine and the Ripple Effects of Change." J. P. Shedd, Jr. *George Washington Law Review* 32:62, October 1963.

LIST OF LEGAL CITATIONS

E.14

METHODOLOGY

Several sources were used to identify the court decisions and state Attorneys General's opinions that are included in this List of Legal Citations. The National Association of Attorneys General provided valuable assistance by identifying, through its members, Attorneys General's opinions and leading cases in the public purchasing field. Other sources consulted to identify additional court decisions included: *American Jurisprudence, Corpus Juris Secundum, American Law Reports,* and West's *Decennial Digests.* Additional Attorneys General's opinions were identified by consulting annotations to state statutory codes, Shepard's state citations, state digests, and indices to bound volumes of State Attorneys General's opinions.

Some of the sources supplied information concerning public purchasing in only one State; other sources dealt with state and local government purchasing as part of a larger topic, such as state or municipal law. Consequently, this list of citations relates exclusively to the distinct subject of state and local government purchasing.

STRUCTURE

The list of legal citations is presented in two sections—Case Law and Attorneys General's Opinions—which are further subdivided into topic areas that are as specific as practicable. Whenever appropriate, the same topic headings are used in both sections.

Court decisions are cited according to the format delineated in *A Uniform System of Citation,* Eleventh Edition. Within each topic, state cases are cited first, in alphabetical order by state name, and federal cases are cited last. When either several cases from one State or several federal cases are cited under one topic, they appear in order of descending court rank (i.e., decisions from higher order courts precede decisions from lower order courts). Several opinions from the same court appear in reverse chronological order.

The format for the citations of Attorneys General's opinions was created to make this listing an easily usable tool (i.e., one that supplies enough information to enable the researcher to locate the reference). Two types of citations are used in the listing because two distinct types of information concerning Attorneys General's opinions were included.

The first type of citation concerns opinions published in bound volumes by the States. These references were gathered and several checks on them made throughout the course of the study at the law libraries of the Library of Congress and the United States Department of Justice. These opinions are cited showing: The volume number (if applicable); the designation "Op. Atty Gen." to represent the volumes of collected opinion; the page number on which the opinion appears; and, in parentheses, the State and years included in the volume in which the opinion is located. These opinions are cited within each topic in alphabetical order by state name. If there are several opinions from the same State within a topic, they are cited in reverse chronological order.

The second type of citation, Attorneys General's opinions not published in bound volumes and not available from the above libraries, are cited last within each topic group. Because all of this group of Attorneys General's opinions are in letter form, they are cited under a subheading "Letter from Attorney General to:" followed by the addressee and, in parentheses, the State and exact date of the opinion. Like the other Attorneys General's opinions, these are cited in alphabetical order by state name with several opinions from a State being listed in reverse chronological order.

CASE LAW

Central Purchasing Authority and Responsibilities

R. G. Wilmott Coal Co. v. State Purchasing Commission, 246 Ky. 115, 54 S.W.2d 634, 86 A.L.R. 127 (1932)
Griswold v. Ramsey County, 242 Minn. 529, 65 N.W.2d 647 (1954)
State *ex rel.* Great Falls Mr. Klean v. Montana State Board of Examiners, 153 Mont. 220, 456 P.2d 278 (1969)
Holtz v. Babcock, 143 Mont. 341, 389 P.2d 869 (1963)
State v. Kollarik, 22 N.J. 558, 126 A.2d 875 (1956)
State *ex rel.* S. Monroe & Son Co. v. Baker, 112 Ohio St. 356, 147 N.E. 501 (1925)
State *ex rel.* Junk v. Herrick, 107 Ohio St. 611, 140 N.E. 314 (1923)
Yohe v. City of Lower Burrell, 418 Pa. 23, 208 A.2d 847 (1965)
McIntosh Road Materials Co. v. Woolworth, 365 Pa. 190, 74 A.2d 384 (1950)
Schull Construction Co. v. Board of Regents, 79 S.D. 487, 113 N.W. 2d 663 (1962)
Robbins v. City of Rapid City, 71 S.D. 171, 23 N.W.2d 144 (1946)
Savage v. State, 74 Wash. 2d 618, 453 P.2d 613 (1969)
Petschl v. Century 21 Corp., 61 Wash. 2d 283, 377 P.2d 991 (1963)
State *ex rel.* Hercules Tire & Rubber Supply Co. v. Gore, 152 W. Va. 76, 159 S.E.2d 801 (1968)

Exemptions from Central Purchasing

Parkin v. Day, 250 Ark. 35, 463 S.W.2d 656 (1971)
Los Angeles Dredging Co. v. City of Long Beach, 210 Cal. 348, 291 P. 839, 71 A.L.R. 161 (1930)
Comley v. Board of Purchase, 111 Conn. 664, 149 A. 410 (1930)
Parker v. Panama City, 151 So. 2d 469, 15 A.L.R.3d 725 (Fla. 1963)
Eggart v. Westmark, 45 So. 2d 505 (Fla. 1950)
McNay v. Town of Lowell, 41 Ind. App. 627, 84 N.E.778 (1908)

Fisk v. Board of Managers, 134 Kan. 394, 5 P.2d 799 (1931)

State v. Smith, 334 Mo. 396, 67 S.W.2d 50 (1933)

Holtz v. Babcock, 143 Mont. 341, 389 P.2d 869 (1963)

Miller Insurance Agency v. Porter, 93 Mont. 567, 20 P.2d 643 (1933)

Scatuorchio v. Jersey City Incinerator Co., 14 N.J. 72, 100 A.2d 869 (1953)

Mullen v. Town of Louisberg, 225 N.C. 53, 33 S.E.2d 484 (1945)

State ex rel. Small v. Hughes County Commission, 81 S.D. 238, 133 N.W.2d 228 (1965)

Jibben v. City of Sioux Falls, 79 S.D. 143, 109 N.W.2d 252 (1961)

Washington Fruit & Produce Co. v. City of Yakima, 3 Wash. 2d 152, 100 P.2d 8, 128 A.L.R. 159 (1940)

Specifications

White v. McDonald Ford Tractor Co., 287 Ala. 77, 248 So. 2d 121 (1971)

Berryhill Office Equipment Co. v. Phillips, 35 Ariz. 180, 276 P. 4 (1929)

Fones Brothers Hardware v. Erb, 54 Ark. 645, 17 S.W. 7 (1891)

Town of Mill Valley v. Massachusetts Bonding & Insurance Co., 68 Cal. App. 372, 229 P. 891 (Dist. Ct. App. 1924)

Bader v. Sharp, 36 Del. Ch. 89, 125 A.2d 499 (Sup. Ct. 1955)

Hinds vs. State ex rel. Knight, 59 So. 2d 634 (Fla. 1952)

Wester v. Belote, 103 Fla. 976, 138 So. 721 (1931)

Tousey v. City of Indianapolis, 175 Ind. 295, 94 N.E. 225 (1911)

Walker & Brothers v. Manning, 6 Iowa 518 (1858)

Meahl v. City of Henderson, 290 S.W.2d 593 (Ky. 1956)

Commissioners of Sewage v. National Surety Co., 145 Ky. 90, 140 S.W. 62 (1911)

Standard Highway Co. v. Police Jury, 158 La. 294, 103 So. 819 (1925)

Gunning Gravel Co. v. City of New Orleans, 45 La. Ann. 911, 13 So. 182 (1893)

Dewey Jordan, Inc. v. Maryland National Capital Park & Planning Commission, 258 Md. 490, 265 A.2d 892 (1970)

Board of Education v. Allender, 206 Md. 406, 112 A.2d 455 (1955)

Pacella v. Metropolitan District Commission, 339 Mass. 338, 159 N.E.2d 75 (1959)

Pascoe v. Barlum, 247 Mich. 343, 225 N.W. 506 (1929)

Foley Brothers, Inc. v. Marshall, 266 Minn. 401, 123 N.W.2d 387 (1963)

Nielsen v. City of St. Paul, 252 Minn. 12, 88 N.W.2d 853 (1958)

Otter Tail Power Co. v. Village of Elbow Lake, 234 Minn. 419, 49 N.W.2d 197 (1951)

Coller v. City of St. Paul, 223 Minn. 376, 26 N.W.2d 835 (1947)

Hillig v. City of St. Louis, 337 Mo. 291, 85 S.W.2d 91 (1935)

West Virginia Coal v. City of St. Louis, 324 Mo. 1021, 25 S.W.2d 466 (1930)

Pasche v. South St. Joseph Town-site Co., 190 S.W. 30 (Kan. City, Mo. Ct. of App. 1916)

Glennon v. Gates, 136 Mo. App. 421, 118 S.W. 98 (Kan. City Ct. of App. 1909)

Ruehl Co. v. Board of Trustees, 85 N.J. Super 4, 203 A.2d 410 (1964)

Gerzof v. Sweeney, 16 N.Y.2d 206, 264 N.Y.S.2d 376, 211 N.E.2d 826 (1965)

Grimm v. Troy, 60 Misc. 579, 303 N.Y.S.2d 170 (Sup. Ct. 1968)

Rodin v. Director of Purchasing, 38 Misc. 2d 362, 238 N.Y.S.2d 2 (Sup. Ct. 1963)

Tinston v. City of New York, 17 App. Div. 2d 311, 234 N.Y.S.2d 730 (Sup. Ct. 1962)

Columbus Blank Book Co. v. Maloon, 116 Ohio App. 393, 188 N.E.2d 431 (1963)

L&M Properties v. Burke, 152 Ohio St. 28, 86 N.E.2d 768 (1949)

Page v. King, 285 Pa. 153, 131 A. 707 (1926)

Commonwealth v. Sanderson, 40 Pa. Super. 416 (1909)

Duke v. Bruce Independent School District, 77 S.D. 568, 96 N.W.2d 172 (1959)

Vilbig Brothers v. City of Dallas, 127 Tex. 563, 96 S.W.2d 229 (1936)

Hoffman v. City of Mt. Pleasant, 126 Tex. 632, 89 S.W.2d 193 (Comm. App. 1936)

Smith v. Seattle, 192 Wash. 64, 72 P.2d 588 (1937)

A.A.B. Electric, Inc. v. Stevenson Public School District, 5 Wash. App. 887, 491 P.2d 684 (Ct. App. 1971)

Use of Bidders Lists

Taylor v. Parker, 302 S.W.2d 125 (Ky. 1957)

Advertising

Berryhill Office Equipment Co. v. Phillips, 35 Ariz. 180, 276 P.4 (1929)

Parks v. City of Pocatello, 91 Idaho 241, 419 P.2d 683 (1966)

Meahl v. City of Henderson, 290 S.W.2d 593 (Ky. 1956)

City of Hartford v. King, 249 S.W.2d 13 (Ky. 1952)

Jenkins v. City of Bowling Green, 39 Ky. 119, 64 S.W.2d 457 (1933)

Bennett v. Baltimore City, 106 Md. 484, 68 A. 14 (1907)

Anderson v. Board of Public Schools, 122 Mo. 61, 27 S.W. 610 (1894)

State v. Kuhner, 107 Ohio St. 406, 140 N.E. 344 (1923)

State ex rel. Dacek v. Cleveland Trinadad Paving Co., 35 Ohio App. 118, 171 N.E. 837 (1929)

Verardi v. Borough of Sharpsburg, 407 Pa. 246, 180 A.2d 6 (1962)

Dillingham v. Mayer, 75 S.C. 549, 56 S.E. 381 (1907)

Reiter v. Chapman, 177 Wash. 392, 31 P.2d 1005 (1934)

Competitive Bidding

Kimbrell v. State, 272 Ala. 419, 132 So. 2d 132 (1961)

Brown v. Phoenix, 77 Ariz. 368, 272 P.2d 358 (1954)

Parkin v. Day, 250 Ark. 35, 463 S.W.2d 656 (1971)

Fones Brothers Hardware v. Erb, 54 Ark. 645, 17 S.W. 7 (1891)

McRoberts v. Ammons, 104 Colo. 96, 88 P.2d 958 (1939)

Eggart v. Westmark, 45 So. 2d 505 (Fla. 1950)

Inskip v. Board of Trustees, 126 Ill. 2d 501, 187 N.E.2d 201 (1963)

Wickwire v. City of Elkhart, 144 Ind. 305, 43 N.E. 216 (1896)

Iowa-Nebraska Light & Power Co. v. City of Villisca, 220 Iowa 230, 261 N.W. 423 (1935)

Fisk v. Board of Managers, 134 Kan. 394, 5 P.2d 799 (1931)

Board of Education v. Hall, 353 S.W.2d 194 (Ky. 1962)

Board of Regents v. Cole, 209 Ky. 761, 273 S.W. 508 (1925)

Boxwell v. Department of Highways, 203 La. 760 14 So. 2d 627 (1943)

Hall v. City of Baltimore, 252 Md. 416, 250 A.2d 233 (1969)

Pacella v. Metropolitan District Commission, 339 Mass. 338, 159 N.E.2d 75 (1959)

Lasky v. City of Bad Axe, 352 Mich. 272, 89 N.W.2d 520 (1958)

Hunt v. Fenton, 313 Mich. 644, 21 N.W.2d 906 (1946)

Detroit Free Press Co. v. Board of State Auditors, 47 Mich. 135, 10 N.W. 171 (1881)

City of Hattiesburg v. Cobb Brothers Construction Co., 183 Miss. 482, 184 So. 630 (1938)

Hillig v. City of St. Louis, 337 Mo. 291, 85 S.W.2d 91 (1935)

Miller Insurance Agency v. Porter, 93 Mont. 567, 20 P.2d 643 (1933)

State v. Cote, 95 N.H. 428, 65 A.2d 280 (1949)

Township of Hillside v. Sternin, 25 N.J. 317, 136 A.2d 265 (1957)

Poling v. Roman, 86 N.J. Super. 484, 207 A.2d 219 (1965)

Mullen v. Town of Louisberg, 225 N.C. 53, 33 S.E.2d 484 (1945)

Allied Paint Manufacturing Co. v. Bradley, 21 Pa. D&C.2d 747,75 Dauphin 63 (Dauphin County Ct. 1960)

Duke v. Bruce Independent School District, 77 S.D. 568, 96 N.W.2d 172 (1959)

Fonder v. City of South Sioux Falls, 76 S.D. 31, 71 N.W.2d 618, 53 A.L.R.2d 493 (1955)

Tri-State Milling Co. v. Board of Commissioners, 75 S.D. 466, 68 N.W.2d 104 (1955)

Gostovich v. City of West Richland, 75 Wash. 2d 583, 452 P.2d 737 (1969)

United States Wood Preserving Co. v. Sundmaker, 186 F. 678 (C.A. 6th Cir. 1911)

Bid Security/Bid Bonds

M.F. Kemper Construction Co. v. City of Los Angeles, 37 Cal. 2d 696, 235 P.2d 7 (1951)

Inyoken Sanitation District v. Haddock Engineers, 36 Cal. 2d 450, 224 P.2d 709 (1950)

Petrovich v. City of Arcadia, 36 Cal. 2d 78, 222 P.2d 231 (1950)

Town of Mill Valley v. Massachusetts Bonding & Insurance Co., 68 Cal. App. 372, 229 P. 891 (Dist. Ct. App. 1924)

Boise Junior College District v. Mattefs Construction Co., 92 Idaho 757, 450 P.2d 604 (1969)

Commissioners of Sewage v. National Surety Co., 145 Ky. 90, 140 S.W. 62 (1911)

Board of Education v. Hooper, 350 S.W.2d 629 (Ky. Ct. App. 1961)

Board of Education v. Allender, 206 Md. 406, 112 A.2d 455 (1955)

Detroit Free Press Co. v. Board of State Auditors, 47 Mich. 135, 10 N.W. 171 (1881)

Bolivar Reorganized School District v. American Sun Co., 307 S.W.2d 405, 70 A.L.R.2d 1361 (Mo. 1957)

School District v. Olson Construction Co., 153 Neb. 451, 45 N.W.2d 164 (1950)

State v. Bartley, 50 Neb. 874, 70 N.W. 367 (1897)

Township of Hillside v. Sternin, 25 N.J. 317, 136 A.2d 265 (1957)

People v. McDonough, 173 N.Y. 181, 65 N.E. 963 (1903)

Union Free School District #1 v. Gambs, 20 Misc. 315, 191 N.Y.S.2d 183 (Sup. Ct. 1958)

Board of Education v. Maryland Casualty Co., 277 App. Div. 936, 98 N.Y.S.2d 865 (Sup. Ct. 1950)

Board of Education v. Sever Williams Co., 22 Ohio St. 2d 107, 51 Ohio Op. 2d 173, 258 N.E.2d 605 (1970)

State v. State Office Commission, 123 Ohio St. 70, 174 N.E. 8 (1930)

Altschul v. City of Springfield, 48 Ohio App. 356, 193 N.E. 788 (1933)

State v. State Construction Co., 203 Ore. 414, 280 P.2d 370, 52 A.L.R.2d 779 (1955)

Hedder v. Northampton Area Joint School Authority, 396 Pa. 328, 152 A.2d 463 (1959)

A.J. Colella, Inc. v. County of Allegheny, 391 Pa. 103, 137 A.2d 265 (1958)

McIntosh Road Materials Co. v. Woolworth, 365 Pa. 190, 74 A.2d 384 (1950)

Harris v. City of Philadelphia, 283 Pa. 496, 129 A. 460 (1925)

Dillingham v. Mayer, 75 S.C. 549, 56 S.E. 381 (1907)

State v. Union Construction Co., 9 Utah 2d 107, 339 P.2d 421 (1959)

City of Newport News v. Doyle & Russell, Inc., 211 Va. 603, 179 S.E.2d 493 (1971)

Puget Sound Painters v. State, 45 Wash. 2d 819, 278 P.2d 302 (1954)

A.A.B. Electric, Inc. v. Stevenson Public School District, 5 Wash. App. 887, 491 P.2d 684 (Ct. App. 1971)

State ex rel. Printing — Litho, Inc. v. Wilson, 147 W. Va. 415, 128 S.E.2d 449 (1962)

State of Connecticut v. F. H. McGraw & Co., 41 F. Supp. 369 (D.C. D. Conn. 1941)

Receipt and Control of Bids

Huddleston v. Humble Oil & Refining Co., 260 Ala. 384, 71 So. 2d 39 (1954)

Coller v. City of St. Paul, 223 Minn. 376, 26 N.W.2d 835 (1947).

McIntosh Road Materials Co. v. Woolworth, 365 Pa. 190, 74 A.2d 384 (1950)

Schull Construction Co. v. Board of Regents, 79 S.D. 487, 113 N.W.2d 663 (1962)

State ex. rel. Yahn Electric Co. v. Baer, 148 W. Va. 527, 135 S.E.2d 687 (1964)

United States v. Lipman, 122 F. Supp. 284, 52 A.L.R.2d 792 (D.C.E.D. Pa. 1954)

Bid Opening and Recording

Huddleston v. Humble Oil & Refining Co., 260 Ala. 384, 71 So. 2d 39 (1954)

James v. Humphrey, 226 Ark. 325, 289 S.W.2d 691 (1956)

Adams v. Town of Leesville, 210 La. 106, 26 So. 2d 370 (1946)

Nielsen v. City of St. Paul, 252 Minn. 12, 88 N.W.2d 853 (1958)

Pangla Construction Co. v. Cinnaminson Township, 136 N.J.L. 284, 55 A.2d 260 (1947)

United States v. Lipman, 122 F. Supp. 284 (D.C.E.D. Pa. 1954)

Processing Bids and Award of Contract

Boseker v. Wabash County Commissioners, 88 Ind. 267 (1880)

Adams v. Town of Leesville, 210 La. 106, 26 So. 2d 370 (1946)

Otter Tail Power Co. v. Village of Wheaton, 235 Minn. 123, 49 N.W.2d 804 (1951)

Page v. King, 285 Pa. 153, 131 A. 707 (1926)

Savage v. State, 75 Wash. 2d 618, 453 P.2d 613 (1969)

State ex rel. Printing — Litho, Inc. v. Wilson, 147 W. Va. 415, 128 S.E.2d 449 (1962)

Criteria for Evaluation and Award

White v. McDonald Ford Tractor Co., 287 Ala. 77, 248 So. 2d 121 (1971)

Townsend v. McCall, 262 Ala. 554, 80 So. 2d 262 (1955)

Huddleston v. Humble Oil & Refining Co., 260 Ala. 384, 71 So. 2d 39 (1954)

Brown v. Phoenix, 77 Ariz. 368, 272 P.2d 358 (1954)

Berryhill Office Equipment Co. v. Phillips, 35 Ariz. 180, 276 P. 4 (1929)

James v. Humphrey, 226 Ark. 325, 281 S.W.2d 691 (1956)

McRoberts v. Ammons, 104 Colo. 96, 88 P.2d 958 (1939)

Bader v. Sharp, 36 Del. Ch. 89, 125 A.2d 499 (Sup. Ct. 1955)

Eggart v. Westmark, 45 So. 2d 505 (Fla. 1950)

Willis v. Hathaway, 95 Fla. 608, 117 So. 89 (1928)

Parks v. City of Pocatello, 91 Idaho 241, 419 P.2d 683 (1966)

People ex rel. Assyrian Asphalt Co. v. Kent, 160 Ill. 655, 43 N.E. 760 (1896)

Boseker v. Wabash County Commissioners, 88 Ind. 267 (1880)

Urbanay v. City of Carroll, 176 Iowa 217, 157 N.W. 852 (1916)

Williams v. City of Topeka, 85 Kan 857 (1911)

City of Hartford v. King, 249 S.W.2d 13 (Ky. 1952)

Baskett v. Davis, 311 Ky. 13, 223 S.W. 2d 168 (1949)

Bancamerica — Blair Corp. v. State Highway Commission, 265 Ky. 100, 95 S.W.2d 1068 (1936)

R. G. Wilmott Coal Co. v. State Purchasing Commission, 246 Ky. 115, 54 S.W.2d 634, 86 A.L.R. 127 (1932)

Adams v. Town of Leesville, 210 La. 106, 26 So. 2d 370 (1946)

Standard Highway Co. v. Police Jury, 158 La. 249, 103 So. 819 (1925)

Gunning Gravel Co. v. City of New Orleans, 45 La. Ann. 911, 13 So. 182 (1893)

Board of Education v. Allender, 206 Md. 406, 112 A.2d 455 (1955)

Lasky v. City of Bad Axe, 352 Mich. 272, 89 N.W.2d 520 (1958)

Leavy v. City of Jackson, 247 Mich. 447, 226 N.W. 214 (1929)

Pascoe v. Barlum, 247 Mich. 343, 225 N.W. 506 (1929)

Electronics Unlimited, Inc. v. Village of Burnsville, 289 Minn. 118, 182 N.W.2d 679 (1971)

Foley Brothers Inc. v. Marshall, 266 Minn. 401, 123 N.W.2d 387 (1963)

Nielsen v. City of St. Paul, 252 Minn. 12, 88 N.W.2d 853 (1958)

Otter Tail Power Co. v. Village of Elbow Lake, 234 Minn. 419, 49 N.W.2d 197 (1951)

Coller v. City of St. Paul, 223 Minn. 376, 26 N.W.2d 835 (1947)

State ex rel. Johnson v. Sevier, 339 Mo. 483, 98 S.W.2d 677 (1936)

Anderson v. Board, 122 Mo. 61, 27 S.W. 610 (1894)

State ex rel. Woodruff — Dunlop Printing Co. v. Cornell, 52 Neb. 25, 71 N.W. 961 (1897)

Commercial Cleaning Corp. v. Sullivan, 47 N.J. 539, 222 A.2d 4 (1966)

Township of Hillside v. Sternin, 25 N.J. 317, 136 A.2d 265 (1957)

Scatuorchio v. Jersey City Incinerator Co., 14 N.J. 72, 100 A.2d 869 (1953)

Armitage v. Mayor, 86 N.J.L. 5, 90 A. 1035 (1914)

Faist v. Mayor, 72 N.J.L. 361, 60 A. 1120 (1905)

Mal Brothers Contracting Co. v. Kohl, 113 N.J. Super. 144, 273 A.2d 357 (App. Div. 1971), cert. denied, 58 N.J. 94 (1971)

Motorola Communications & Electronics, Inc. v. O'Connor, 115 N.J. Super. 317, 279 A.2d 855 (1971)

Poling v. Roman, 86 N.J. Super. 484, 207 A.2d 219 (1965)

Ruehl Co. v. Board of Trustees, 85 N.J. Super. 4, 203 A.2d 410 (1964)

Gerzof v. Sweeney, 16 N.Y.2d 206, 264 N.Y.S.2d 376, 211 N.E.2d 826 (1965)

Dictaphone Corp. v. O'Leary, 287 N.Y. 491, 41 N.E.2d 68 (1942)

Futia Co. v. Office of General Services, 39 App. Div. 2d 136, 332 N.Y.S.2d 261 (Sup. Ct. 1972)

Zara Contracting Co. v. Cohen, 23 App. Div. 2d 718, 257 N.Y.S. 2d 118 (Sup. Ct. 1965)

Caruci v. Dulan, 41 Misc. 2d 859, 246 N.Y.S.2d 727 (Sup. Ct. 1964)

Albro Contracting Corp. v. Department of Public Works, 13 Misc. 2d 846, 181 N.Y.S.2d 402 (Sup. Ct. 1958)

Picone v. City of New York, 176 Misc. 967, 29 N.Y.S.2d 539 (Sup. Ct. 1941)

Weiner v. Cuyahoga Community College District, 19 Ohio St. 2d 35, 249 N.E.2d 907 (1969)

L&M Properties v. Burke, 152 Ohio St. 28, 86 N.E.2d 768 (1949)

State v. Board of Public Service, 81 Ohio St. 218, 90 N.E. 389 (1909)

Altschul v. City of Springfield, 48 Ohio App. 356, 193 N.E. 788 (1933)

McIntosh Road Materials Co. v. Woolworth, 365 Pa. 190, 74 A.2d 384 (1950)

Wilson v. City of New Castle, 301 Pa. 358, 152 A. 102 (1930)

Douglass v. Commonwealth ex rel. Senior, 108 Pa. 559 (1885)

Kuhn v. Commonwealth, 291 Pa. 497, 140 A. 527 (1928)

Gostovich v. City of West Richland, 75 Wash. 2d 583, 452 P. 2d 737 (1969)

Petschl v. Century 21 Corp., 61 Wash. 2d 283, 377 P.2d 991 (1963)

Stern v. Spokane, 60 Wash. 325, 111 P. 231 (1910)

A.A.B. Electric, Inc. v. Stevenson Public School District, 5 Wash. App. 887, 491 P.2d 684 (1971)

State ex rel. Waller Chemicals, Inc. v. McNutt, 152 W. Va. 186 160 S.E.2d 170 (1968)

Butler v. Darst, 68 W. Va. 493, 70 S.E. 119 (1962)

State *ex rel.* Printing — Litho Inc. v. Wilson, 147 W. Va. 415, 128 S.E.2d 449 (1962)

Automatic Merchandising Corp. v. Nusbaum, 60 Wis. 2d 362, 210 N.W. 2d 745 (1973)

State *ex rel.* Democrat Printing Co. v. Schmiege, 18 Wis. 2d 335, 118 N.W.2d 845 (1963)

Lefkowitz v. Turley, 414 U.S. 70, 94 S. Ct. 316, 38 L.Ed. 2d 274 (1973)

United States Wood Preserving Co. v. Sundmaker, 186 F. 678 (C.A. 6th Cir. 1911)

Fulton Iron Co. v. Larson, 171 F.2d 994 (C.A. D.C. Cir. 1948), *Cert. denied,* 336 U.S. 903, 69 S. Ct. 489, 93 L.Ed. 1068 (1949)

Pittman Construction Co. v. Housing Authority, 167 F. Supp. 517 (D.C. W.D. La. 1958)

Errors in Bids

City of Hattiesburg v. Cobb Brothers Construction Co., 183 Miss. 482, 184 So. 630 (1938)

School District v. Olson Construction Co., 153 Neb. 451, 45 N.W.2d 164 (1950)

Kenneth E. Curran, Inc. v. State, 106 N.H. 558, 215 A.2d 702 (1965)

Cataldo Construction Co. v. County of Essex, 110 N.J. Super 414, 265 A.2d 842 (1970)

Smith & Lowe Construction Co. v. Henara, 79 N.M. 239, 442 P.2d 197 (1968)

Union Free School District #1 v. Gambs, 20 Misc. 315, 191 N.Y.S.2d 183 (Sup. Ct. 1958)

Board of Education v. Sever Williams Co., 22 Ohio St. 2d 107, 51 Ohio Op. 2d 173, 258 N.E.2d 605 (1970)

State v. State Construction Co., 203 Ore. 414, 280 P.2d 370, 52 A.L.R.2d 779 (1955)

Hedder v. Northampton Area Joint School Authority, 396 Pa. 328, 152 A.2d 463 (1959)

A. J. Colella, Inc. v. County of Allegheny, 391 Pa. 103, 137 A.2d 265 (1958)

James T. Taylor & Son, Inc. v. Arlington Independent School District, 60 Tex. 617, 335 S.W.2d 371 (1960)

State v. Union Construction Co., 9 Utah 2d 107, 339 P.2d 421 (1959)

City of Newport News v. Doyle & Russell, Inc., 211 Va. 603, 179 S.E.2d 493 (1971)

Puget Sound Painters v. State, 45 Wash. 2d 819, 278 P.2d 302 (1954)

Moffett, Hodgkins & Clarke Co. v. Rochester, 178 U.S. 373, 20 S.Ct. 957, 44 L.Ed. 1108 (1900)

State of Connecticut v. F. H. McGraw & Co., 41 F. Supp. 369 (D.C. D. Conn. 1941)

United States v. Lipman, 122 F. Supp. 284 (D.C.E.D. Pa. 1954)

Alta Electrical & Mechanical Co. v. United States, 90 Ct. Cl. 466 (1940)

Bidders' Failure to Bid to Specifications

White v. McDonald Ford Tractor Co., 287 Ala. 77, 248 So. 2d 121 (1971)

Urbanay v. City of Carroll, 116 Iowa 217, 157 N.W. 852 (1916)

Commissioners of Sewage v. National Surety Co., 145 Ky. 90, 140 S.W. 62 (1911)

Pascoe v. Barlum, 247 Mich. 343, 225 N.W. 506 (1929)

Coller v. City of St. Paul, 223 Minn. 376, 26 N.W.2d 835 (1947)

Foley Brothers, Inc. v. Marshall, 266 Minn. 401, 123 N.W.2d 387 (1963)

Nielsen v. City of St. Paul, 252 Minn. 12, 88 N.W.2d 853 (1958)

Otter Tail Power Co. v. Village of Wheaton, 235 Minn. 123, 49 N.W.2d 804 (1951)

Township of Hillside v. Sternin, 25 N.J. 317, 136 A.2d 265 (1957)

Caruci v. Dulan, 41 Misc. 2d 859, 246 N.Y.S.2d 727 (Sup. Ct. 1964)

Allied Paint Manufacturing Co. v. Bradley, 21 Pa. D&C 2d 747, 75 Dauph. 63 (Dauphin County Ct. 1960)

A.A.B. Electric, Inc. v. Stevenson Public School District, 5 Wash. App. 887, 491 P.2d 684 (Ct. App. 1971)

State of Connecticut v. F. H. McGraw Co., 41 F. Supp. 369 (D.C.D. Conn. 1941)

Authority to Reject All Bids

Townsend v. McCall, 262 Ala. 554, 80 So. 2d 262 (1955)

Brown v. Phoenix, 77 Ariz. 368, 272 P.2d 358 (1954)

Stanley-Taylor Co. v. Board of Supervisors, 135 Cal. 486, 67 P. 783 (1902)

McRoberts v. Ammons, 104 Colo. 96, 88 P.2d 958 (1939)

Hanlin v. Independent District, 66 Iowa 69, 23 N.W. 268 (1885)

Baskett v. Davis, 311 Ky. 13, 223 S.W.2d 168 (1949)

Bancamerica-Blair Corp. v. State Highway Commission, 265 Ky. 100, 95 S.W.2d 1068 (1936)

Trapp v. City of Newport, 115 Ky. 840, 74 S.W. 1109 (1903)

State *ex rel.* Irondale Chert Paving & Improvement Co. v. City of New Orleans, 48 La. Ann. 643, 19 So. 690 (1896)

Gunning Gravel Co. v. City of New Orleans, 45 La. Ann. 911, 13 So. 182 (1893)

Leavy v. City of Jackson, 247 Mich. 447, 226 N.W. 214 (1929)

Electronics Unlimited, Inc. v. Village of Burnsville, 289 Minn. 118, 182 N.W.2d 679 (1971)

Foley Brothers, Inc. v. Marshall, 266 Minn. 401, 123 N.W.2d 387 (1963)

State *ex rel.* Johnson v. Sevier, 339 Mo. 483, 98 S.W.2d 677 (1936)

Anderson v. Board of Public Schools, 122 Mo. 61, 27 S.W. 610 (1894)

State *ex rel.* Woodruff-Dunlop Printing Co. v. Cornell, 52 Neb. 25, 71 N.W. 961 (1897)

State v. County of Saline, 19 Neb. 253, 27 N.W. 122 (1886)

Commercial Cleaning Corp. v. Sullivan, 47 N.J. 539, 222 A.2d 4 (1966)

Scatuorchio v. Jersey City Incinerator Co., 14 N.J. 72, 100 A.2d 869 (1953)

Armitage v. Mayor, 86 N.J.L. 5, 90 A. 1035 (1914)

Faist v. Mayor, 72 N.J.L. 361, 60 A. 1120 (1905)

Motorola Communications & Electronics, Inc. v. O'Connor, 115 N.J. Super 317, 279 A.2d 855 (1971)

Poling v. Roman, 86 N.J. Super. 484, 207 A.2d 219 (1965)

Ruehl Co. v. Boards of Trustees of Schools, 85 N.J. Super. 4, 203 A.2d 410 (1964)

Bielec Wrecking & Lumber Co. v. McMorran, 21 App. Div. 2d 949, 251 N.Y.S.2d 331 (Sup. Ct. 1964)

Zara Contracting Co. v. Cohen, 45 Misc. 2d 497, 257 N.Y.S.2d 479 (Sup. Ct. 1964)

People ex rel. Shay v. McCormack, 167 App. Div. 854, 153 N.Y.S. 808 (Sup. Ct. 1915)

Weiner v. Cuyahoga Community College District, 19 Ohio St. 2d 35, 249 N.E.2d 907 (1969)

State v. Board of Public Service, 81 Ohio St. 218, 90 N.E. 389 (1909)

Gross v. State Capital Commission, 11 Wash. 174, 39 P. 972 (1895)

Bellingham American Publishing Co. v. Bellingham Publishing Co., 145 Wash. 25, 258 P. 836 (1927)

Stern v. Spokane, 60 Wash. 325, 111 P. 231 (1910)

State ex rel. Democrat Printing Co. v. Schmiege, 18 Wis. 2d 335, 118 N.W.2d 845 (1963)

Fulton Iron Co. v. Larson, 171 F.2d 994 (C.A.D.C. Cir. 1948), cert. denied, 336 U.S. 903, 69 S. Ct. 489, 93 L.Ed. 1068 (1949)

United States Wood Preserving Co. v. Sundmaker, 186 F. 678 (C.A. 6th Cir. 1911)

Preferences

St. Louis Quarry & Construction v. Von Versen, 81 Mo. App. 519 (1899)

Pasche v. South St. Joseph Town-Site Co., 190 S.W. 30 (Kan. City, Mo. Ct. of App. 1916)

State ex rel. Great Falls Mr. Klean v. Montana State Board of Examiners, 153 Mont. 220, 456 P.2d 278 (1969)

Taylor v. City of Philadelphia, 261 Pa. 458, 104 A. 766 (1918)

Emergency Purchases

Los Angeles Dredging Co. v. City of Long Beach, 210 Cal. 348, 291 P. 839, 71 A.L.R. 161 (1930)

McNay v. Town of Lowell, 41 Ind. App. 627, 84 N.E. 778 (1908)

West Virginia Coal v. City of St. Louis, 324 Mo. 1021, 25 S.W.2d 466 (1930)

Scatuorchio v. Jersey City Incinerator Co., 14 N.J. 72, 100 A.2d 869 (1953)

Grimm v. Troy, 60 Misc. 579, 303 N.Y.S.2d 170 (Sup. Ct. 1968)

Rodin v. Director of Purchasing, 38 Misc. 2d 362, 238 N.Y.S.2d 2 (Sup. Ct. 1963)

Columbus Blank Book Co. v. Maloon, 116 Ohio App. 393, 188 N.E.2d 431 (1963)

Hoffman v. City of Mt. Pleasant, 126 Tex. 632, 89 S.W.2d 193 (Comm. App. 1936)

Stern v. Spokane, 60 Wash. 325, 111 P. 231 (1910)

Single-Source Purchases

Comley v. Board of Purchase, 111 Conn. 664, 149 A. 410 (1930)

Hinds v. State ex rel. Knight, 59 So. 2d 634 (Fla. 1952)

Tousey v. City of Indianapolis, 175 Ind. 295, 94 N.E. 225 (1911)

Pacilla v. Metropolitan District Commission, 339 Mass. 338, 159 N.E.2d 75 (1959)

Glennon v. Gates, 136 Mo. App. 421, 118 S.W. 98 (Kan. City Ct. App. 1909)

Gerzof v. Sweeney, 16 N.Y.2d 206, 264 N.Y.S.2d 376, 211 N.E.2d 826 (1965)

Tinston v. City of New York, 17 App. Div. 2d 311, 234 N.Y.S.2d 730 (Sup. Ct. 1962)

Vilbig Brothers v. City of Dallas, 127 Tex. 563, 96 S.W.2d 229 (1936)

Washington Fruit & Produce Co. v. City of Yakima, 3 Wash. 2d 152, 100 P.2d 8, 128 A.L.R. 159 (1940)

Informal Purchases

Trapp v. City of Newport, 115 Ky. 840, 74 S.W. 1109 (1903)

State ex rel. Small v. Hughes County Commission, 81 S.D. 238, 133 N.W.2d 228 (1965)

Seim v. Independent District of Monroe, 70 S.D. 315, 17 N.W.2d 342 (1945)

Edwards v. City of Renton, 67 Wash. 2d 598, 409 P.2d 153 (1965)

Performance Bonds

Boseker v. Wabash County Commissioners, 88 Ind. 267 (1880)

Meahl v. City of Henderson, 290 S.W.2d 593 (Ky. 1956)

R. G. Wilmott Coal Co. v. State Purchasing Commission, 246 Ky. 115, 54 S.W.2d 634, 86 A.L.R. 127 (1932)

Nielsen v. City of St. Paul, 252 Minn. 12, 88 N.W.2d 853 (1958)

Biondo v. City of Rochester, 18 App. Div. 2d 78, 238 N.Y.S.2d 7 (Sup. Ct. 1963)

Haff v. Hjelle, 130 N.W.2d 217 (N.D. 1964)

McIntosh Road Materials Co. v. Woolworth, 365 Pa. 190, 74 A.2d 384 (1950)

State ex rel. Printing — Litho, Inc. v. Wilson, 147 W. Va. 415, 128 S.E.2d 449 (1962)

Renewal, Renegotiation, and Modification

Lassiter & Co. v. Taylor, 99 Fla. 819, 128 So. 14, 69 A.L.R. 689 (1930)

Griswold v. Ramsey County, 242 Minn. 529, 65 N.W.2d 647 (1954)

State v. Kollarik, 22 N.J. 558, 126 A.2d 875 (1956)

Seim v. Independent District of Monroe, 70 S.D. 315, 17 N.W.2d 342 (1945)

Savage v. State, 75 Wash. 2d 618, 453 P.2d 613 (1969)

Miller v. State, 73 Wash. 2d 790, 440 P.2d 840 (1968)

Surplus, Excess, and Scrap Disposal

Taylor v. Balderston, 57 Idaho 771, 68 P.2d 761 (1937)

Administrative Settlement of Disputes and Claims

Commercial Cleaning Corp. v. Sullivan, 47 N.J. 539, 222 A.2d 4 (1966)

Mal Brothers Contracting Co. v. Kohl, 113 N.J. Super. 144, 273 A.2d 357, cert. denied, 58 N.J. 94 (1971)

Motorola Communications & Electronics Inc. v. O'Connor, 115 N.J. Super. 317, 279 A.2d 855 (1971)

Splitting Purchases

State ex rel. Woodruff — Dunlop Printing Co. v. Cornell, 52 Neb. 25, 71 N.W. 961 (1897)

Op. Atty. Gen. 155 (Nevada, 1950-1952)
Op. Atty. Gen. 112 (New Mexico, 1970)
6 Op. Atty. Gen. 105 (Texas, 1944)
2 Op. Atty. Gen. 295 (Texas, 1940)
51 Op. Atty. Gen. 696 (West Virginia, 1965-1966)
Letter from Attorney General to:
Chairman, Board of Land and Natural Resources (Hawaii, September 22, 1966)
Commissioner, Dept. of Finance (Kentucky, December 3, 1964)
State Representative — District 33 (Missouri, October 9, 1968)
State Auditor (Washington, February 22, 1972)

Specifications

Attorneys General's Opinions
31 Op. Atty. Gen. 161 (California, 1958)
Op. Atty. Gen. 149 (Colorado, 1941-1942)
Op. Atty. Gen. 27 (Delaware, 1964)
Op. Atty. Gen. 636 (Florida, 1961-1962)
Op. Atty. Gen. 363 (Florida, 1953-1954)
Op. Atty. Gen. 181 (Maine, 1961-1962)
Op. Atty. Gen. 208 (Maine, 1949-1950)
Op. Atty. Gen. 164 (Nevada, 1952-1954)
42 Op. Atty. Gen. 129 (North Carolina, 1972)
36 Op. Atty. Gen. 39 (Washington, 1961-1962)
49 Op. Atty. Gen. 178 (West Virginia, 1960-1962)
44 Op. Atty. Gen. 318 (Wisconsin, 1955)
Letter from Attorney General to:
Rocky Mountain Engraving Co. (Colorado, October 21, 1941)
Executive Director, State Purchasing Commission (Florida, February 15, 1967)
Dept. of Purchasing (Maine, October 25, 1962)
St. Louis County Purchasing Agent (Minnesota, January 9, 1968)
Ramsey County Attorney (Minnesota, June 12, 1967)

Administration of Bidders Lists

Attorneys General's Opinions
Op. Atty. Gen. 374 (Florida, 1965-1966)
Op. Atty. Gen. 373 (Florida, 1965-1966)
51 Op. Atty. Gen. 845 (West Virginia, 1964-1966)
Letter from Attorney General to:
Executive Director, Dept. of General Services (Florida, March 8, 1971)
State Comptroller (Hawaii, October 22, 1964)
State Comptroller (Hawaii, September 21, 1964)
Commissioner, Dept. of Finance and Administration and Director, Div. of Purchases (West Virginia, October 3, 1966)

Competitive Bidding

Attorneys General's Opinions
Op. Atty. Gen. 716 (Georgia, 1969)
Op. Atty. Gen. 2-160 (Kentucky, 1968)
Op. Atty. Gen. 2-536 (Kentucky, 1965)
Op. Atty. Gen. 2-148 (Kentucky, 1964)
Op. Atty. Gen. 2-294 (Kentucky, 1960)
Op. Atty. Gen. 15 (New Mexico, 1968)
41 Op. Atty. Gen. 527 (North Carolina, 1971)

40 Op. Atty. Gen. 504 (North Carolina, 1971)
Op. Atty. Gen. 459 (North Carolina, 1969)
Op. Atty. Gen. 632 (Ohio, 1959)
40 Op. Atty. Gen. 52 (Washington, 1970)
Letter from Attorney General to:
Principal, Doss High School (Kentucky, June 26, 1969)
Assistant Superintendent of Public Instruction (Kentucky, October 5, 1961)
State Public Examiner (Minnesota, February 19, 1971)
Montevideo City Attorney (Minnesota, August 22, 1969)
Prosecuting Attorney, Osage County (Missouri, June 23, 1971)
State Purchasing Agent (New Mexico, August 4, 1969)
State Purchasing Officer (North Carolina, August 3, 1970)
Butler County (Ohio, September 8, 1970)
Licking County (Ohio, February 11, 1969)
Prosecuting Attorney, Montgomery County (Ohio, February 7, 1969)
Prosecuting Attorney, Lucas County (Ohio, July 26, 1966)
Prosecuting Attorney, Lucas County (Ohio, May 8, 1958)
District Attorney, Yamhill County (Oregon, September 11, 1958)
District 11-A State Representative (Washington, October 26, 1970)

Bid Security

Letter from Attorney General to:
Secretary, Dept. of Property and Supplies (Pennsylvania April 18, 1973)
Secretary, Dept. of Property and Supplies (Pennsylvania, April 2, 1973)

Bid Opening and Recording

Attorney General's Opinion
Op. Atty. Gen. 19 (Texas, 1966)
Letter from Attorney General to:
State Purchasing Officer (North Carolina, March 6, 1972)
Director, Div. of Purchasing and Contract, Director of Budget Bureau and Acting President of Univ. of North Carolina (North Carolina, June 9, 1950)

Criteria for Evaluation and Award

Attorneys General's Opinions
48 Op. Atty. Gen. 112 (California, 1966)
Op. Atty. Gen. 67 (Colorado, 1956)
Op. Atty. Gen. 120 (Colorado, 1938)
Op. Atty. Gen. 633 (Florida, 1962)
Op. Atty. Gen. 718 (Florida, 1960)
Op. Atty. Gen. 549 (Florida, 1960)
Op. Atty. Gen. 110 (Maine, 1961)
Op. Atty. Gen. 61 (Maine, 1956)
Op. Atty. Gen. 13 (Minnesota, 1966)
Op. Atty. Gen. 12 (Minnesota, 1966)
Op. Atty. Gen. 2-192 (Ohio, 1970)
Letter from Attorney General to:
Director, Div. of Supply (Alaska, June 15, 1966)

Director, Youth Services Commission (Delaware, June 12, 1963)

Acting Director, Statewide Data Processing System (Hawaii, March 16, 1965)

Purchasing Agent (Maine, May 25, 1962)

Board of Education Supervisors and Board of County Commissioners of Garrett County (Maryland, January 6, 1956)

Corporation Counsel, City of St. Paul (Minnesota, December 27, 1952)

Commissioner of Highways (Minnesota, May 15, 1952)

Henderson County Attorney (North Carolina, June 3, 1971)

State Purchasing Officer (North Carolina, October 10, 1969)

Secretary of Property and Supplies (Pennsylvania, February 24, 1941)

No Bid Response

Attorney General's Opinion
Op. Atty. Gen. 388 (Florida, 1966)
Letter from Attorney General to:
Eden City (North Carolina, May 25, 1970)

No Bid Received

Attorney General's Opinion
Op. Atty. Gen. 32 (Delaware, 1964)

One Bid Received

Attorney General's Opinion
Op. Atty. Gen. 527 (North Carolina, 1971)
Letter from Attorney General to:
Executive Secretary, State Purchasing Council (Florida, September 28, 1953)
Executive Secretary, State Purchasing Council (Florida, September 15, 1953)

Errors in Bids

Attorneys General's Opinions
Op. Atty. Gen. (Maryland, 1953)
Op. Atty. Gen. 141 (South Dakota, 1969)
Letter from Attorney General to:
Delaware State Hospital (Delaware, May 6, 1965)
Acting Director, State Purchasing Commission (Florida, November 8, 1966)
Executive Director, State Purchasing Commission (Florida, January 5, 1957)
Board of Control (Iowa, October 5, 1962)
Rock County Attorney (Minnesota, December 7, 1954)

Bidders' Failure to Bid to Specifications

Attorneys General's Opinions
34 Op. Atty. Gen. 217 (Maryland, 1949)
Op. Atty. Gen. 107 (Nevada, 1970)
Op. Atty. Gen. 32 (Nevada, 1967)
Op. Atty. Gen. 72 (Nevada, 1964)
Op. Atty. Gen. 459 (Oregon, 1966)

Letter from Attorney General to:
Dept. of Finance (Kentucky, January 26, 1968)
Assistant Director of Purchases (Minnesota, June 2, 1950)
State Purchasing Agent (Missouri, May 20, 1959)

Late Bids

Attorneys General's Opinions
Op. Atty. Gen. 134 (Georgia, 1968)
Op. Atty. Gen. 2-488 (Ohio, 1965)
Op. Atty. Gen. 189 (Ohio, 1929)
Letter from Attorney General to:
Superintendent of Purchases, Dept. of Finance and Control (Connecticut, March 10, 1955)

Tie Bids

Letter from Attorney General to:
Purchasing Agent (Maryland, May 25, 1962)
Secretary of Property and Supplies (Pennsylvania, May 26, 1936)
Secretary of Property and Supplies (Pennsylvania, December 16, 1935)

Preferences

Attorneys General's Opinions
53 Op. Atty. Gen. 72 (California, 1970)
Op. Atty. Gen. 12 (Nevada, 1970)
Op. Atty. Gen. 135 (Nevada, 1967)
Op. Atty. Gen. 310 (Nevada, 1955)
Op. Atty. Gen. 64 (New Mexico, 1969)
Op. Atty. Gen. 146 (New Mexico, 1968)
Op. Atty. Gen. 73 (New Mexico, 1968)
Op. Atty. Gen. 15 (Texas, 1958)
Op. Atty. Gen. 445 (Texas, 1939)
Op. Atty. Gen. 599 (West Virginia, 1965)
Letter from Attorney General to:
State Purchasing Director (Colorado, August 7, 1968)
State Purchasing Agent (Colorado, September 24, 1957)
State Purchasing Agent (Colorado, April 17, 1957)
Div. of Purchases (Colorado, January 26, 1949)
Comptroller, Dept. of Accounting and General Services (Hawaii, April 13, 1965)
Dept. of Transportation (Hawaii, January 25, 1963)
Superintendent of Public Works (Hawaii, August 27, 1958)
State Representative, 38th District (Missouri, December 9, 1970)
State Senator Lamb (Nevada, August 17, 1970)
Counsel, Las Vegas Valley Water District (Nevada, June 9, 1967)

Emergency Purchases

Attorney General's Opinion
Op. Atty. Gen. 883 (West Virginia, 1966)
Letter from Attorney General to:
Legislative Auditor (Kentucky, November 10, 1970)
Sheriff, Fayette County (Kentucky, August 25, 1960)
State Auditor (New Mexico, September 12, 1969)
Director, Div. of Purchases (West Virginia, February 9, 1966)

Single-Source Purchases

Attorneys General's Opinions
  Op. Atty. Gen. 169 (Georgia, 1968)
  Op. Atty. Gen. 489 (South Dakota, 1968)
  Op. Atty. Gen. 303 (South Dakota, 1967)

Negotiation

Attorney General's Opinion
  42 Op. Atty. Gen. 102 (Maryland, 1957)
Letter from Attorney General to:
  Director, Div. of Supply (Alaska, May 31, 1966)
  Deputy Director, Dept. of Centralized Data Processing (New Hampshire, August 17, 1971)
  Henderson County Attorney (North Carolina, June 3, 1971)

Informal Purchases

Attorney General's Opinion
  Op. Atty. Gen. 65 (Delaware, 1965)

Renewal, Renegotiation, and Modification

Attorney General's Opinion
  Op. Atty. Gen. 2-265 (Ohio, 1969)
Letter from Attorney General to:
  Assistant Superintendent of Public Instruction, Dept. of Education (Kentucky, September 17, 1962)
  Director, Capital Outlay Budget Board (Louisiana, August 14, 1972)
  Div. of Public Buildings (Missouri, February 3, 1953)
  Farmville Town Attorney (North Carolina, December 8, 1970)
  Secretary, Property and Supplies (Pennsylvania, January 14, 1974)

Surplus, Excess, and Scrap Disposal

Attorneys General's Opinions
  Op. Atty. Gen. 214 (Florida, 1967-1968)
  Op. Atty. Gen. 126 (Indiana, 1968)
  Op. Atty. Gen. 148 (Massachusetts, 1963-1964)
  Op. Atty. Gen. 168 (Massachusetts, 1961-1962)
  3 Op. Atty. Gen. 519 (Michigan, 1957-1958)
  1 Op. Atty. Gen. 490 (Michigan, 1955-1956)
  Op. Atty. Gen. 390 (Michigan, 1949-1950)
  Op. Atty. Gen. 539 (Ohio, 1952)
  25 Op. Atty. Gen. 290 (Oregon, 1950-1952)
  49 Op. Atty. Gen. 232 (West Virginia, 1960-1962)
  Op. Atty. Gen. 145 (Wisconsin, 1970)
Letter from Attorney General to:
  Director of Purchasing and Property (New Hampshire, January 24, 1952)
  Auditor General (South Dakota, May 22, 1972)

Splitting of Purchases

Attorneys General's Opinions
  Op. Atty. Gen. 534 (Delaware, 1964)
  Op. Atty. Gen. 2-333 (Kentucky, 1969)
  Op. Atty. Gen. 2-1286 (Kentucky, 1963)

Letter from Attorney General to:
  Judge, Hardin County Court (Kentucky, January 13, 1971)
  Judge, Owsley County Court (Kentucky, October 18, 1962)
  Assistant Superintendent of Instruction, Dept. of Education (Kentucky, September 26, 1962)
  Adam Village Attorney (Minnesota, March 22, 1971)
  State Purchasing Agent (New Mexico, January 26, 1968)
  Hon. C. M. Williams, "Director" (North Carolina, February 3, 1953)
  22nd District State Representative (Washington, November 15, 1971)

Combinations, Collusions, Conspiracies

Letter from Attorney General to:
  Commissioner of Dept. of Business Research and Development (Minnesota, February 5, 1951)
  Assistant Director of Purchases, affirming opinion of June 10, 1940 (Minnesota, July 25, 1941)
  Director of Purchases, Dept. of Administration (Minnesota, June 10, 1940)
  Comptroller of Public Accounts (Texas, November 12, 1959)
  Acting Supervisor, Div. of Purchasing (Washington, April 21, 1964)
  Military Dept., Assistant Finance Officer (Washington, January 9, 1962)

Conflict of Interest

Attorneys General's Opinions
  Op. Atty. Gen. 194 (Georgia, 1965-1966)
  Op. Atty. Gen. 2-626 (Kentucky, 1968-1970)
  Op. Atty. Gen. 113 (Maine, 1963-1964)
  Op. Atty. Gen. 132 (Nevada, 1967-1968)
  Op. Atty. Gen. 219 (New Mexico, 1969)
  Op. Atty. Gen. 176 (New Mexico, 1967)
  Op. Atty. Gen. 29 (Ohio, 1959)
Letter from Attorney General to:
  State Purchasing Agent (Idaho, May 27, 1969)
  Acting Chairman, Idaho State Board of Correction (Idaho, March 21, 1969)
  State Purchasing Agent (Idaho, December 4, 1959)
  Chairman, Idaho State Board of Correction (Idaho, December 28, 1954)
  Commissioner, Dept. of Finance (Kentucky, October 20, 1970)
  Trimble County Attorney (Kentucky, May 9, 1967)
  Commissioner, Dept. of Finance (Kentucky, November 6, 1964)
  State Auditor (Maine, January 17, 1950)
  State Controller (Maine, July 18, 1945)
  Director, Dept. of Civil Service (Minnesota, April 16, 1940)
  Senator Hazelbacker and Senator James (Montana, May 25, 1972)
  Chief, Purchasing Bureau (Montana, March 14, 1972)
  State Purchasing Director (Oklahoma, November 14, 1961)
  Administrative Div. of State Purchasing and Supplies (Oklahoma, April 1, 1950)

Chairman, State Board of Public Affairs (Oklahoma, August 16, 1947)

Chairman, South Carolina Wildlife Reservation Committee (South Carolina, November 26, 1963)

Record Retention

Attorneys General's Opinions
Op. Atty. Gen. 396 (Florida, 1965-1966)
Op. Atty. Gen. 368 (Florida, 1965-1966)
Op. Atty. Gen. 125 (Georgia, 1971)
Op. Atty. Gen. 13 (Georgia, 1970)
Op. Atty. Gen. 220 (Georgia, 1969)
Op. Atty. Gen. 105 (Nevada, 1965-1966)
41 Op. Atty. Gen. 479 (North Carolina, 1971)
Op. Atty. Gen. 11 (Texas, 1953)
52 Op. Atty. Gen. 15 (West Virginia, 1966-1968)
51 Op. Atty. Gen. 690 (West Virginia, 1964-1966)
Letter from Attorney General to:
State Purchasing Agent (Missouri, February 5, 1957)

Index to Key Subjects

Index to Key Subjects